MW00791310

LOSING ISTANBUL

LOSING ISTANBUL

Arab-Ottoman Imperialists

and the End of Empire

———

MOSTAFA MINAWI

Stanford University Press

Stanford, California

STANFORD UNIVERSITY PRESS

Stanford, California

© 2023 by Mostafa Minawi. All rights reserved.

No part of this book may be reproduced or transmitted in any form or by any means, electronic or mechanical, including photocopying and recording, or in any information storage or retrieval system, without the prior written permission of Stanford University Press.

Printed in the United States of America on acid-free, archival-quality paper

Library of Congress Cataloging-in-Publication Data

Names: Minawi, Mostafa, 1974- author.

Title: Losing Istanbul : Arab-Ottoman imperialists and the end of empire / Mostafa Minawi.

Description: Stanford, California : Stanford University Press, 2022. | Includes bibliographical references and index.

Identifiers: LCCN 2022012268 (print) | LCCN 2022012269 (ebook) | ISBN 9781503633162 (cloth) | ISBN 9781503634046 (paperback) | ISBN 9781503634053 (ebook)

Subjects: LCSH: Arabs—Turkey—Istanbul—History. | Ethnicity—Turkey—Istanbul—History. | Istanbul (Turkey)—Ethnic relations—History. | Turkey—History—1878-1909. | Turkey—History—Mehmed V, 1909-1918.

Classification: LCC DR727.A73 M56 2022 (print) | LCC DR727.A73 (ebook) | DDC 305.892/7049618—dc23/eng/20220802

LC record available at https://lccn.loc.gov/2022012268

LC ebook record available at https://lccn.loc.gov/2022012269

Cover design: Rob Ehle

Cover photo: Nimet Hanım, wife of Shafiq al-Mu'ayyad Azmzade, on her wedding day, 1901. Source: Marmara University, Taha Toros Archive.

Typeset by Newgen in Adobe Caslon Pro 10.25/15

To the memory of my great-grandmother and great-grandfather
Teté Bader Doghan (Doğan) and Jiddo 'Abd al-Ghani
[a.k.a. 'Abed] 'Uthman (Osman).
They survived the famine and Seferberlik of World War I, the end of Ottoman rule
and French colonialism in Beirut, British colonialism and exile from Palestine,
a number of wars in Lebanon, and the heartache of futures imagined and lost.

CONTENTS

ILLUSTRATIONS

PREFACE

Processing Times of Transition

This book is the product of over a decade's worth of research that took me across archives and libraries from London to Damascus. I spent years re-membering the fragments of the lives of Arab-Ottoman imperialists and their family members who lived over a hundred years ago in Istanbul. Even though they lived lives that could not be more different than mine—privileged elites born and raised in a wealthy provincial notable family who spent their careers near the pinnacle of a bygone imperial world—I have been driven by more than academic curiosity to understand their experiences. It took me years to understand that a large part of my interest was personal. They occupied a liminal space in a dying imperial world order; spent their lives adjusting to global forces of political, cultural, and social change that were well beyond their control; and eventually found themselves having to make very difficult life choices as the home they knew no longer existed and the society they understood themselves to be a part of rejected them for the intimate recent past they represented.

As the great-grandchild of Beirutis who lived through the loss of the end of the Ottoman Empire, never acknowledged national borders that separated the people of Bilad al-Sham, and raised a global family through decades of regional instability; as the grandchild of a Beiruti grandmother and a Jeru-salemite grandfather who started a family in Jaffa and never quite recovered from their sudden exile from Palestine; as the son of Palestinian refugees who grew up "stateless" in Beirut and as a queer man in search of a tribe across Southwest Asia, Europe, and North America, I was drawn to the story of Arab-Ottomans in Istanbul and their experience of tenuous belonging, rejection, and loss. Though more than a century and a continent removed, I understood what it meant to live through global changes that render one disoriented, one's loyalties suspect, and one's very existence the subject of debate and controversy.

Just like the path a human life takes, the course of researching this book was long and winding. There was no plan, no ultimate goal, and no roadmap to follow. It was in many ways similar to exploring what architect Somaiyeh Falahat called *hazar-tu*, or a "thousand insides," of cities like old Tunis, Isfahan, and Fez.[1] At every turn, a new part of the city presents itself to the pedestrian, like a map unfolding a thousand times. Although Shafiq and Sadik belonged to a global imperial class of men and women who left some archival traces, they did not leave the historian a roadmap of their lives across social spaces, time, and continents. They were grand historical characters but also ordinary people whose lives were thousands of insides folded upon themselves. At every turn, a new detail revealed itself that took me to a discovery or led down a dead end.

Even with a historian's patience, endless starts and stops made this research a long-term project that had to accompany me as I researched other projects. Along the way, I wrote and published *The Ottoman Scramble for Africa* and a few articles on Ottoman imperialism and international relations—important detours that also took me on new adventures and challenged my perception of Ottoman history from the inside out.[2] It also liberated me to follow paths that had not been followed before, with no signposts and with nothing to go on but the clues that slowly emerged. Between 2008 and 2021, I gathered and translated data and connected the dots whenever I had the time to do research and look over an interview or a new source of information I had come across. I had to make sense of disparate pieces of data and recognize the moment when I had enough to "know" these Arab-Ottoman families outside of the old theoretical frameworks of late nineteenth-century Ottoman historiography, such as the debates over Ottoman exceptionalism, the decline thesis, identity, anti-orientalist telling of Ottoman history, or the origin of different forms of nationalism in the region. What emerged is a book about the complexities of lived experiences that require a deep understanding of the ever changing political and social context that Arab-Ottoman imperialists lived in and the embrace of a multitude of dimensions, often contradictory and fuzzy, the sum total of which makes up a colorful human life.

It took exceptional circumstances for me to finally embark on the writing process. As I experienced major events over the past couple of years—living in Beirut during the Lebanese October 2019 revolution, surviving the Beirut Port blast in August of 2020, and navigating the perils of a global pandemic—it all started to make sense. Working on a laptop that bore the scratches and scrapes of flying shards of glass from the Port blast, it occurred to me that history, for most people, is about recounting intimate experiences of lived moments. When it comes down to it, people often want to understand, empathize, or imagine how an event *felt* and how it impacted real people's lives. How was it to experience a revolution from the inside? What was it like to live through a pandemic? How did the blast feel, and what impact did surviving it have on personal and professional priorities? That is how most people internalize history—the sum total of experiences of lives lived. It is rarely about figures or dates or large sociopolitical patterns or epic wars observed from above.

In the safety and isolation of Ithaca and then Budapest, I wrote to process this moment of global and personal crisis the best way I knew how. The result is a book that approaches the study of humanities at its most essential essence—an attempt to make sense of one's experience in the world, through the understanding of others' experiences, even people who might otherwise seem far removed temporally, geographically, and morally from one's own life.

Lastly, I wanted this book to be an invitation to reconsider the history of the Ottoman Empire as the shared heritage of the *peoples* of all successor states and not as it is mostly taught now, a prehistory of modern Turkey alone. Forced amnesia about the diversity of the ruling elites of Istanbul has distorted a relatively recent history of belonging that has contemporary real-life implications. Perhaps the dire effects of this unchecked amnesia can best be felt when former members of the same empire, like citizens from Syria and Turkey, find themselves living in close proximity in Istanbul. One has to wonder how a better understanding of the history of the empire as a shared past that people of many countries can claim, "warts and all," would impact the lives of Syrians, Lebanese, Bulgarians, Palestinians, Iraqis, Armenians, Turks, Kurds, and others living, once more, side by side in their former imperial capital.

ACKNOWLEDGMENTS

A great deal of support from friends, colleagues, and biological and chosen family members was poured into this work. I have also received much institutional support that allowed me to travel, live, and conduct research in Southwest Asia, Europe, and the United States. I will do my best to recall and acknowledge all the support I received, but I know that I will inevitably forget some. For those that I forget: I beg your forgiveness and keep my fingers crossed for a second edition to make sure I have the chance to correct any mistakes I might have made.

The past two years have been very trying, forcing me to face my mortality and to pause to reassess my priorities in life and the way I approach my scholarship. As someone who has gotten used to writing in coffeeshops while traveling around the globe, by staying put—first in the safety of Ithaca, New York, and later in the historical beauty of Budapest—I cut down external distractions without eliminating inspiration. One of the things that kept me grounded through the writing process was the daily virtual check-ins with my friend and fellow historian, Nilay Özok-Gündoğan. Whether it was to discuss our work, to laugh about the quirks of our chosen profession, or whether she gave me self-care advice or reminded me to stay true to my vision when I hesitated, I could not have written this kind of book, now, without her friendship and advice.

None of my work would be possible without the support of family and friends. I am grateful for my mother and father, Firyal Shourafa and Adel Minawi, who remind me what it means to remain proud and resilient in the face of loss; my sisters, Rima and Nahed Minawi, who lovingly listened to me as I tried to work though my complicated relationship with academia; my friends Spencer Halperin, Pinar Gnepp, Leena Dallasheh, Alper Rozanes, Corey Gutch, Rob Morache, Jamie Morrisey, Alex Lenoble, Randall Chamberlain, and many other kind souls whose paths have crossed mine and helped me recognize the strength in me.

I am ever so thankful for the support, wisdom, inspiration, and encouragement of Virginia Aksan, Amal Ghazal, Salah Hassan, Christine Philliou, Janet Klein, Ilham Khuri-Makdisi, Jens Hanssen, Nadia al-Bagdadi, Nadya Sbaiti, Eve Troutt Powell, Hasan Kayalı, and William O'Reilly. These are but a few in a long list of scholars who have believed in me, inspired me, and challenged me over the past few years to want to write this book during these very turbulent times. I owe them all a debt of gratitude.

I am also lucky to have brilliant and supportive colleagues like Ernesto Bassi, Julilly Kohler-Hoffmann, Robert Travers, Eric Tagliacozzo, Russell Rickford, Larry Glickman, Saida Hodžić, Aaron Sacks, Lucinda Ramberg, Tamara Loos, Judith Byfield, Maria Cristina Garcia, and Claudia Verhoeven; and blessed to have wonderful graduate and undergraduate students. I learn so much from them every day.

Putting the final touches on the book while sitting at a café a few feet from where the Azmzades lived in fashionable Teşvikiye, I am aware of how lucky I am to have access to the travel and research resources of Cornell University and the financial backing of the Cornell Society for the Humanities, the Cornell Center for Social Sciences, the Department of History, and Koç University's ANAMED.

A resident fellowship at the Institute for Advanced Studies at the Central European University in 2020–2021 allowed me the time and space to think, write, and discuss my work with brilliant scholars like Gina Caison, Somogy Varga, Petr Vašát, Tyrell Caroline Haberkorn, Zsuzsa Hetényi, Raluca Iacob, Lorenzo Sala, and the Crow family. What a lucky man I was to have had them as my neighbors and captive intellectual circle during months of lockdown in Budapest.

Durba Ghosh, Kent Schull, and Cemil Aydın exemplify the academic excellence and generosity of spirit that I aspire to. I am very lucky to have had their encouragement to write this book and their invaluable feedback on earlier drafts. Last, but not least, I would like to thank the blind reviewers for their invaluable comments and suggestions, and Kate Wahl for her advice, vision, and patience as she shepherded this book to publication. The book is infinitely better because of the advice I got from everybody mentioned above, and I am confident that any of its shortcoming are entirely of my own doing.

NOTE ON TRANSLITERATION

Since language plays a key role in the argument I am making in this book, I have had to pay extra attention to transliteration, and in the process have sometimes sacrificed uniformity in favor of honoring the specificity of context and the meaning a word conveys beyond the limits of its literal definition. The following paragraphs offer a brief guide to the transliteration system.

If a place-name had a common English spelling, I used it; otherwise, the transliteration depended on the geographical context. For example, I used Istanbul, not İstanbul, and ʿAjlun, not Aclun. Similarly, if a given name of a person had a common English spelling, I used it. For example, I used Ali instead of ʿAli, and Izzet instead of ʿIzzet. If historical figures left examples of how they rendered their own names in the Latin alphabet through signatures, letterheads, or business cards that have survived, I remained loyal to that. Prioritizing surviving documents written in French over the accuracy of pronunciation if I had used the modern Turkish alphabet for specific vowel sounds or the modern Arabic transliteration system was a difficult decision but one I had to make in order to avoid the anachronistic use of a writing system that did not exist during a person's lifetime. Thus, for example, I used Vassik instead of Vasık or Wathiq.

In cases where there were no written records with the Latin alphabet, I used the modern Turkish spelling or the Arabic transliteration of a given name, based on cultural context or explicit identification. As a less than satisfactory compromise, I gave the Turkish version or the Arabic transliteration of a name in parenthesis the first time I used it. In a time of layered notions of cultural belonging and a quickly changing geopolitical map of the region, this decision was often difficult. For example, for Sadik's children, who lived into the republican period and adopted Turkish nationality, I used the modern Turkish spelling instead of the French or a transliteration from Arabic. Thus, I used Giyas, not Ghiyath, and Masune, not Massouné or Masuneh. However, for Sadik's eldest son, who moved to Damascus after the end of the empire and adopted Syrian citizenship, I used Jelal, not Djelal, Celal, or Jalal.

In general, I used the simplified Arabic transliteration system followed by the *International Journal of Middle Eastern Studies* with rare exceptions when I wanted to emphasize Levantine (*Shami*)–Arabic pronunciation. For example, instead of "Tashwiqiyya," I use "Tashwiqiyyeh." I avoided the use of diacritical marks with the exception of the accent ' for the letter 'ayn and the accent ' to indicate a hamza in the middle or at the end of a word. For Ottoman-Turkish transliteration, I used modern Turkish orthography, with minor exceptions. The following is short guide to the pronunciation of Turkish letters:

a like *a* in star.

e like *a* in slay.

c like *j* in joy.

j like *s* in measure.

ç like *ch* in **ch**ocolate.

ş like *sh* in sa**sh**ay.

ı like *o* in butt**o**n.

i like *ee* in qu**ee**n.

o like *o* in p**o**se.

ö like the German *ö* in K**ö**ln.

u like *u* in B**u**dapest.

ü like the French *u* in Br**u**xelles.

g like *g* in wi**g**.

ğ is silent and often serves to extend the vowel it follows.

Transliteration decisions are never perfect, not least because they inevitably contribute to the privileging of European languages and sounds over non-European ones. I ask the specialist reader to consider the context of each case and not to be distracted by transliteration choices they might disagree with.

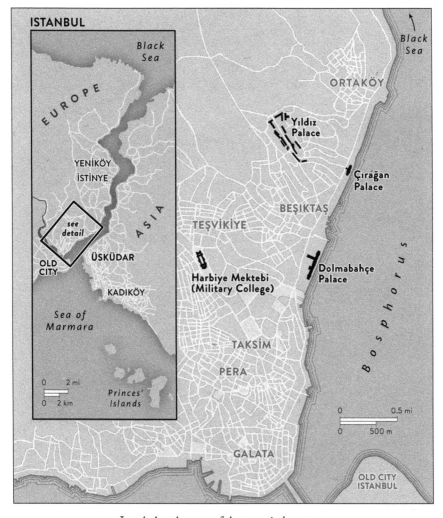

Istanbul at the turn of the twentieth century.

LOSING ISTANBUL

INTRODUCTION

ON THE 27TH OF APRIL 1909, THREE OFFICERS ARRIVED AT Yıldız Palace to the sound of wailing and weeping from the harem and the sultan's private quarters. They came to deliver official notification of the military court's decision to exile the sultan and his family to Salonica (Thessaloniki), with immediate effect. As soon as he heard the news of their arrival, the sultan came out and sat on a throne. The color had drained from his face and he was shaking. *Miralay* (Colonel) Galib (Ar. Ghaleb) Bey, from the 1st regiment of the Ottoman Army (the Macedonia Regiment), approached the sultan and repeated to him the military council's decision and asked him to prepare to leave the palace immediately.[1] Sultan Abdülhamid II (Ar. 'Abd al-Hamid) (r. 1876–1909) reportedly asked the men to help him find another way, maybe even moving him to the Çırağan Palace instead of being completely exiled from his beloved Istanbul. When he could not get any positive response, he went silent for a few minutes, then asked if it was certain that his life would be spared. Galib assured him that his life was in no danger. The sultan's youngest son, Abdürrahim (Ar. 'Abd al-Rahim), seemed not to trust Galib's word and continued to ask the officer over and over if his promise of safe passage was true. Hearing the fear in his son's voice, Abdülhamid's eyes welled up with tears that began to flow down his gray beard. He seemed unable to understand, asking why he was being punished in a way none of his ancestors had been. The officers answered that his fate was in fact better than that of many of his ancestors. Sending him into exile at that moment, they argued, was better than putting his life in danger—a subtle reference to a history of regicide in the empire that went back to the reign of Sultan Osman (Ar. 'Uthman) II in the early seventeenth century.[2]

Around 1 a.m., the sultan, along with three princes, three princesses, four concubines, and a few members of his entourage and palace servants, were loaded into a convoy of armored automobiles. While the people of the imperial capital slept, the sultan's convoy slowly made its way to Sirkeci, the last station on the European railway system, which terminated a short walk from the church-turned-mosque Aya Sofia and the old royal residence and center of the Ottoman dynasty's power, Topkapı Palace. The convoy was flanked by members of the cavalry, with foot soldiers lining the street. When it arrived at the station, the sultan and his companions boarded the train in almost complete silence. Within minutes it took off under cover of darkness, destined for Salonica, which would be the deposed sultan's residence until 1912.[3] It was said that Sultan Abdülhamid II tried to take one last look at the walls of the city he had lost, but it was difficult—the curtains on the train windows were tightly closed. However, one of his young sons was able to sneak one last look through a gap in the curtains with sadness in his eyes.[4]

This story is a dramatic recounting of the last few hours of the longest reign of any Ottoman sultan, as reported in a Beirut-based Arabic-language newspaper, painting a vivid picture of the end of an era and the beginning of what was to be a hopeful fresh start for the people of this ailing empire. The sultan's exile came a few months after the military coup, usually referred to as the Young Turk Revolution, that effectively ended his reign and reinstated the Ottoman constitution. Along with him, the coup took down a substantial number of loyalists who had built their careers around service to the palace. Many of the closest advisors to the sultan were Ottoman imperialists who came from Arabic-speaking majority provinces in the Levant and whose fates were tied to his.

This book offers an experiential history of some members of the Arab-Ottoman community who set up households in Istanbul in the 1880s, worked for the Yıldız Palace in various capacities, and deeply identified with Ottoman imperial rule.[5] They held on to the possibility of an alternative future for their children under the large tent of an imagined diverse and inclusive

Ottoman state until their hopes were dashed with the collapse of the last
Muslim imperial rule in the region.

Collecting pieces of the lives of two men and their extended families, this
book aims to construct an intimate history of global circumstances through
public and private experiences of the last four decades of the Ottoman Empire. It argues that the two men, Shafiq (Shafīq) al-Mu'ayyad (Tr. Şefik el-
Müeyyed) Azmzade (1861–1916) and his nephew Sadik (Sādiq) al-Mu'ayyad
(Tr. Sadık el-Müeyyed) Azmzade (1858–1910), and their families embodied
the trials and tribulations of the empire they identified with, whose strengths
and weaknesses were refracted through their careers and whose loss meant

FIGURE 1. Sadik al-Mu'ayyad Azmzade, late nineteenth century.
Source: Azmzade Private Family Archive. Reprinted with permission.

FIGURE 2. Shafiq al-Mu'ayyad Azmzade, late nineteenth century.
Source: The public al-'Azm Facebook page. Reprinted with permission.

the end for a community of *İstanbul'lu* Arab-Ottoman imperialists (figures 1 and 2).

Few could have felt the winds of change more than the Arab-Ottomans who worked and lived in the heart of the empire, through the fast and dramatic events of the last four decades of Ottoman rule. This was the last generation to spend its entire life under Ottoman rule, taking their last breaths in the dying days of the empire. The very last generation to be born under Ottoman rule was their children and grandchildren—old enough to remember living in imperial Istanbul but young enough to have a post-Ottoman afterlife in the new geopolitical realities of the age of the nation-state.[6]

A Brief Sociopolitical Context of the Hamidian Period

The political movements that Abdülhamid tried to suppress in the last two decades of his reign spun out of his administration's control in its last few years. They took the sultan and a whole generation of palace loyalists down, changing the demographic makeup of Istanbul's ruling elites.[7] A decade after his exile, vast territories of the empire that his family had ruled for more than six hundred years became part of the contested history of Southeast Europe and Southwest Asia.[8] Abdülhamid did not live long enough to witness the fateful dissolution of the empire and the end of the institution of the caliphate, which he had reinvented as a modern political institution of a global racialized Muslim community in response to claims of racialized Hellenistic Christian superiority.[9] Although he had warned of European designs on the empire, he could not have imagined that the region would be almost unrecognizable within a decade of his departure.[10] Arabs, Kurds, Armenians, Greeks, Bulgarians, Albanians, Jews, and Turks would splinter and be divided between nation-states with contested territorial boundaries, European colonial mandates, and a settler-colonial ethnostate embedded in the heart of the Levant.

European victors of World War I, American representatives, and a handful of former citizens of the empire decided the fate of the majority of the population in Southwest Asia.[11] Ottoman state policies enacted during Sultan Abdülhamid II's reign against the Armenian-Ottoman population foreshadowed the ethnic cleansing of the native Armenian and Greek populations of Anatolia in this polyglot empire.[12] However, it would have been much harder for contemporary observers to predict that the empire's largest

Muslim population, from which some of his closest advisors hailed, would also break off. Even though a variety of political opposition movements came to light under Abdülhamid's rule, the "Arab versus Turk" style of ethnoracial differentiation became a real threat to the unity of the empire only a few years after his departure.[13] Soon after World War I, Southwest Asia was carved into a puzzle of nation-states that left many former members of the empire marginalized, alienated, or displaced.[14]

Shafiq and Sadik's Generation

The penultimate Ottoman generation at the center of this book was the one that experienced the internal centralization efforts of the Hamidian administration; major defeats and territorial losses in the late 1870s; desperate and often violent efforts to silence perceived threats to the rule of the Ottoman dynasty; the second constitutional revolution; and finally a fleeting alternative possibility of twentieth-century inclusive Ottoman citizenship that transcended the ethnic and religious hierarchies of the past. This generation was as comfortable in Beirut, Damascus, or Sofia as in Istanbul. They skillfully negotiated a multilingual world of late nineteenth-century imperialism, allowing them to advance their careers as palace bureaucrats, diplomats, and policy advisors. They lived a life of privilege, affording them the opportunity to imagine an ideal existence of an Ottoman—not as a member of the ruling dynasty but as a citizen who identified with an Ottoman fatherland that honored its multicultural and multilingual reality; a precarious idea that rose and fell during their lifetime.[15] By no means was this generation of imperialists limited to Arab-Ottomans or Turkish-Ottomans.[16] However, the Arab-Ottomans of Istanbul did hold a unique place in the history of late Ottoman imperialism, which will become clear as the reader follows the lives of Sadik and Shafiq and their families throughout the book.

As the Ottoman Empire moved toward a more centralized and bureaucratized system of governance and administration in the second half of the nineteenth century, men from notable Levantine families found new career options to consider as the power of their provincial families was being curtailed. With the right pedigree, education, and transimperial connections, they could follow career paths that took them to the imperial center, allowing them to break away from their families' traditional provincial careers as municipal councilors, provincial administrators, land-owning elites, and wealthy merchants. Those traditional family roles, which often passed down from one generation to the next, accumulated a great deal of social and political capital. This history also came with the burden of decades worth of decisions, alliances, and missteps that their ancestors had made. Public memory was long, Istanbul's loyalty contingent, and the palace and the Sublime Porte often used events from the past to justify investing in one family's future success versus another's.

The Azmzades had centuries worth of provincial experience and history they carried with them. During the reign of Sultan Abdülhamid II (the Hamidian period), a new generation of Azmzades used their education and connections to forge a new kind of career in the metropole, in the process extending the family's network of power to the capital and beyond. Some established their households in the city, close to the palace and among other palace favorites. Moving away from the comfort of ready-made opportunities available to them in their family's homestead was not the only or the most obvious option for a young Azmzade in the 1880s. Many chose to stay in the Levant and continue the tradition of provincial and municipal careers while holding on to the vestiges of a bygone golden era of provincial notables.[17] However, after the 1860s, opting for a career in imperial service became an attractive option, which allowed some of the more ambitious members of the family to build their careers, far away from the safety and constraints of the family's powerful bases in provinces like Aleppo, Syria, Egypt, and Beirut.

As Sadik rose through the ranks, he developed a reputation for his negotiation skills on some of the most sensitive diplomatic assignments—whether accompanying a Russian grand duke to Jerusalem and the German kaiser to Damascus or representing the sultan in the Sahara Desert, Germany, Abyssinia, western Arabia, Russia, Bulgaria, eastern Anatolia, and Macedonia. The records Sadik left behind paint a picture of a proud and conflicted man struggling to maintain his relevance as the empire crumbled. It all came to a sudden end during World War I, with his family being one of the casualties of war, splitting along newly established national borders, never again to be reunited.

Shafiq's life gives the reader an example of a sedentary civil service career in the palace. Shafiq was able to amass political and financial capital, which he spent in support of his business dealings and his relatives in Istanbul,

Cairo, and Damascus. After reinstatement of the constitution, he reinvented himself as a deputy elected to represent the Province of Syria.[18] His luck ended with the arrival of World War I, when he was charged with treason and executed in 1916. Members of his family were interned in Bursa during the war, but they eventually returned to the Levant and reestablished their political influence under the Amir Faisal administration and the French colonial government.[19]

Shafiq and Sadik were only two of many Arab-Ottoman imperialists working for the Hamidian administration. One of the most (in)famous in this generation was their relative and the sultan's close advisor Izzet (Tr. İzzet/Ar. 'Izzat) al-'Abid (al-'Ābid).[20] Izzet greatly influenced the way Arab-Ottoman imperialists like the Azmzades perceived their role in the empire, and how they would later be perceived as the embodiment of the corruption of the Hamidian period. His memoirs, which were made available by his family only in 2019, provide insight into the sociopolitical world of Arab-Ottoman men of the palace.[21]

Losing Istanbul Three Ways

Losing Istanbul operates on three levels. The first is the voyeuristic level of a curious spectator observing the colorful lives of this generation of Arab-Ottoman imperialists unfold on the pages of the book. A deep dive into the details of the lives of Sadik and Shafiq shows how significant events were experienced on the individual level and, conversely, suggests an alternative understanding that takes an individual's disposition as a driving force behind some of the state's policies. One level deeper brings the reader to the complex topics of ethnicity, race, and the anxiety of life under a creeping Western political and cultural hegemony and in an increasingly ethnoracialized Ottoman center. Yet one level deeper uncovers the operation of microhistory to get at a "total history" in the tradition of the Annales school.[22]

One way to approach *Losing Istanbul* is as a story of two handsome, well-educated, well-traveled Arab-Ottoman men who spent the bulk of their careers working for the palace and living a privileged life with their families in Istanbul, from the mid-1880s to the mid-1910s. It affords readers a "fly on the wall" perspective on the inner workings of the Ottoman state through the personal lives of Arab-Ottoman statesmen. Shafiq and Sadik hailed from a powerful provincial family that was a feature of regional politics in Damascus and Aleppo and one that has been extensively studied but only as a provincial or Syrian phenomenon.[23] This book turns the spotlight on Istanbul's Arab-Ottoman community through the social spaces of the Azmzades—their careers and the intimacies of their quotidian life set against the dramatic background of Istanbul's glamorous high society; the political intrigue of the palace; and the near-constant existential anxiety that came with living at the center of a vanishing imperial world order. Marriages and births; palace receptions and circumcision ceremonies; corsets and medal-adorned uniforms; travel and (mis)adventure—all are part of the story. The ugly side of imperialism also features prominently, including classism, corruption, slavery, the rise of racism, ethnoracial discrimination, and ethnic cleansing.

The goal is to give the reader a street-level understanding of the *experience* of the final four decades of an ailing empire through the eyes of a small community of Arab-Ottomans in Istanbul that identified with the idea of an Ottoman Empire until the end. I use *experience* throughout in both its passive and active senses.[24] The word *tajruba* (Tr. *tecrübe*) is better suited for what I mean because it encompasses both passive and active meanings. One meaning refers to something that a person goes through passively, in the process impacting one's senses, disposition, and character. The other refers to experimentation, in which one partakes in "tests," constructs, and ponders one's condition, often acting as the subject, object, and in some cases narrator of perceived reality.

Another layer of analysis is meant for students of Ottoman history interested in themes such as imperial identification(s), ethnoracialization, and racism in the late Ottoman Empire. First, however, a note on the term "Arab-Ottoman imperialist" and why it is fundamental to the arguments I present. I use *imperialist* to refer to Arab-Ottomans who built their careers, social connections, and sense of self around the Hamidian-era palace and who pegged their survival to the success of Ottoman imperialism. They stood in contrast to others from Arabic-speaking majority provinces who opposed Hamidian rule or were not as invested in Ottoman imperialism, who lived too far away from the political currents of the time to care, and who gradually became invested in alternative futures, with Arab separatist nationalism being an extreme version of these futures.

The other choice of terminology is the hyphenated *Arab-Ottoman* signifier, which risks coming across as an anachronistic borrowing from the hy-
phened identifiers of countries that tout their multicultural heritage. Having lived in Canada, I see terms like *Arab-Canadian* or *French-Canadian* as
culturally acceptable ways to acknowledge difference without causing offense.
Canada's "multiculturalism" policies were initially proposed as a way to address the grievances of Canadians of French origin who had always felt that
their cultural identity was under threat. Then they were extended to include
an increasingly diverse immigrant population. The country's "multiculturalism"
remains controversial for many reasons, including the message it sends about
the need for some Canadians to explicitly identify their ethnic or national origins. In contrast, the majority—White Canadians of Anglo/Irish origin—do
not need an additional marker to signify their national belonging. In order to
avoid replicating a similar logic in the Ottoman case, where an "Ottoman" is
often, erroneously, assumed to mean "Turk" while the rest of the ethnic groups
need to be more finely ethnically or religiously identified, I follow the same
naming convention for Turkish-Ottomans as I do for others like Armenian-,
Greek-, or Kurdish-Ottomans, whenever it is relevant to the discussion.[25]

I also insist on the use of the hyphenated signifier to reflect the way public discourse acknowledged and emphasized the different *'anaser/anasır* (sing.
Ar./Tr.: *'unsur/unsur*). *Unsur* literally meant "element," but in the context
in which it was mostly used in the early twentieth century, it better corresponded to the English use of *ethnies* or *ethnic groups* that made up the Ottoman peoples. I argue that outside of the official state discourse the discussion
was less about the various religious sects and increasingly about the various
ethnic groups. By 1908 the use of *al-'unsur al-'arabi*, which means the Arab
ethnic group, was a common way of referring to Ottomans who identified
themselves or were identified as having an Arab origin. Turks were similarly referred to as an *unsur*. Both one's ethnic group—Arab, Greek, Kurdish,
Albanian—and its belonging to a wider Ottoman fatherland—Ottoman—
were important signifiers at this juncture in imperial history, particularly in
the context of the life of statesmen living in Istanbul. To make both elements
visible and indivisible, I use *Arab-Ottoman* throughout the book. To avoid
the perils that the modern use of the hyphen presents in Canada, I use this
method to signify all ethnic groups, including Turkish-Ottomans.

Unsur is not to be confused with *millet*, which was inherited from the early days of the Ottoman state, initially referring to state-recognized non-Muslim populations of the empire: the Greek Orthodox (*Rum*), the Armenians, and the Jews. The meaning of *millet* changed over time, and in the late nineteenth century the state used *millet* to refer to any legally recognized "nationality of people."[26]

Historian Ussama Makdisi argues that "religious difference" plagued an unsuccessful nineteenth-century Ottoman project of "equal citizenship."[27] In addition to religious difference and the nineteenth-century notion of *millet*, I argue that *unsur* was a necessary addition to the vocabulary of public discourse, which acknowledged the rise of an ethnoracial identification beyond the Ottoman state–recognized *millet* or an evolving sectarian system. *Unsur* reflected a new social reality that acknowledged the ethnoracial identification of peoples and a global trend of racialization and ethnonationalism. Istanbul was not immune to this late imperial mentality, where a person's *unsur*, or ethnicity, became rigid categories and had real implications for urban Ottoman society. It is telling that in Arabic *'unsuriyya*, from *'unsur*, developed to also mean *racism* in the twentieth century.[28]

There is a sentiment in the Ottoman history field to minimize the loaded meaning of ethnoracial markers, such as *Arab* and *Turk*, before the emergence of widespread ethnonationalism in the region during World War I and after.[29] I argue that the exclusive focus on political organization and the rise of nationalism has left us blind to the rise of ethnoracial differentiation in Ottoman society well before the rise of populist nationalism. In the last decade of the nineteenth century, Ottoman society's self-perception was undergoing a transformation. *Arab* or *Turk*, for example, were not innocuous signifiers but critical ethnoracial markers deployed in the Ottoman metropole with positive and negative connotations. They were also embraced by some and avoided by others in the small circle of Arab-Ottoman statesmen well before the 1908 Young Turk Revolution, the 1911 loss of Libya to Italian colonialism, the 1912 Balkan losses, or World War I. *Arab-Ottoman* and *Turkish-Ottoman* acknowledge and amplify this reality.

It is important to distinguish the rise of ethnoracial differentiation in the Ottoman center and the often-parallel rise of "isms," whether Arabism, Turkism, or nationalism. To borrow the famous adage from statistical sciences, correlation does not imply causation. Political and intellectual projects such as what came to be known as *al-Nahda* (the Awakening), Arab nationalism, Turkification, and Turkish nationalism have been hotly debated in Ottoman historiography.[30] For example, historian Erol Ülker argues that there was no uniform policy of Turkification employed by the ruling Committee of Unity and Progress (CUP) between 1908 and 1918. He contends that, even though many different methods were used in a nation-building project across the empire, one can only talk of Turkification as a form of Turkish nationalism after 1913.[31] Similarly, historian Hasan Kayalı, in his seminal book *Arabs and Young Turks*, argues that what was perceived by Arab-Ottoman politicians and intellectuals as an attack on Arabism was in fact a form of state central-ization. He suggests that Arab politicians' accusations of the CUP forcing Turkification were not driven by nationalist ideology. They were "new games of politics" deployed as opposition to the government and were expressed in an "anti-Turkish idiom." The charge of Turkification was meant to hurt the CUP and its standing in Arab public opinion.[32] However, the rise of Arabism and the various ideas of nationalism in the Arabic-speaking major-ity provinces were in fact a long precipitative process that began well before World War I and was ultimately usurped by a few Hijazi Arab-Ottomans with dreams of grandeur.[33] Even after World War I, a political imagination and centuries of history and social ties that connected different parts South-west Asia continued in various parts of the former empire during the long period of separation that stretched into the early 1920s.[34]

Thus, even though Turkification and Turkish nationalism might not have been influential state-sponsored projects before World War I, one cannot ignore the informal currents of ethnoracial differentiation taking place well before then. The sense of marginalization of Arab-Ottomans did not emerge overnight after the Young Turk Revolution; nor was it manufactured by local politicians. It was a much longer process that spilled out into the open after 1908, particularly after the disappointment of the unfulfilled promises of the revolution.[35]

Acts and ideation of ethnoracial differentiation in Istanbul came through the details of daily life, coloring Arab-Ottomans' experiences there. Eth-noracial differentiation, which was a feature of late imperialism around the globe, and which some historians have pointed to along the frontiers of the

Ottoman Empire, manifested itself in the Ottoman metropole as well.[36] I have argued elsewhere that much of the derogatory rhetoric of difference employed by Ottoman statesmen in describing the Bedouins of the Hijaz, for example, should not be measured against British or French methods of colonial rule as normative examples of late imperialism. The particularity of the Ottoman case should give us pause before making a sweeping generalization about Ottoman impressions of inhabitants of the frontiers.[37] In this book, however, I do not shy away from noting where ethnoracial identification, which is often associated with frontier regions or colonial possessions, was reflected in the society of the Ottoman metropole as well.[38]

The third layer of *Losing Istanbul* addresses historians interested in the theoretical underpinnings of an experiential history of a group of people outside of the tradition of historical biographies. I use sociologist Pierre Bourdieu's concepts of habitus and social space because they provide a rich and malleable framework for understanding the lifeworld of a group of individuals who adapted to a changing world, across empires, cities, and cultures. A social space, though often aligned with a physical space, such as a neighborhood, a place of work, or even a nation-state, is not a physical space. A social space is produced and reproduced through individuals' engagement in social practices, which often mirror their perspectives, positionalities, relationships to one another, and strategies for mobility.[39] Perhaps most important, it is not static as a space, but changes over time based on the positionality of a particularly social agent in relation to society and other social agents.[40] A habitus is an embodied orientation to the world and a position in social space that is often long-lasting.[41] It is a "system of dispositions" and a long-lasting structure of perception and action that comes as the product of social and historical conditions that are constantly changing. Although dispositions are long-lasting and tend to perpetuate themselves, they can be changed through historical events, education, intentions, and consciousness. This collective system of perceptions creates a habitus, making it equally vulnerable and susceptible to change.[42]

Habitus and social space are concepts developed in tandem. They are best understood together in order to navigate the multitude of layers of the turbulent late nineteenth and early twentieth centuries. It bears repeating that this book is *not* a biography of two men. It is a glimpse into the changing lifeworld of men and women who shared overlapping social spaces, systems of disposition, and a patchwork of fractured habitus. Even though the Azmzades were only a few of many Arab-Ottomans who established themselves in Istanbul in the late nineteenth century, their lives provide an excellent case study of a community that had to continuously negotiate a place for itself in a quickly changing empire.

Since the sources did not explicitly deal with the inner lives of these imperial men and women, I had to rely on tools developed by literary scholars for "inscribing fragments of . . . consciousness" in a text that at first glance might appear devoid of any hidden meaning.[43] Reading the texts "against the grain" has allowed me to shine a light on the social consciousness of Arab-Ottomans in Istanbul, and at times their subconsciousness, as they performed who they thought they were and where they thought they fit in or wanted to. In particular, I attempt to understand their habitus, changing positionality, and the emergence of notions of difference that have, with a few notable exceptions, eluded scholars of the Ottoman Empire.[44] Leaning on the work of thinkers from a variety of fields, I investigate Sadik's identification or purposeful (dis)engagement with "Ottoman-ness," "European-ness," "Arab-ness," and "Whiteness" from his writings during his travels in Africa and Europe and while accompanying Russian and German royalty in the Levant.[45] I highlight Sadik's response to the European gaze on "the Orient," as well as his evolving understanding of his subject position in an imperial world order. As he pondered what I call the "intimate other" in the Sahara and North Africa, I learned more about him and his self-conscious obsessions and social anxieties than about the objects of his observations.[46] I put Sadik's habitus in conversation with historical events of the period and the textual and pictorial evidence that Sadik and his family left behind.[47] The result is a surprising insight into where a Muslim, Arab-Ottoman member of a global imperial class positioned himself and how that positioning evolved as the empire's internal and external political and social dynamics changed.

Sources, Analysis, Scale

Putting a person's life at the center of a historical narrative is not new to Ottoman historiography. Several works have highlighted historical characters' lives during the Ottoman era, spanning geographies from Sudan to Bulgaria and Tunisia to Syria, and many were part of the inspiration for this book.[48] *Losing Istanbul* offers a new intervention in the field of Ottoman studies in three important ways. The first is the use of microhistory methodology, which examines all evidence, from the seemingly insignificant to the obviously pivotal, in order to bring to life an entire world out of the intimate details of people's lives. This book puts biographical details in conversation with global events to provide a total history of an empire at the scale of human experience—a dialectic relationship between the experiences of individual lives and the unfolding of significant events.[49] In the tradition of total history (*histoire totale*), it envisions history over the long and medium term that is not divided into sub-historical categories such as economic, social, diplomatic, or cultural.[50] I have chosen "total history" to describe my approach to the totality of experience, which incorporates several historical disciplines over the *durée* of a human life.

On the one hand, the book zooms in on the impact of historical events on the individual level. It analyzes how the traumas of wars, local political conflict, international conflicts, and natural and human-made catastrophes were *experienced* by historical figures living in the empire and how they were reflected in the unique and shared conditions that defined each person's lifeworld. It refracts through the microcosm of the rich lives of flawed human beings who influenced the making and unmaking of the Ottoman state in the 1880s, 1890s, 1900s, and 1910s. On the other hand, the book sees "the world in a grain of sand,"[51] constantly "[playing] with the scale"[52]— examining the minutiae of daily life to construct a total history of the last four decades of the Ottoman Empire, zooming in to provide a street-level view and zooming back out to give a bird's-eye view—an experiential history of a moment in the life of the empire.

I have employed hundreds of archival sources directly related to or intersecting with the families whose lives I attempt to re-member. Sources from Turkish, British, Bulgarian, Lebanese, French, and Syrian archives and libraries helped contextualize photos, and two manuscripts of travelogues written in Ottoman-Turkish, which I found or were given to me by the Azmzades' descendants. I analyzed those manuscripts in relation to several versions of the published travelogues in Ottoman-Turkish, modern Turkish, and Arabic.

The various versions differed significantly, helping to shed light on the political, social, and cultural contexts in which they were written, modified, censored, and (re-)published. Additionally, I remedied some biographical gaps and incorporated some family memories through interviews with descendants residing in Damascus, Istanbul, Qatar, and California. Inspired by historians who have adapted an experiential approach to the study of traumatic moments of ruptures and violence in history, I wove all of these sources together to provide the reader with an experiential narrative of the end of the Ottoman Empire from the perspective of Arab-Ottomans as they fell from the pinnacle of power to become objects of suspicion in the span of one generation.[53]

Finally, following Shafiq and Sadik from birth to death, through their rise and fall in the inner circles of the Ottoman metropole, *Losing Istanbul* offers more than a new analytical take on well-known events. It offers what I think of as a "slow burn," narration of the delicious details in order to present an almost sensory experience of the past—a "sense" of life in its joys and sorrows, triumphs and losses, generosity of spirit, and moral depravity that stems from pride, prejudice, and the confusion of losing one's place in the world.[54] Ultimately, my hope is that readers of this book will take the time to delve as deeply into the details as they choose to while maintaining an empathetic perspective of the human dimension of late nineteenth- and early-twentieth-century Ottoman history.

Names, Titles, and the Social Context

After the collapse of the Ottoman Empire, the Azmzade family was fractured, with some staying in what would become the Republic of Turkey and others living across Syria, Lebanon, and Egypt, forever losing the center of their imperial world, Istanbul. Now their descendants live across the world, but they trace their background to the Azmzades of Istanbul or the al-'Azms of Syria: two names for the same family. The duality of how Azmzades represented their family names in many ways reflected their layered habitus as they appeared to seamlessly transition from Arabic in Damascus—al-'Azm—to Ottoman-Turkish (from Persian) in Istanbul—Azmzade (Azm-zade).

Azmzade was a well-known surname that took on new political meaning in the aftermath of the empire. *'Azm* (also transliterated as *Azım, 'Azem,* or *'Azim*) is an Arabic word with a complicated history. Some claim that it came from *'azama*, meaning greatness, and others claim that it came from *'adem or 'azem*, meaning bones, in reference to the broad stature of one of the Azmzades' ancestors. The name and its origin are entangled with ethnon-ationalist claims on both sides of the Turkish-Syrian border. Some Turkish scholars and Turkish members of the family insist on the Anatolian ancestry of the family and that *'Azm* was an Arabic translation of the Turkish *kemik*, meaning bone, and that the family was originally known as *Kemikoğlu* (the family of *kemik*—literally the son of *kemik*). In this theory, the name was changed to the Arabic form *Banu al-'Azm* and later simply *al-'Azm* once the family moved to Syria in the sixteenth century.[55] Other members of the family, mostly those who identify with the Arab side, claim that the name came from that of an Arab tribe. They insist on their Arab ethnicity, telling stories of how they came from Ma'arrat al-Nu'man in northern Syria, and some even claim the family originated on the Arabian Peninsula.[56]

What is important to me as a historian is not the ethnic or national iden-tification of the descendants. What matters is understanding the how and the why of family members representing themselves, over the last few de-cades of the empire, through written records. After all, Sadik and Shafiq lived through major sociocultural transitions at the center of the empire. While they passed through major political upheavals after the Young Turk Revolution in 1908, World War I, and the breakup of the empire, they im-pacted their own notion of belonging and identification. This is especially evident after 1908, when the family name again became an issue, with Shafiq using not Azm-zade, the Ottoman form (derived from Persian), which most of the family members used during the Ottoman period, but rather al-'Azm, the Arabic form.

I consistently use the Ottoman-Turkish form Azmzade, which was most commonly used by the family. This choice is not meant to imply their Turk-ishness or non-Turkishness; I believe it to be the most faithful to their im-perial persona. I make an exception for bibliographical references in order remain faithful to the rendering as it appears in the published source.

Sadik had a daughter named Masune (Levantine Ar. Masuneh) and two sons—(Ahmed) Celaleddin aka Celal (Ar. Jelal al-Din; hereafter Jelal) and (Mehmed) Giyasuddin aka Giyas (Ar. Ghiyath al-Din; hereafter Giyas).[57]

They were all born in Istanbul and grew up with Turkish as their mother tongue. They all learned Arabic, and the boys became fluent French speakers. When writing in French, they adopted the second part of their name, al-Mu'ayyad, to honor the patriarch of the family, Ahmed al-Mu'ayyad, transliterated in modern Turkish to el-Müeyyed. As is often the case with Arabic-origin names in republican Turkey, how a name was pronounced and the way it was written became a way to express identitarian belonging to an ethnic Turkish nationality.[58] However, little discussed in the literature is how Arab-Ottoman imperialists, well before the end of the empire, had to navigate language and self-representation, often code-switching in a multilingual Istanbul. Code-switching is "adjusting one's style of speech, appearance, behavior, and expression in ways that will optimize the comfort of others in exchange for fair treatment. . . ."[59] In the Azmzades' case, it involved knowing when it was advantageous to speak Turkish, classical Arabic, Levantine (*Shami*) Arabic, or French. Code-switching was in many ways about signaling a particular set of cultural, national, and class belongings that also applied to their pronunciation of certain words, including their names, which might register as Arabophile, Turcophile, or transimperial Francophile.

While in most cases it is impossible to be certain of how Ottoman-Turkish sounded—written with Arabic letters with no diacritical marks that would indicate which vowels to use when transliterated—the debate about the transliteration of Ottoman-Turkish continues, and it is often tainted with political bias and nationalist fervor. One of the best-known examples is the writing of the name of the founder of the Khedival dynasty in Egypt, an Albanian-Ottoman soldier from Kavala, a town in Ottoman Macedonia in the Province of Salonica (today part of Greece). The debate is over whether his name should be written and pronounced in Arabic or Turkish form—Muhammad 'Ali or Mehmed/t Ali. The Turkification or Arabization of pronunciation is a sensitive topic for Egyptians because it goes to the heart of the official story of the creation of the modern Egyptian state.[60]

In most cases, the implications of how a name or a word is transliterated do not carry the heavy weight of national, racial, and ethnic belonging. A simple explanation of the transliteration system adopted at the beginning of a book suffices. However, in a multigenerational history of an Arab-Ottoman family, where linguistic and cultural identifications are part of the story, it becomes much more complex. With the help of written records that show how members of the family transliterated their names into French, we get a better insight into the way they uttered their names, allowing for a rare opportunity to "hear" them. A clear move toward a Turkish pronunciation took place for Sadik's children, who were born and raised in Istanbul. Thus, al-Mouayad (Arabic pronunciation), the way Sadik in 1908 signed his name in Latin letters, became el-Mueyed (Turkish pronunciation) when his children signed it in 1919, similar to the way present-day Turkish historians have taken to denoting it—el-Müeyyed. Bank records and correspondence with the Ottoman Imperial Bank written in French in 1919 show Sadik's children's names as A. Ghiassedine el-Mueyed and Mehmed Djelaleddine el-Mueyed, while Sadik's was still al-Mouayad (figure 3).[61]

Those were all written records. The way the Turkish sounded, however, is much harder to come by, but we do have a clue from 1904 when Sadik arrived in Sofia. He (or his staff) sent a formal telegram to the grand vizier announcing his arrival at his post and commencement of his "sacred duty."[62] The telegram was a transliteration of Ottoman-Turkish into Latin letters, allowing a truly phonetic representation of how Sadik and the people around him sounded. The use of certain letter combinations betrayed the diplomatic core's Francophone education: "Chimdi Sofiyaya vassil vé vézaifi mir kioulei tchakranámin ifacina besmélékechi ibtidar oldiguim marouzdir ferman. Signed Sadik Almouayet."[63] This is a rare opportunity to hear a historical subject, approximating how an Ottoman, French-educated member of the imperial foreign service pronounced certain words in Ottoman-Turkish. Two words were particularly unexpected. The first is *oldiguim*, in which he sounds the "g" as what today, using modern Turkish pronunciation rules, would be a silent, or *yumuşak* "g," giving us *olduğum*, a form of the verb *olmak*. In the sentence, it comes at the end to add the meaning of "I have . . . arrived . . . and commenced. . . ." The second seems to indicate the softening of the last consonant in his name, al-Mouayad, turning the "d" into a "t" (al-Mouayet). This was a common way of softening endings, turning a "b" into "p" and a "d" into "t" in spoken Ottoman-Turkish, and it became the rule in modern Turkish. The significance of these word forms is an auditory sense of spoken Turkish at the turn of the century. The second is a reminder that spoken Ottoman-Turkish, even by *İstanbul'lu* elites, did not necessarily sound the

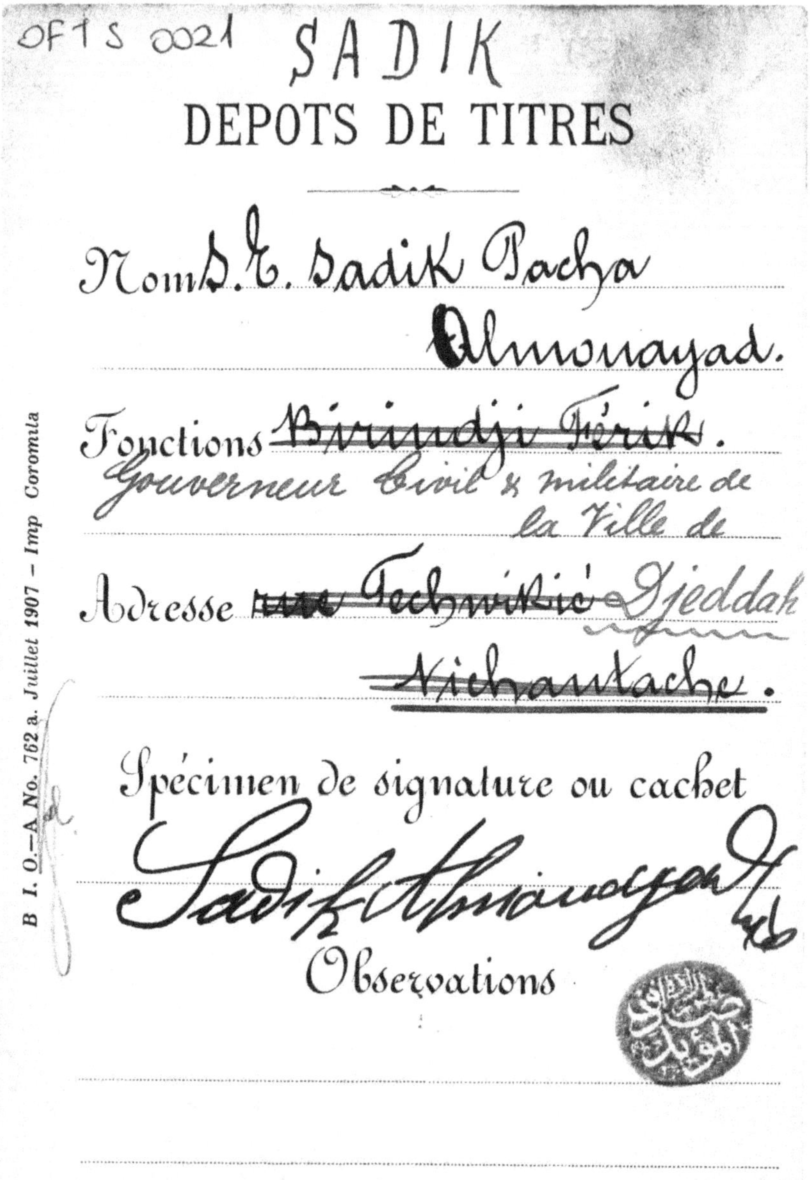
OFTS 0021 SADIK

DEPOTS DE TITRES

Nom S.E. Sadik Pacha Almouayad.

Fonctions ~~Birindji Férik~~. Gouverneur Civil & militaire de la Ville de

Adresse ~~rue Techvikié~~ Djeddah ~~Nichantache~~.

Spécimen de signature ou cachet

Sadik Almouayad

Observations

B I. O.—A No. 762 a. Juillet 1907 – Imp Coromila

FIGURE 3. Sadik's Signature Card from the Ottoman Imperial Bank.
Source: Salt Research, Ottoman Bank Collection, OFTS0021.

same as modern Turkish, or what many refer to as Istanbul Turkish, today. Additionally, the common use of modern Turkish to transliterate Ottoman documents, which I follow, should remind us of what we lose when we erase spoken sounds that Turkish had in common with neighboring languages like Arabic, Kurdish, and Persian.

With all that said, Azmzade was in fact not a legal surname. Even though some household names like Azmzade were well known and were usually used in the same way surnames are today, it is important to remember that there were no legally recognized surnames in the Ottoman Empire. In fact, they did not become a requirement until more than a decade after the dissolution of the empire.[64] This, however, meant that titles that often followed the first name in formal written and spoken forms were especially crucial sociocultural markers.

Titles such as *Bey* (Ar. *Bek*), *Pasha* (Tr. *Paşa*), *Efendi*, *Usta*, *Agha* (Tr. *Ağa*), and *Hanım* (Ar. *Khanom* or *Hanem*) implied belonging to a certain class, guild, or even a form of nobility.[65] These were generally societal, and often professional titles that announced an individual's status, and they changed as the person ascended or descended the social, political, or professional ladder.

I refrain from using titles except when an individual is first mentioned or when explaining the significance of how a title was earned or lost. This is meant to maintain the focus on the individual and not rank or status, keeping the reader on a first-name basis with characters with whom the reader will become intimately familiar. It also avoids confusion for the nonspecialist reader only familiar with the much less nuanced use of titles in today's Turkey and other Ottoman successor states.

Content and Chapter Organization

In Chapter 1, I focus on the path taken by Shafiq and Sadik Azmzade from their childhood homes in Damascus to their new households and careers in the capital. I follow them from their formative years in post-pogrom Syria of the 1860s through their education in Mount Lebanon, Beirut, and Istanbul between the 1870s and the early 1890s. Along the way, I offer the reader a peek into their homes, meeting Sadik's wife, Esma; Shafiq's wife, Nimet, Sadik's *evlatlık*, Bilal, and his three children living in the new neighborhood of Teşvikiye, where class and gender segregation were practiced, and different forms of indentured domestic labor made their luxurious lifestyle affordable.

In Chapter 2, I delve into what careers in the empire meant for Shafiq and Sadik. Starting with the quotidian corruption that came with power, I focus on Shafiq's career in the palace and how he used his position for personal benefit. I demonstrate how Shafiq, as a loyal imperialist, believed that the empire's strength corresponded to his personal success, and, by the same token, the wealth of the empire was his wealth. In the second part of the chapter, I focus on Sadik's involvement in the dark events between 1893 and 1897, including a cholera outbreak in the more impoverished neighborhoods of Istanbul and the Armenian massacres in the Ottoman east.

In Chapter 3, I offer an alternative view of the post-1878 Ottoman defeat by Russia. Starting in 1888 and ending in 1903, I cover three events in which Sadik was involved and that played an essential role in shaping his view of the world. The first came a decade after the defeat, when a Russian grand duke and his entourage traveled throughout the Levant in what can only be described as a belated victory tour on Ottoman soil. The second was Sadik's years in Berlin and his subsequent accompaniment of the German emperor to his childhood home in Damascus. The third was Sadik's official travels in Russia, Crimea, and Ottoman Macedonia on behalf of the government, witnessing firsthand the long-term impact of the Treaty of Berlin and twenty-five years of failed Ottoman policies in the Balkans.

In Chapter 4, I argue that Sadik constructed a discursive illusion of the Saharan "native" using broad strokes meant to distance a familiar Other, one with whom he shared a mother tongue, a religion, and, by his own assessment, a political allegiance. I analyze the text to show how Sadik followed a strategy that granted him the status of an outside observer who shared a frame of reference with his readers in Istanbul while acting as an expert who could interpret the natives for the people back in the Ottoman metropole. As I interrogate Sadik's word choices, I ask: What's in a word? How does one understand the social implications of a signifier such as "Arab" in the context of events in Istanbul at the time? In the final section of the chapter, I shift the focus to Sadik's relative, Izzet al-'Abid, also infamously known as Arap İzzet, to delve deeper into the appellation *Arap* as an ethnoracial marker in late Ottoman Istanbul.

In Chapter 5, I show how Sadik negotiated a complex set of identifications with Muslims, Syrians, Ottoman imperialists, Western Europeans, and, most important, what he called "Whites," which he constructed against an African Other that he described in his Abyssinia travelogue. I argue that by 1904 racialization was playing a substantial role in explaining what Sadik considered the negative characteristics of "Black" Africans and his superiority as a self-identified "White" man.

In Chapter 6, I concentrate on Sadik's assignment as the Ottoman special commissioner to Bulgaria between 1904 and 1908. The challenges of the turbulent eastern Balkans, coupled with intraimperial government quibbling and Sadik's pride, would contribute to the unfolding of disastrous events for the empire and his own career. In Chapter 7, I catch up with Shafiq as he reinvented himself as the representative of the Province of Syria in the Ottoman parliament. He became a leader of an Arab-centered political party adamant about working within the system to fight against what they saw as the ruling party's anti-Arab prejudice in Istanbul. The final years of his career give the reader the chance to reexamine those turbulent years, in which cultural identification became an issue of public debate and ethnoracial identification became a political factor, leaving no doubt that anti-Arab sentiment was perceived by many in the Levant to exist well before World War I.

In the concluding chapter, Chapter 8, I address the end of Shafiq and Sadik's generation of Arab-Ottoman imperialists and its aftermath. I briefly discuss the fate that befell their children and grandchildren during the Great War, where the family members ended up after the end of the war, and how the Azmzades transformed themselves after the dissolution of the Ottoman Empire. Even though the breakdown of the family is a story of loss of home, prestige, and an imagined future, I show how this is also a story of survival, adaptation, and transformation, as family members on both sides of the newly created Turkish-Syrian border found a way to reinvent themselves while claiming different versions of the family's long history.

CHAPTER 1

FROM MEYDAN, DAMASCUS,
TO TASHWIQIYYEH, ISTANBUL

He soon appeared and took me upstairs. . . . It was a very
hot day, and Sadik Bey took down the lattice, and the
whole beautiful view burst on me of the green hill opposite,
crowned by the white kiosks of Yildiz Palace, and the
Mosque where the Sultan goes for Selamlik, and to the
right the waters of the Bosphorus, sparkling over the brown
roofs of the houses in Beshiktash quarter.

—Georgina Adelaide Müller, 1893[1]

THE SMALL WORLD OF ITINERANT GLOBAL ELITES OF EMPIRE
meant that the British socialite and wife of the famous philologist, Max Müller, happened to be in Sadik's Istanbul home on a sunny afternoon in 1893,
leaving us some of the most colorful descriptions of this private space. It was
a long way from Sadik's childhood home in Damascus where he and Shafiq
grew up. In the last quarter of the nineteenth century, like Sadik and Shafiq,
many Arab-Ottoman men from notable urban families in the provinces had
a choice of paths to pursue: a career in the imperial capital or one closer to
home in the Levant.[2] They came from cities like Aleppo, Damascus, Beirut,
Jerusalem, and Tripoli and built their careers in Istanbul during the Hamidian period. Their paths often intersected at a missionary school in Mount

Lebanon, followed by some form of higher education in Beirut. If they were academically inclined and, perhaps more important, had the right pedigree and familial connections, they had the choice to join the imperial civil service or the military in Istanbul. Otherwise, they would follow in their fathers' and grandfathers' footsteps in local and regional governance and commerce.

As state centralization accelerated in the second half of the nineteenth century, so did the need for powerful provincial families to establish themselves in the imperial center. The Azmzades were not unique in this respect; the famous Melhamés and al-'Abids, for example, were two other families from Beirut and Damascus who left an indelible mark on turn-of-the-century Istanbul and whom the reader will meet as their lives overlapped with the Azmzades.[3] Although they took different paths once they made it to Istanbul, they all shared many aspects of their rise, running in the same social spaces with overlapping ambitions. They often made political alliances with one another, and at times they found themselves in competition for the same position or the same lucrative contract for government infrastructure projects. This generation of Arab-Ottoman imperialists also had front-row access to some of the most significant global events that the empire witnessed between 1883 and 1919.

This chapter's focus is on the road taken by two Azmzades, Shafiq and Sadik, and their relative, Izzet al-'Abid, from their childhood homes in Damascus to their new homes in Istanbul. I follow them from their early formative years in the post-pogrom Damascus of the 1860s through their education in Mount Lebanon and Beirut in the 1870s and early 1880s and on to their careers in the second half of the 1880s.

I also introduce the reader to Sadik's wife, Esma, and Shafiq's wife, Nimet, and some of their children, and I provide a glimpse of their private lives as young palace officials who left their mark on the newly established neighborhood of Teşvikiye—their "Tashwiqiyyeh." Tashwiqiyyeh was most likely the way a native Levantine-Arabic speaker pronounced Teşvikiye. The name of the neighborhood comes from the Arabic root *tashwiq* (Tr. *teşvik*) meaning excitement, incitement, encouragement toward something, a fitting name for this new and "modern" neighborhood in Istanbul. I highlight the Levantine-Arabic pronunciation of the name here to draw attention to the fact that imperial Istanbul was also a part of Arab-Ottoman experience

in the late Ottoman Empire and to emphasize that a number of the original Hamidian-era Teşvikiye/Tashwiqiyyeh inhabitants were native-Arabic-
speaking Ottoman families.

Alternative Paths to Power

Shafiq was born in early 1861 into a Damascus reeling in the aftermath of
the anti-Christian pogroms of 1860,[4] and he was raised amid turmoil and instability for the family. Weathering the ups and downs of provincial politics,
his family had risen to significant influence in the eighteenth century, when
the Azmzades had held the governorship of Damascus nine times between
1725 and 1808.[5] Like most notable families who depended on the goodwill
of the central government for their legitimacy, they also faced their share of
punishments, including executions, exile, and property confiscations during
the times they fell out of favor with Istanbul. For example, the first time
Shafiq's father, Ahmed al-Mu'ayyad, ran afoul of the Ottoman government
a decade after the end of Egypt's governor-general Mehmet Ali's rule of the
Levant, which lasted from 1832 to 1840. At that time, al-Mu'ayyad was investigated for irregular tax collection and then fired from his position as the
kaymakam (district governor) of Qal'at al-Akrad (Krak des Chevaliers) and
the village of Humais in what is today northern Lebanon.[6] Eight years later,
in early 1858, he was exiled to Nicosia in Cyprus, but this time as a punishment for what was described as unspecified violent acts committed by him
and his men.[7]

In 1861, the year of Shafiq's birth, many of the Azmzades were exiled yet
again, and many of their properties were confiscated. This time the punishment was in response to their inability to prevent the anti-Christian pogroms and to the participation of their own armed militias in the atrocities
in Damascus and elsewhere in the spring and summer of 1860.[8] In an effort
to appease European observers and send a signal to its own population, the
Ottoman central government had to demonstrate its willingness to punish
anybody considered a culprit in the massacres, even members of a family as
firmly rooted in the Ottoman traditional power structure as the Azmzades.
The central government cast a wide net, confiscating the property of several men of the family who were exiled to Cyprus, Rhodes, and Chios. The

Azmzades were seen as silent observers or collaborators in the massacres.[9] Even though some of the elders died in captivity, most returned to the Syrian provinces within a year or two, although often they were not allowed to live in the city they had left. For example, 'Abd al-Qadir (Tr. Abdülkadır) Azmzade, the son of Shafiq's grandfather's brother, who was forgiven in 1862 and allowed to leave Chios and return to the Levant, was not granted permission to return to his home in Damascus, at least at that time.[10] Time and time again, the Azmzades found their way back to prominence, competing with other factions for power and influence in the Levantine provinces. All of this turbulence must have left an impression on young Shafiq, who learned that one had to adapt to political changes, which meant that sometimes one had to jump from a sinking ship and follow a new political course in order to survive. That would come in handy for Shafiq and Sadik as they negotiated the cutthroat political world of Istanbul in the early 1900s.

Shafiq received his elementary education in Damascus before being sent to Mount Lebanon, where he studied at the oldest French Catholic missionary school in Southwest Asia, Le Collège Saint Joseph. The college had been established by Lazarist[11] priests in 1835 in the village of 'Aintoura (Antoura) in Mount Lebanon and continues in operation today.[12] Going to the Collège Saint Joseph was one of the most effective ways to become proficient in French, which was the language of international diplomacy at the time and the marker of an educated Ottoman class. Most of the Levantine men of the state who ended up building a career in Istanbul in the late nineteenth century started their educational trajectory there before diverging later on to join either the civil service, the military, or the vast Yıldız Palace bureaucracy. Like many other members of elite Damascene families, after finishing his studies in 'Aintoura, Shafiq moved to Beirut to further his education at the Greek Catholic Collège Patriarchal, followed by a stint at what some Ottoman sources referred to as the "American College" but was better known as the Syrian Protestant College.[13]

The Syrian Protestant College opened its doors to students in 1866 and in 1870 moved to its permanent home on land reportedly donated by Shafiq's father and Sadik's grandfather, Ahmed al-Mu'ayyad.[14] Al-Mu'ayyad, like many Damascene notables, had a second house in Beirut and a summer house in Mount Lebanon and owned a great deal of land in what used to be the hinterland of Beirut, outside the old city walls. The college's campus was built in the neighborhood of Ras Beirut, where the city's shoreline juts out slightly into the Mediterranean. Standing on top of a hill just above the seashore, the university, along with many large houses, was beyond the noise and congestion of the old city and had spectacular views of the sea. The campus, which has expanded considerably since its establishment, still stands on one of the most beautiful and valuable pieces of real estate in Beirut.[15]

By the time Shafiq had finished his education, he was fluent in Arabic, Turkish, French, and English—language skills that would eventually boost him to one of the most important offices in the empire. After graduating, he worked in municipal and provincial governments; first as a clerk in the Municipality of Beirut in 1879 at a modest salary of 300 kurush (Kr) per month and then, in 1880, as head clerk of the customs office in Beirut at 450Kr, raised in two years to 520Kr. By the end of his career, he would be making sixty-five times that amount. In 1882, at the young age of twenty-one, he was hired at triple his former salary at the Directorate of Land Register of the Province of Syria in Damascus. He stayed in Damascus for five more years until fate intervened, catapulting him from obscurity as a provincial governmental employee into one of the centers of power at the time: the translation office in Yıldız Palace.[16]

Even though Sadik was Shafiq's nephew, he was his senior by a few years and must have had more vivid memories of the massacres of 1860–1861 and the crisis that followed. Sadik followed a similar path to his uncle's by going to Saint Joseph, but instead of the Greek Catholic Collège Patriarchal, he went to al-Madrasa al-Wataniyya (the National School) in Beirut, which had notably been founded by the Protestant convert and Arab-Ottoman patriot and intellectual Butrus al-Bustani.[17] That was where Sadik's and Shafiq's educational paths diverged, for Sadik took the military education route, heading to the military school in Istanbul. In 1883 he graduated at the rank of *mülazım* (lieutenant) and later joined the elite Office of Aides-de-Camp to the sultan (*Yaver-i Sultan*).[18] He was fluent in Arabic, Turkish, and French, and after a few months' stint in Berlin later in his career he also became fluent in German. He was a peripatetic man and an ardent imperialist who represented the sultan on many missions in Europe, Russia, Arabia, and Africa. He also wrote extensively in Ottoman-Turkish, translating several books from French and Arabic and publishing two popular travelogues. The manuscripts that survived the first fire in his Istanbul home did so because they were given as gifts to the sultan and are now preserved in Istanbul University's Nadir Eeserler Kütüphanesi (Rare Works Library).

Shafiq and Sadik were not the only members of the Azmzade family to hold important positions in the Ottoman government during the turbulent years of Abdülhamid's rule, the transition to the second constitutional period, and World War I. Some of Sadik's brothers, cousins, and other relatives held important positions, but most did not break out of the provincial power structure. For example, one brother, Sa'id, joined the Ottoman military and later served on the Damascus municipal council and would eventually become known for being one of the first people to drill for oil in the Syrian desert. Another brother, Iklil (Tr. İklil), held the position of *kaymakam* (district governor) of the districts of Duma, 'Ajlun, Nabek, and Baalbek in the Province of Syria, and he would survive internment in World War I to return to his vast property and wealth in Damascus after the war ended. Later he would be named governor of Hawran under the rule of Amir Faisal. A third brother, Safuh, held several local positions, including that of police inspector and director of prisons.[19] I will come back to Sadik's brothers and other family members in the coming chapters; however, next I briefly turn to a very (in)famous relative of the Azmzades, one of the most influential Hamidian-era imperialists and a figure who cast a long shadow on Arab-Ottomans of Istanbul even years after he had fled the city.

Izzet (bin Holo) al-'Abid was born in Damascus in the early 1850s.[20] He completed his elementary education and then followed a path similar to that of his relatives of the same generation, Shafiq and Sadik, entering St. Joseph in 'Aintoura in Mount Lebanon and later studying Arabic under the supervision of the famous Arabic-language linguist and author Nasif al-Yaziji at the Greek Catholic Collège Patriarchal in Beirut.[21] He worked his way through the local and provincial governments, distinguishing himself in the justice department for reforming the court system in Mount Lebanon, and was later briefly assigned to Konya and Salonica before arriving in Istanbul. There he became the head of Istanbul's court of the first instance, then the court of appeals, and finally he had a short stint at the commercial court. In 1895 he was appointed to the Council of State (*Şura-i Devlet*). More important, nine years after his arrival in Istanbul, he was officially employed as a second secretary and close advisor to the sultan, earning 20,000Kr a month—the highest recorded level of "official" salaries that I came across for that period. He received too many honors and medals from Ottoman and foreign states to enumerate. Between 1897 and 1903, he was a member of the Committee for Fiscal Reforms and a major part of the Istanbul-based commission organizing the global logistics of constructing the Hijaz telegraph and railway lines.[22]

Legend in the 'Abid family says that Izzet's first encounter with the sultan took place in the mid-1880s, when his father Muhyi al-Din Abi al-Hawl, known as Holo (Hawlo, Hulu) Pasha, sent him to Istanbul with two "lions" from Yemen to give to the sultan (though most likely they were Arabian leopards or some other wild feline native to the region).[23] Holo Pasha was a nominal ally of the Azmzade faction in Damascus from the Meydan neighborhood. He distinguished himself by playing a decisive role in protecting Christians during the 1860 pogroms. He married Makkiyyeh Azmzade, the granddaughter of the last Azmzade to serve as the governor-general of Syria. The marriage solidified the ties between these two families, a mutually beneficial alliance, especially after the Azmzades temporarily fell out of favor with Istanbul following the pogroms.[24] Makkiyeh had five children—half-sisters and brothers to Izzet.[25] Izzet and his brother Mustafa, who became the district governor of Mosul, were born to a mother from the Kharbutli (Tr. Harputlu) family.[26]

Holo's first major governmental post was as district governor of the Beqaa, where he reportedly collected taxes in a repressive and unfair fashion, prompting locals to complain about him. He was able to save himself by going to Istanbul to plead his case, and somehow, he came back with the honorary title of Pasha and the governorship of Nablus. He also served as a *mutasarrıf* (district governor) of Hama and Tripoli (now in northern Lebanon) and as a member of the *Meclis-i Ayan* (Assembly of Notables) in Damascus, among other positions.[27] Holo was accused of maladministration through which he amassed a sizable fortune and was even imprisoned several times, yet he seemed to always survive. Along the way, his wealth continued to grow, reportedly thanks to smart investments in projects like the Suez and

Panama canals. He lived until 1895, long enough to witness Izzet reaching the pinnacle of his career.[28] Izzet had a large impact on how Arab-Ottomans in the capital and beyond were viewed, first by the Hamidian administration and later by the Committee of Unity and Progress (CUP) administration.

A Founding Myth for the Azmzades of Istanbul

Like Izzet's, Shafiq and Sadik's opportunity to work in the sultan's court took on a mythical quality in the family history. According to Shafiq's son-in-law 'Abd al-Qadir Azmzade, Shafiq did not seek the glamour or power associated with working close to the sultan at the time; it fell into his lap by accident. The story starts with Shafiq's father, al-Mu'ayyad, traveling on business to the imperial capital. While in Istanbul, "he happened to perform his Friday prayer at the Yıldız Palace mosque at the same time as Sultan 'Abd al-Hamid Khan the Second. That was when al-Mu'ayyad Bey's augustness drew the attention of the sultan. Namık Pasha, the Head of Ministers (Ar. Sheikh al-Wuzara', Tr. *Şeyh-ül-Vüzera*), who happened to be accompanying the sultan, inquired about his identity. Namık Pasha, who had served as governor-general of Syria before, recognized the family name. So, the sultan sent one of his companions to invite al-Mu'ayyad Bey to visit him. . . ."[29]

Eventually, the story continues, al-Mu'ayyad got an audience with the sultan, which lasted more than an hour, during which the sultan bestowed on him the title of Pasha at the rank of Beylerbey and awarded him with an unspecified medal. The sultan reportedly also insisted that al-Mu'ayyad make any request of him. Out of an abundance of pride and humility, initially, al-Mu'ayyad declined the sultan's offer. The sultan reportedly had to ask him three times before al-Mu'ayyad agreed, stating that he did not need anything for himself. However, he continued, "I have a son named Shafiq who graduated from institutions of higher learning where he perfected Turkish, French, and English. I also have a grandson by the name of Sadik who works in your majesty's Aides-de-Camp office." That was when the sultan ordered the appointment of Shafiq as a translator in the palace and raised Sadik's rank. The story goes on to say that the sultan even invited al-Mu'ayyad to stay in Istanbul as his guest until the Eid celebrations, when the sultan would have offered him the title of vizier. Al-Mu'ayyad, reportedly knew better and left Istanbul as fast as possible, knowing well what fate might eventually befall a vizier if he were to fall out of favor with the sultan.[30] This story was passed down from generation to generation in the Azmzade family. It was relayed to me by the late philosopher and professor Sadiq Jalal al-'Azm, one of Sadik's grandchildren, when I interviewed him in Damascus in the winter of 2009.

The notion that the Azmzades fared better in the imperial period, in this case being divinely positioned at the right time and the right place, was something the family felt was symbolic of their fortune during imperial times. The notion that some elite families did much better under Ottoman rule than under the nation-state system is not rare. It is shared by many large Sunni Muslim families of Syria, Palestine, and Lebanon. However, one cannot rely on the impressions of the past when one has other sources. In Ottoman history, there are always other sources, and in this case the Ottoman archives give a more complex story of how al-Mu'ayyad came to be in the sultan's presence.

Al-Mu'ayyad was indeed in Istanbul a few months before his son moved there; that much was true. However, as a letter he sent to the palace upon his return to Damascus indicates, al-Mu'ayyad was there to ask for the intervention of the palace on his behalf in a land inheritance dispute languishing in the local Damascus courts. Thus, like most mythologies, the story was partially based on fact. He did travel to Istanbul but only after having petitioned the sultan to intervene and then must have found it necessary to have an audience with him. There was no coincidence or divine intervention. The rest of the story is much less clear, and the land dispute issue would be passed on to Shafiq a couple of years later.[31]

Upon al-Mu'ayyad's return to Damascus, he sent the sultan an eloquent letter in Arabic. In it he unleashed line after line of poetic compliments singing the virtue of living under Abdülhamid II's rule. He thanked the sultan for the hospitality and kindness he had shown him and assured him that he was back at home in good health and singing his praise at every social gathering. He said that since there was no way to return the favor by hosting him in Damascus, all that was left was for him and his family to "increase their prayers for [his] highness."[32]

Thus, whether or not the rest of the story's details as told by 'Abd al-Qadir and Sadiq Jalal al-'Azm are accurate is hard to tell. The story paints the family as loyal servants of Sultan Abdülhamid II and shows that the influence of the family was strong even before the rise of Sadik and Shafiq in the palace. We know for sure that Shafiq was hired and moved to Istanbul in 1887, the same year as al-Mu'ayyad's visit. Similarly, Sadik was promoted that year; however, his promotion came on the heels of a critical mission that he had successfully completed, getting the attention of the sultan. The mission, which I discuss in detail in Chapter 4, was a diplomatic one, where he was entrusted with the delicate task of bringing the Grand Sanusi in the eastern Sahara to the side of the Ottoman Empire. By the time Sadik went on this mission to the Sahara, he had already become a *kolağası* (lieutenant commander).[33] Sadik's return to Istanbul after this first major successful mission to the eastern Sahara coincided with the arrival of his grandfather, al-Mu'ayyad. Thus, it is hard to know with any certainly whether al-Mu'ayyad's visit had anything to do with Sadik's promotion to the rank of *binbaşı* (lieutenant colonel) as al-Mu'ayyad had claimed. However, it much more likely was a result of the success of this critical diplomatic mission to meet with the Sanusi than with a tale of the sultan granting favors to a provincial strongman.[34]

Setting Up Home in Teşvikiye

Both Shafiq and Sadik established their households in the neighborhood of Teşvikiye. They became well-known loyal imperialists who believed in the dynasty's continuity and worked in the tight-knit circle of advisors surrounding the sultan. Sadik became known as a diplomat who served the sultan as his emissary in several places, starting with the mission to the Sahara in 1886 mentioned above, and from that year on, he spent very little time at home. Shafiq rose through the ranks in the office of the secretaries of the palace, remaining in Istanbul for all of his career except for occasional trips back to Syria and to Egypt for family business. Sadik and Shafiq lived one block away from each other. We have much more detail about Sadik's habits and lifestyle, inferred from his travelogues, than about his uncle's. We are also fortunate to have a rather intimate description of a young Sadik in the prime of his life from an unusual source: the travelogue of a British woman who visited Istanbul with her husband, a famous German orientalist, along with their grown son. The palace assigned Sadik as the family's companion and tour guide in Istanbul, leaving quite an impression on the curious British tourist and becoming the unintended star of her popular book.

Sadik lived in a multistory house, a *konak,* on one of the main streets in Teşvikiye, next door to the famous Teşvikiye Mosque and the local police station, claiming his place among the movers and shakers at the empire's center of power.[35] Like his uncle Shafiq and many other bureaucrats and military officials who worked in the offices of the Yıldız Palace and Sublime Porte, the *konak* was offered to him by the palace. The Azmzades became part of a history of privilege in this unique neighborhood, which had been connected to the royal court since its establishment in the first half of the nineteenth century. Even though a humble mosque had been initially built there in 1795, indicating the official establishment of a new neighborhood (Tr. *mahalle*), it was not until 1853–1854 that the ornate Teşvikiye Mosque, which was designed by the famous Armenian-Ottoman architect Krikor Amira Balyan, was built on the site of the original mosque.[36]

The Teşvikiye Mosque was built in the neoclassical architectural style of the new royal palace at the time, the Dolmabahçe, which stood a couple of miles down a hill on the shores of the Bosphorus. When Sultan Abdülmecid (Ar. ʿAbd al-Majid; r. 1839–1861) moved into the Dolmabahçe Palace, many of the high-ranking government officials and the staff who worked in the palace also made the move from the crowded old city across the Golden Horn to this new part of a quickly expanding European Istanbul, in the process establishing several prestigious residential neighborhoods. Teşvikiye was built on a part of Sultan Bayezid II's land *vakıf* (Ar. *waqf*), a charitable endowment established centuries earlier. Initially, Circassian refugees were allowed to stay on the land after the Crimean war. However, it was quickly transformed by members of the royal family and high-ranking officials allowed to live on land parcels, with their *konaks* built and paid for by the palace, coinciding with the expansion of infrastructure projects commissioned to service the neighborhood.[37]

Teşvikiye truly came to life in the 1880s, after Sultan Abdülhamid II moved to his new residence, the Yıldız Palace. The palace was built on a hill opposite to the one where Teşvikiye stood. Even though historians Alan

Duben and Cem Behar argue that neighborhoods in Istanbul were not seg-regated by class until after the end of the empire, Teşvikiye must have stood as an exception—a purpose-built neighborhood for palace-associated elites.[38] First, construction material stores, furniture stores, and even piano-building businesses moved there to cater to the luxurious "modern" houses being built. They were followed by theaters, cafes, restaurants, grocers, and other staples of an elite neighborhood in Istanbul.[39] During the 1890s, the neighborhood expanded south toward the military college and east toward the Bosphorus. The *konaks* were awarded by special permission of the sultan, with the un-derstanding that they would be handed over after the official's death or upon retirement or dismissal. They varied in size and grandeur, from what could be described as an above-average house to a large mansion, but they all had lux-ury elements in common: large gardens and salons for entertaining and three stories' worth of rooms to house the officials' families and household staff. A description of one of these houses from the inside comes from Georgina Adelaide Müller during her visit to Istanbul in 1893. As mentioned earlier, Sadik accompanied her and her husband, the famous German philologist, sixty-nine-year-old Max Müller during their time in Istanbul.[40] She was so impressed by Sadik and curious about his private life that she asked to come for a visit. She noted the following:

> His house was small, but loftier than most Turkish houses and built on the very edge of the steep hill opposite Yildiz Palace. Here again a narrow pas-sage shut off all view of the entrance door from the interior of the house. I was shown in to what was evidently his sitting-room on the ground floor, for there was no lattice. The room was plainly furnished, but there was a book-case full of French and German books, for Sadik Bey had been some time in Berlin, and French he had learned in Pera, he did not understand English. He soon appeared and took me upstairs. . . . It was a very hot day, and Sadik Bey took down the lattice, and the whole beautiful view burst on me of the green hill opposite, crowned by the white kiosks of Yildiz Palace, and the Mosque where the sultan goes for Selamlik, and to the right the waters of the Bosphorus, sparkling over the brown roofs of the houses in Beshiktash quarter.[41]

A colorful description by a contemporary of Sadik from the most intimate of places, his home.

By World War I, this relatively small neighborhood boasted twenty-eight *konaks* and mansions. Some of the famous historical figures who lived there included the four-times grand vizier Kıbrıslı Kamil Pasha; a president of the Council of State, Kürt Said Pasha; and the head secretary in the palace for more than a decade, Süreyya (Ar. Thureyya) Pasha.[42] Teşvikiye became the neighborhood where some of the honored guests of the sultan were housed (some without their consent to ensure that they did not pose any threat to Abdülhamid II's authority). Perhaps the most famous "hostage" who lived there was the Muslim intellectual and political reformist Jamal al-Din al-Afghani, who died and was buried in Teşvikiye in 1897.[43]

Teşvikiye was the perfect location for the who's who of Istanbul. It was a short walk from the military college, Harbiye Mektebi, where the sons of Sadik and Shafiq would go for their higher education. A twenty-minute walk, or a ten-minute tramway ride, further down Şehit Muhtar Bey Boulevard (today's Cumhuriyet Boulevard) put them at the top of the Grand Rue de Pera (today's İstiklal Boulevard) in Beyoğlu, the principal arts and entertainment district. Pera boasted a nightlife that was unmatched in the rest of the empire. It had a mixture of Christian-, Jewish-, and Muslim-owned businesses that catered to the varied tastes of the city. Wine bars, piano bars, brothels, traditional Turkish cafes, and Parisian-style patisseries stood side by side.[44] Ballrooms, theaters, and dancehalls lined the side streets that branched out from the main boulevard, where many American and European celebrities like Sarah Bernhardt graced the stage. The famous Arab-Ottoman cartoonist Yusuf Franko (Kusa), whose family hailed from Mount Lebanon in the middle of the nineteenth century, beautifully captured the who's who of Pera in his cartoons depicting the cosmopolitan high society's life in this legendary entertainment district.[45]

One street over, on Tepebaşı Boulevard (today's Meşrutiyet Boulevard), new luxury hotels began to be built, catering to the local elites and foreign diplomats and tourists, some arriving from Europe on the famous Orient Express. Perhaps the two most famous meeting places were the Pera Palace

Hotel, built in 1895, and the Grand Hotel de Londres, built in 1892, where tea rooms, cigar bars, restaurants, and ornate lobbies were the spaces that hosted intellectuals, politicians, diplomats, and foreign dignitaries.[46] During the age of Abdülhamid II, that meant that it was also the perfect place to catch people off guard, with many of the sultan's spies infiltrating gatherings of unsuspecting people.[47]

In the opposite direction, a carriage ride from Teşvikiye, stood the Yıldız Palace complex. The palace was not only the residence of the sultan and his family; it employed many of the residents of Teşvikiye, including Shafiq, his son Vassik, and Sadik when he was not away on a diplomatic mission. The ride to the palace must have provided some spectacular views of the Bosphorus. Before the heavy construction of Art Nouveau and Art Deco residential buildings in the districts of Şişli and Fulya in the 1920s and 1930s obstructed the view, one must have been able to see all the way to Asia and to the bustling neighborhood of Üsküdar and the grand summer houses in Beylerbey on the shores of Anatolia and what would become the Asian side of metropolitan Istanbul.[48]

A block away from Sadik, Shafiq's family lived in a three-story konak on Bostan Street, up from the large mansion of the sultan's right-hand man and second secretary, Izzet al-'Abid, who was granted his large mansion after the sultan's head secretary passed away at the age of fifty in 1890. Izzet stayed there until he had to flee after the Young Turk Revolution.[49] Sadik and his family lived a block away on the main stretch, across the street from the police station, which stands to this day.[50]

Georgina Müller filled page after page with Sadik's praises in her famous Letters from Constantinople, initially published in London in 1897. She left some of the liveliest descriptions of Sadik's personality that we have on record. Georgina's descriptions were not limited to Sadik's official persona. Indeed, they give us a vivid picture of Sadik as a young man, and they allow the reader to get a sense of him from this British woman's perspective, coming across as a worldly man well versed in Western cultural understanding of "the Orient" and thus especially equipped to render Istanbul legible to Europeans. Sadik inhabited the global transimperial social spaces that had a common language, both symbolically and literally. Speaking in French, Sadik made foreigners feel comfortable while exuding a sense of pride in his own country. Georgina took note of his skill when she visited his home and met his wife, mother-in-law, and children.

At the time of Müller's visit, Sadik was a thirty-five-year-old man, whom Georgina described as "one of the most eager as well as one of the best dancers" she had met.[51] She noted that he cared deeply about his looks and wore a "marvelously tight uniform (he must have been poured into his trousers) [that] made any out-of-the-way exercise an effort."[52] He enjoyed partaking in merriment, despite his devotion to his religious practice, and "did not rigorously abstain from drinking . . . saying he considered it 'a little sin.'"[53] In Georgina's assessment, "Sadik evidently knew his Koran and the tenets of his faith very perfectly. But though a devout follower of his Prophet, he is by no means a bigot."[54]

She went on to describe him as "a highly cultivated Turk, or rather Arab, [who] was not only able to act as interpreter, but such was the prestige of his uniform that all doors were readily thrown open, and treasures seldom or never exhibited were freely shown to us. Sadik Bey spoke German, French, Turkish and Arabic, and having lived at Berlin for some time he could readily enter into the feelings with which we regard Oriental life, and point out objects that would be of special interest to Europeans."[55] This is an astute observation and carefully thought-out statement in two ways.

First, European cultural influence on Sadik was evident, but not in a way that inspired mimicry. The complete opposite was true, in fact, as Georgina described him as a man who could inhabit European disposition when he chose to, to literally "enter into the feeling" that allowed him to understand the way that Europeans "regard Oriental life." Sadik, by all accounts, lived a liminal life. An imperialist from the center who was in many ways an outsider, often finding himself in a foreign land, which made him question which identarian categories he belonged to. He was also part of generation that chose to partake in some European cultural practices as a form of belonging to a global imperial class, but he did not accept them as "universal" or as a "yardstick for all things." This was an age in which most people, including elite members of society, had not yet forgotten that many of the cultural habits that they had conditionally adopted from Europe's elites had "their roots in the complex and controversial realties of a particular historical society."[56] In other words, although some European cultural habits were adopted, they were not taken to be universal, and this understanding colored Sadik's observation of Europeans and non-Europeans during his travels in Europe, Anatolia, Arabia, the Sahara Desert, and the Horn of Africa.

Second, Georgina was careful to correct her description of all Ottomans as "Turks" by including a caveat that Sadik's ethnic origin was "Arab." She then returned to the original signifier, "Turkish," which fit the context of her perception of what he represented, what many Europeans mistakenly called the Ottoman government, as the "Turkish" government. She stated: "He was a Turkish officer and, in every sense, a Turkish patriot, truly devoted to his sovereign, and willing, if need be, to fight and die for him, for his country, and his religion."[57] Considering that Sadik was accompanying the Müllers in an official capacity assigned by the palace, one might take such a description as an expected performance. However, Sadik indeed lived his life as a true Ottoman imperialist, as she described him.

Esma and Nimet

According to Georgina's observations, Sadik's family was "really happy . . . and there could be no doubt of the affection between husband and wife, and the perfect content of the wife [Esma] in her round of home duties."[58] Georgina seemed to have a multitude of emotions about Esma that betrayed a level of admiration, pity, and even perhaps a hint of jealousy. She described her first impression of Esma as follows:

> At the top of the staircase stood his very pretty wife, small, with fine eyes, and masses of dark hair, in which she wore a natural rose. She was dressed in white muslin, with white satin shoes, the dress trimmed with pink ribbons and a scarlet sash, whilst the rose was deep crimson. She wore very fine diamonds, and was evidently got up in her very best, and in her eyes my black brocade must have seemed very dingy. The room into which we went was small and tightly latticed. She seemed bright and happy, and cast looks of adoring affection on her lord and master, who sat opposite her, and opened the conversation by asking: "What do you think of her?" I could truly say she was the prettiest woman I had seen in Pera.[59]

She noted that when Sadik opened the window, "his wife moved back, and sat where she could not see anything out of window but the sky."[60] Georgina seemed convinced that all women in the Ottoman Empire were weak and treated as property, projecting a distorted notion of the gendered high society in Istanbul. Of course, she knew nothing of Esma and her upbringing. Luckily, I do (figure 4).

Esma came from an illustrious branch of the Azmzade family started by Khadija (Tr. Hatice) Hanım in the early eighteenth century. Khadija was the daughter of Nasuh Azmzade and the sister of (Ahmed) al-Mu'ayyad Azmzade, Sadik's grandfather and the founder of the Mu'ayyad branch of the family. She was married to Ali Agha, a "Turk in the Ottoman service in Damascus" who had considerable ties with the ruling family in Egypt. During Egyptian rule in Syria, he served as a close ally and advisor to Ibrahim Pasha, the son of Mehmed Ali Pasha, the governor-general of Egypt and the Khedival dynasty's founder. One of Khadija's daughters, Farlan, was married to an Egyptian plenipotentiary in Damascus, and her sister-in-law was the wife of Ibrahim himself. Khadija inherited the Azmzades' substantial charitable endowments (*awqaf*) in Egypt, left to her by her father.

The family ties started and nourished by Khadija were very helpful to the Azmzades during the Mehmed Ali dynasty's rule in Syria (1832–1840), but would cost the family dearly after the reestablishment of direct Ottoman control.[61] Giving her maiden name to her children was unusual, but considering the importance of the Azmzade name and the history that it carried, it was more advantageous for Khadija's children to adopt her name instead of their father's.

The great-great-granddaughter of Khadija, Esma was also the sister of Haqqi (Tr. Hakkı) Azmzade, a famous politician and prolific writer. Haqqi grew up with Esma in Damascus and spent his adult life between Istanbul, Damascus, and Cairo, the three nodes of the Azmzade family. Like his relatives, he began his career in the Ottoman provincial government in Damascus and then worked for the imperial government in Istanbul. In 1908 he became a member of the CUP and was appointed as an inspector in the Ministry of Charitable Endowments. Soon after, he left for Egypt when he grew disheartened by the CUP's agenda toward Arab-Ottomans, becoming one of the founders of the Decentralization Party. During French colonial

FIGURE 4. Esma Azmzade at home, early twentieth century.
Source: Azmzade Private Family Archive. Reprinted with permission.

rule of Syria, he was appointed to several high-level administrative positions, becoming the prime minister of Syria in 1932. He died in 1955 in Cairo, where he had retired to look after the charitable endowments left by his great-great-grandmother Khadija.[62]

From the family's perspective, Sadik and Esma were a perfect match. Their union further consolidated the wealth and political capital of the family. Esma, who grew up in Damascus, learned Arabic and Turkish, but not French, unlike many women of her generation and socioeconomic status in Istanbul. Georgina described Esma's daughter Masune as "a little girl of about eight, the most fantastic figure, whose dress and hat would have suited Madge Wildfire [a rather mean-spirited reference to a mentally unstable young woman in a Sir Walter Scott novel].[63] She went to school every morning, and in the afternoon learned music and needlework from her mother, who is particularly skillful with her needle. Like her mother, the child only speaks Turkish and Arabic." According to Georgina, Sadik commented that he would not educate Masune in French, for "what is the good? It only makes them unhappy." A strange statement from a man who was fluent in German and French to a foreign woman conversing with him in French at the time. It is hard to understand whether Sadik was performing a certain machismo to a ready audience of one or whether he genuinely believed in what he said. In a decade, his wife and daughter would accompany him to a diplomatic post in Bulgaria, where knowing French would have come in very handy. Even in Damascus, the times in the Azmzade households were changing. According to Sadik's grandson, his aunts (Sadik's nieces) were so insistent on learning French that they found a way to sneak a French tutor into their house without their father's knowledge. Their father was Iklil, who had the reputation of being a religiously conservative man. He never left the region yet accumulated a large fortune, making his daughters and sons attractive marriage prospects.[64]

During Georgina's visit, Sadik's mother-in-law, who lived with his family, came into the salon to offer the guest a glass of cold almond drink. Georgina wrote of "a dear old lady, with a white linen covering over her head and a shapeless gown of some soft dark material, came in, bringing me the most delicious iced-almond drink, rather like almond sherbet one gets in Sweden. I should have liked to have seen more of the little house, but felt shy about asking to go into other rooms, as I did not know how far it might be liked." The white linen shawl worn loosely over the head and the black dress were typical fashion items worn by older upper-class ladies who were widowed—a sort of dignified fashion statement.[65]

It must have been difficult for Georgina to have access to the kind of informal political networking that women in Esma's position would have partaken in. What seemed to Georgina to be informal homosocial events bringing women of high society together, often accompanied by their children and a female servant, were often carefully orchestrated social interactions meant to promote the family's standing in the halls of power. Georgina noted women picnicking, gathering at the *hammam* (better known in the West as Turkish baths), or enjoying the waters of the Bosphorus by boat. However, she had very little access to the events in the palace's harem.

Khaled Azmzade, a distant cousin of Sadik and another future prime minister of the Arab Republic of Syria, provided a rare description of those events. As a young child, he accompanied his mother and aunt to women-only social events and celebrations in the palace, which often occurred parallel to events where statesmen and foreign guests met with the sultan. Esma did not interact with many foreign diplomats' wives because of the language barrier, which I mentioned earlier. However, with her knowledge of Turkish and Arabic, meetings with the royal family and the wives and daughters of Ottoman officials often took place. Here is a vivid description of the world of aristocratic women, their fashion, homosocial interactions, and a brief understanding of what that must have been like, in Khaled's words:

> While the sultan received an audience in one of the main reception halls of the palace, the same rituals would take place in the haramlik section, where the sultan's wife (Yasin Kadin Efendi, that is the first wife), and the sultan's daughters met the rest of the princesses and the wives of ministers and other important men in the government. Of course, the ladies would take this opportunity to wear the most beautiful dresses and don their crowns decorated with diamonds, emeralds, rubies, and pearls on top of a kind of headdress made of a thin layer tulle called *hotoz*. Neck and chest were covered with precious jewelry of pearl and diamond necklaces, and the bejeweled medals that are only given to women (*Şefkat Nişanı*) that hang on a white sash

with red and green edges and come in five different levels [*sic*]. From their ears hung precious earrings of pearls and emeralds. The same was true of arms and wrists, carrying the heavyweight of gold and bejeweled bracelets. Tradition states that nobody turns his back to the sultan when walking away. The same was true for women when they took leave of the "first wife." They often tripped on the long tails of their dresses and almost fell to the floor. That is why they would practice walking backward in their own home until they perfected it to avoid facing the good-natured laughter or ridiculing of other ladies there who were both friends and foes. Of course, my mother, my aunts, and my older sister spent long times in preparations to attend a party, whether through beauty regiments or practicing how to walk. Face powder and *düzgün* [a white liquid to paint the face to make it look whiter] and eyeliner. Lipstick was not common back then. Hair was kept long and uncut, which allowed women to put it up without having to puff it up. . . . As for formal dresses for evening events and celebrations, they were made from expensive brocade which reached the floor and had a long tale. . . . Sleeves covered the arms, and in general, dresses covered the women so that only the chest and neck were shown. However, one could see the beautiful definition of her waist using a corset that was structured through iron rods or whale bones. A lady would tighten it so much until her belly and the rest of her organs moved up towards her chest. She would tolerate shortness of breath in order to show a tiny attractive waist. Below the waist, their behinds looked wide and plump.[66]

A rare description of the private lives of women, which are often hard to access through traditional archival sources.

Searching through memoirs, travelogues, and even bank records gives a general impression of the Azmzade women, but their storied lives remain a mystery. It is worth noting that every member of the family I spoke with, whether they were descendants of what became the Syrian side or the Turkish side of the family, insisted that women in the Azmzade family were known to be strong-willed, often on the leading edge of women's rights movements in Turkey and the Levant. If Khadija, the founder of the Egyptian arm of the family, was any indication, women were indeed at least as powerful as the men at promoting the family's political and social interests.

Less is known about the internal workings of Shafiq's household and his wife with the exception of a major tragedy that took place in 1903 discussed later. A couple of years before then, things were looking up for Shafiq and his family. Along with a new position and the substantial raise it garnered, he also got married for the second time. His bride was a young and beautiful socialite named Nimet (Ar. Ni'mat), the widow of the famous grand vizier Kabaağaçlızade Ahmed Cevad (Ar. Jawad) Pasha.[67] He was a Turkman native of Syria and a star military man–turned–politician in the Hamidian administration, serving as grand vizier between 1891 and 1895. He spent most of his final years in his native Syria and died from tuberculosis complications at the age of 51 in 1900.[68] According to 'Abd al-Qadir, a son-in-law of Shafiq, many asked for Nimet's hand in marriage after Ahmed Cevad Pasha's death, but she passed them all up for Shafiq, stirring animosity among many of Istanbul's elites.[69]

Nimet was born and raised in a Circassian-majority village close to Samsun called Hurdaz (now Havza Cevizlik). Even though she came from a wealthy and well-known family, in the book Şakir Paşa Ailesi, written by a famous Turkish actress and descendent of the family, Şirin Devrim, Nimet was described in terms that give the impression that she was a Circassian concubine. Devrim states that Nimet was "bought" and then educated in "Ottoman manners," French, and the piano before she was considered worthy of presenting to Cevad for marriage.[70] Cevad died within a year of marrying her. He and Nimet happened to have lived on the street that Shafiq lived on in Teşvikiye.[71]

Nimet was a well-known socialite interested in philanthropy, earning her the Ottoman Medal of Compassion (Şefkat Nişanı) before marrying Shafiq in 1901.[72] Her father Karden İsa Efendi owned a mill and a hotel among other properties. One of the family's claims to fame was the story of Mustafa Kemal (Ataturk) staying in their hotel during the war of independence. Nimet was not the only one in her family to marry a well-known statesman; her three sisters married an Ottoman diplomat, a statesman, and a military man, creating a robust influential network through marriage relations.[73] So it makes sense that Nimet had plenty of suitors once she became available. Shafiq, a widower himself at the time, might have been a convenient but not obvious choice. Though we do not have a record of her birth year, if her

FIGURE 5. Nimet Hanım, wife of Shafiq al-Mu'ayyad Azmzade,
on her wedding day, 1901.
Source: Marmara University, Taha Toros Archive, document no: 001560153008,
permanent link: http://hdl.handle.net/11424/. Reprinted with permission.

picture is any indication, she was a fairly young woman when she was married to Shafiq, a man in his early forties (figure 5).

Paid and Unpaid Domestic Help

Missing from Khaled's memoir and Georgina Müller's travelogue were the lives of the large number of workers in elite households, paid and unpaid, in formal and informal labor. In a household like Sadik's, a rising star in the Office of the Aides-de-Camp for the sultan, there would have been at least some hired help in the form of a female housemaid, a male servant, a carriage driver and stableman, and others who were hired as the need arose, such as a nanny or a milk mother. In late nineteenth and early twentieth-century Istanbul, however, not all household labor was paid. Even though the African slave trade had been outlawed in in 1857, domestic slavery continued to be a staple feature of many well-to-do households in the Ottoman Empire, and Istanbul was no exception.[74] Enslaved persons were often written out of late nineteenth-century narratives of that period, but they are there waiting for us to take a closer look. Memoirs recalling lives inside the big households attest to this.

In her memoir, Halide Edib (Edivar), the daughter of Edib Pasha, one of the bureaucrats who worked in the palace at the same time as Shafiq and Sadik, described how enslaved people were bought and sold and manumitted as an everyday occurrence. She talked of manumitted enslaved people from the palace who themselves at times owned slaves. She also talked about enslaved people whom her grandmother owned over the years. Some were still in her service and others she manumitted and with whom she maintained a form of patronage relationship extending down to their children and grandchildren.[75]

Patronage indicates an unequal relationship between someone of higher status in society, usually from a wealthy or politically powerful household, a benefactor or master who extended her or his "moral protection, assistance and benefits" to a person of lower status, in this case, manumitted slaves. In return, the protégé was expected to offer his or her "personal service, loyalty, and affection." The relationship between the manumitted slave and the household was supposed to be a more "noble" form of attachment that was based on *vela* (loyalty) or a special kind of kinship. Enslaved people were entirely reliant on their owners since they were severed from their culture, language, and familial ties upon enslavement.[76] As slavery became less acceptable in Ottoman society and enslaved people started to fight for their right to freedom after 1908, the complexity of this relationship and the inherent violence of its patronage were laid bare.[77]

The enslaved people that Halide mentioned in her memoirs were either White and assumed to be of Circassian origin, or Black from sub-Saharan Africa and often assumed to be from Abyssinia or the Sudan. A nanny of African origin was referred to as an *Arap Bacı*.[78] They were not explicitly referred to as slaves, as most were given a title based on their job. They were supposed to look after the children, and their persona, usually depicted as large, warm, and well-tempered, was often similar in the imagination of Ottomans of that time to the persona of a mammy in the American Jim Crow South.[79] Halide explained the term as "an appellation for a negro nurse," referring to her own nanny as a child growing up not far from Sadik's house.[80]

Halide herself, born in 1885, owned an enslaved girl as a teenager. A jarring description of this is perhaps necessary to understand how the upper society in Istanbul perceived themselves. The year was not given, but based on the context from her memoir, it would have been late in the last decade of the nineteenth century when, as she described, "I heard of a rather exciting event. Two Abyssinian girls, one bought for abla [appellation for "older sister" in Turkish] and the other for me, were shortly to arrive from Yemen. . . . Abla was not interested in the creature, but Reshe, the one bought for me, was as pretty as an Abyssinian girl could be."[81] She continued to describe the girl in what she considered affectionate terms, but today's reader would find them disturbingly dehumanizing. At one point, Halide learned Reshe's story of capture when she asked Reshe about a song she was singing: "I never learned what this wonderful song meant, for by the time she learned Turkish she had forgotten her own Abyssinian. But it had indefinite pathos and longing. From it I caught a glimpse of the misery of her past days before she was able to tell me about the way she had been stolen with her little brother from a wonderful Abyssinian Forest and made to walk for months under the lash of the slave-dealers. There was that in her song, especially in the way she sang it, which made one guess the dreary suffering through the meaningless words."[82]

Khaled, born in 1902, was of a socioeconomic background similar to Halide's. He grew up in Damascus and Istanbul and described a similar relationship to workers in his household. His father Muhammad Fawzi (Tr. Fevzi) worked in the palace, then worked with Sadik and other members of the imperial government to extend the Hijaz railway, and later moved back to Istanbul to take up the post of minister of religious endowments in 1911.[83] Like Halide, Khaled remembers having a "Black nanny (*murabiya zinjiyya*)" called Mankasheh who was tasked by his mother to look after him and stay by his side all the time, to the extent that she would sit next to him in the classroom. Along with Mankasheh, he also had private French and Swiss tutors after he left the local school, whom he credited with his excellent knowledge of French, a sign of wealth and status at the time.[84]

Note the use of different terms for a Black person. Halide used the common term *Arap* (like in *Arap Bacı*), the Turkish word for Arab, to describe a Black person. However, Khaled used the Arabic word *zinji*, which is also used in Turkish (*zenci*) and is often translated in English as "Negro." Arab-Ottomans never used the word Arab, whether they wrote in Turkish or Arabic (Ar. pl. *'Arab*, sg. masc. *'Arabi*, sg. fem. *'Arabiyya*) to refer to a Black person. Language matters, and the choice of words often betrays the complex, sometimes unspoken, societal beliefs or prejudices. The multiple meanings of *Arap* in late nineteenth-century Istanbul and how they interplayed with the racialization of Arabs, including the Arab-Ottomans of Istanbul, will be discussed in Chapter 4.

As for the staff who worked in Sadik and Esma's houshold, there is very little information. Only one picture gave me clues as to the workings of their household, which seems on the whole not very different from households of other members of the same class in Istanbul described above.

In Figure 6, Sadik's sons Jelal and Giyas are wearing school uniforms, boots, and fezzes. They must have been between ten and thirteen. In the same picture, however, is a Black child, wearing a buttoned-up uniform,

FIGURE 6. Giyas (*left*), Sadik's younger son; Bilal, Sadik's *evlatlık*;
and Jelal, Sadik's older son, 1903.
Source: Azmzade Private Family Archive. Reprinted with permission.

white shirt, leather boots, and a fez. There was no mention of this child anywhere in the private or public correspondence of Sadik or other members of the Azmzade family, but the note on the back of the photo, written much later by Giyas, states his name as Bilal, who was "my late father's *evlatlık*. He died in World War I." According to Sadik's great granddaughter, all she knew was that Bilal was brought from Sudan.[85] She did not have any details about how Bilal was "brought" to Istanbul. In the early twentieth century, the slave trade had been illegal in the Ottoman Empire for more than fifty years. However, that did not mean it was not still practiced. In the late Ottoman Empire, the line between slave labor and waged domestic labor was very thin, and the two existed in parallel.[86]

Evlatlık was a form of adoption or fostering of children from families with little or no means to provide for a child. The meaning and the range of acceptable and legal forms of this practice changed drastically over time.[87] A family that had fallen on a hard time, often refugees, such as Muslim refugees from the Russian Empire following the Crimean War and Balkan Muslims following the Balkan Wars, would give the child over to a wealthier family, sometimes for a fee, in order to offer the child better living conditions and opportunities. Similarly, a child without capable relatives, requiring a foster home, would be taken in under the same system. This practice was widespread and was thought of as a form of social service without much legal consequences. The child's labor was used to help the homeowner, and in exchange he or she would be fed and clothed and sometimes even educated. When he or she was old enough, a suitable marriage would be arranged. However, the line between fostering a child and domestic slavery was very fine.[88]

A famous Turkish historian of African origin who died in 2016, Mustafa Olpak, wrote about the Afro-Turkish community in the province of Aydın. To him, the *evlatlık* system, especially for children of African descent (like Bilal), was in many ways a continuation of domestic slavery by another name. It became more common after 1854, when slave markets were outlawed, but it was not until 1889 that the practice of Black slavery itself was made illegal, and not until 1908 that White slavery was made illegal.[89] It was only after 1926 that it genuinely stopped in Turkey, although the practice of *evlatlık* persisted.[90]

Personal Tragedies

In 1903, the same year the photo of Bilal, Jelal, and Giyas was taken, tragedy hit both Shafiq's and Sadik's households and would have a lasting impact on the standing of the Azmzades in Istanbul for a decade to come. First, in the early days of the year, while Sadik happened to be with his family in his sultan-assigned *konak* in Teşvikiye, a fire was intentionally set in the house while the Azmzades and their staff slept. The shock and despair that Sadik felt was captured by a note he wrote to his employer at the palace a few hours after the flames were extinguished. This was not like his usually meticulous handwritten notes to the palace. He wrote the words with jagged edges and smudged ink, betraying his mental state, describing what happened and asking for help. The fire had consumed his house and all his possessions; within minutes all that he had owned was up in flames. He wrote:

> This evening around eleven o'clock, an unknown person who wishes us ill set the house on fire. As the smoke quickly engulfed us from all directions and I was on the verge of passing out, I took my wife and children from their beds, and while barefooted and bareheaded, we ran to my dear uncle Shafiq Bey's house to take refuge. There was no time to save anything. The three horses I had in the stable slowly (*deri deri*) burnt, and now I do not have a penny on me.

He asked for immediate financial help from the palace and sure enough a money note of 10,000Kr was issued within a few days.[91]

There were some speculations as to the cause of the fire, and rumors abounded. Even when I discussed the fire with one of Sadik's late grandsons in Istanbul in 2008, he did not want to elaborate but was sure it was a deliberate act of arson. In an interview with Sadiq Jalal al-'Azm in Damascus in 2009, he remembered that this incident was talked about in his family, and he had assumed that it must have been politically motivated as an anti-Abdülhamid incident. His Turkish relative, a great grandson of one of Sadik's brothers who happened to be present at the interview, jumped in. "It was the *seyis*," he said with certainty. It was the stableman who had been recently fired. He insisted that it was a matter of a disgruntled ex-employee who wanted to exact revenge on the Azmzades. He seemed confident that it was not political, such as an act of sabotage by anti–Abdülhamid II activists.

Sadik himself did not elaborate on what took place, and I could not find any mention of the fire in the newspapers, even though fires were standard items of interest reported in the dailies at the time. Sadik's only reference to it came up in his travelogue, which he wrote a little over a year later. He lamented his lost travel equipment and the travelogue he had kept on his mission of extending the telegraph line between Damascus and Medina in 1900 and 1901.[92] This would not be the only time the house would burn down, however. It burnt down along with many other *konaks* on the street in a massive fire in 1919.[93]

That same year, 1903, tragedy followed Sadik's family into Shafiq's household. Three months after they took refuge in Shafiq's *konak*, his wife Nimet died, along with their newly born child, under suspicious circumstances. This incident, which I discuss in detail in Chapter 7, turned into a legal investigation that would haunt Shafiq until he left public office and moved to Damascus a decade later.

The Azmzades lived in Teşvikiye for close to a quarter of a century, danced at large balls, debated in political meetings, attended weddings and wakes, and experienced the ups and downs of Istanbul's political life, surviving a revolution and a counterrevolution, and weathering public scandals, inheritance disputes, and an existential crisis that eventually caught up with their vanishing imperial world. Throughout their time in Istanbul, Shafiq and Sadik's connections to their family in Syria remained strong. They often used their growing influence in the palace to advocate for their family members back home, who seemed to have been regularly involved in land disputes and power struggles with other influential families and members of the provincial government.

In this chapter, I offered a glimpse into the lives of Shafiq and Sadik as they worked their way from their provincial upbringing in Damascus through their education in Mount Lebanon and Beirut, and, finally, settling into their respective careers in Istanbul. While Sadik's success on his diplomatic career path meant that he barely spent any time with his family in Istanbul, Shafiq spent most of his time close to the sultan as part of the well-established Arab-Ottoman community, propelling himself up the palace ladder rather quickly. In the following chapter, I delve into a number of episodes that spanned both of their careers to give the reader a better sense of the good, bad, and ugly of their work lives and what it meant to have empire as a career in the 1890s.

CHAPTER 2

A CAREER IN EMPIRE

I learned from a newspaper translation that the English
have just entered Transvaal. Knowing this, look into
sending a man to meet the English prime minister, secretly
and unofficially, to propose that we transfer Armenians
living in Anatolia to Transvaal, and in exchange, we relocate
Transvaal inhabitants to Anatolia.

—Sultan Abdülhamid II as recalled by
Izzet al-'Abid in his memoirs[1]

THE TREND TOWARD ROMANTICIZING THE PAST RISES WHEN
the realities of the present seem especially oppressive. Whether it is an economic downturn, war, or even a pandemic, populist politicians and public
intellectuals often resort to a reimagined notion of the past as a time of glory
and moral certitude that the nation must work to regain. Over the past few
years, the popular portrayal of an imagined past that whitewashes some of
the sins of imperialism has become prevalent. Politicians, artists, and even
some scholars cast the British, French, and the Ottoman empires as lost uto-
pias where peaceful coexistence and prosperity under the benevolence of a
strong sovereign was the norm.[2]

This chapter focuses on the dark side of working for the empire during the Hamidian era. From rampant nepotism and privileges that were afforded to the few, to the debates around methods for ethnic cleansing (as the chapter epigraph shows), Izzet, Shafiq, and Sadik were members of a cadre of global imperialists laboring on the dark side of turn-of-the-century imperialism. Starting with the mundane corruption that came with the concentration of power in the hands of a few men at the top of the imperial food chain, I focus on Shafiq's career in the palace and how he was able to make it work to his personal benefit. From 1888 until World War I, Shafiq remained a loyal imperialist who believed that the strength of the imperial center reflected his own strength and, by the same token, that the wealth of the empire was also his wealth. As loyalists worked for what they believed was the good of the empire, it also meant that they worked for their own personal gains. This was a common form of understanding how imperial administration operated and was embodied in the few men who stayed close to the center of power. However, as will become clear, capital did not present itself through financial accumulation only. Political capital was the true sign of power, allowing Shafiq to unduly influence various forms of administrative and judicial decision-making. Among other things, he used his power to influence land ownership disputes in his family's favor, garner at least one sultanic pardon to overturn the criminal conviction of one of his brothers, and allegedly usurp the inheritance of one of his sisters.

The second part of the chapter focuses on Sadik's involvement in the dark years between 1893 and 1895. The year 1893 witnessed a cholera outbreak in the poorer neighborhoods of Istanbul, highlighting the difference in living standards between a neighborhood like Teşvikiye, where the rich and influential lived, and a neighborhood like Yeniköy, on the northern outskirts of the city, where many destitute refugees first arrived from Russia. Sadik was assigned to the commission tasked with solving the cholera problem, which was blamed on the unhygienic conditions in some neighborhoods.

The years of 1894–1896, as any Ottoman history specialist can attest, automatically bring to mind the Hamidian massacres of Armenians in central and southeastern Anatolia. In the final part of the chapter, I focus on Sadik's role in the Ottoman commission tasked with assessing damages in Urfa after the massacres and his attitude toward the Armenian victims. His disposition toward this episode might be jarring to some readers, though it should not be surprising considering his loyalty to the sultan. Sadik's sins were not related to the physical violence but to his role in accepting the official narrative and promoting anti-Armenian propaganda. Sadik continued to harbor strong anti-Armenian opinions years after his mission to the eastern provinces as a state representative, promoting a common opinion of many statesmen of the era: that the Ottoman government was the victim rather than the aggressor.

An Ambitious Climb to the *Mabeyn*

While Sadik was quickly rising through the military ranks, his uncle Shafiq, who had moved to Istanbul in late 1887, was hard at work at the Translation Bureau of the Yıldız Palace's *Mabeyn-i Hümayun*, or *Mabeyn* for short, which first appeared in records in the late eighteenth century. *Mabeyn* means "that which lies in between," in reference to the office that occupied the space between the private part of the palace, the imperial *haramlık*, or *Harem-i Hümayun*, and the public part of the palace where the official state visits took place, the *selamlık*.[3] The *haramlık*, as the name might indicate, was where the harem was located. In English, the term carries a fictionalized notion of an exclusively female domain of the sultan's concubines. In reality, the harem was a complex and highly influential social and political institution that included the concubines' domain and the private quarters of the royal family, both men and women.[4]

During the time that Sadik and Shafiq were employed, the *Mabeyn* was made up of two sections. One section was headed by a *başmabeyinci*, the equivalent of a head chamberlain, who headed a staff devoted to looking after the internal functioning of the palace, which encompassed everything from cuisine and the grooming of the sultan to large-scale banquets and catering to the personal needs of the royal family. Most of this staff, known as *mabeyincis*, lived in the palace. The other section of the *Mabyen* was devoted to state affairs. It grew exponentially during the reign of Abdülhamid II, who wanted to centralize the decision-making process and reduce the power of the *Bab-ı Ali*, the Sublime Porte, which encompassed the office of the grand vizier and other ministries. The head of this section was known as the *başkatib*, or head secretary to the sultan. It was a very important position occupied by someone in whom the sultan had complete trust and who possessed a great deal of power by having one foot in the real world while having the sultan's ear. All the rest were known as *katibs*, state secretaries or clerks of different ranks divided into several offices. Two of the most important offices were the Translation Bureau, where Shafiq worked, and the Office of the Aides-de-Camp to the sultan, to which Sadik belonged. It was reported that the *Mabeyn* staff swelled to 424 people during Abdülhamid II's reign, reflecting the sultan's need for control over state decisions.[5] It also meant that Sadik and Shafiq were at the pinnacle of the imperial decision-making center from 1883, when Sadik first entered the service followed by his uncle in 1887, until the end of the Hamidian period.

Shafiq's arrival in Istanbul must have been a shock on many levels. First, he had to take a substantial cut to his salary, earning two-thirds of what he was making in Damascus at the Land Registry Office. It was also his first time working away from his family's traditional center of power in the Levant. At the palace's translation office, he was one of many individuals who came from across the diverse empire. Working in such an unusual environment with other translators who hailed from various ethnic and religious backgrounds must have been difficult to become accustomed to. The physical environment of the translation office was described in detail by a fellow palace worker, Ali Ekrem, who joined the *Mabeyn* in 1888, less than a year after Shafiq's hiring:

> A rectangular room about nine or ten meters in length, with eight windows, containing a large office desk with six drawers as well as three smaller writing desks, six gilded highbacked chairs from the time of the Sultan Abdülaziz II, each fitted with gold brocade cushioning, two sofas and two armchairs, a capacious mahogany cupboard for the storage of documents, a large porcelain stove with pipes, an ordinary rug on the floor, two candelabra each with six candles, and an extraordinary collection of papers and notebooks of all shapes and sizes covering the items of furniture and the floor.[6]

Despite the decrease in Shafiq's reported income, one cannot put a figure on the social and political capital that came with being a palace employee working in the secretary office. An ambitious man, Shafiq was not shy about advocating for himself and his family, regularly asking for raises and demanding recognition. Within two years of his arrival in Istanbul, his salary had tripled to 3,000Kr, followed by a third-rank *Mecidiye* medal two years after solidifying his position as one of the favorites in the translation office in 1891.[7] Over the next decade, Shafiq and other members of the Azmzade family would rise through the palace ranks, thanks in part to Shafiq's penchant for negotiating and network-building.

A good example of his political prowess was his ability to walk the fine line between portraying a humble loyalty to the sultan while asking for what he believed he deserved. His first request came in the form of petitions to the palace asking for fair compensation for his role, soon after being promoted in the *Mabeyn*. Shafiq stated his linguistic credentials and proudly touted his coming from Arab regions (*aktar-ı arabiye*) and his family's record of loyalty to the Ottoman dynasty for "two or three hundred years," contributing "over twenty viziers" during that time. He confidently added that he would not have dared send his petition if he had not thought he was perfect for his position.[8] A few months later, he received a silver *Liyakat Madalyası* (Medal of Merit) followed by confirmation of his position.[9] Within a year, he again wrote asking for a raise, for which he had been passed up while others, according to him, had gotten their due. It took a year, but he was eventually promoted and given a 500Kr raise.[10] Two years later, he wrote yet again asking for a raise, claiming that he had a great deal of debt and financial responsibilities to address.[11] This time it took a couple of years, but then he was promoted to one of the most influential roles in the administration when he was assigned in 1896 as a representative of the Ottoman state in the Public Debt Administration.[12]

Shafiq remained at the Public Debt Administration until 1901, when he took the unusual step of resigning. According to his son-in-law, he was brought on as a financial consultant for a railway extension project from Riyaq to Aleppo. The sticking point was that the fiscal earnings from taxes levied on agricultural products of the provinces of Aleppo and Syria, known as *uşur* (Ar. *'oshor*), or a tenth of the income, was to be directed to the Public Debt Administration in support of financing the railway. Shafiq refused to throw his support behind this scheme, supposedly because of the unfair burden it placed on local farmers. However, the sultan overrode him and approved it despite his objections, forcing him to resign to save face. Nevertheless, he was rewarded for his "gallantry" by being assigned to the commission representing the palace in another arm of the Public Debt Administration, the Tobacco Régie, with a respectable salary that reached 4,410Kr. Shafiq remained in this position until just before the Young Turk Revolution in 1908.[13]

It is important to note that all of the salaries I have quoted were officially reported; that is, they were what he was registered to be paid as a monthly salary and what his pension would eventually be based on. However, like many men in high positions, his income also came from several sources, including free housing and informal gifts and favors. According to his son-in-law, Shafiq reported that his income was in fact 20,000Kr per month.[14]

The Régie, where Shafiq worked until 1908, was a consortium of the Ottoman Bank, Crédit Anstalt, and Bleichröder banking groups. It had the exclusive right to the lucrative tobacco production processed in the empire. The origin of the Régie goes back to the establishment of the Public Debt Administration, which had the right to the tax revenue of the empire's tobacco production and the right to grant a monopoly over this production to be administered by a third party. This was what happened in 1883 when the Public Debt Administration gave the rights to the newly formed Régie for an annual payment of 750,000 Ottoman lira and a share of the profits divided between the government and the Public Debt Administration. By the early 1890s, the Régie's several tobacco factories were hiring thousands of Muslim and non-Muslim men, women, and children.[15] During his time there, Shafiq secured a position for one of his nephews, Badiʿ al-Muʾayyad Azmzade, who had just graduated from law school in Istanbul. Badiʿ would go on to make a name for himself in Istanbul a few years later, after the Young Turk Revolution.[16]

Normalization of Corruption

In a crowded office of secretaries vying for the attention of the all-powerful head secretary and the sultan, it was not easy to stand out. Not only was Shafiq an expert self-promoter but he was also an expert at finding the right channels to exert pressure in support of family members back in the Levant. Whether it was putting a thumb on the scales of justice in Damascus or pushing the palace to hire his relatives, it is important to keep in mind that Shafiq was not exceptional. Not unlike his relative and neighbor, the powerful Izzet, he simply exercised what he believed to be an earned privilege for his service to the sultan. Izzet was known for taking over major imperial projects, such as the Commission for Fiscal Reforms (*Islahat-ı Maliye Komisyonu*) and then blurring the line between his personal finances and those of the state, collecting many enemies along the way who accused him of blatant embezzlement. He had one of the busiest offices in the palace and remained close to the sultan, who seemed to trust him with the most sensitive of state secrets and large-scale projects.[17] From Izzet's vantage point, he believed himself to be a man who embodied all the potential that the empire had on the world stage, which he and the empire were unfairly prevented from achieving. The difference between the imperial state and the men of the state often seemed very fine, reflected in memoirs and autobiographies that blurred the line between the personal and the political and between their financial ambition and the empire's prosperity. The following are but a few cases where this privilege played a defining role in the power and wealth of the extended Azmzade family.

In the early 1890s, Shafiq wrote several letters asking the palace and the grand vizier to intervene in a legal dispute over land inheritance and purchase between the inheritors of al-Mu'ayyad's estate and the Quwatli (Tr. Küvvetli) family. At the same time, fourteen members of Shafiq's extended family in Damascus felt emboldened to write the sultan to complain about what they felt was a bias against them, particularly held by the head of the Court of Appeals in Damascus, Abdullah Efendi. They claimed that they and their supporters were being targeted in the most "savage" and "illegal" ways because they had raised the alarm against the head of the court and the governor-general Giritli Mustafa Asım (Ar. 'Asem) Pasha (Ar. al-Kriti, En. Cretan), who had them detained on some drummed up charges.[18] Like Shafiq in his petitions, the other Azmzades never missed a chance to remind the palace that they had been "loyal to the Ottoman government for two or three hundred years." The Ministry of Interior wasted no time sending a request for a commission to be set up to investigate the head of the Court of Appeals.[19]

Meanwhile, the requests for their release kept coming, with the most interesting one from six women who belonged to the family of Ahmed (Shafiq) Azmzade, who appealed to the authorities in Istanbul, stating that Ahmed (Shafiq) looked after a household made up of sixty people who depended on

him.[20] Because the family was not satisfied with the first investigative commission, another one was sent to Damascus.[21] The archival trail for this case
ends here, but it is enough to demonstrate the attention that the Azmzades
commanded in Istanbul.[22] While this was going on, two other cases were
brought to the attention of the Ministry of Interior, the Council of State, and
the palace. One was about the land inheritance dispute, which had started in
1887, as mentioned earlier, and the other was a double homicide.

Shafiq's petitions often reaped some results, but not without some pain.
The land dispute case mentioned earlier was taken up by the Council of
State. It was even ruled on by *Şeyhülislam* (Ar. *Sheikh al-Islam*) himself, the
müftü (Ar. *mufti*) of Istanbul and the highest religious legal authority in the
land, who stated that the court should take up the case in Aleppo and that
Damascus should hand over all records about the case.[23] This was a radical
change, for the Council of State had made it clear that, without the necessary documentary evidence from the Azmzades, the land would stay in the
hands of the Quwatlis, who had documentation to show their right to it. This
initial ruling enraged Shafiq, and he wrote what was seen as an insult to the
courts—a felony under Ottoman law—for which at one point the Council of State even recommended that he be charged.[24] Yet upon the palace's
request, the council was asked to look further into the case, especially after
Shafiq handed over his own documentary evidence.[25] The Syrian provincial
court conducted an investigation and a full trial was called with tens of witnesses and experts and extensively documented witness statements. After all
this, the judge yet again decided in favor of the Quwatli family due to a lack
of convincing evidence from the Azmzade family.[26] Surprisingly, however,
five months after this ruling, the administration in Syria changed. The new
governor-general instructed the district governor of Duma to hand the land
back to the Azmzades.[27] There was no legal evidence that I could find that
would support such an action, which had gone against consecutive court rul-
ings in the past.

Thus, a court case that was initially decided by local authorities in Damascus was taken up by the Council of State and weighed on by the palace, the office of the grand vizier, and even the office of *Şeyhülislam*. Then
it was sent back to a sharia court in Damascus, all with similar outcomes.
They privileged the paper documentation of rent of the land produced by the

Quwatli family over the verbal witnesses presented by the Azmzade family. Nevertheless, the ruling for the Quwatli family was ultimately overturned when a friendly governor-general was transferred from Beirut to Damascus. Whether this was because of the direct intervention of Shafiq in Istanbul or other legal reasons not documented in the archives, it is hard to tell. It definitely could not have hurt that the palace was on the side of the Azmzades. A mere three years after his arrival in Istanbul, Shafiq had become so influential as to have the central government investigate its provincial legal apparatus in what was essentially a power struggle between two influential families in Syria, the Quwatlis and the Azmzades. Using his influence and proximity to the levers of power in Istanbul and his intimate knowledge of the inner workings of the palace proved helpful indeed.

Once Shafiq retired from politics, his sister, Hajjeh (Tr. Haci) Munira, wrote to complain about the usurping of her inheritance, the same land he fought to keep in the family twenty-five years earlier. Munira requested that the land register be opened, something that had been blocked by her brother when he had influence, first as a palace man and later as a deputy of the Province of Syria. She was finally able to petition for her share of the land that, up until the case was brought to the Ministry of Interior in 1914, had been withheld from her, first by her father and then her brother. She claimed that the land had initially belonged to her husband but upon his death was taken from her by her father, al-Mu'ayyad, with the support of the sultan as the reader saw in Chapter 1, and, after his death, by her brother, Shafiq. Thus, she was allegedly deprived of her share of the inheritance of this land twice over.[28]

Crime and (In)Justice

Shafiq's influence went far beyond financial interest or inheritance. It stretched to criminal matters, including assault and murder. Shafiq's brother and Sadik's uncle, Ali al-Mu'ayyad Azmzade, had killed two members of the famous Jaza'iri (Tr. Cezayirli) family over an apparent land dispute in the Province of Aleppo. The Jaza'iri (literally, "The Algerian") family was first established in Damascus by 'Abd al-Qadir al-Jaza'iri after his exile, albeit with a handsome financial incentive, due to his active resistance to the French colonial occupation of Algeria.[29] He won great fame and favor with Istanbul during the 1860 pogroms when he helped save hundreds of Damascene Christians.[30] This stood him in sharp contrast to other families, including the Azmzades, who were partially blamed for not doing more to stop the pogroms and, in some cases, for supporting the mob with their private militias. As a result, some of the family's patriarchs were exiled and their properties confiscated, at least for a while, as I mentioned in Chapter 1.

'Abd al-Qadir al-Jaza'iri lived on a generous stipend from the French government, allowing him to establish his household in Syria, which included a small armed militia. The killing of two al-Jaza'iri family members by a member of another notable family, supported by its own strongmen, caused a great deal of turbulence that rippled all the way to Istanbul. According to Shafiq's son-in-law, after "being cursed by an incident with the migrant Algerian amirs," Ali Azmzade, "of pure faith, who worked in agriculture and of strong build, a courageous man" went on the run, leaving on horseback through Anatolia to Istanbul, then on to Greece, ending up in British-occupied Egypt, where he remained for a while and reportedly started a newspaper.[31]

Members of the al-Jaza'iri family who lived in Istanbul and the police commissioner of the Province of Syria painted a much less romanticized picture of Ali and the murders. On July 6, 1893, three members of the al-Jaza'iri family, all aides-de-camp to the sultan, two of them at the rank of *ferik* (lieutenant general) and one at the rank of *yüzbaşı* (lieutenant), wrote to the palace detailing the incident and requesting its intervention to ensure that justice was served. The police commissioner also wrote to the Ministry of Internal Affairs on July 10, 1893, a week after the incident. The commissioner made sure to note that the suspect was the brother of "one of the translators who work in the *Mabeyn-i Hümayun* Shafiq Bey," and described the killings in detail, adding that Ali and his companions had also burnt the village Taliftaya, consisting of twenty-five houses, to the ground before fleeing. This village was in the *kaza* (county) of al-Nabek, an eight-hour ride from Damascus. The commissioner requested that the perpetrators be arrested and returned to Syria to stand trial.[32] Having escaped from territories under direct Ottoman control, Ali would eventually be tried in absentia, with a guilty verdict handed down, punishable by death. However, almost eight years from the date of the incident, Ali was given a royal pardon by Sultan

Abdülhamid II and allowed to return to Syria (though not the city of Damascus) as a free man.[33]

This would not be the end of this story. Like Shafiq's sister Munira, the al-Jaza'iri family would also have to wait until 1913, after the influence of Shafiq in Istanbul had waned, to complain about the fact that Ali was back in Damascus walking freely and causing trouble, even though he was supposed to stay away from the city. They described incidents of aggression by him toward members of the al-Jaza'iri family and asked the Ministry of Interior to intervene. They insisted that he had been able to get away with murder because of his family's close ties to the local government and his brother's former position in Istanbul, and they wanted this to be rectified.[34] As will become clear in Chapter 8, Ali and his family would eventually be rounded up; however, it would not be for the reasons mentioned above but for suspicion of disloyalty to the Ottoman government during World War I.

In 1902, yet another Azmzade, Rif'at (Tr. Rıfat), a nephew of Shafiq, was accused of a series of crimes that could "fill volumes," including theft, murder, beatings, and breaking the sanctity of people's honor. The file of crimes committed by Rif'at, the son of Shafiq's brother 'Abd al-Hamid, reached the office of the grand vizier when Rif'at wrote complaining about the local justice system and the verdict against him. The governor-general of Syria also wrote explaining why Rif'at and his companions should be arrested and exiled for the safety of the people of Hama. The response from the Council of State accused the government in Syria of not following the proper legal procedure. Thus, the order to exile Rif'at to Cyprus could not be executed. It seems that the influence of the Azmzades in the imperial center had yet again won over the local provincial authorities' demands.[35]

It was not only Shafiq's star that was rising in the early 1890s; Sadik continued to lead missions abroad as part of some of the most historically important events of the late Ottoman Empire. Next, however, I turn to the rare occasions that Sadik was in Istanbul.

A Pandemic of the Poor

After playing host to the Müllers in Istanbul in 1893, Sadik was promoted to the military rank of *kaymakam* (lieutenant) in 1894, and less than a year later he was promoted yet again to the rank of *miralay* (colonel) for his work on the cholera commission in 1895.[36] This meteoric rise primed Sadik to take the lead in some high-profile missions within and without the empire. His noticeably quick promotion would also come to haunt Sadik after the Young Turk Revolution, when the records of promotions of palace loyalists were scrutinized, which I discuss in Chapter 6. While the Müllers were touring Istanbul under the guidance of Sadik, cholera was quietly spreading in the poorer northern outskirts of the city. The Ottoman Empire was initially spared the worst of the pandemic, which hit most of Western Europe, Russia, and Iran very hard. According to a conference report from the end of 1892 in St. Petersburg, cholera was first reported in Mashhad in May of 1892 and then "was once again imported across [Russia's] frontiers, and rapidly spread to almost every corner of her immense territories. From Russia, cholera passed to Germany, Austro-Hungary, Belgium, Holland, and France."[37] Mention of the Ottoman Empire was notably absent from this report; the initial assumption was that the *Memalik-i Mahruse*, or Well-Protected Domains, as the Ottoman Empire was often called, had been spared.

Complaints rose about the arrival of Jewish refugees from Russia who had to find temporary shelters in Synagogues and Jewish-Ottomans' homes in Istanbul after being expelled from Odessa with little notice. The Ottoman state assumed that the refugees coming from Russia in the middle of 1892 could be carriers of cholera and tried to stop the influx to Istanbul and relocate them to other places in the empire.[38] By August of 1893, cases of cholera appeared in Istanbul that were blamed on the Russian refugees, as well as a British ship that did not follow quarantine practices when it docked in the city. By mid-September, a pandemic was officially declared in Istanbul that lasted until May 1894, when it was declared under control. Of those hospitalized, 1,597 were Muslim; 505, Greek; 386, Armenian; 173, Jewish; and 17, foreign, reflecting the number of non-Muslims living in the neighborhoods where cholera had hit the hardest. Of a total of 2,683 patients hospitalized, 1,537 succumbed to the virus.[39] Sadik was one of two Arab-Ottoman statesmen who worked on a health commission put together to get the disease under control. The other Arab-Ottoman who was involved was a fellow graduate of Saint Joseph of 'Aintoura, Selim Melhamé,[40] from the famous Beiruti Maronite family. He approached the French virologist Louis Pasteur to come to Istanbul to help with the cholera outbreak as early as 1893. Pasteur did not come himself, but sent Dr. Maurice Nicolle in his stead. With the Ottoman government's support, mediated through Selim, Nicolle established l'Institut Pasteur de Constantinople (Tr. Pasteur Enstitüsü).[41]

Cholera cases reemerged in 1895 in a district in the far northern part of the city on the Bosphorus, particularly in İstinye and Yeniköy. That is when German virologist Rudolf Emmerich from Munich University was invited to investigate the cause of this re-emerging epidemic. Sadik, who had acquired fluency in German by that time, was assigned to a team headed by Emmerich; the Public Health Commission's inspector, Ömer (Ar. 'Umar) Bey; and a Dutch physician who worked on the local quarantine board, referred to as Doctor Stéculis. They were sent to the affected neighborhoods to determine the reason for the reoccurrence of this disease.[42]

The pandemic was the impetus for many cities in Europe, Russia, and the Ottoman Empire to implement public hygiene measures and raise their pandemic preparedness. Germany was one of the hardest-hit countries, with Hamburg becoming an example of the horrors a pandemic could bring to a city unprepared for such a public health disaster.[43] The investigation in Istanbul made several recommendations that focused on rehabilitating the sewer system and eliminating open sewers, which were contaminating the water supply in the far northern neighborhoods.[44] Many of the older neighborhoods in Istanbul still relied on archaic or nonexistent sewerage infrastructure, making disease breakouts in these neighborhoods possible.

In another part of the city, the more affluent part where top governmental officials, including Sadik and Shafiq, lived, life could not be more different. In fact, in 1896, Teşvikiye was equipped with its very own *bakteriolojihane*, a bacteriology laboratory that tested the water supply to the neighborhood to ensure that no pathogens contaminated it. In addition, the doctors and nurses who worked in this neighborhood were given a raise by the government to ensure that any pathological illnesses would be immediately treated.[45]

While on duty on this health commission, however, death also visited Sadik's family, though it was unclear whether it was related to the cholera outbreak. In July 1895, Sadik asked permission to take leave and return to Damascus to look after some of his mother's affairs after her passing.[46] Death hung over other territories of the Ottoman Empire in the mid-1890s too. The infamous 1894–96 massacres were taking place at the time, and they,

too, would touch the Azmzades in their capacity as loyal imperialists in the
service of the palace.

The Bloody Work of Late Nineteenth-Century Imperialism

The mid-1890s were dark years in the Ottoman Empire. While Ottoman
diplomats and international law experts were engaged in a desperate battle
to reclaim parts of the Red Sea coast of Africa in the South and news of a
Macedonian separatist movement was coming from the West, the Hamidian regime began perpetrating one of the worst atrocities committed in
modern time against its own people in the East. The mistrust between
Armenian-Ottomans and their neighbors had been growing for months,
instigated by Armenian nationalist groups—like the Dashnaktsutyun and
the Hunchakian—and the local Kurdish Aghas and Muslim religious leaders (mullahs).[47] The "events," as many Ottoman documents referred to them,
started in the summer of 1894 in Zeytun and quickly spread to other provinces in the Ottoman East. In the summer and fall of 1895 violence broke out
in what was known as the Six Provinces—Sivas, Erzurum, Ma'murat al-'Aziz,
Diyarbakir, Bitlis, and Van, as well as neighboring cities and villages that had
a substantial Armenian population, such as Sasun, Zeytun, Urfa, and 'Aintab.
The third wave of violence unfolded in October 1895 in Trabzon on the
northeast Black Sea coast of Anatolia. More important, it manifested itself in
pogroms against Armenians in Istanbul itself.[48] Even though many Mosques
were burnt down and many Muslims were killed while their properties were
destroyed or stolen, the Armenian population bore the brunt of the violence.
That violence was committed mostly by the Hamidiye Light Cavalry Regiments, who were recruited from mostly Kurdish tribes in the region, by local
Kurdish and Turkish community leaders, and was aided by local government
officials.[49] News of the massacres spread quickly and made it to the foreign
press, forever marking Abdülhamid in Europe as an anti-Christian sultan,
labeled the "Great Assassin" in Britain and "Le Sultan Rouge" in France.[50]

The Cyprus Convention, the San Remo Treaty, and the Treaty of Berlin
all stipulated that the Ottoman government had to enact immediate reforms
in the Ottoman East or face European (particularly British) intervention.[51]
This was viewed by staunch Ottoman imperialists as a blatant interference
in the internal affairs of the empire. They feared a repeat of what had taken

place in the Balkan provinces, where separatist movements of Greeks, Serbians, Montenegrins, and Bulgarians were supported and, in some cases, instigated by the Russian and British empires. After news of the initial massacres had spread, the sultan announced reforms to guarantee the safety and
security of the Christian population. His administration was adamant not to
allow further European interference. The fear of another Bulgaria or Serbia
in the heart of Anatolia led to a different approach to questions of Armenian separatism. The emergence of "committees" made up of revolutionaries
supported by Russia and the location of the Six Provinces with substantial
Armenian populations being so close to the three provinces taken over by
the Russians after the defeat of 1877 made the so-called Armenian Question
even more threatening to an Ottoman administration in a perpetual state of
existential panic.[52]

An announcement of reforms that were supposed to appease European
critics led to even more violence in the provinces. It fueled anti-Armenian
sentiment, confirming local Muslims' suspicions that Armenian-Ottomans
were somehow a tool of foreign powers determined to undermine Ottoman
sovereignty and intent on humiliating the Muslim population.[53] As international organizations like the Red Cross, the English Society of Friends, and
many American missionaries and relief agencies spread across eastern Anatolia, the Hamidian administration's fears seemed to materialize—foreign
powers were ignoring Ottoman authorities in a region where foreign influence and separatism were rife.[54] The massacres led to the death and displace-
ment of tens of thousands of Armenians, as well as the forcible conversion
of many who wanted to be spared the violence unleashed on their villages.
Many Armenian-Ottoman villagers escaped to the Russian Empire and even
farther afield if they had the means—to Britain, the United States, Abyssinia,
and South Africa.[55]

Izzet reported in his private journal a conversation he had with Sultan
Abdülhamid II on the question of forcible deportation of Armenians to Africa. According to Izzet, on November 18, 1900, he was summoned to meet
with the sultan. As soon as he entered the room, the sultan said, "I learned
from a newspaper translation that the English have just entered Transvaal.
Knowing this, look into sending a man to meet the English prime minister, secretly and unofficially, to propose that we transfer Armenians living in

Anatolia to Transvaal, and in exchange, we relocate Transvaal inhabitants to Anatolia."[56]

Government-censored newspapers in Istanbul, like İkdam, seemed obsessed with events taking place in Transvaal, highlighting British defeats and the destruction the second Boer War brought to the local population.[57] It was not unusual for Ottoman newspapers to cover international events. Still, the detailed coverage of what at first glance seemed not to have anything to do with Ottoman interests becomes clearer when considering how European imperialism was always, in one way or another, an issue of immediate concern for Ottoman statesmen. According to Izzet, he immediately thought the exchange of Armenians and South Africans was a bad idea and dissuaded the sultan. He reasoned that the Armenians who wanted to set up an independent state would turn to the Russians if the Ottomans were to turn to the British, incentivizing the Russians to support the establishment of a satellite state in eastern Anatolia. Instead, he proposed that the empire take the opportunity of the Russo-Japanese war to secure its position in the eastern provinces.[58] What Izzet claimed to have taken place would have been a very controversial proposition, but it would not have been outside of the realm of possibilities. Violence continued to flare up in the eastern provinces until at least 1897, and the palace remained obsessed with the Armenian Question right through the end of Abdülhamid's reign and after. Izzet, like many advisors close to the sultan, did not mince words when it came to describing his mistrust of the Armenian-Ottomans of Anatolia. He felt that the Armenian Question was just another ploy for the Great Powers to weaken the empire's sovereignty.

Sadik's attitude toward the Armenian Question was no less hostile than Izzet's. He looked at what was taking place in the eastern provinces as an extension of no less than a global conspiracy to undermine the empire's sovereignty. For him, and I would argue for many statesmen who deeply identified with the imperial project, the empire had been in an existential crisis since the Treaty of Berlin in 1878. They fought against anything and anyone they perceived as a threat to the empire, leaving no room for moral or humanitarian considerations in their rush to accept the palace's version of events.[59]

An incident that took place a few years after the meeting between Izzet and the sultan sheds light on Sadik's attitude toward the Armenian-Ottomans of Anatolia. In a travelogue from 1904, Sadik wrote that he had run into some of the Armenian refugees of the 1895 massacres, or "the events" as he referred to them, who were living in Addis Ababa. His attitude was defiant and explicitly resentful toward them, as he made clear:

> We received the leaders of the Greek Orthodox [*Rum*] and Armenians who are here. The Armenians had migrated to Addis Ababa after the well-known events. This led about three hundred of them to move to Addis Ababa. Some migrated alone, and others brought their women. Many of them regret what had happened and are resentful against those that have tricked and deceived them. I found them lamenting and moping when Istanbul or Anatolia was mentioned in front of them. Some admitted their fault and the patience and mercy shown to them by the government. However, what is the point now when it is all too late. I learned that the Armenians here had wanted to start an association that would have its own board of directors and a private administration, but the [Abyssinian] emperor told them, "It seems to me that you are a group of people who have gotten used to evil-doing, because if it weren't for that, your own state would not have kicked you out of your homeland. That is why I will ask you to bring me an attestation, either from the Ottoman government or from other foreign governments. Barring that, you will have to leave my country." That is when they had to ask his majesty for a few months extension to write the Patriarch asking for his attestation on their behalf.[60]

Though I was surprised by the tone of Sadik's description of this encounter, I initially assumed it was a result of his efforts to appease his audience—the sultan and his readership back in Istanbul. This travelogue was widely consumed upon his return to Istanbul: It was serialized in the daily newspaper *İkdam* before being published as a book in Ottoman-Turkish in Istanbul and was later translated and published in Arabic in Cairo.[61]

My assumption was wrong on two counts. First, I learned that the Arabic translation, which I quote, was based on the manuscript and not the Ottoman-Turkish book. Comparing the Ottoman-Turkish version with the manuscript showed me that the former had been heavily censored. In fact, this whole incident was completely excised from the Ottoman-Turkish version. An Ottoman official's hostility toward Armenian refugees could not have sat well with the Hamidian administration claiming innocence at every turn. The second reason I was wrong was the belief I had held for many years, that Sadik was not involved in the "the events" of 1895–1896. It was based on an extensive search of the Ottoman archives for every Ottoman government-related mission he had ever been on between 1890 and 1900. There was no substantial evidence of him being assigned to any mission in the eastern provinces that I could find—that is, until I came across his name in a passing mention in the British National Archives.

Sadik's name came up in a dispatch from Bulgaria to London that referenced his work with the Ottoman commission after the 1895–1896 massacres. A certain Charles Marling, in a confidential note to the Marquess of Lansdowne, described Sadik as a former "member of a Commission sent to enquire into the conditions of the Armenians in 1896."[62] Sadik was part of the Ottoman commission in Urfa, assigned to assess the damages and distribute aid to Ottoman inhabitants (according to the British claim, mostly Muslims) who were affected by the violence. Ottoman officials often accompanied international organizations, at times trying to control the distribution of aid and asserting Ottoman authority on the ground.[63] Sadik's presence in Urfa could only be confirmed in the archives by one document that did not mention the reason for his being there but mentioned his presence in Birecek, a small town near Urfa and an order to deposit an extra 10,000Kr to his bank account in Aleppo, on top of the initial 15,000Kr he had already received for an unmentioned job.[64]

Sadik was also featured on the front page of the Sunday edition of one of the most popular illustrated newspapers in Europe covering the 1894–1896 massacres (figure 7).[65] In a charm offensive by the Ottoman government, the Ottoman ambassador in Paris landed the front page, where he, with the help of the newspaper's editor, complained of European journalists purposely misrepresenting what was happening in the Ottoman East as an indication of Ottoman state oppression:

> In the presence of this deliberately tendentious campaign, the imperial Ottoman Embassy in Paris believes it should warn the public against all sensational rumors. The authorities had to suppress, as happens in such a case in

ARMÉE OTTOMANE

SADIK-BEY
Colonel d'infanterie, aide de camp de
S. M. I. le Sultan.

RIZA-BEY
Commandant de cavalerie, aide de camp
de S. M. I. le Sultan.

CHEFKET-BEY
Lieutenant-colonel d'artillerie.

FIGURE 7. Front cover of *Le Petit Journal*'s *Supplément du Dimanche*, November 25, 1895, featuring Sadik on the left.
Source: gallica.bnf.fr / Bibliothèque nationale de France.

all the world countries, some local skirmishes that are not of the scope that
warrant attributing them to the general situation of the empire. Additionally,
the imperial government will not fail in its duty to work against disturbers
of public order if new disturbances were to occur. His Majesty the sultan's
generous intentions for all his subjects, without distinction of race or religion,
are well known to everyone, which every civil servant has the duty to draw
inspiration from to ensure the progress and tranquility of the populations.[66]

The newspaper stated that the Ottoman government had the military
power necessary to "suppress the sedition of the Armenians." The "director"
of the newspaper visited Tophane, a weapons factory in Istanbul, and reported that it produced some of the "most excellent" weapons. He also stated
that he spoke at length with the sultan and with Sadik himself and two other
members of the military whose portraits were also on the front page of the
weekend edition. He was "struck by their education, the extent of their military knowledge as well as their love of the soldier's profession."[67] The author
continued with Ottoman propaganda aimed at the French audience, stating
that if the situation worsened, "the sultan whose high wisdom and firmness
are universally recognized would easily triumph. Europe, therefore, has no
reason to worry about the famous [potential] spark of which we speak too
much" because the sultan would know how to put down any revolt by himself. While the front page featured three Ottoman officers, including Sadik,
the back cover had a drawing titled "Attack on a Mosque by Armenians,"
to ensure that the propaganda was complete, cover to cover. The article was
published during the height of the massacres, and the violence would continue for several more months (figure 8).[68]

Like many palace advisors, Sadik was on the front lines of this conflict
as a representative of and close aide to the sultan. His interaction with his
European counterparts in eastern Anatolia would influence his impression of
the fading sovereignty of the sultan, which he saw as a personal existential
threat. Anti-Ottoman sentiment had been running high, with some British
politicians and missionaries advocating a strong anti-Ottoman policy as early
as the 1870s, greatly impacting public opinion in Europe. He also witnessed
the dirty business of international politics when the British Empire used
the pain and suffering of Christian communities in the Ottoman Empire as

ÉVÉNEMENTS D'ORIENT
Attaque d'une mosquée par les Arméniens

FIGURE 8. Back cover of *Le Petit Journal's Supplément du Dimanche* headlined
"An Attack on a Mosque by Armenians," November 25, 1895.
Source: gallica.bnf.fr / Bibliothèque nationale de France.

leverage for its own political and economic goals. Even though the Treaty of Küçük Kaynarca (1774) and the Treaty of San Stefano (1878) made watching out for the well-being of Christians in the Ottoman Empire the privilege of the Russian Empire, the Cyprus Convention in 1878, some argue, gave the British Empire the ability and the excuse to exert pressure on Istanbul.[69] It also meant that the British government was in a position to claim the violence against the Armenian-Ottoman population as its own cause, seeking compensation and restitution on their behalf.

Witnessing Transimperial Profiteering

European powers were quick to demand financial compensation for damages their subjects' businesses suffered during the 1896 Istanbul pogroms, using them as a way of settling old political scores. One example was the claim of compensation for property damages and the lost lives of Armenian-Ottomans who worked for British businesses in Istanbul. Here the secret negotiations between the Sublime Porte and the British government give us a clear picture of how the suffering of Armenian-Ottomans was leveraged to the benefit of some European governments.

After refusing to entertain any talk of compensation, lest that be considered an admission of guilt, in 1899 the Sublime Porte signaled to the British ambassador that the palace was willing to negotiate over certain issues as a way of appeasing the British government in return for closer ties. The ambassador bundled together a few demands—granting a license to a British steamer company asking for special rights to operate on the Tigris River and the prevention of local authorities from constructing irrigation canals with their mouths at the river, lest they impede their ability to operate; financial settlement for an English steamer's losses because they were prevented from operating a line between Istanbul and Bartin; granting the Eastern Telegraph Company a license to construct submarine lines between Istanbul and Constantine; giving a certain Mrs. Simmons who owned a farm in Ottoman domains a fair price for her land; giving a certain Reverend Martin, a British subject, financial compensation for mistreatment on one of his trips by local authorities; and last but not least financial compensation for the improper treatment of Reverend McCallum, who in 1897 was expelled from the country while distributing relief payments in Zeytun after the massacres.[70]

None of these claims were considered controversial, with the exception of the last one, which the Ottoman government made clear it was unwilling to entertain in its current form. The initial claim was worded in a way that tied it directly to the massacres and was provided as an enclosure to the main memorandum proposed to the head secretary of the palace, the famous Süreyya Efendi. The memorandum stated:

> The Imperial Government has not yet acceded to the demand of pecuniary compensation in favor of the British subjects who suffered a loss in the recent *disturbances* [the author's italics], though claims for damage sustained in similar disturbances have before now been paid by the United States Government to China, by France to Italy, and by England to France; it would therefore be in accord with the principles of international law and the well-known sentiments of justice of the Imperial Government to follow these precedents, and it is therefore requested that the claims of British merchants and subjects for the losses sustained by them may be met.[71]

It is important to note the language used in this memo. The massacres were referred to with the vague term "disturbances." They also did not name the perpetrators, rendering intentional acts of violence as passive events. However, that was not enough. Süreyya wrote back, stating in unequivocal terms that if the British government wanted any of the other financial compensation claims to be considered, the last one, relating to the Armenian massacres, had to be taken off the table. The British representative, Mr. Block, wrote back with threats of his own: "The money would have eventually to be paid, and it was better to settle the question now than allow it to drag on. The Armenian question was dormant, but until this money was paid, reference would perpetually be made to the massacres, which in the interests of the Ottoman Government were better forgotten. Other nations had paid money under similar circumstances, and the fact of indemnifying the sufferers did not imply responsibility." The sultan's head secretary understood the blackmail, and he diplomatically assured the British representative that there would be a better time to settle this issue. Mr. Block was convinced and took the issue of indemnity off the list. Sure enough, three of the requests were immediately approved and the other three were referred to the Sublime Porte for more consideration.[72]

Within a couple of years, the British and Ottoman governments had found a way to pay the requested amounts, without any admittance of guilt, with the help of the British representative. The idea of folding the payment into a bigger project that would benefit British businesses had come up, but the British government was not the originator of this scheme. Someone known only as R. P. M. writing on February 21, 1901, suggested an alternative approach than continuing to request the amount owed as indemnity, which according to British calculations amounted to £63,938. Five official requests were submitted to the Sublime Porte over a six-year period, with no success. Other European powers and the United States, however, were much more successful. The key was discretion. The French government received 35% of its requested amount, with the condition that a French contractor receive a larger "kilometer guarantee" on the railway extension of the Beirut-Damascus line, something the Porte had been adamantly against. The rest of the amounts were to be handled through the railway company and indirectly funneled to the claimants. The American claim of $90,000 in indemnity requested in 1895 was only approved once it was bundled into a deal for the purchase of a cruiser from an American contractor, the first payment for which would be supplemented by the indemnity money the Americans had demanded. Other European powers affected, Ambassador Nicolas O'Conor claimed, had a great deal of business between their industries and the Ottoman Empire and would most likely get their payments in similar ways.[73] For example, with the Germans acting as mediators, the Porte signed a contract with an Italian firm to rebuild the ironclad Mesudiye as a way of satisfying the Ottoman government's obligations for property destroyed during the pogroms.[74]

In early 1901 a deal was struck with the Ottoman foreign minister, Tevfik (Ar. Tawfiq) Pasha. He proposed to instruct the director of the Ottoman Navy to purchase a cruiser from a British supplier by the name of Messrs. Armstrong, a process through which the indemnity money would be indirectly funneled to the British government. He insisted that "nothing would induce the sultan to consent to a direct payment under the heading of Compensation for Outrages and Massacre." Tevfik insisted on the condition that the details of this deal be kept out of the press.[75]

The news was leaked to the British press, but Ambassador O'Conor insisted that the matter not be discussed in parliament. The signing of the contract for the cruiser took place in June 1901, and the first installment was immediately transferred. In order for the indemnity payments not to be traced back to the Ottoman government, the agreement was that they would pay Messrs. Armstrong, in installments, a sum that included both the fee for the cruiser and the indemnities. Messrs. Armstrong would deposit a portion of the payments into the personal account of the British ambassador at the Ottoman Imperial Bank. The ambassador would then distribute the money to British subjects affected by the massacres. It is important to note that most of these British subjects were in fact local Ottoman residents, many of whom were Armenian-Ottomans, working under the extraterritorial legal protection of the British Empire.[76] A few months later, the ambassador reported that he had had the very rare opportunity to dine with the sultan, when he thanked him for the sensitivity he had shown on the issue of payments. He also expressed his eagerness to have this whole matter settled and put behind them. The foreign minister reiterated the importance of keeping the arrangement secret so as not to alert other powers to the favorable deal the British had obtained. To speed up the process, the sultan issued a special decree to make sure the rest of the payments were immediately settled.[77]

Even though it might seem that this agreement allowed both parties to save face, it ultimately made very little difference in the perception of the Ottoman Empire, particularly under the rule of Abdülhamid II. The Armenian Massacres of 1895–1896 would forever be tied to the sultan as one of the worst atrocities in the empire's recent history. As an advisor to the sultan who was involved in crafting the Ottoman response to European intervention in the eastern provinces after the massacres, Sadik was privy to the inner workings of Ottoman-European relations. His resentment toward what he perceived as blackmail and a double standard that the Ottoman government had to adhere to would color his outlook for the remainder of his career. This included his interaction with Armenian refugees whom he met with in Addis Ababa in 1904 and his attitude toward Bulgarian independence during his 1904–1908 tenure as Ottoman special commissioner in Sofia, which I discuss in Chapter 6. Even though the massacres were shocking in their scale, they, along with Abdülhamid II's idea to relocate the entire Armenian population to Transvaal, foretold of a much larger atrocity to come twenty years later in which the vast majority of the Armenian population of Anatolia would be killed, converted, or deported.[78]

Arab-Ottoman's Fingerprints on Hamidian-Era Policies

Whether it was working on public health initiatives, advising the sultan, or representing the empire, the influence of Arab-Ottoman imperialists on the Hamidian-era Ottoman Empire is hard to overestimate. The cholera outbreak and the large difference between the recently built neighborhoods of those closest to the imperial government and the poor neighborhoods meant the difference between life and death. The privilege of living in a neighborhood like Teşvikiye was but one of many fringe benefits of working in the palace.

By today's standards, nepotism, accepting gifts, and using one's influence to make things better for oneself and one's family are tantamount to corruption. In Hamidian Istanbul, they meant doing what was expected in a system that rewarded loyalty, not necessarily with high salaries but with opportunities to advance one's personal interests. Thus, Shafiq was not ashamed of bragging that he earned four times what his official salary was to his son-in-law, who considered him a symbol of nobility and honor. That was what a man in his position was expected to do. There were lines he was not willing to cross, though, as the incident with the railway funding demonstrates, and he was willing to risk his job for what he believed. However, Shafiq did nothing that was not calculated, which allowed him to reinvent himself several times. Even when people around him fell, he always seemed to land on his feet.

By 1895 Sadik was established in his position as a member of the sultan's advisory office. In this chapter, the reader discovered how his experience as the sultan's representative and an imperial loyalist impacted his view of the Armenian massacres. He seemed to lay the blame at the feet of Armenians only. He thought of the massacres not as the plight of fellow Ottomans but simply as policy abstracted into "events" or "disturbances" that amounted to a threat to the empire and, by extension, to himself as an imperial statesman. In Chapter 3, the reader will follow Sadik on several high-profile assignments to Germany, the eastern Balkans, and Russia, and when accompanying important European dignitaries in the Levant. On average, Sadik spent nine out of twelve months on the road, which no doubt affected his personal life and relationships. As for most travelers, time abroad as a foreigner allowed him the space to reflect on his own country, his personal life, and where he fit in a vanishing imperial world order.

CHAPTER 3

AN OTTOMAN IMPERIALIST'S

GLOBAL SOCIAL SPACE

We took shelter in a [German] friend's place not far from
where we were staying. The rain came down so heavily that
the streets turned to rivers. A little after that, the [Berlin]
municipal employee tasked with spraying the streets with
water using a horse-drawn carriage passed by. He stopped
in front of the public water tap and filled his carriage. He
then started spraying the streets, not seeming to notice the
fact that it was raining. When our host came into the living
room, we asked him what the man was doing, spraying
the street with water, despite the heavy rain. He simply
answered us: "He is just doing his job!"

—Sadik al-Mu'ayyad Azmzade, writing in 1904[1]

LIKE MANY ELITE MEMBERS OF HIS GENERATION, SADIK WAS
greatly influenced by and well versed in western European languages and
cultures. Despite his admiration for many European cultural habits, as the
epigraph taken from his 1904 Abyssinian travelogue shows, he was not blind
to some of what he considered to be illogical behaviors in the West. He was
also bitterly aware of the power differential between the Ottoman Empire

and its European counterparts and the way that played in weakening Ottoman sovereignty and prestige.

This chapter offers an alternative perspective on the post-1878 Ottoman defeat against the Russian Empire that invites the reader to imagine the world through the eyes of a young up-and-coming Ottoman patriot a decade after the Congress of Berlin. Starting in 1888 and ending in 1903, it covers three episodes that Sadik witnessed and, I argue, played an important role in shaping his worldview. The first was the decade after the defeat, when Sadik accompanied a Russian grand duke and his entourage on their travels in the Levant in what can only be understood as a belated victory tour on Ottoman soil. The second, which the epigraph refers to, was Sadik's years in Berlin and his subsequent accompaniment of the German kaiser to his childhood home in Damascus. The third was Sadik's involvement in the so-called Macedonian Question as a representative of the empire in the eastern Balkans and negotiations with the Russian tzar in the Crimean Peninsula.

The notion that the Ottomans were unfairly treated by the European powers seemed to permeate the rank and file in the palace. In his diary, Izzet regularly referenced nineteenth-century agreements that the Ottoman Empire signed with European powers in good faith, only to be unjustly treated by them. The three most frequently referenced conferences he wrote of were the Paris Peace Conference in 1856, the Congress of Berlin in 1878, and the Conference of Berlin on Africa 1884–1885—where the European powers most egregiously betrayed agreements with Istanbul and norms of international law.[2] Izzet often pointed out how the Great Powers manipulated facts on the ground to suit their needs and weaken the sovereignty of the empire. Whether it was the British in northeast Africa and the Red Sea basin; the French in Syria, Mount Lebanon, and Central Africa; or the Russians in the Balkans, his diary reads like a list of international grievances. Like Sadik, Izzet took Ottoman imperialism seriously and, some would say, personally.[3]

In 1878, Sadik was most likely a young cadet in military college when the humiliating conditions stipulated in the Treaty of Berlin were announced. A decade later, as a thirty-year-old man, Sadik accompanied a Russian grand duke, his wife, and his brother to Palestine. He witnessed the consecration of Russian influence in the Holy Land and the deference shown to Russian imperialists on Ottoman soil. Although it is impossible to know the extent of the emotional or psychological impact this mission had on an impressionable Sadik, we can empathize with this ardent imperialist and better understand the contradictions of belonging to a transimperial global social space dominated by a rising European political hegemony.

The second mission, in 1898, should be understood in the context of German-Ottoman military cooperation and the cultural impact it had on members of the Ottoman military. Sadik was one of many promising Ottoman officers to spend a few years in Berlin, becoming very familiar with German culture, which influenced his view of the West. As he accompanied the German kaiser on a visit to Damascus, the Azmzades' center of power and his childhood home, he witnessed his home through a "Western" gaze. He operated as a language and cultural interpreter and a Damascene "native informant." Remembering what Georgina Müller said in Chapter 1, Sadik was a perfect tour guide because he understood how the "Orient" was perceived from a European perspective.

The final part of the chapter follows Sadik on missions to the Ottoman Balkans and Russian Crimea. As a negotiator with the Russian tzar, he had come a long way from his days as a tour guide for the Russian grand duke in Jerusalem fifteen years earlier. The early 1900s marked a shift in Sadik's career, as he became mired in the complicated world of the Balkans' ethnic nationalism and interimperial disputes. His perspective on Ottoman weakness and European opportunistic interference in domestic affairs that he had acquired over the previous two decades shaped his work in Macedonia and later in Bulgaria.

An Ottoman Officer and a Russian Grand Duke

In 1888, Sadik was assigned to accompany Grand Duke Sergei Alexandrovich, the son of Tzar Alexander II and the brother of Tzar Alexander III of the Romanov dynasty. The grand duke was on his second tour of the Levant with his brother, Grand Duke Paul Alexandrovich, and his wife Grand Duchess Elizabeth Feodorovna, the granddaughter of Queen Victoria of Britain and the niece of Empress Victoria of Germany. By all accounts, it was a very delicate mission, accompanying this royal family a mere decade after the end of the Russian-Ottoman War of 1877–1878, which was a decisive victory by the

Russians over the Ottoman forces. Sergei and Paul had fought against the Ottomans in the famous battle and siege of Plevna in 1877, in which the Ottomans were able to gain a rare win against the Russian coalition army.[4] However, after a five-month siege, the Russians forced the Ottomans to retreat.[5]

The Ottoman defeat was monumental, prompting some historians of the late Ottoman Empire to call it "the beginning of the end."[6] While I disagree that the Ottoman Empire faced an inevitable demise after the 1878 Treaty of Berlin, I agree that this defeat and the subsequent treaties forever changed the character of the empire. Most of the Balkan provinces—the historic heart of the Ottoman Empire and one of the oldest territories to be conquered by the early Ottoman dynasty—were engaged in a slow and painful process of separation. This defeat cast a long shadow over the empire and the Ottoman dynasty that lasted until the very end of their rule and arguably even after, when the Treaty of Berlin was used as the basis for the Paris Peace Settlement at the end of World War I.[7]

As part of the San Stefano Treaty, later replaced by the Treaty of Berlin (1878), Serbia and Montenegro expanded territorially and, along with Romania, were given complete independence. An autonomous, though decidedly not independent, Bulgaria was declared a principality, and Batumi, Kars, Ardahan, and Doğubayazıt were ceded to Russia. The Ottoman administration also agreed to design and enact reforms that would ensure protection of the rights and safety of the Christian population in Thessalia and Epirus, and, perhaps most consequentially, the Armenian population in the heart of Anatolia. Act 61 of the treaty specified that if it were to be determined at a future date that these reforms had not been carried out and the safety of these populations could not be guaranteed, Russian and European parties had the right to intervene.[8] Act 61 was used to intervene during the 1894–1896 massacres and later during the Macedonian rebellion in 1903, which I discuss later in this chapter.

Sadik was around twenty years old at the time of the Ottoman-Russian war and the Congress of Berlin that followed. He probably was in the first year of military college in Istanbul, having had recently moved from Beirut to pursue a career in the Ottoman military. Such a significant defeat and loss of territories, one that irreparably changed the standing of the Ottoman Empire in the world, must have had an impact on an impressionable young and, by all accounts, patriotic Sadik. Assigning him a decade later to accompany the Russian grand duke was a vote of confidence in his ability to maintain his diplomatic composure as a rising star in the Office of the Aides-de-Camp. Sadik's fluency in French was no doubt one of the factors in assigning him to such a mission, and his familiarity with the region and native fluency in Levantine-Arabic was another.

Another reason this was a sensitive mission for the Ottomans was the announced purpose of the grand duke's visit. Sergei was there to bolster the global reach of Russian religious and political influence. Perhaps more dangerously, Russia sought closer ties with the Orthodox Arab-Ottoman population in one of the most important cities in the empire, Jerusalem. Sergei was there to consecrate the Church of St. Mary Magdalene, a new Russian Orthodox church that he had partially funded and that was registered as a charitable, religious endowment in 1882, after his first trip to Jerusalem.[9] He also established the Imperial Orthodox Palestine Society to support Russian pilgrims in Jerusalem and promote the Russian Orthodox Church's interests there. Additionally, he founded a hostel for Russian Christian pilgrims to the Holy Land.[10]

The purpose of the Imperial Orthodox Palestine Society, as outlined in a memo submitted to the United Nations in 1949, was to protect Russian properties in Palestine. The society was established to "study the Holy Land and spread information on it in Russia;" to build schools, churches, and monasteries that would provide "enlightening activity to the Orthodox population in Palestine;" and to assist Russian pilgrims. In 1949, Russian properties were plentiful and stretched across all of Palestine, but their biggest concentration was in Jerusalem. They had been registered under the names of Ottoman citizens on behalf of the Russian Empire as well as members of the monarchy because the laws at the time did not allow the purchase of immovable properties in the Ottoman Empire by ordinary non-Ottoman citizens.[11] The Russian presence, including the registration (but not necessarily purchase) of lands and properties in the name of the Russian Empire after the 1878 Congress of Berlin and continuing until the British Mandate, was about establishing Russia's imperial presence on some of the most symbolically and politically important real estate in the world. Perhaps the foreign minister of the Russian Federation, Sergey Lavrov, said it best when, in 2015, he described the establishment of the society by the grand duke as "not only for facilitating Russians' travel to the holy places, but also in the interests of creating [a] Russian presence in the Holy Land . . . a 'Russian Palestine'. . . . In addition to the spiritual aspects of 'Russian Palestine,' this is also a very important tool for the strengthening of Russia's position . . . in this very important area."[12]

St. Mary Magdalene was built in Muscovite style, with white limestone and seven gold onion domes, each topped with a Russian cross. It stood on the western slope of the Mount of Olives (figure 9).[13] Such a sizeable, conspicuous structure built on this symbolically important land ensured that "Russian subjects performing a pilgrimage and those simply voyaging along the territory of the Ottoman State [were] elevated," as stated in Article 8 of the 1774 Treaty of Küçük Kaynarca. The treaty, signed after the defeat in the second half of the eighteenth century, included a provision to allow the Russian Empire to build two other churches and a consulate in the heart of

FIGURE 9. St. Mary Magdalene church in Jerusalem, with the Dome of the Rock in the background, ca. 1940s.
Source: G. Eric and Edith Matson Photograph Collection. Library of Congress, Prints & Photographs Division (LC-DIG-matpc-12524).

the capital.[14] This established a precedent for European powers claiming religious custodianship of Christian Ottoman imperial subjects. In the case of tsarist Russia, the claim was to be able to intervene on behalf of the Orthodox Christian population of the empire and act as the sponsor of Orthodox Christian churches in Ottoman lands.[15]

The Russian church took advantage of the cleavages arising between the Arab Orthodox and Greek Orthodox populations in the Levant by supporting the former in a bid to weaken the Istanbul-based Greek Orthodox Church's hold over such a large and influential population. The Russian Empire also competed with France by attempting to increase the power of the Orthodox Church through the sheer number of Russian pilgrims. Indeed, in a bid to outperform other Christians in Jerusalem, the Russian Empire increased the number of pilgrims by several fold, such that by the turn of the nineteenth century seven thousand Russian pilgrims were dwarfing the fewer than one thousand Catholic pilgrims from Italy, Austro-Hungary, and France.[16]

An Ottoman Office on the Russian Victory Tour

Since his first visit to the Levant, Grand Duke Sergei had become the governor-general of Moscow and had married Elizabeth (Ella) of Hesse, now known as Grand Duchess Elisabeth Feodorovna. Sergei was known as a proud, fanatically religious, ardent anti-Semite. By all accounts, he had a rigid understanding of protocol and a taste for luxury, fashion, jewelry, and art. He had a complicated public image, with rumors circulating that blamed his unhappy marriage on his sexual affairs with officers in the Russian army.[17] Sergei's trip to the Ottoman Empire in 1888 can be interpreted as a victory tour, part of a broader symbolic program of signaling Russian power in the empire, as the Russians competed with the other Great Powers for the right to represent Christian Ottomans. The clause in the Treaty of Berlin that affirmed Russia's role as protector of Orthodox Christians in the empire was especially offensive to the Ottoman elites, not only because of the acknowledgment that it was simply a pretense for interference in Ottoman affairs but also because it attempted to carve out Ottoman Orthodox Christians, with the argument that they needed protection from the Ottoman state. One of the closest international relations advisors to the sultan and a master negotiator, Kara Todori Pasha, had been the plenipotentiary at the Congress of Berlin. He recalled that he explicitly protested the notion that the Orthodox population needed protection in the Ottoman Empire, reminding Prince Bismarck that everybody knew that he was an Orthodox Christian Ottoman:

> For as long as the Ottoman Empire has been around, Christians could freely and publicly perform their rituals and display of their religion without any problems. Bells tolling inviting Christians to worship in Churches and Monasteries could be heard. On Easter and other feast days, Christian inhabitants go out on the street and publicly perform their religious rituals with total freedom. Nobody has ever witnessed any kind of persecution, abuse, or obstacles erected to stop such displays. For this reason, there is no need for what the Russian plenipotentiary proposed [to assign Russia as the protector of Orthodox Christians].[18]

Despite fervent Ottoman protests, the clause remained and was carried over in the subsequent treaty with the British Empire in the Cyprus Convention.

The church in Jerusalem was only one Russian monumental project to be built on Ottoman soil following the defeat of the Ottomans in 1878. In 1892 the building of a Russian victory monument commenced on the western doorstep of Istanbul, in today's Yeşilköy, and it was completed in 1898. For Ottomans, this was a bitter reminder of their defeat and how close the Russians came to taking Istanbul before the sultan sued for peace in 1878. The Russians insisted on keeping the building of the monument as a clause in the Treaty of Berlin after it replaced the Treaty of San Stefano. The Ottoman ambassador to Berlin, Sadullah (Ar. Sa'd Allah) Pasha, wrote about this in his memoirs, recalling how hard he tried to excise this clause requiring the building of a "victory monument," saying that it would be a "monument of shame" that would "scream every day at Ottoman faces their shameful defeat."[19] The monument was so bitterly despised that in 1914 it was blown up by the Ottoman government. This event was recorded in the first Ottoman documentary film directed by an Ottoman citizen.[20]

The sultan reportedly paid the Russians' expenses during their first visit to Jerusalem in 1881. On their second trip, they stopped in Istanbul for two days, where they were the personal guests of the sultan and were treated to a number of banquets. The grand duchess even met one of Abdülhamid's wives and his daughters.[21] When the Russians left Istanbul, they were sent off with official salutes and the firing of the cannons. In Izmir, they docked briefly, met the governor-general and refueled and resupplied before continuing to Beirut. The same day that the grand duke and his companions left Istanbul, the accompanying Ottoman delegation, including Sadik, left to meet them in Beirut. Sadik wrote a firsthand account of this trip. The following section is based on this account, which was cosigned by his companions, giving the historian a firsthand description of the power that the Russians enjoyed a decade after their defeat of the Ottomans and the deference that had to be demonstrated by officials at every level of government—all at the Ottoman taxpayers' expense.

When the delegation made it to Beirut on the evening of September 21, it was welcomed by local officials, including the governor-general, and then headed into the city to visit several churches and a Russian girls' school. The visitors rested in a hotel for the night, and the following day the Ottoman delegation left with consultants from the Russian embassy to Haifa to prepare for the grand duke's arrival. The grand duke and his companions continued their tour, heading to Damascus but first stopping in Shtoura, the largest town in the agricultural center of the Beqaa Valley. The next day they continued and were met in Damascus by the governor-general and other dignitaries. They stayed as guests of the *Amir al-Hajj* (director of the Hajj) for several days and were taken to all the tourist sites and several churches. Then they returned to Beirut, immediately boarded the ship, and headed for Haifa. In Haifa they were met by district governors—the *kaymakam* of Haifa and the *mutasarrıf* of 'Akka—and then continued on to Nazareth and other areas of northern Palestine.[22]

From Nazareth, they headed to Jaffa and then on to Jerusalem. They spent many days there, where they performed official visits to the various Russian Orthodox sites and archeological digs that Sergei had paid for when he visited Jerusalem the first time. The governors of each administrative zone welcomed him and his wife, and he was met with pomp and circumstance by every official he met along the way, for which he rewarded those officials with medals. He also consecrated St. Mary Magdalene, where they had the first mass.

From Jaffa, the grand duke and his companions headed to Alexandria. At the same time, the Ottoman officials had to wait for the Egyptian mail boat to take them to Beirut and then wait five more days for a Russian mail boat that would take them back to Istanbul.[23] While Sadik and his companions waited to head home, the grand duke's ship returned empty via Istanbul to Russia, refueling at the port of Harem on the Asian side of Istanbul before continuing to the Black Sea.[24]

Sergei wrote to the palace, thanking the sultan for his hospitality. He also complimented the service of the accompanying Ottoman soldiers, who included Sadik, a *binbaşı* (lieutenant colonel) at the time, as well as another *binbaşı* and a *ferik* (lieutenant general), all from the Office of the Aides-de-Camp.[25] Four soldiers also accompanied them, all of whom were also there to greet the grand duke upon his arrival in Jaffa.[26] Each member of the Ottoman delegation was compensated for their efforts by the Ministry of Interior, with Sadik given a respectable 10,000Kr, the lieutenant general given 30,000Kr, and each officer given a humble 2,500Kr. Sadik's 10,000Kr for such an arduous mission was a far cry from the 20,000Kr he would claim for a return journey in the comfort of the train between Sofia and Istanbul toward the end of his career. The Ministry of Exterior estimated that in all 60,000Kr was spent on hosting the grand duke and duchess in Jerusalem in 1888.[27]

Here one should not look at the Russian visitors and the Ottomans accompanying them exclusively as old enemies. It has to be kept in mind that they shared a code of behavior and a particular cultural orientation held by all elite members of a transregional imperial world. Sadik could have easily found common interests with the grand duke, and they might have even liked one another or liked what they symbolized as members of an exclusive social space of global imperialists. They were men and women who shared a common code of behavior and protocols, a learned sense of superiority and entitlement, and an admiration for all things "modern," which they discussed in glamorous salons and luxurious hotel lobbies from Istanbul to Paris. They communicated in French, the global lingua franca of the elites at the time.

Sadik, an increasingly staunch imperialist, also had a front-row seat to the power differential between the Russians and the Ottomans. European entitlement, enabled by the imperial and provincial government, was on full display. Sadik witnessed how powerful Russian imperialists had free rein in Ottoman lands, including his birthplace, Damascus. He was in the process of fashioning his future as a diplomat. A year after the departure of the grand duke, Sadik was on his way for further education in Berlin, where he became acculturated to specific habits that he would feel conflicted about for a long time. More tangibly, he also learned the most useful language for dealing with the empire's closest European ally, Germany.[28]

An Ottoman Officer in Berlin

The military cooperation between the Ottoman and German empires in the late nineteenth century went back to the 1877 defeat of the Ottomans by the Russian army. Following that humiliation, the Sublime Porte and the palace agreed that acquiring German military assistance was crucial to the survival of the empire. Sultan Abdülhamid II reportedly had been very impressed by the Germans when he visited in 1867 as a young prince, even stating that "the Germans and the Ottoman Turks had similar characteristics: he considered them brave, honest, and hospitable."[29]

Chancellor Otto Von Bismarck was initially opposed to any cooperation with the Ottomans. However, in 1882 a military cooperation agreement was signed, allowing German military advisors to be dispatched to the empire and millions of kurush to be spent on arms purchases from German manufacturers.[30] During the early 1890s, under contract with the German military and through the leadership of Colmar Freiherr von der Goltz, the Ottoman army was thoroughly reorganized along the German model. This reorganization and the arms bought from Germany during this period were credited with the Ottoman victory against the Kingdom of Greece in 1897.[31] Arms sales meant frequent visits by Ottoman inspectors to Germany. They proved so lucrative that Mauser, a rifle manufacturer, built a unique guesthouse to host the Ottoman inspectors sent to Germany, complete with an "oriental" architectural design and a crescent-shaped moon on top of one of the steeples.[32]

In addition to the German military advisors sent to reform the training of a new generation of Ottoman military personnel, high-ranking and promising Ottoman military officials were sent to Germany for further education. Starting in the late 1880s, many of the most famous Ottoman military personalities spent some time in Berlin in training, in the process acquiring a degree of fluency in German. As the number of soldiers in Berlin grew, the need for a large Muslim cemetery became apparent, so the "Turkish cemetery" constructed in the Neuköln neighborhood in 1866 was expanded to replace a smaller one built at the end of the eighteenth century. It still stands next to a mosque, with many headstones dating back to the heyday of Ottoman military education in Berlin.[33]

Sadik's time in Berlin had a lasting impact on him. While he was deeply impressed by the industrial advancement and technology he saw in Germany, he remained uneasy about what he described as the people's machine-like qualities. To him, stern predetermined schedules and the repetitiveness of a regulated world in the city seemed to replace common sense. He admired the order that discipline instilled, but feared its effect on people who could not control their own actions anymore. It also exposed a deeply engrained classism between the common person, with whom he did not identify and often described as unthinking and machine-like, and a person of his class, to whom he attributed faculties of reason and agency. He documented his ambivalence in a travelogue he wrote on his way from Istanbul to Addis Ababa in the spring of 1904, which is the subject of Chapter 5. His travels provided him the space to reflect on a world that was quickly vanishing and the threats that he felt were creeping closer, threatening the Ottoman Empire's place in the world. While he was in transit in Marseille, he recalled an incident from his time in Berlin:

> On Friday morning, while I sat outside one of the country club's cafes observing passersby, the servant of the business's owner came out and started to unfurl the sun screen tent all the way to the ground. When I asked the servant why he did that, he simply pointed to the clock. When I looked up, it was 7.30 am. I understood that the habit in this place is to put down the shades at 7.30 am every day to block the sun's rays. Even though the sun was absent that day and there was no need to put down the shades, this worker, who resembles a mechanical instrument, did not have the capacity to recognize that. This reminded me of a similar incident that I witnessed in Berlin. For I once was taking a walk with a bunch of my officer friends, when the weather suddenly took a turn for the worse, and there were signs of impend-

ing rain, so we took shelter in a friend's place, not far from where we were staying. The rain came down so heavily that the streets turned to rivers. A little after that, the municipal employee tasked with spraying the streets with water using a horse-drawn carriage passed by. He stopped in front of the public water tap and filled his carriage. He then started spraying the streets, not seeming to take notice of the fact that it was raining. When our host came into the living room, we asked him what the man was doing, spraying the street with water, despite the heavy rain. He simply answered us: "He is just doing his job!"[34]

Such incidents betrayed Sadik's refusal to blindly accept European ways of life as superior to his own. As he rose through the ranks and had to travel there to meet with his European counterparts, he adopted more of the habits and attitudes of global imperialists, often praising European elites' behavior. However, it was not at all a simple adoption of "Western" ways. It was a complex notion of belonging to a particular social structure that operated under specific rules of behavior that transcended cultural specificity and was elevated to the performativity of a globalized imperial ruling class.

Over the following decade, Sadik's experience in Berlin and his knowledge of German helped propel him to the forefront of the empire's diplomatic relations. As Istanbul's economic and military ties with Berlin deepened, personal relations between the sovereigns warmed. Emperor Wilhelm II (r. 1888–1918), a fan of old-world regal ceremonial performances, took great pleasure in his visits to the Ottoman Empire. His first visit was in November of 1889, barely a year after his coronation. As a battered sovereign who often found himself unsupported on the international stage, Abdülhamid greatly appreciated the symbolism of the kaiser's visit, which did not go unnoticed by the Great Powers. Newspapers from Paris to New York followed the European monarch's visit to Istanbul with great interest.[35] Wilhelm II himself telegraphed several messages to the German chancellor describing the joy he felt at Abdülhamid's hospitality, which he described as "paradisical."[36] More important, this trip solidified political, economic, and military ties between Istanbul and Berlin that led to a noticeable increase in German imports to the empire and planted the seeds for the kaiser's second trip. On his first journey, Wilhelm was granted a prime piece of real estate in Jerusalem, where the first German protestant church was to be built. There is no evidence of Sadik's involvement in the first visit, but he was front and center during the better-known second *Orientreisse*, when the kaiser paid another visit to the sultan in Istanbul and then embarked on a lavish tour of the Levant. The highlight of that trip was the consecration of the German protestant Church of the Redeemer in 1898.[37]

An Ottoman Officer and a Kaiser

After the 1894–1896 massacres, one European government remained conspicuously silent about the atrocities committed; this was the German government. The old friendship between Wilhelm and Abdülhamid and Wilhelm's "sentimental attachment to the Ottoman Empire" seemed to have only strengthened since the early 1890s.[38] In fact, while Britain, France, Russia, Italy, and the United States were busy negotiating indemnities and reparations for damages they claimed were caused by the massacres, preparations for Wilhelm and Empress Victoria's visit were well under way. This official trip was carried out against the advice of the German chancellor Bismarck, who wanted Germany to stay away from the mire of the Armenian Question. He feared that such a trip would send the wrong message, complicating Berlin's relationship with its European neighbors and impacting its colonial ambitions in Africa.[39] As historian Sean McMeekin explains, this was not an indication of Bismarck's hostility toward the Ottomans; rather, it was an example of Bismarck's realpolitik approach. He was simply uninterested in Ottoman internal affairs, determined not to see Germany caught up in intra-European disagreements, all the while quietly expanding German economic and military influence in the empire.[40] In fact, one can say that Bismarck was personally supportive of policies toward non-Muslim Ottomans. He advocated "assimilation," which he believed would, with time, lead to a "diminishing" of the "non-Turk" influence, possibly forcing them to completely "merge with Turks" until the state became "a solely Turkish State," regaining its former glory in the process.[41] Bismarck even pushed for further military support for the empire, where during the five years following the kaiser's first visit, German exports to the Ottoman Empire would rise by 350 percent.[42]

Bismarck's approach of quietly expanding German markets and influence in the Ottoman Empire contrasted with Wilhelm's flair for public displays of loyalty.

Wilhelm's first stop in 1898 was Istanbul, where he stayed for a jam-packed five days before continuing to the Levant. Part of the preparation for his visit was handled by a rising star of the palace, another Arab-Ottoman imperialist and Shafiq and Sadik's fellow alumnus of the College Saint Joseph, who the reader met in Chapter 2, Selim Melhamé. Selim was part of the large welcoming committee that met Wilhelm's yacht upon its arrival at Gallipoli. Wilhelm continued his trip accompanied by an honorary flotilla until arriving at the Dolmabahçe Palace's private dock on the Bosphorus. The sultan was there to welcome him, along with a large number of dignitaries and advisors. Several carriages took Wilhelm and his entourage from Beşiktaş up the hill to the sultan's palace complex. A large, lavishly furnished, and electrified guest villa known as the Yıldız Şale Köşkü had been doubled in size and redesigned by Italian architect d'Aronco at a reported cost of 25,000 pounds sterling in anticipation of the arrival of the honored guests and their eighty-eight-member entourage.[43]

The next few days were filled with one extravagant reception after another. One of the unconfirmed reports was by the famous gossip writer known as Count Paul Vasili. Vasili included the report in a letter to the Ottoman government in which "he" criticized the extravagance of the kaiser's visit, which the count learned cost the Ottoman government 6 million francs, not including the salaries of soldiers and personnel who accompanied the German visitors. Count Vasili was a nom de plume that some attributed to a Frenchwoman named Juliette Adam, the founder of *La Nouvelle Revue*; others attributed it to a Russian princess by the name of Catherine Radziwi. Both lived in Berlin in the late nineteenth century. Count Vasili published a series of high-society gossip columns formatted as letters to a young diplomat in *Nouvelle Revue*. The letter on the kaiser's visit made its way to the Ottoman Ministry of Foreign Affairs and was translated and preserved in the archives. In it, the writer complained about the censorship of her recent "article" in *Nouvelle Revue* and the punishment of those who brought the article into the realm through illegal means, suggesting that the empire had to loosen its censorship laws sooner or late. After providing an analysis of

European powers' disagreement over the status of the Ottoman Empire, the writer devoted the second half of the letter to what she considered the unnecessary expenses of the German emperor's visit. She described this "out of the ordinary" extravagance shown by the sultan as a waste, even pointing out that Abdülhamid went as far as dipping into his personal savings to cover some of the costs. She wondered why the empire would spend more than six million francs to host a foreign dignitary when it was having trouble paying soldiers' salaries, even in active conflict zones such as Crete. The letter is a fascinating exposé that deserves much more attention, written with a tone of irony and a very astute understanding of the personal nature of international diplomacy.[44]

Interestingly, the heavily censored Istanbul dailies reported similar expense figures and gave further details about where all this money was spent. It went to things like hundreds of bottles of Champaign and wine bought for the occasion, with reports of the amount spent ranging from one-half to 6 million francs.[45] Regardless of the amount spent, what matters here is the impression of extravagance that, in Europe, was considered scandalous and in keeping with stereotypes of an excess-prone Orient. The image-conscious sultan might have wanted to project strength and glory, but in many ways, in the European press, it was interpreted as a form of waste and blatant pandering to a foreign power.

However, if the sultan's goal was to impress the kaiser in order to encourage economic and military cooperation with the Ottoman Empire, the record shows that he mostly succeeded. Military, infrastructure, and financial services were only some of the multimillion-franc deals signed. Most important, buying an ally for Istanbul when it desperately needed one and providing new markets for an expanding German Empire were the real benefits. As a result, a Treaty of Friendship, Trade, and Shipping was concluded a few months after Wilhelm's tour. In addition to the well-known Anatolian train expansion and the Berlin-Baghdad railway, new contracts for telegraph lines from Berlin to Istanbul were given. Similarly, exports from the Ottoman Empire to Germany increased by 717 percent.[46]

As one can imagine, Wilhelm's trip caught the attention of the press across the empire, including front-page, step-by-step coverage by İkdam. Fifty journalists from Southwest Asia, Europe, and North America also accompanied him, sending daily telegrams back with descriptions of Wilhelm's tour of the "Orient." To facilitate the transmission of what they hoped would be a positive image of the empire to readers worldwide, the Ottoman government assigned four telegraph operators in Wilhelm's service.[47] Most of the newspaper coverage in Europe and the United States seemed to go from describing what it considered the exotic to a subtle criticism of this show of solidarity and friendship between the German kaiser and the Ottoman sultan. The palace kept a close eye on foreign coverage of the trip, translating what it could get its hands on into Ottoman-Turkish. Coincidentally, some dispatches were translated by none other than Sadik's uncle Shafiq, by then firmly entrenched in his position in the Translation Bureau of the palace.[48]

Leaving Istanbul for the Levant, the emperor and empress were met at every port by local notables, provincial government officials, high-ranking members of the military, as well as members of the local regiment. Additionally, the elite Ertuğrul Regiment, 543 members strong, was mobilized from Mecca and dispatched to Palestine to meet up with the emperor and provide protection on his tour of the region (figure 10).[49]

With his fluency in German and French and his familial connections in Beirut and Damascus, Sadik was the obvious companion to the emperor and empress as they toured the Levant. He first met the German party when they docked at the port of Haifa.[50] The Turkish-language press continued to follow the trip with its reporters and the translation of newspaper articles from Germany.[51] However, Sadik's role was primarily emphasized in the Arabic-language media, where he was claimed as the son of a local notable family. One of the journalists who wrote about the emperor's trip with the most colorful and embellished prose, was the editor of the Arabic-language newspaper *Lubnan*, Ibrahim al-Aswad. In a short book published the same year, he used the full flexibility, poeticism, and wit that the Arabic language allowed to shower the emperor and empress with compliments. For example, as the emperor arrived in Damascus, al-Aswad wrote, "As the sun set on Monday, the 7th of November, the light brought by the arrival of the emperor replaced it, shining out from the train car and [filling] the atmosphere of Damascus, so cannons were fired in celebration in their honor. Then his majesty stepped off the train car, disembarking in Baramkeh station [on the outskirts of the city], where the train came to its final stop."[52]

FIGURE 10. Wilhelm II of Germany (*center*) with his entourage and Sadik
(*rear left, facing camera*) at the Tomb of Kings in Jerusalem, 1898.
Source: American Colony, Photo Department, *State visit to Jerusalem of Wilhelm II
of Germany.* The Library of Congress, www.loc.gov/item/2019694898/.

In Sadik's hometown, the emperor was feted for two days. Every neighborhood he visited was decorated with banners and torches, welcoming him
and the empress. Wilhelm was so impressed he later noted: "My reception in
Damascus was astonishing and astounding, and I wished the others would
learn from Damascus how to make a king feel welcome."[53] He showed his
appreciation by showering many of the people in power in the Levant with
German medals of various ranks.[54] Sadik and his family could take much
credit for this glowing review.

The special advisory committee for the emperor's visit to Damascus was
headed by the governor-general and ten men: the head of the Land Registry
Office, the amir of the Hajj, the commander of the gendarmerie, the minister of foreign affairs, and several others, including two of Sadik's relatives.[55]
One was a member of the local executive council at the time, (Muhammad)
Fawzi Azmzade, the father of Khaled Azmzade, whom the reader encountered in Chapter 1. Fawzi would eventually become the minister of religious

endowments during World War I.[56] The other was a high-ranking member of the Ottoman military, Khalil Azmzade.[57]

Perhaps the highlight of the visit for Sadik was hosting the emperor and empress in the family's ancestral palace in the heart of old Damascus. The royal couple stopped for tea and toured the Azmzade palace, where they were gifted some of the family's Chinese porcelain that the empress admired. Their visit was preserved in a photograph taken while they had coffee in the courtyard; Sadik most likely took it since he was not in front of the lens.[58] The palace was constructed by As'ad (Tr. Esad) Pasha, one of the most famous and influential members of the family. He ruled as the governor-general of Damascus for a very long time in the early eighteenth century.[59] The palace remained in the family's hands until after World War I, when 'Abd al-Qadir, Shafiq's son-in-law, had to sell it. As the family was trying to financially recover after being interred in Bursa during the war, he said he had no other choice but to sell the palace to the French colonial government at the time. Then it was transferred to the Syrian government and is in operation as a public museum today.[60]

While in Damascus, the German emperor stopped at the tomb of Saladin to pay his respects. After heading back to Germany, he asked Sadik, personally, to lay a wreath on his behalf that had the following note, albeit written in German: "Wilhelm II, the Kaiser of Germany, and the King of Prussia in memory of the hero, Sultan Salah al-Din al-Ayyubi."[61] His recognition of Salah al-Din al-Ayyubi (Ibn Ayyub), better known in the West as Saladin, the Muslim Kurdish warrior who ousted the crusaders from the Levant in the twelfth century, was a risky political move, particularly for his audience in Europe. It was a calculated risk, however, when one considers that Saladin was not only known as the Muslim leader who took Jerusalem back from Christian crusaders; he was also famous for his benevolent and diplomatic approach to dealing with the Christian rulers and the Christian population after his victory.[62] Wilhelm invoked Saladin again when he gave a speech during a large lunch reception in his honor at the Damascus City Hall. He delivered it in German, with Sadik as his interpreter in Arabic. He began by showing his thanks for all of the elaborate displays of respect and adoration he had been met with in Damascus and other cities in the Levant. He continued:

I feel joy from the bottom of my heart when I remember that I am in a city where one of the greatest of noble, heroic kings . . . Sultan Salah al-Din al-Ayyubi lived. I would like to take this opportunity before everything else, with happiness that cannot be any greater, to declare my gratitude to his majesty Sultan 'Abd al-Hamid Khan whose love and the hospitality he has shown us I take with great pride. Let his majesty the sultan, 'Abd al-Hamid Khan the Second, and the three hundred million Muslims spread worldwide, who are steadfastly loyal to his great caliphate, know that the emperor of Germany will forever love them. Now, I will toast his majesty the sultan, 'Abd al-Hamid Khan the Second.[63]

A year later, Wilhelm sent a small German delegation to Damascus to lay a permanent metal wreath, with inscriptions in German and Quranic verses in Arabic.[64] Izzet, who was a massive fan of the Germans, ridiculed the Syrian governor-general for having to ask for permission from the sultan to accept such a gift, stating that only "ignorance" could possibly lead to such a question.[65]

Sadik accompanied Wilhelm from Damascus to the Roman temple in Baalbek, where he again acted as interpreter for the historical expert who walked them around the site's ruins.[66] Wilhelm was so enamored by the fully intact Roman temple that he would bring it up with the Ottoman ambassador two years later, asking to send German archeologists to study the site.[67] During his visit, a plaque nailed to the temple entrance was revealed, in German and Ottoman-Turkish, commemorating his visit and Abdülhamid II's rule. It still stands today. While the emperor was in Baalbek, the Greek Orthodox archbishop of Zahleh, a town in the Beqaa Valley, greeted him. He delivered a short speech in which he conveyed how much the "Syrian Ottomans" appreciated the support of the German emperor and the friendship between the German people and the Ottoman people. He expressed it as a perfect harmony between Germany, "a land known for being a source of philosophy and science," and "Eastern countries" where "the divine message was declared."[68]

This kind of description must have resonated with Sadik, a man living in the empire in a time of great cultural flux, hailing from the so-called East, traveling around the world, and often identifying with many aspects of what he considered European culture. It must not be forgotten that he had been born and raised in Syria and had spent his early adult years in Istanbul, but a great deal of his mental mapping took place while living in Berlin, traveling through the Sahara and Arabia with what he referred to as the "Bedouins," accompanying Russian royalty to the Levant, and finally leading German allies through his childhood stomping grounds. Men like Sadik, Izzet, and even Shafiq, who had Istanbul at the center of their lives yet maintained their mental and familial ties to different parts of the world, allow us to reimagine the fracturing of the Arab-Ottoman habitus as the imperial order they were so loyal to stood in stark contrast to the power of its European enemies and allies alike. There were many occasions for Sadik to represent the empire in Europe.[69] Next, I turn to one that would entangle him in yet another "question" in the eastern Balkans in the early twentieth century.

An Ottoman Imperialist, Macedonia, and the Tzar

Sadik started the new millennium on a secret mission to Skopje, the capital of the Province of Kosovo and the future capital of Northern Macedonia. Insurgencies, open rebellions, and foreign agitation in Ottoman Macedonia had been rising for over a decade. By the turn of the twentieth century, the Macedonian Question was part of the broader so-called Eastern Question that was supposed to have been remedied with the Treaty of Berlin in 1878 but was in fact exacerbated by it.[70] The newly drawn or redrawn boundaries of Ottoman provinces, as well as autonomous and semiautonomous states, set up the grounds for years of further conflict over territory and national belonging. This meant countless incidents of mass violence and deportations of peoples who did not fit into notions of ethnic and/or religious homogeneity in the newly found independent Balkan states.[71]

Similarly, the conflict over what would make up a Macedonian territory was being defined and redefined, causing seemingly endless human hardship.[72] The very word, Macedonia, was discouraged in official Ottoman correspondence during the Hamidian period, lest it be considered an acknowledgment of the insurgents' claim to identarian separatism.[73] While Istanbul fought against local separatist movements across the Balkans, the 1903 Ilinden uprising became a pivotal event that made the Macedonian Question a popular issue in Europe, ultimately leading to further partition of Ottoman territories.[74] The uprising was eventually put down, but the threat of what it represented enticed Abdülhamid II's regime to plot out the long promised reforms that ultimately remained on paper only.[75] As historian İpek Yosmaoğlu puts it: "The struggle for Macedonia ... was not simply a war fought between states with conventional armies. It was not purely a diplomatic crisis either. It was a protracted conflict, finally, a civil war, fought as an insurgency, where the lines separating fighter from civilian, perpetrator from victim, traitor from hero, were not clearly drawn."[76] It was also a complex web of intercommunal conflicts supported and, in some cases, instigated by external states such as the Russian Empire, the Bulgarian Principality, and the Kingdom of Greece. Ottoman Macedonia, or the Macedonian Question, was also at the center of four delicate international relations vectors—Ottoman-Russian, Ottoman-British, Ottoman-Austro-Hungarian, and Ottoman-Bulgarian.[77]

Sadik's involvement started in early 1900, when he was assigned to an investigative unit sent to handle a sensitive assignment at a time when reports of suspicious political organizations, paramilitary activity, and anti-Ottoman agitation were coming in. With a generous allowance of 10,000Kr to each member of the unit to cover travel expenses, Sadik, who had been promoted to the rank of *mirliva* a year earlier, earning him the honorific of Pasha, was asked to join the mission to Macedonia by the head of the Ottoman army, Şakir (Ar. Shaker) Pasha.[78] He was part of a small committee headed by another Office of the Aide-de-Camp member, *ferik* (lieutenant general) Edib Pasha,[79] tasked with the difficult mission of removing the sitting governor-general, Hafiz Pasha (r.1894–1900). It was based on complaints by local notables and reports of mismanagement of local tensions and support of some Macedonians, which in light of international interference and intercommunal tensions, some locals referred to as treasonous. Sadik and the delegation announced a general amnesty, but a few strongmen still resisted. Ottoman measures in the eastern Balkans were an incredibly delicate issue, with the eyes of the Great Powers focused on Istanbul's response to local non-Muslim subjects' demands and Muslim rulers' call for military aid. The Russian consulate in Skopje was in direct contact with various *juhhal*, (literally "ignorant people"), a term used to describe rebels or any who opposed the rulers' policies.[80] Further enforcement of Ottoman military presence was sent from the neighboring province of Salonica to control the situation and to implement martial law until a new governor-general could be appointed. This had to take place immediately, without triggering interference by the Great Powers. Sadik's sensitive mission took a little over a fortnight, and then he was back in Istanbul to get ready for an extended deployment to the other side of the empire, the Province of Hijaz.[81] Yet these two weeks would mark the beginning of Sadik's involvement in the turbulent politics of the Balkans, which lasted almost until the end of his career.

In November of 1902, Sadik was a party to the secret Ottoman mission to the emperor of Russia, Nicholas II, at the Livadia Palace in Yalta on the southern coast of the Crimean Peninsula. This short summit came by invitation to the palace facilitated through the Russian Embassy in Istanbul and Grand Duke Nicholas Nikolaevich (1856–1929), a cousin of the tzar and commander-in-chief of the Russian Imperial Army. According to Sir G. Bonham, the grand duke stopped in Istanbul on the way back from the commemoration of the Shipka Pass battle in Bulgaria, which had taken place in 1877 between the Bulgarian and Russian armies on one side and the Ottoman army on the other.[82] Following a meeting with the Ottoman minister of foreign affairs, Ahmed Tevfik (Ar. Tawfiq) Pasha, it was agreed that a delegation "of appropriate level" men would be sent to discuss issues that had to do with the "neighboring" states. Sadik was included on this sensitive mission, along with the governor-general of Monastir, Ali Rıza Pasha, to meet with the emperor and other members of the Russian government.

The primary purpose of the discussions was the seemingly uncontrollable events in Ottoman Macedonia. According to the Ottoman ambassador to Russia, Turhan Pasha (Perometi), an Albanian-Ottoman diplomat and later prime minister of an independent Albania, discussions with the emperor went on for hours. The talks concluded with the agreement that the Russian Empire and the Ottoman Empire would cooperate to control the situation in the Balkans and that "the rights of the sultan would no longer be touched."

The occasion was not all work. Much dining and entertaining with the emperor, empress, and the grand duke took place. They took walks in the forest surrounding the palace with the empress and her young daughters. They even had a memorial photograph of Sadik, Ali Rıza, and Empress Alexandra taken.[83]

In December, the Russian government put out a conciliatory statement. It asserted its goodwill toward the "neighboring" empire while insisting that the promised reforms be put in place to protect the Orthodox population against "all acts of violence and cruelty." However, "the fact must not . . . be lost . . . that so long as the present disturbed condition of the province continues, by which the Ottoman Government are given legitimate grounds for the measures taken against their rebellious subjects, there is considerable practical difficulty in putting into execution any administrative reforms, and in completely guaranteeing the population against the very harsh means of repression exercised by the local authorities."[84] With this, the delegation returned to Istanbul on a hopeful note. Sadik was decorated with the St. Anne Medal of the first order by Tzar Nicholas II for his efforts in the negotiations and was awarded the *Osmani Nişan Alisi* of the first order by the sultan.[85] But his celebratory mood would not last too long. Soon after his return to Istanbul to spend time with his wife and children, tragedy struck: his house was burnt to the ground, as described in Chapter 1.

In spite of his tragedy, Sadik was assigned soon after to an advisory committee (*hay'at-i nasiha*) that met with locals from across Ottoman Macedonia in an effort to make informed recommendations to the General Inspectorate of Rumeli (*Rumeli Umumi Müfettişliği*), which was responsible for recommending and implementing reforms not only in the three "Macedonian" provinces, which included Monastir, Salonica, and Kosovo, but also in the three other provinces of Ottoman Europe: Yanya (Ioannina), İşkodra (Shkodër), and Edirne. A monumental task and a last-ditch effort to keep the European powers from interfering and forcing their version of reforms, the mission was headed by Hüseyin (Hussein) Hilmi Pasha, a veteran Ottoman administrator who had previously been the governor-general of Yemen, another restive province in the empire.[86] Sadik, an experienced negotiator and now an expert on the turmoil in the Balkans, was one of the stars of the advisory committee, traveling extensively to gather information and provide recommendations to the inspectorate.[87] He remained in Macedonia for a short time before he abruptly returned to Istanbul "to clear his name." Although he provided no details,[88] two events could have caused this issue. One was a vaguely worded letter he received before he left for Istanbul in which he was reminded that nobody in the delegation was to appear in public in civilian clothes. It was a seemingly insignificant order about clothes that surprisingly would come back to haunt him five years later, which I discuss it in detail in Chapter 6.[89] The alternative explanation for his sudden departure was a scandal that was enveloping his uncle at the time, having to do with suspicious conditions under which his young wife had passed away, which I discuss in Chapter 7.

The Inner Struggle of an Arab-Ottoman Imperialist

In this chapter, the reader witnessed Sadik's experience as his personal and professional worlds merged. First, he guided a member of Russian royalty, a former soldier who fought against the Ottoman army and won, to one of the holiest cities in Islam. He saw how a treaty signed a decade earlier had a long-term impact on the ground as he accompanied the victor to the Levant at the expense of the Ottoman taxpayers and the pride of an empire still reeling from the loss of much of the Balkan territories. He also witnessed the celebration of European royalty in his adopted home, Istanbul, and in his childhood home, Damascus. One can only imagine how all these layers that he identified with must have merged, clashed, or worked in harmony as he attempted to interpret a world that he knew so intimately to a royal foreigner. Pride, discomfort, a feeling of distance, or one of belonging? One can only speculate how his experience as an itinerant Arab-Ottoman, who had lived a part of his life in Berlin and was part of a transimperial elite culture, helped him understand the spectacle or made it all the more difficult. Sadik was able to move between worlds, an insider/outsider, though he publicly promoted one version of who he was—*İstanbul'lu*, Ottoman, imperialist.

Those experiences can be looked at as a rich well of cultural competencies to draw on. They also make it difficult to pin down where Sadik belonged or felt his home was. His perspective was not simply a hybrid of perspectives. Like many imperialists of his generation, I argue in the following chapter, he was part of a "fractured habitus," as Bourdieu called it, that allowed space for adaptation. It also left an individual scared and uncertain. That was due not simply to the number of experiences he had in his lifetime but to the number of places he had to work to fit into and spaces he had to inhabit. His roles as a negotiator with the Russian emperor, consultant to the reform committee in Macedonia, and inspector in the eastern Balkans added to his reputation as a flexible man with consistent loyalty to Hamidian imperialism. He would eventually go back to the Balkans for the most important assignment of his career in Bulgaria. Before that happened, he developed a reputation for successfully negotiating with "Arabs"—a term that, I argue in the following chapter, he consciously avoided, exposing the tip of an iceberg of a complex set of ethnoracial identifications emerging in the Ottoman Empire at the time.

{ CHAPTER 4 }

COMING TO TERMS WITH *ARAP*

These people who have just left their homelands, towns,
relatives, and traditions had signs of agitation and sadness
on their faces that completely changed after putting on
their fancy military uniforms. They became so pleased
that many of them dumped their old clothes into the sea.
As soon as they found their places and the boat started to
move, the singing, harmonizing, and the *Aman Amans* came
from all directions that when I heard them together it felt
like I was at a very strange concert.[1]

—Sadik al-Mu'ayyad Azmzade, writing in 1895

THE EPIGRAPH, TAKEN FROM SADIK'S 1895 TRAVELOGUE FROM
his mission to Jaghbub in the Libyan Desert describes a moment of rebirth,
when subjects from different parts of the empire were reincarnated as Ottomans, discarding their old identities into the sea. It is a passage that betrays
Sadik's internal struggle as he came to terms with the complexity of his subject position. This travelogue from his mission deep into the eastern Sahara
is the focus of the first part of this chapter. It examines his choice of words,
turns of phrase, and observations, which I argue expressed his anxieties, desires, and insecurities as an Arab-Ottoman in an increasingly ethnocentric
metropole. Sadik painted a picture of the Saharan local in very broad strokes

that I contend were meant to distance a familiar Other, one with whom he shared a mother tongue, religious identification, and, by his assessment, political allegiance. Relying on the work of sociologist Pierre Bourdieu, humanist Homi Bhabha, and philosopher Jacques Derrida, I deconstruct the text to show how Sadik's discursive strategy granted him the status of an outside observer who shared a frame of reference with his readers while acting as a subject matter expert who could colorfully interpret "the natives" to fellow urbanites in the Ottoman metropole. I pay special attention to references about his life in Istanbul, cultural notions he identified with, and identarian signifiers he held up for his readers to see. I argue that the most important cultural category, glaringly obvious by its absence, was the category of "the Arab." His cultural and linguistic roots—Arabic-speaking Damascene—cast a shadow over every word he wrote about the Bedouin "other" or the "exotic" *Urban*, avoiding the one word that might indicate a commonality between him and them. Sadik attempted to discursively disassociate himself from the object of his inquiry.

Arap, Turkish for Arab, was also a loaded term in late nineteenth-century Istanbul. Thus, in addition to interrogating Sadik's choice of terms, I also ask: What's in a word? How does one understand the social implications of a signifier in the context of what was happening in Istanbul at the time? How can we better understand the individual-level experience of being signified as *Arap* in the elite social spaces of Istanbul? To explore these question, in the second part of the chapter, I touch on another project that Sadik was involved in, the Hijaz telegraph and railway lines. I use this occasion to further explicate Arab-Ottoman imperialists' involvement in infrastructure projects, which relied on their familial networks across the empire. More important, I delve deeper into the idea of *Arap* as an ethnoracial marker in late Ottoman Istanbul and the layered meaning it carried in the social space of Ottoman imperialists, focusing on the case of the (in)famous Izzet, who was often referred to as Arap İzzet and happened to have been one of the main drivers of the Hijaz telegraph and railway lines project. I disagree with the notion that there is no place for a productive discussion of the identarian signifier "Arab" in the nineteenth century because it only emerged as a mass-organizational political concept in the early twentieth century. I contend that the focus on mass political and intellectual history erases the experience of some historical actors who were identified as and/or meaningfully identified with the word Arab. Historians like James Gelvin, Hasan Kayalı, and Michael Provence have made a convincing argument against the previously held notion that Arabism and Arab nationalism emerged from some collective dormant or suppressed national identity that "reawakened" as the empire weakened.[2] However, investigations into collective political movements and ideas do not pay enough attention to the *individual experience*. Of course, identifying someone as an Arab did not make one less Ottoman; it just made one a particular kind of Ottoman. I argue that the word itself, however, had weighty social implications before it had political ones, which disproportionately impacted an Arab-Ottoman *İstanbul'lu* trying to fit into a global class of imperialists in an increasingly ethnoracially differentiated world.

The Diplomatic Mission

Sadik's first mission to meet with the Sanusi leadership was in 1886, following the Conference of Berlin (1884–1885). This long trip deep into the Libyan Desert was part of a larger multilayered approach to assert Ottoman territorial claims over what was considered the hinterland of Ottoman Libya. The 1886 trip set the cornerstone of a relationship between Istanbul and the Sanusi Order—an alliance that proved essential to Ottoman allegations of "effective occupation" of the Lake Chad basin. Upon his return from this mission, Sadik wrote a short report in which he described the conditions on the ground and the level of enthusiasm for Ottoman rule in Benghazi and at various other stops on the way in the Libyan Desert.[3] A decade later, Sadik departed on another mission to the Sahara to meet with the Sanusi leader, this time with years of experience behind him and the weight of what he perceived as an empire under attack on his shoulders. The empire's status in the world had become even more precarious since the first time he visited the Sanusi, on the heels of the Conference of Berlin. Between 1886 and 1894, Ottoman attempts at asserting the empire's claim to the eastern Sahara by relying on international agreements bore no fruit. Despite their continuous reassurances to the contrary, London and Paris ignored Istanbul's territorial claims, precipitating unsuccessful protests by Ottoman lawyers and diplomats.[4] An alliance with the Sanusi was a crucial component of the palace's plan to regain some of the empire's international status and maintain Istanbul's political capital beyond the so-called Eastern Question. With the British advancing from the Nile Valley on one side and the French advancing from West Africa on the other, the delicacy of Sadik's missions to maintain Istanbul's claim to the eastern Sahara becomes clearer. Add to this the volatile domestic conditions on the western Balkan and the eastern Anatolia frontiers, and the importance of maintaining control over the empire's southern African frontiers takes on a new level of urgency.

Sadik communicated the sultan's desire for an alliance with the Sanusi and advised the palace not to do anything that might undermine the Sanusi's local hold on power. The Ottomans desperately needed the Sanusi's allegiance to claim "sovereignty by proxy" in the face of French and British advances. Sadik provided counsel on ways to assert Ottoman control without raising the ire of the local powers, which he portrayed as passionate and loyal subjects of the sultan.[5]

With only three days to prepare for this long journey, signaling the urgency of this mission, Sadik was given his marching orders on the evening of October 1, 1895. The next morning, he headed to the palace to receive further instructions, after which he began purchasing the equipment he needed for the trip. In his travelogue, he gave little information about the political and diplomatic aspects of the mission, choosing to concentrate on his personal experience and observations.

As an educated member of a transimperial class of gentlemen, he often referenced his passionate engagement with the technical and mechanical innovations of his time. One of them was photography. Even though he had very little time to prepare for his mission, one of his main concerns was securing a camera that was "easy to use and can withstand the heat."[6] He stressed his need for no less than "the latest technology and lightweight camera" that used film, not glass plates.[7] To secure one, he took a boat across the Bosphorus to the neighborhood of Haydarpaşa on the Asian side of Istanbul to drop by the house of one of his closest friends (*bir ahbabım*) to borrow his camera.[8] When he arrived, he found him oiling his Velocipede bicycle. He wondered whether such a modern form of transportation could help him on the flat parts of the journey in the desert, but dismissed the idea when he considered that he would not be able to mechanically maintain it on the road.[9]

Technological innovations were common themes of discussion for men of his class. They were often the subject of editorials in journals like *Servet-i Fünun* and daily newspapers such as *İkdam*. Sadik took his passion for photography a bit further than a casual hobbyist. He wrote a book, *Fen-i Fotoğraf* (*The Science of Photography*), which was an illustrated guide to equipment and techniques of photography that remained in manuscript form and was eventually gifted to the sultan.[10]

Sadik was not alone in writing books intended as gifts to the sultan, a well-known bibliophile. Other men in Sadik's family who lived and worked in Istanbul also wrote, dedicating their work to the sultan and drawing inspiration from their world experiences about topics that ranged from history to the applied sciences. In addition to the book on photography, Sadik translated novels and history books into Ottoman-Turkish and wrote on various interests. He wrote a chemistry book, most likely translated from Arabic, *Al-Kimya' fi Tahlil al-Hawa' wa-l-Ma'* (*Chemistry in the Analysis of Air and Water*), which also stayed in manuscript form.[11] The rest of his works were translations of French books, including the children's books *Küçük Henri* (*Le Petit Henri*) and *Fernando*, as well as a translation of the Arabic history book by Imam Muhammad al-Waqidi titled *Tarikh Futuhat al-Sham* (*The History of the Conquest of Syria*). All were dedicated to the sultan, a big fan of literature.[12] However, the most famous of Sadik's publication was *Habeş Seyahatnamesi* (*The Abyssinia Travelogue*), which I discuss in detail in Chapter 5.[13] This travelogue solidified Sadik's status as a pioneer of Turkish-language travel literature of his time.[14]

Having access to several versions of Sadik's Sahara travelogue in different languages, I compared and contrasted them to offer an otherwise inaccessible historical understanding of how and why he and the editors who followed chose certain themes and terminology to highlight or exclude. I was also able to contextualize the changes made to the versions based on the historical and geopolitical environment in which they were published. I do not have his original notes, which most likely burned along with his other possessions in the 1903 fire, so I had to satisfy myself with a manuscript that he presented to the sultan as the earliest version, now housed at the Rare Books Library at Istanbul University. Although this version was written with an audience of one in mind, I believe it gives the historian the least censored, reinterpreted, or otherwise manipulated version available. The second version was meant for the consumption of the general educated public familiar with the genre of travelogues of "exotic" destinations, which were very popular in Europe in the nineteenth century. It was edited and published in Ottoman-Turkish in Istanbul in 1899 after it was initially serialized in the popular journal *Servet-i Fünun*.[15] In a handwritten note to the palace, which he sent with the published version for which he had received the approval of the Ministry of Education first, Sadik stated that he wrote his book to inspire further "ties between the people of the Sanjak of Benghazi and subjects of the caliph, and it included a list of reforms and means of progress to address the development and infrastructure projects the sanjak needs."[16] The third is an Arabic translation published in Tripoli by the Libyan national archives in 1998.[17] The fourth is a transliteration into modern Turkish published in Istanbul in 2008.[18]

Thus, I view this trip as more than just a diplomatic mission; it was also a personal odyssey. The documents he left behind allow the historian an entry point to his mental state at the time and his perception of his place in the world in relation to both the Ottoman Empire and the local Bedouin population he spent weeks traveling with through the desert. Thus, what I offer here is not an analysis of that mission's political and diplomatic dimensions but a close reading of the text in a multitude of versions: a manuscript, and published Ottoman-Turkish, Arabic, and modern Turkish versions of his travelogue.

A Journey Inward

Within weeks of returning from his mission in southeastern Anatolia in October 1895, discussed in Chapter 2, Sadik had to leave on his second diplomatic journey to the eastern Sahara. As the turmoil dragged on at home, Sadik took off to the oasis of Kufra, which was the new headquarters of the Sanusi Order in Africa. Sadik left Istanbul for Benghazi by sea and then by caravan from Benghazi to the Sahara, past Jaghbub, the original headquarters of the Sanusi Order, to the desert oasis of Kufra, in the southeastern corner of modern day Libya. He carefully documented his journey and observations along the way, often in the manner of many European adventure travelers, adding flourish and highlighting the exoticism of the Arabic-speaking nomadic people of the Libyan Desert. His reference to them as "the natives" and, more often than not, either collectively as *Urban* or individually as *Bedevi* (Bedouin) was an exacting choice of terms that, once translated into Arabic in 1998, were more often than not changed to Arab or Arabs (*'Arab*). Sadik, an Arab-Ottoman officer of Damascene origin, paid much attention to *not* referring to those that he met in 1895 as Arabs.

Choosing terminology that allowed for what the sociologist Pierre Bourdieu called a "system of dispositions,"[19] Sadik created a two-dimensional rendition of another world that was colored by his particular social experience up to that point. He discursively constructed a seemingly distant and utterly exotic habitus, not only unfamiliar to the reader but seemingly unrelated to his own life experience. This was an important strategy for travel writers in general and, I argue, was of particular importance for Sadik in 1895. It allowed him to act as an outside observer who shared a frame of reference with the reader in the metropole while also acting as the traveling subject matter expert, which meant having to un-recognize this familiar Other who, after all was, among many things, an Arabic-speaking Sunni Muslim—subject of the caliph, just like he was. This is not to imply that he was doing this to fool the reader or even to fool himself. It was, however, a discursive construction of signs (his words) and the signified (his experience of reality), which, as the philosopher Jacques Derrida argues, superseded logic as the foundation of making meaning of reality itself. As Derrida puts it: "The exteriority of the signifier is the exteriority of writing . . . there is no linguistic sign before writing."[20] In other words, this form of discursive distancing created its own reality and did not describe a pre-existing one. Sadik needed to express his understanding of himself—in this case, Ottoman, urban, worldly, *İstanbul'lu*—by discursively creating an exoticized Other—native, desert-dwelling Bedouin, Saharan. This allowed him to imagine an alternative world, an exotic way of being, one that he could simultaneously observe, describe, and interpret on behalf of members of his Istanbul social circles.

Even before starting the description of his trip, Sadik began to construct a kind of time-distance from his subjects. He described the environment as

alien and distant from his reality: The extreme heat that the Bedouins could
endure but he could only suffer through; the long distance and time it took
to cross the desert, which the Bedouins did not mind (three months on the
road but an eternity for him); and what he continuously portrayed as the
alien habits of "the natives." Starting his travelogue by relying on memories
from his first trip nine years earlier, he evoked what would become a common theme in his travel writing—the strangeness of local cuisine and eating habits. He described how local food tasted, how it was prepared, how
it was consumed, and, predictably, how he considered it to be inedible. For
example, he told the reader that the Bedouins were not familiar with "the
hors d'oeuvres [his words], and soups that we know, and the salads, bifthèque
[his words], filets, Karnıyarıks, and other dishes that we crave. Their lives
are very plain (*sade*)."[21] He did not understand why they liked a simple dish
that they made on the go called *Zmita* more than what he considered Ottoman sophisticated cuisine. He described how they made it and how they
"huddled around" and "ate it in a hurry in big mouthfuls (*koskocaman lokma-
lar*)." Sadik was well aware of how his description of the local habits might
be interpreted by his readers, admitting it in a sentence at the beginning of
the travelogue. For he followed the above description with the one statement
that acknowledged that what he described was a unidimensional pejorative
characterization of Bedouins: "My aim when I say Bedouin is not to say they
are savage. After months spending time with them, one sees that they have
very good moral turpitude (*ahlak*)."[22] This was the only indication that he
understood the impact of the picture he painted and the terms he chose, but
it did not stop him from using them for the remainder of the travelogue. This
section of the travelogue was one of many that were modified in the Arabic
translation, stripping away the condescending tone and much of the details
that aimed to compare the supposedly sophisticated taste of Sadik with the
underdeveloped taste of the locals.[23]

Sadik's description of how the Bedouins prepared and ate meat was also
edited out of the Arabic version. Sadik started by stating that he and his
"Ottoman companions" had their own cook, whom they instructed to cook
the "Ottoman way." He liked meat well-done and lightly seasoned in contrast to the people from "Benghazi and other hot places," whom he stated
liked their food very spicy and that their "servants or slaves cook it for

them" that way. The Arabic version took out the essentializing description about Benghazi, replacing it with a sentence that simply stated: "Our hosts whose local food is known for the plentiful use of hot pepper and black pepper" and eliminating the reference to enslaved people. Unlike the Arabic version, in the published Ottoman-Turkish and modern Turkish versions, the editors preferred to elaborate on Sadik's description, adding that the local food was so spicy it was inedible. In contrast, the Ottoman food they shared with the caravan workers was, according to them, only consumed after the workers spiced it to their taste.[24]

The Violence of Letters

In his criticism of Lévi-Strauss's account of "the native's" relationship to writing while on one of his anthropological research trips, Derrida coined the term "anthropological war," where the violence is partially that of the letters that narrate the Other. What Derrida called the "violence of the letters" was in reference to the words used in the narration of incidents or "of relationship among individuals and among groups, among cultures or within the same community" of the "native," which were tainted by "tones of violence repressed or deferred, a violence sometimes veiled, but always oppressive or heavy."[25] Sadik's violence of narration about a primitive Other he constructed for a primed reader was certainly understood by the editors of *Servet-i Fünun*, who chose to embellish it, and by the Libyan translators, who chose to eliminate it. For example, he described a scene that can only be understood as rhetorical violence, dehumanizing Bedouins in a tradition of the "savage native." In this case, it was the notion that the locals, whom he contrasted with Ottomans, ate raw or undercooked meats and what he described as their "fanatical (*mutaassıb*)" approach to the Muslim ritual of halal slaughter before consumption. A practicing Muslim himself, he described their way of preparing meat as a misunderstanding of Muslim ritual because they washed the carcass repeatedly in what he thought was a waste of precious water that stemmed from blind fanaticism.[26]

Sadik continued the discussion of the Bedouins' eating habits by painting a vivid picture of the locals huddled around the fire, cooking and eating meat in what he considered "the strangest way." According to him, they cut the carcass into large pieces of meat and then sat around the fire waiting for it to cook. "While the meat was still hot and before it was fully cooked, one of them would pick up the piece and hold it with both hands, and start to pull, break, and gnaw at it with his teeth (*çıkar, kopar, çiğnemeye başlar*) with great eagerness (*hevesle*) and when one person was done with one piece of meat, they would put it aside leaving it for another to taste and start with another piece. Nothing was left except for the bare bones." While most of this description was considered vulgar by Libyans who censored it out of the Arabic version, it was embellished and highlighted with exotic touches in the Ottoman-Turkish version. An expression in broken Arabic added for effect stated what the Bedouins thought about meat: "*Kul dakhil yanfa'*! (All that is in it [sheep, goat, or camel] is fit to eat!)."[27]

The deferred violence of the letters narrating "difference, of classification, and of the system of appellation" turned to immediate corporal violence toward the end of Sadik's journey.[28] He described an incident when, after some kind of joke or teasing between two workers, one hit the other with a blunt instrument causing the other to bleed and call out in pain. As punishment, Sadik ordered that they both be whipped to make an example of them to the rest. He was careful to report that all those around him thought the punishment of twenty lashes to the person who caused the injury and three to the one injured was fair. He proudly noted that the crowd watching the punishment shouted "*Allahu Akbar*! (God is Great!)" instead of "*Aman!*" (often an exclamation of emotional pain or longing used by some Turkish and Arabic speakers at the time) after every strike. At the end of the whipping, Sadik reported that the Bedouins all said in Arabic, "May God keep the sultan victorious! (*Allah yansor al-sultan!*)" He interpreted these exclamations from the crowd as signifying their satisfaction with the fairness of the corporal punishment he had ordered.[29] It is worth noting that in the published version, the reference to the sultan was eliminated, possibly not to associate the image of the sultan with any act of extrajudicial violence.[30] After all, this act of violence was committed on the orders of an Ottoman state representative without any reference to the law. Additionally, it was exacted on the body of a population within the Ottoman sphere of influence but only as far as its loyalty to the sultan could be enticed. Sadik, who spent the bulk of his travelogue discursively constructing a persona of savage Bedouins for his readers in Istanbul, did not need to explain his actions in "teaching [them]a lesson." He simply ended his description of this incident by stating that the victims of his violence, after the punishment, simply packed up to start moving early the next day. His narration of violence was as commonly handled as any other description of chores completed that day.

As Sadik wrote and revised his travelogue, first for the consumption of the sultan and later for the consumption of the Ottoman-Turkish-reading Istanbul public, he was simultaneously producing and inhabiting what Homi Bhabha called a "Third Space."[31] This space was filled with gray ambivalence, a complicated self-conscious and self-referential space where the similarities and differences between the observer and the observed were much harder to discursively produce and defend than for a European traveler. It was a much more complicated situation than what Edward Said described in *Orientalism*, where the notion of difference between an "Occident" and an "Orient" was assumed.[32] The production of a Third Space, "a process of signification through which statements of culture or on culture differentiate, discriminate and authorize the production of fields of force, reference, applicability, and capacity,"[33] was a discursive space that Sadik as an Ottoman explorer performed simultaneously with the production of the Other, in this case the Bedouin.

The Third Space necessitated Sadik's simultaneous enunciation of his own belonging to the urban/Ottoman/modern while writing about the rural/Bedouin/not-modern. It was by no means stable. It disrupted the imagined notion of an accurate and timeless representation of both the Bedouin and Sadik himself. Sadik and Shafiq were constantly changing how they represented themselves, both having a self-conscious, some would even say reactionary, understanding of the world around them, with the baggage of history weighing down every action they took and every word they wrote.

Sadik also described the non-Arab Tebu people as dropping their "Bedouin habits" once they benefited from the Sanusi's teachings. In the printed version of the travelogue, the expression "Bedouin habits" was reinterpreted as "those with savage conditions and habits" for added impact—that is, until they were brought onto the straight path by following the Sanusi Order, which he considered the proper way of being a Muslim.[34] The third layer of reinterpretation was added in the Libyan version, where the harsh "savage conditions" was replaced with "those who have primitive characteristics and harmful backward tradition," and became "modern/urbanized (*mutamadinin*)"—perhaps a form of postcolonial linguistic compromise that reflected contemporary sensitivity to language and the notion that the Bedouins, who ultimately became Libyan citizens after all, had already been brought into the fold of Libyan modernity.[35] Similarly, in the section about the Sanusi Order's benefits to the locals and how the order's teachings and projects aligned with the Ottoman state, which was added to the Ottoman-Turkish printed version, the expression "savage local tribes" was changed in the Libyan version to "primitive African tribes." This way, the translators created a discursive distance between the contemporary Libyan reader and what Sadik wrote about their ancestors.[36] The Ottoman-Turkish and the Arabic versions of the same travelogue were made to appeal to a particular reader. The kinship of the author—an *İstanbul'lu* Ottoman in the Ottoman-Turkish version and a Muslim Damascene Arab in the Arabic version—created a double persona; both personas were true and coexisted. However, only one was emphasized by the author.

The flip side of distancing the Bedouins was the necessity to emphasize Sadik's "Ottoman-ness" as a cultural determinant of belonging. Sadik highlighted his imperial loyalty, shedding a tear when he heard praise of the sultan on the road, shouting in exhilaration, "Long Live Ottomanism! (*Yaşasın Osmanlılık!*)"[37] Sadik seemed to have been a believer in his mission and in the benefits of Ottoman imperialism's reach, taking every opportunity to remind the reader (and himself) that he and his soldier companions were more than citizens of the same empire; they were all culturally undifferentiated Ottomans. This careful discursive construction of a collective "us, Ottomans" versus them "them, Bedouins" was hardly an obvious choice. His companions were from places as different as Aydın, Sivas, Prizren (Kosovo), and Bursa.[38] They were all members of the Ottoman military, but they hailed from places with varying traditions, customs, cuisines, dialects, and mother tongues. He regularly referred to them as "the Ottomans," who shared habits and tastes— a myth of a uniformity of Ottomanism in which he was deeply invested.

Early in his trip, while still on the boat taking him to Benghazi, via Izmir and Crete, Sadik recounted a vision of Ottoman uniformity that he equated with progress, highlighting the positive impact it had on the people it touched:

> As we moved from the Kale-i Sultaniye [Çanakkale] 1,063 new conscription recruits came on board. They were heading to Crete, Benghazi, and Tripoli. They were from many different places, which one can see from the large variety of clothing they wore. When they came onboard, they were given their military uniform to change into. They all changed into their uniforms at the same time. One has to note the difference between how they looked before, and the beautiful sight they became after wearing their uniforms. These people who have just left their homelands, towns, relatives, and traditions had signs of agitation and sadness on their faces that completely changed after putting on their fancy military uniforms. They became so pleased that many of them dumped their old clothes into the sea. As soon as they found their places and the boat started to move, the singing, harmonizing, and the Aman Amans came from all directions that when I heard them together it felt like I was at a very strange concert (*konser*).[39]

The Ottoman uniform was not just a tool of discipline meant to erase differences and present a united front. For Sadik, it seemed that wearing fancy uniforms was about pulling people out of their ignorance about the possibilities that Ottoman uniformity allowed. He painted them as people who were initially sad that they had to let go of their customs and their place of origin until they understood that a uniform Ottoman identity brought them something better. They were not asked to throw away the costumes they came to the ship with, but they spontaneously did it as soon as they experienced the joy of being Ottoman.

Arabs, *Urban*, and Bedouins

Izzet took pride in having secured funding for the Hijaz telegraph and railway lines without foreign assistance.[40] Besides convincing the provincial governments of Beirut and Syria to make up part of the deficit, he needed to reach out to the wider public for funds. The donors' names were celebrated on the front page of Istanbul's newspapers in an effort to entice Muslims from across the empire and beyond to participate in the project's financing.[41] *İkdam* was a leader in this regard, starting with a rousing column announcing the Assistance Commission (*İaanat Komisyonu*) headed by Reşad (Ar. Rashad) Bey.[42]

This was where Izzet was able to shine, tasking himself with finding sources to fund the project without resorting to European loans. It meant taxing localities, fundraising across the empire, and, perhaps most interesting, fundraising among Muslims in the British Empire, who looked at this project as the embodiment of the *ummah*, the global Muslim community, coming together. Thousands of small contributions came pouring in from ordinary Ottoman citizens and Muslims from as far as Indonesia, South Africa, and Morocco.[43] Izzet took his responsibility seriously, boasting of it as "what Sultan Selim Han the First started but did not finish," which was the unification of the *ummah*.[44] Building a telegraph line to him was a rejection of British and French bids and, perhaps more notably, the diminishing of the influence of other Arab-Ottoman brokers of empire like the Melhamés, with whom he competed for influence and lucrative contracts. He conveniently painted them as traitors or as susceptible to bribery, never missing a chance to point out that they were not Muslim. To him, the British and the French were engaged in an anti-Ottoman project, specifically referencing their policies in Africa and the Levant.[45] With the Hijaz telegraph and railway project, many members of Izzet's extended family in Istanbul and the provinces of Aleppo and Syria came together in its service. It was a massive project that should have been considered impossible given the financial crisis the government was facing. Despite many offers, the palace was adamant about not outsourcing such a religiously symbolic project to a European contractor.[46]

Five years after his trip to the Libyan Desert, in April of 1900, Sadik was assigned to lead the construction of the telegraph line from Damascus to Mecca.[47] It was a career-defining project for which he was rewarded handsomely with a tripling of his monthly salary for the period he was working on the line, several medals, and a promotion.[48] It was also an exceptionally challenging mission, where he had to contend with technical problems, supply shortages, funding difficulties, inhospitable terrain, and, most important, the difficult task of convincing functionally autonomous Bedouin tribes in Arabia to buy into an imperial infrastructure project that passed through their domains.[49] The Hijaz telegraph line became a landmark project of the Hamidian period and one that Sadik became identified with, particularly in his hometown of Damascus. A monument commemorating the extension of the telegraph line stands in the middle of Marjeh Square, one of the main squares in Damascus, today.[50] In 1902, after fulfilling his mission in the Hijaz, Sadik was awarded the highest order of the highest honor medal, *Osmani Nişanı Alisi*, and was promoted to the rank of *ferik* (lieutenant general).[51] He was very proud of his accomplishment and celebrated it as the first time "the people of the City of the Prophet (Madinat al-Nabi), peace be upon him" could communicate with "the rest of the developed world."[52]

The Hijaz telegraph extension project was only the first step in a much larger project to connect the holy cities Mecca and Medina with Istanbul. The Hijaz railway construction project began shortly after the telegraph line commenced. The two projects, usually referred to together as the Hijaz lines or the Hamidian lines were at the core of the Hamidian government's hope for self-reinvention. It was a domestic project designed, built, and operated by Ottomans. It was meant to connect the geopolitically strategic southern reaches of Ottoman Arabia to the imperial capital—a massive undertaking that had much sentimental resonance with Ottoman Muslims and Muslim subjects of other empires worldwide. While it mostly facilitated the central government's control in the region and the quick transportation of soldiers and goods to the western Arabian coast, the project was usually described in terms of the service it provided for Muslim pilgrims to travel to Mecca in the comfort of modern technology. Due to complicated local politics and competition between local, provincial, and imperial interests, neither the telegraph line nor the railroad was allowed to go past Medina.[53]

The construction, operation, and political implications of the Hijaz telegraph and railway have been well-studied. What I am interested in here is understanding how Arab-Ottoman family ties and government networks came together in Istanbul to make the project a success. The Hijaz line construction provides an ideal example of how several members of the Azmzades and their extended networks, which were fundamental to the success of public landmark projects, were utilized by the empire.[54] Family members based in Istanbul and in the provinces of Aleppo and Syria, were involved and left their fingerprints on the Hijaz lines. For example, two Azmzades from Damascus were recognized for supporting funding and logistics, including

(Muhammad) Fawzi, who was awarded the *Rumeli Beylerbeyi*, an honor-ary *Paşalık* (Pasha title),[55] and a second-rank *Mecidiye* medal. The other was Khalil Azmzade, who was also promoted to the rank of *miralay*.[56]

Having lost his notes from the 1900 Hijaz assignment in the fire that de-stroyed his home in 1903, Sadik left some notes in his Abyssinian travelogue, reminiscing about his time in the Arabian desert. For example, while passing through the Red Sea, he recalled:

> Every day, I took out the map and followed the path of the battleship. When
> it passed by certain areas in the Hijaz, like Yanbu and Rabigh and Jeddah,
> I could picture all the fortresses and areas along the hajj route in my mind's
> eye. I spent hours remembering the days that I spent in these remote places.
> I roamed around like a nomad, living in tents for 6 months when I was as-
> signed the task of extending the Hijaz telegraph line with a technical mili-
> tary mission. At that time, I was used to the region, the weather, and the
> *Urban* who live in the desert.[57]

As in his Saharan travelogue, he never referred to any of the nomads in Arabia as Arabs. Always Bedouins, natives, or *Urban*. As an Ottoman official whose native tongue was Arabic and adopted tongue was Turkish, a man who hailed from Damascus and lived in Istanbul, Sadik was well aware of the power of appellation and the Turkish language's nuances understood by the elites in the metropole. According to Redhouse, *Bedevi* is defined as "1. Pertaining to the open country or the desert. 2. An Arab of the wilderness, a Bedouin."[58] Another standard reference for Ottoman-Turkish, the famous Albanian-Ottoman linguist Shamsuddin Sami's *Kamus-ı Türki* defines a *Be-devi* as "a person who lives in a tent and wanders the desert, the opposite of sedentary (*hazari*) and urban (*medeni*)."[59] *Urban* is defined in Redhouse as "the primitive and pureblooded Arabian[s],"[60] while *Kamus-ı Türki* defines it simply as an "Arab Bedouin," with no singular form in Turkish.[61]

In contrast, the Arabic translation of Sadik's travelogue replaced *Urban* with *ʿArab* (Arabs) or *ʿArab al-badiya* (Arabs of the desert) depending on the context.[62] The Arabic version was originally published in 1908 Cairo by Sadik's brother-in-law Haqqi Azmzade and his cousin Rafiq (Tr. Refik) Azmzade.[63] They were self-exiled in Cairo at different times before and after the Young Turk Revolution of 1908. They first escaped with their lives in

1894 when their political activities were noticed by spies who worked for
the Hamidian regime. What is important to note here is that Haqqi and
Rafiq's translation came out of the original manuscript and not the published
Ottoman-Turkish language book. Sadik supplied the original manuscript to
his rebellious family members for publication without the weight of redac-
tions and censored terminology of the published version.

In the manuscript, Sadik boasted of his ability to communicate with
members of the Bedouin tribes, even working as a negotiator, bringing peace
to ensure the successful continuation of the Hijaz project. This time, I use the
Arabic translation to highlight the difference in the appellation:

> Any of the ships that have to sail close to the Red Sea coast has to take an
> *Arab* guide for fear of a collision, and those that do not, often lose their way
> and drown. The small boats of the *Arabs* are made of long wooden boards,
> each carved in the middle to fit one person. A coastal *Arab* uses it in the day
> to go fishing in the sea, and when he comes home to his humble shack, he
> carries it with him like a pole on his shoulder.[64]

Then he continued to describe his relationship with the locals:

> On many occasions, I invited the chiefs of warring tribes to have dinner with
> me. During the dinner, they behaved like there was no animosity between
> them. When I was in Mada'in Saleh, I invited the heads of the tribes of al-
> Yada, al-Faqir, and al-Bali and asked them to declare a truce for a year (which
> the *Arabs* call *'utwa*), so they agreed and did indeed have a year-long truce. I
> had to interfere because we needed their help in extending the telegraph line.
> . . . We needed the camels of the *Arabs* of these two tribes to transport am-
> munition, the soldiers' needs, the wooden poles, and the [telegraph] cables.[65]

All the italicization of the word "Arab" are mine and they are meant to
highlight occasions when *Urban* was replaced with *'Arab* in the Arabic version, even though both words were commonly used at the time.[66] This is not
about linguistic differences between Arabic and Turkish use of *'Arab/Arap*
or *'Urban/Urban*. It is about the social context in which *Arap* was deployed
in the Ottoman center of power by Turkish speakers versus the rest of the
empire. In the following section, the stakes of deploying *Arap* in turn-of-the-
century Istanbul should become clearer.

As an Arab-Ottoman officer, Sadik was attentive to the use of certain identity signifiers in Arab-majority administrative zones like Benghazi and the Hijaz. In 1896, the signifier *Arap* had not yet caught on as an ethnonational one. However, even in the 1890s, those signifiers were not always innocuous categories meant to identify the place where a person hailed from. In a multiethnic empire, where the very diversity of the population was thought of as a source of both strength and peril, such distinctions were often highlighted. Even Sadik was sometimes referred to as Şamlı Sadık (Damascene Sadik) before becoming well known in Abdülhamid II's administration and adopting his grandfather's name (al-Mu'ayyad) as his middle name. Both Izzet and Sadik came from Damascus, but only Izzet was referred to as Arap İzzet. Why was that the case, and why does it matter?

Close analysis of Sadik's choice of words begs the obvious counterfactual question: What if it was indeed an accident of writing rather than an intentional disassociation? What if the term was so commonplace and innocuous that it did not register for a man like him? What if the obvious omission of "Arab" was not because of the identarian or cultural weight in the late nineteenth century as I argue it had? To investigate this further, I return to Izzet, who had to live with the appellation *Arap* until his death.

What's in a Name?

Most historians have assumed that the attachment of *Arap* to Izzet's name was insignificant. A special characteristic, like physical appearance, character trait, or place of origin, was given to individuals with common names such as Izzet or Mehmet, particularly since most Ottoman subjects did not have a family name. Examples include some of Izzet's contemporaries and neighbors in Teşvikiye. One was Tunuslu (Tunisian) Hayreddin (Ar. Kheir al-Din) Pasha, who hailed from Tunisia in 1878 and became a member of the Assembly of Notables and lived in one of the most iconic villas in the neighborhood until his death in 1890.[67] Another was a minister of foreign affairs who then served as the head of the Council of State between 1895 and 1907—known as Kürt (Kurdish) Said Pasha, hailing from Sulaymaniyah in today's northern Iraq.[68]

However, unlike these two, Izzet was well-known by his family name "al-'Ābid," and many even included his father's name, Holo, as his middle name. His official name was Ahmed Izzet (Holo) al-'Abid (figure 11). In other

FFT 730 061E001

دور حميديده سلطان ثانى عزت پاشا

FIGURE 11. Izzet al-'Abid, early twentieth century.
Source: Salt Research, Feridun Fazıl Tülbentçi Archive, FFT730061.

words, his place of origin was not necessary at all, even using contemporary Ottoman logic. Also, as with Sadik, the vast majority of the time, the place of origin referred to a city, a province, or a region someone came from. Even *Kürt* in Kürt Said Pasha referred to Kurdistan. Following this logic, *Arap* would have referred to *Arabistan* (the Arabian Peninsula) and not Damascus. Keeping all this in mind, I want to suggest that Izzet's title referred to the other use of *Arap* in colloquial Turkish.

In informal discussions with some Turkish historians, they argue that *Arap* as a form of insult is a present-day colloquial appropriation associated with the derision that grew out of anti-Arab sentiment after World War I. The idea was in reference to the so-called Arab Revolt, when the amir of Mecca, Sharif Hussein Pasha, rebelled against Ottoman rule with the support of the British Empire during the war. The association of Arabs with backstabbing, a popular racist essentialism in Turkey, is well known. One only needs to search the terms *Arap ihaneti* (Arab betrayal) or *hain Arap* (Arab traitor) on Google to get hundreds of racist entries and comments about "the nature" of Arabs.[69] However, the attribution to World War I as the origin of this practice is inaccurate. The use of the term goes back to the dark history of African slavery in Istanbul.

According to Redhouse's *Turkish and English Lexicon*, originally published in Istanbul in 1890, *Arap* means "1. The Arabian people and race. 2. An Arab. 3. A negro.[70] The third meaning, "negro" or even just "Black," was used as a term of derision, stemming from the association of African-origin men and women with slavery. Redhouse gave suggestions on how it was used in quotidian sayings, for example, "*Arap Ardında*—The Black man is behind you (said [to scare] children as a form of restraint). . . . *Arap Olayım*—May I be a negro if I understand [what you said]. *Arap Babası*—A kind of fit of fury, also a fit of sullen obstinacy, to which negro slaves are subject. . . ."[71] Thus, when a highly disliked official like Izzet, who had a dark complexion and did not hail from Arabia, was given the informal title *Arap*, it makes little sense to assume that the word was not, in fact, in reference to its derogatory meaning. All of the above is meant to highlight the word *Arap*. Its use, or in Sadik's case its avoidance, points to something brewing in Ottoman society at the turn of the century that would become even more defined a decade later, as the reader will see in the following chapter.

Understanding Self by Inscribing Other

Sadik was primarily in the Sahara to observe, negotiate, and recommend ways to strengthen the empire's position there. Some of his recommendations survived in a neat list he prepared upon his return to Istanbul in early 1896. The list was comprehensive. From political advice on the sensitive issue of Ottoman presence on the ground in places like Kufra and Jaghbub to a number of reforms and investments that he believed the Sanjak of Benghazi needed, Sadik did not seem shy to share his thoughts. These included detailed recommendations on expanding the port of Benghazi, extension of the telegraph line between Tripoli and Benghazi, reform of the courts and schools, among others—recommendations that showed a commitment to Ottoman goals and a nuanced approach to governing from the center.[72]

In 1998 the Libyan editors uncritically labeled Sadik an "Arab Muslim from the Syrian Lands,"[73] which was a part of who he was after all but a part that did not make it to the pages of the travelogue—and not because he did not talk about himself. Quite the opposite, his self-reference was present in every description and comment he made. Taking into consideration deployment of *Arap* as a form of derision in the politically fraught landscape of imperial Istanbul—as I argue was the case for Sadik's famous relative Izzet—I investigated why he made no reference to it when traveling in a part of the world that was tied to his personal life by tongue, religion, and, arguably, culture. I suggest that the conspicuous absence of any reference to familiarity or personal similarity indicated a conscious decision influenced by his own social spaces and those of his readers. It was not a binary choice, Arab versus Ottoman, neither of which is a predetermined monolithic identitarian category. This makes his emphasis on one and complete silence on the other ever more telling.

Sadik reflected his disposition vis-à-vis Istanbul's political and social spaces and the anxieties that they induced. A nuanced understanding of what each word meant and, more important, what the choice of words implied was not lost on a man like Sadik. His use of terms to differentiate himself from the "Arabs of the desert" was peculiar and perhaps confusing to Libyan translators of the travelogue, who might not have understood the significance of the term in the context of late nineteenth-century Istanbul. They often changed his awkward use of *Urban* and Bedouin to the simpler and more straightforward *'Arab*. The sensitivities around "Arab" as an ethnoracial signifier and its implication of otherness in late-Ottoman Istanbul did not hold in 1998 Tripoli.

Finally, what I present in this chapter is not meant as the last word on the issue, but hopefully an instigation to come to terms with the wider implications of what the multiple uses of *Arap* meant and the academic silence around it. In the following chapter, I delve into Sadik's third diplomatic mission to Africa, this time to Abyssinia, where the subject of appellation and identification intersected with the complicated issue of race in the early twentieth century.

CHAPTER 5

RACIALIZING SELF, RACIALIZING OTHER

They are more savage than we are; which, again, means they
are further away from the white man. It is said that the
Negros love to jabber. . . . I think of the word jabber I see a
gay group of children calling and shouting for the sake of
calling and shouting—Children in the midst of play, to the
degree to which play can be considered an initiation into
life. The Negro loves to jabber, and from this theory, it is not
a long road that leads to a new proposition: The Negro is
just a child.

—Frantz Fanon in *Black Skin, White Masks*, 1952[1]

FRANTZ FANON BRINGS UP THE COMPLICATIONS OF INTERNAL "dislocation" when he discusses the way a Martinican man described Guadeloupians, in the epigraph above.[2] This analysis brings up the complicated situation that arises when an identification with a shared global imperial "White" habitus seems incongruent with a person's identification with another racialized group that he, under different circumstances, would have identified with. "Racializing self/racializing Other" explores some of the complexities of what Homi Bhaba called "the liminal problem of colonial identity"[3] where an Arab-Ottoman traveler's notion of his racialized self and his belonging to a global "White" habitus was challenged on his travels through the Horn of Africa, and, with the rise of further racialized differentiations closer to home, in the imperial metropole.

Sadik's writing style and the themes he explores were not dissimilar from those of contemporaneous European travel writers. However, it is important to situate him within this tradition of European travel writing without erasing the important differences between his subject position and that of his European counterparts. He was forthcoming in his admiration for European travel writers and in his envy of the support and fame they got in Europe. In his Saharan travelogue, he even lamented that the world was an unequal place where "the natives" walked barefoot, alone, across the desert for one hundred and fifty hours, yet they had no witness to such feats. In contrast, he added, a European traveler would have been celebrated for such an accomplishment, gaining fame and recognition. Using the story of one man he met on the road, he seemed to project his own lack of fortune in not getting the same coverage he felt he would have received if he had been in Europe. "Sübhanallah!" he exclaimed:

> In Europe, a man can travel with a wallet full of banknotes, on a planned route, with breaks along his journey during the day, and nights spent in comfort at a hotel, an inn, in a village, or someone's house. He can have his meals at restaurants that he finds along the way, where he can eat, drink, and enjoy himself as much as he wants. If he travels by foot from one city to another, the newspapers would be full of the coverage of his journey. Dedicated reporters would send telegrams about when so and so left one place and when he arrived in another. His travels would gain the attention and the admiration of the people.[4]

Sadik tried, with some success, to become known for his work as an explorer. He seemed to have been particularly influenced by famous orientalists and explorers who wrote in German. He recalled having met the famous Hungarian Turkologist Ármin Vámbéry (1832–1913), who traveled extensively in Central Asia and promoted the idea of a common ancestry for Hungarians and Turks.[5] He also met and spent time with the German philologist Max Müller and his wife, as discussed in Chapter 1. He must have consumed a great deal of European literature, particularly German travel literature written as part of the tradition of *Afrikareisende* (African explorers) like Alexander Von Humboldt, Heinrich Barth, Gerhard Rohlfs, and Gustav Nachtigal. Historian Tracey Reimann-Dawe argues that German travel writers were unique among European explorers, particularly before the entry of the German Empire into colonial competition in Africa. What made them unique was their continuous negotiation of their own identity. Since they were not yet a colonial power, they were not like other European colonialists who made a sharp distinction between themselves and "African otherness." They were in a liminal space, describing an African Other while constructing their own "German identity as it assert[ed] itself in colonial space," not unlike Sadik.[6]

In 1904, Sadik was an established member of a global social space of imperialists who identified with a wide range of cultural influences. Through his narration during his travels in Africa, he performed an Ottoman imperial identity while negotiating a complex set of identifications with Islam, Ottoman imperialism, European imperialism, and what he called Whiteness. Historian Mustafa Serdar Palabıyık rightfully points out that Ottoman travel writers in Africa had a different relationship to race or physical taxonomy than their European counterparts. However, where I depart from his analysis is his conclusion that when Ottoman travelers discussed what they perceived as the "backwardness of the African people . . . the emphasis [was] on external reasons, instead of intrinsic ones, unlike in most of the European Orientalist literature."[7] Based on Sadik's travelogue, the "backwardness" and "ignorance" among other negative traits were implicitly or explicitly attributed to essential racial characteristics and not environmental or circumstantial ones. In other words, I argue that late nineteenth-century notions of race played a substantial part in explaining what Sadik considered negative characteristics of Black natives and, perhaps more explicitly, his superiority as a self-identified White man.

Unlike his Saharan travelogue, the manuscript that survived Sadik's 1904 journey was not written to give to the sultan, allowing him a much less self-censored space to be more reflective. It was penned in the tradition of European explorers of the time, with a detailed description of what he observed and the occasional advice to future travelers. Unlike his 1895 record of travel, where Sadik often referred to himself as an Ottoman in contrast to the Bedouin Other, his 1904 account often referred to him as one of the Whites (*Beyazlar*) in contrast to the locals, whom he usually referred to simply as natives (*yerliler*) or by their ethnicity: Somali, Abyssinian (*Habeşi*), and so forth. This shift in self-portrayal marked a significant change from his Saharan travelogue. His intended audience remained the same, namely Ottoman-Turkish readers in Istanbul with whom he assumed he shared a set of commonly known cultural references and particular urban tastes. That meant that he did not have to explain or describe certain landmarks he named or cultural references he made, which only residents of Istanbul would have been familiar with. However, even though his audience remained the same, nine years later his dominant self-identification became as a White man, and he assumed that his readers in Istanbul were fellow Whites as well.

An Arab-Ottoman's Fractured Habitus

Between 2004 and 2011, I collected several versions of Sadik's Abyssinian travelogue, allowing me to analyze the changes that were made to the original text and to draw a conclusion as to how and why certain terms, topics, and themes were deemed appropriate for some audiences and not others. The first version is a facsimile of the original 1904 manuscript.[8] The second is the heavily edited and censored version, first published as a serial account of his trip in the daily newspaper *İkdam* and later as a book in 1906.[9] The third is an Arabic version of the original manuscript translated by family members and published in Cairo in 1908 and republished in Dubai in 2001.[10] The fourth version came out in 1999, transliterated and edited for a contemporary Turkish reader and published in Istanbul.[11]

Sadik's journey to the recently established capital of the Ethiopian Empire in the spring of 1904 was an official mission, part of an open diplomatic channel between Istanbul and Addis Ababa that had been established shortly after the Abyssinian victory over invading Italian forces in the famous 1896 Battle of Adwa.[12] Both the Ottoman and the Ethiopian empires were battling European colonial expansionism while attempting to enlarge their spheres of influence in the Horn of Africa. Italy, France, Britain, Russia, and even Spain were at some point vying for political influence and footholds in the Horn of Africa in the final decade of the nineteenth century. The Ottoman Empire was no different, resorting to older agreements with its

European counterparts to maintain its tenuous claim to key territories that were nominally under Ottoman rule on the African Red Sea coast and in the Lake Chad basin.[13]

By then, Sadik had built himself a reputation as a capable negotiator with local powers, whether the head of the Sanusi Order in central Africa or the chiefs of Bedouin tribes in the Hijaz. In both cases, his knowledge of Arabic was cited as one of the many reasons he was chosen for these missions. As an Arabic, Turkish, German, and French speaker, Sadik was able to communicate with some of the locals along the southern frontiers of the empire and with foreign representatives in those regions.

Despite having established his household in Istanbul, with two young sons, a teenage daughter of marriage age, his wife Esma, and his mother-in-law at home, Sadik seemed not to hesitate to stay on the road for most of his career. His gifts were his mobility and adaptability as a loyal representative of the sultan and an advocate for Ottoman imperialism, whether in the Balkans, Russia, or the Sahara. Thus, assigning Sadik a mission to meet with the emperor of Ethiopia, Menelik II, arguably the most important ally the sultan had in the Horn of Africa, could not have come as a surprise. Of course, language mattered; Sadik had the opportunity to practice classical and Levantine-Arabic with Somalis, Yemenis, and Syrians; Turkish with Armenian-Ottoman and Greek-Ottoman migrants and merchants; French with colonialists and other diplomats; and German with Menelik II's Swiss advisor and confidant, Alfred Ilg.[14] However, Sadik's proven experience as a diplomat who enjoyed the pomp and circumstance of official visits almost as much as he enjoyed the long journeys to get to his destinations, made him the ideal candidate for this mission.

I will not delve further into the complicated issue of Ottoman-Ethiopian relations and Ottoman imperial ambition in the Horn of Africa. This chapter instead focuses on Sadik's perception of what he encountered and the experiences he lived through as a way of gaining insight into his changing positionality and morphing habitus. According to Bourdieu, a person develops his habitus as a child and a young adult, informed by factors such as cultural traditions, family values, and class.[15] Sadik's habitus overlapped with that of his Damascene relatives from the same generation, like Izzet and Shafiq. Even though Sadik also shared with them many of the social spaces he inhabited in Istanbul, it is important to keep in mind that Arab-Ottomans of this generation experienced different trajectories in their careers once they arrived in the capital. However, only Sadik left behind two rich pieces of writing that facilitate an insight into his habitus at two junctures in his life—in 1895 and in 1904. Even though they share many themes, it would be a mistake to read the two travelogues as a single set of sources. It is important to remember that they were written at two very different moments in Sadik's life, nine years apart, reflecting the changes Sadik experienced personally and professionally. They also reflect the change in sensibilities toward notions of identifications, the most obvious being the newly gained importance of ideas about race in constructing "the Other" and "the self."

Much had happened since 1895. In the nine years since his second journey to the Sahara, Sadik had hosted Wilhelm in his own ancestral home, witnessing how a European royal reacted to what he saw and how it was perceived in the European press. He also worked on commissions in the Ottoman Balkans whose stated purpose was to find ways to address the grievances of the local Christian populations supported by Russian and other European powers. Sadik represented the sultan on a mission to the Crimea, where he met the Russian tzar. He also lost his house and his mother and had to head back to Syria for a while. Last but not least, he led the Hijaz telegraph line construction project and spent six months negotiating with Bedouin chiefs in Arabia.

His near nonstop mobility must have given Sadik a great deal of time to think about his subject position and life experiences. As he rose through the ranks of the Ottoman military and in the circle of palace advisors, reaching the rank of *birinci ferik* (general) in 1905 and taking up the critical position of Ottoman special commissioner to Bulgaria, his habitus must have been repeatedly "fractured." The dual mobility—upward social mobility gaining him more cultural capital in the Hamidian governmental structure and physical mobility as an itinerant diplomat and military general forcing his shifting perspectives—translated to shifts in his relative position in the social spaces he inhabited and a transition in his perspective on his own life.

Following Bourdieu's analysis, drastic changes in one's relationship to the world around them as they move socially and physically causes a fracture in one's habitus—*habitus clivé*.[16] This is a fracture, not a replacement, of one's original system of dispositions, which is often formed early in life. It is a form of dual habitus that one has to contend with as a price for social and geographic mobility. Thus, the lessons Sadik learned about himself by having to transverse the familiar urban environs of the Levant, the halls of power in Istanbul, his position in the social spaces of the Ottoman elites, and his relationship to the European royals, caused several extreme shifts in his sense of belonging. Plotted on a graph of positional change over time, the significance of where Sadik thought he belonged and his assumed "us" that he described in his travelogues become of interest to the historian.

Africa in One Ottoman Imperialist's Imagination

Sadik was not shy to express his opinion on things he saw, often in thinly veiled sarcasm. While issues of identification continued to be prominent themes in his discourse, the categories of what he observed expanded. Thus, it was no longer about imperial versus native identifications. In 1904, race had become a notable factor for Sadik to observe and to formulate as a way of identifying who he was in relation to an African Other. This was not the only, or even the primary, differentiation method, but it was one that must be noted. While he made sweeping judgments about cuisine, clothing, cultural beliefs, language acquisition, and similar cultural attributes, during this trip he was uniquely positioned to make comments on European as well as African habits, all through a personal and self-conscious lens. Through documentation of his observations, he struggled with his otherness to Europeans while identifying the otherness of the Africans he encountered. As Bhabha notes in his commentary on Fanon's work, the non-White other, probably more in the case of imperialists like Sadik, is always in "a space of splitting." It is not a neat division of us, Whites, versus them, Blacks. For Sadik it was always a "doubling, dissembling image of being in at least two places at once" that made the question of identity almost impossible to pin down.[17] An Arab-Ottoman imperialist's place was necessarily a liminal one, and Sadik constructed his place in opposition to what he saw and experienced on his journey.

The journey started on April 18, 1904. Sadik was accompanied by several Ottoman representatives, but he mentioned two in particular. *Binbaşı* (Lieutenant Colonel) Talib Bey from Tripoli (in today's Lebanon), who was also part of the Office of the Aides-de-Camp to the sultan, and *Tüfek Blok Çavuşu* (Rifle Regiment Sergeant) Yasin Efendi from Nablus (in today's Palestine).[18] They left Istanbul on a French passenger ship owned and operated by Messageries Maritimes, one of the most active shipping companies in the Eastern Mediterranean at the turn of the century. Sadik made a point of informing the reader that he had first-class accommodations as he crossed the Mediterranean Sea to Marseille, the main passenger-shipping hub of long-distance travel at the beginning of the twentieth century, stopping first in Izmir and then in Athens and Napoli. He did not comment on the counterintuitive route, heading west to the south of France to head back east in the direction of Alexandria, a city on the coast of an Ottoman province, or the fact that he had to arrange his own travel from Marseille onward. He had to rely on a British passenger ship and the French navy to get him from Marseille to the Horn of Africa.

This luxurious cruise on the first leg of the journey was a far cry from the Egyptian mail ship Sadik had had to take after accompanying the grand duke in 1888 or the military ship he had taken on his way to Benghazi in 1895. Instead of observing other Ottoman soldiers and commenting on their habits as he had nine years earlier, he had a range of colorful European characters and habits to comment on, particularly of those who shared his dinner table. A reoccurring theme and one of the first things he noted was, yet again, what he considered the oddities of foreign cuisine, in this case European cuisine. In particular, he spilled a great deal of ink discussing the strangeness of eating donkey meat and how similar it might have been to the horse meat he was more familiar with from his time traveling in Paris:

> While at dinner, I learned something that I would like to recount: I admit that I always thought the Europeans were gluttonous for eating horse meat. On many occasions, while in Paris, I noticed the abundance of mule and horse meat, and I saw signs in front of butcher shops advertising fatty mule meat. What surprised me was that they also ate donkey meat. Of course, logically, there is no difference between donkey meat, mule meat, and horse

meat. The similarity is probably due to the fact that their diet is essentially the same, and it is not a big leap from eating horse and mule meat to donkey meat. However, the reason for my puzzlement is the knowledge that donkeys are pretty rare in Europe, and they are usually only found in zoos in major cities under the category of exotic animals. So, I have never heard of donkeys being plentiful in Europe to the extent that their meat was eaten. Well, tonight, before the soup, the waiter brought some "hors d'ouvres," which included some kind of thinly sliced sausage (*Sucuk*) that looked lovely and had great color. Since, at first, I did know what kind of meat it was, I did not have any. Next to me sat a priest possessing a large body, with his fatness, appearance, and health that betrayed his love of food. When he saw that I limited myself to Sardines and butter, he said: "Eat my good sir some of this sausage, for it is some of the most delicious that has ever been made, and it is made of a mixture of mule and donkey meat." Others who were present agreed with him, but I politely declined, thanking him for being concerned for the wellbeing of his neighbors.[19]

Food that he found exotic or inedible was a common theme, always referencing the refined tastes of the cuisine back home. What was "home" also seemed to change. The reader might recall that while he was in the Sahara, he could not stop talking about how basic the tastes of the locals were compared with the tastes of home, what he called "Ottoman cuisine." The tastes of home in 1904 were much more specific and pointed to his original place of upbringing. What he craved and demanded was no longer what he called "Ottoman cuisine" in the 1895 travelogue, an ambiguous term considering the variety of cuisines that spanned a multicontinental empire. He instead talked about how what he and his two companions wanted was "Syrian cuisine," since the companions were also from the Levant. Instead of Karnıyarık, an Anatolian dish he highlighted craving on his Saharan trip, he referenced Bulgur Köftesi (Ar. Kubbeh). He said, "Since the three of us were all Syrian, Bulgur Köftesi, a dish from our Syrian cuisine, was never missing. We taught the cook how to make it right from the first day [while Albanian] Şevket Efendi who was interested in making food would prepare different types of dessert from his hometown."[20]

As for the local Abyssinian food, he relied on the trope of making the cuisine seem strange, often talking about how it required "a strong stomach" to not get sick eating their "undercooked" food. He even interpreted the making of Injera, unleavened soft bread that accompanied some Abyssinian meals, as a sign of the local populations' ignorance of the use of yeast to make the bread dough rise before baking. He described the Abyssinian hired hands' way of eating: "They squatted, always with a jar of hot peppers nearby, and ate quietly, always covering themselves with their shawls as they put food into their mouths." The idea that people "in hot climates" liked spicy food was repeated here, along with the notion that food was consumed while undercooked, making "natives'" stomachs "stronger." Undercooked and over spiced seemed to signal difference and lack of sophistication in taste.[21] Where does this notion come from?

The mid-nineteenth century brought with it much adaptation of elite Western European habits and tastes. The way a member of the Ottoman elites ate, for example, was markedly different in the late nineteenth century than a few decades earlier. Sitting down for meals on chairs, using forks and knives, at a designated table was a foreign appropriation that the elites adopted soon after the Ottoman palace did. Certain Western European eating rituals eventually overtook certain quotidian ways of behavior in the Ottoman Empire, first with elites who performed these rituals in public and then in the elites' intimate environments as a way of asserting a sense of belonging to a global imperial social space. Sadik's generation of men and women had to unlearn old habits and learn new ways of behaving in public in order to perform a specific level of imperial internationalism, contemporaneity with other elites in Europe, and by extension a marker of their class.[22] It was a *performative* aspect of public culture, a way of being that Ottomans termed *alafranga*. Although the term is often translated as "in the French mode," attributing a European aesthetic to France, it was more of a global imperialist class performance, *alaimperial* if you will, a late nineteenth-century way of performing one's class to one's counterparts at home and abroad.

Sadik's generation was not necessarily born with these forms of cultural appropriations, adaptations, and attitudes—they were not part of their original habitus but were a class-conscious addition to or partial replacement of

behavior that they learned in the social spaces they inhabited, starting in
Collège Saint Joseph in Mount Lebanon and then in Pera in Istanbul and
beyond. The embodiment of Western European eating and drinking rituals
were all new modifications that had to be learned within Sadik's lifetime.
Eating what was considered haute cuisine and how one behaved were em-
bodiments of imperial Ottoman modernity, which Sadik was not only careful to perform but also keen to describe in contrast to that of the African
Other. Sadik's describing his way of having a meal versus how others, in this
case Somalis and Abyssinians, did was another form of "performativity" as
philosopher John L. Austin describes it; using words to create an impact
and effect change.[23] Making words do the work for him, Sadik effected an
image of who he wanted to portray himself to be: a member of a global
imperialist class.

Another way performativity was key here was the repetition of details on
how and what he ate. The *repeated* aspect of performativity—as explained by
Judith Butler concerning gender—around the ritual of making and consum-
ing food constructed the image of an elite culture that, for Sadik, happened
to be centered in the metropole.[24] It is worth repeating that this was not
about pretending to be Western; it was about doing acts adopted from elite
Western European culture. What was elite and current became synonymous
with being a member of an exclusive club of imperialists who adapted and
internalized certain elite Western European cultural rituals as universal elite
behavior.

Tropes of Racism

Another reoccurring theme was what Sadik considered his cultural superiority through an acceptance of science and technology, which separated him
from the locals. He pointed out incidents in which the locals did not understand scientific advancements or were puzzled by or afraid of new technology
that they did not like or were skeptical of because they relied on what he saw
as superstitions. He did not investigate the hesitation he encountered; he
simply narrated incidents highlighting his puzzlement, frustration, or dislike
of what he considered a childish stubbornness. In other words, the incidents
of interaction were about his emotional reaction to them, registering them
as opportunities to document what made him different from the Other. That

is, his travelogue was about himself more than anything else. Yes, the observations were plentiful, and one can read a concerted effort to make the travelogue as useful to future travelers and travel literature hobbyists as possible. However, his observations were mostly a reflection of his own anxieties, which did not stem from "the natives" he described but from people he feared identifying with and who pulled him away from his desire to identify with Whiteness as a way to access elite notions of modernity he felt he could lay claim to.

Sadik described many incidents to his readers to highlight what he considered examples of ignorance and lack of global awareness. For example, he was often accosted by an Abyssinian servant who would try to cover him while he ate. He explained it as a superstition of the locals, who thought that an evil eye would strike them if they were not careful to cover themselves while they ate in the open. Sadik mocked this superstition and asked the servant to stop trying to cover him several times until one day, when he wanted to have a cup of coffee by a lake, a servant rushed toward him with a cover. Sadik dissuaded him by stating that he was well-protected from the evil eye because he carried a small amulet of neatly folded Quranic verses wrapped in a cloth (Tr. *Nazar Takmı*, Levantine Ar. *Hijab*) and was wearing blue-colored sunglasses in place of a blue bead (Tr. *Nazar Boncuk*).[25] Catering to his audience back in Istanbul, where both objects were well-known as remedies against people's envious evil eye, Sadik did not consider that superstitions he was familiar with were as culturally and geographically specific as the ones he witnessed in the Horn of Africa. How could an Abyssinian man understand and acknowledge Ottoman superstitious habits? In reality, this story was a discursive tool meant to create another layer of difference. Whether it was real or not, it allowed him to create a sense of familiarity with his readers while portraying Abyssinians as strangely superstitious. The Arabic version of the travelogue left no doubt about Sadik's feelings, adding an explicit condemnation of the locals' superstitions: "How strange are the habits of these people, and how ugly it is for one's mind to surrender to such delusions."[26]

This statement fits into Sadik's pattern of infantilizing the locals. He stated that, even though the youngest of them was at least nineteen years old, they were "like children, with no trace of gloom in their heart, always laughing and playing that they don't let an hour pass by without finding a reason to make a joke."[27] This infantilizing was part of the process of other-ing, describing other cultures as inferior or innocently ignorant, oblivious to the world around them. Similar to Fanon's example of what "Guadeloupe Negros" faced from Martinicans that this chapter opened with, Sadik's dis-tancing himself from the locals was less about what he observed and more about his own ethnoracial anxiety.

Another trope of othering was highlighting what he perceived as the lo-cals' fear or misunderstanding of technology. For example, Sadik highlighted two incidents when the locals were afraid of having their picture taken, but with no explanation of what happened. He was content with ending his ob-servation with an exclamation mark to indicate his puzzlement. One incident occurred upon docking in Djibouti. He mentioned that the local boys were great at swimming and diving, so he and others on the French navy ship entertained themselves by throwing coins into the water to watch the "very black Somali boys" dive to retrieve them. He was amused and wanted to take a photograph of some of the boys, but as soon as he turned his camera on them "they appeared terrified." He did not go any further and continued to the next topic, which happened to be the official welcome he received as he disembarked at the French colony's port.[28] The other incident took place at one of the train stops on the way from Djibouti to Dire Dawa outside the city of Harar. Sadik wanted to take a picture of the Somali children there as well, but "'they would die,' their fathers shouted. Since I would not want them to die either, I gave up on getting their photo." This was a sarcastic response to the locals' superstition. In the Arabic, Ottoman-Turkish, and modern Turkish versions, this statement was followed by several exclamation marks to alert the reader to the sarcasm.[29]

He took a similar attitude when he described an incident that took place at the home of an Albanian advisor to Menelik II. He recalled that the group he was with sat in the garden of the house that was an hour and a half away from Addis Ababa on horseback, listening to songs from Istanbul on a gramophone. "While the gramophone was on," he continued, "our servants and the Abyssinian soldiers came close and started looking in the gramo-phone with confusion and amazement and wondered to one another how did the singer get into the gramophone?! [exclamation point in the original]. They were not convinced when they were told there was nobody inside the machine. It seemed like they had never seen a gramophone before. Truth be told, I too was surprised to find a gramophone in Addis Ababa."[30]

Sadik's most impassioned defense of technology against what he saw as the locals' ignorance was one that hit close to home. The train between Djibouti and Dire Dawa was a French project commissioned by Menelik II to connect the capital, Addis Ababa, with Djibouti, allowing the landlocked empire access to the Port of Djibouti in what was then French Somalia. The construction had started in 1897, and the first section, which terminated in Dire Dawa outside the city of Harar, was completed in 1902, two years before the arrival of Sadik. Of course, Sadik was fresh off the Hijaz project, which, like the French project, had faced a great deal of resistance from the local population. The opposition to these projects was couched by the imperial powers in terms of locals' "ignorance" and resistance to new technology.[31] In this case, Sadik had a stage to narrate his personal frustration and to distance himself, as an Ottoman Muslim, from non-Ottoman Muslims, Somalis, who in his opinion resisted the train under misguided religious pretenses. His tone was one of lecturing the locals on how to be good Muslims and to follow the Ottoman caliph's example of embracing this new technology. He wrote:

> When the train paused, some of the Somalis spotted my Fez, so they descended on the train car from every direction with signs of happiness apparent on their faces, and they started to talk to us. We asked those who knew Arabic how they were doing, so they complained about the railway. I asked: "Why are you complaining about the railway? Isn't it better than your camels?" The man who was best at speaking Arabic came closer and answered with the strangest explanation [*tuhaf tuhaf*]: "No, it is not better than our camels, for if the camel touched a human being, the man does not get injured, and if it got excited it won't inflict any harm on him, in fact, all that would happen is that the camel would start to foam at the mouth. However, this [pointing to the train car] if it happened upon a man or animal while it was moving, it would tear them to pieces. If it got mad, it would make a noise so loud that it scares our camels and cattle, sending them running into the wilderness, even causing the camels to drop their load on the ground. And this [pointing to the steam stack of the train], if it got angry, spews smoke

and fire and covers the field with a layer of soot. Additionally, one can eat camel meat, and camels can reproduce and multiply, as for this [the train] how can one slaughter it and eat it?" In response, I said: "Railways are present in the Well Protected Domains [Ottoman lands], and the Hijaz will soon also be connected to the rest of the empire by railroad." In response, he said: "So the railways that you have are not a Western (*Efrenc*) heretical invention, and so our train must be the same."[32]

In narrating the incident, Sadik was able to show his puzzlement at the lack of acceptance of this technology, assert the superiority of the Ottomans as adopters of it, and finally show the moral authority and influence the Ottomans had over local Muslims. He was quick to distance them from what he considered the true form of Islam. According to him, Somalis' knowledge of Islam was shallow. Even though they were practicing Muslims who would "try" to perform the five daily prayers, they remained "famous for bloodletting and the killing of souls. One of their savage habits is that a man places a feather in his hair, a bracelet or an earring for each person he killed. . . . Additionally, Somalis used to work in the slave trade, but now they have mostly abandoned it."[33] He made these statements to show, based on what he had heard, that the Somalis did not have a grasp of the religion due to practicing slavery and other forms of violence. This was an unusual statement to come from a military man who lived in late nineteenth-century Istanbul, where domestic slavery was not unusual.

Assuming that Sadik accurately reported what the Somali man had said to him—in Arabic, indicating his high level of education—the Somali man was making an excellent point, albeit taking poetic license to compare a train to an animal. He expressed valid concerns about the penetration of the train into Somalis' lands disrupting their habitat and way of life, often striking their animals, and introducing noise and air pollution, and they were not compensated for their lost labor and land. Like the Arab nomads Sadik had encountered during his time in the Hijaz, the Somalis understood that this technology meant the extension of imperial power with little to no benefit for the locals. In the case of the Hijaz, the railway meant the extension of Istanbul's power to the Bedouin tribes' domains, in the Somali case it had a double effect. It meant the extension of Western (*Efrenc*) colonial penetration into the African continent's interior, as well as the extension of Ethiopian imperial domination over Muslim Somali territories, pressuring the local camel herders into choosing submission or migration. Sadik's final statement about the supposed realization of the Somali man that the train was not a foreign "heretical invention (*bid'a*)" seemed to invoke religious reasoning out of nowhere. Of course, the Somali mistrust of foreign technology as a tool of colonial domination and dispossession was well warranted whether Muslim religious authorities sanctioned the technology itself or not. However, Sadik's choice of narration changed the nature of the complaint from a political, environmental, and economic one to one based on religious concerns. It allowed Sadik a chance to narrate Ottoman religious influence over non-Ottoman Muslims, Somali nomads in this case, while reinforcing his superiority as a representative of the empire.

Sadik's narration of the train incident had an underlying assumption that suspicion of new technologies was a self-evident misunderstanding of modern sciences based on ignorance and superstition. His understanding of how Somalis or Abyssinians related to science and technology was always self-referential, highlighting his sense of superiority as a man who prided himself on adopting modern sciences and the benefits of technological innovations, in the process highlighting that his attitude was a reflection of the Ottoman Empire's attitude toward such topics. However, this differentiation took on an added layer of meaning when Sadik referred to himself as a representative of "Whites" as well.

Ethnoracialization in the Ottoman Empire

The adoption of racial appellations in the European travel literature of the early twentieth century was a common occurrence. However, an Arab-Ottoman man repeatedly and explicitly declaring an identification with a specific racial category in contrast to another is noteworthy. Ethnic and religious differentiation by the Ottoman state and within Ottoman society is well-studied as an aspect of the so-called *millet* system. The *millet* system was a form of categorization based on state-recognized ethnoreligious identifications. It traditionally carried with it official and unofficial hierarchies of rights and responsibilities for the Greek Orthodox, Jewish, and Armenian communities.

With the rise of ethnonationalism in the nineteenth century, ethnic identification became more starkly defined in the Ottoman Empire, leading to
further differentiation within the various ethnic and religious communities.[34] For example, the Greek Orthodox Church, which had jurisdiction over
Greeks, Bulgarians, Serbians, and Syrians, among other Orthodox Christian
communities. It began to lose control over a number of them as they petitioned to be recognized as a separate *millet* by the Ottoman state based
on ethnicity, such as Arabic speakers who claimed discrimination by the
Greek Orthodox Church did.[35] While it seemed that ethnoracial differentiation did not play a role in this top-down government organization structure,
often touted as an ideal pluralistic system and a precursor to the notion of
"multiculturalism."[36]

Race as an official category did not appear to be an explicit factor in how
the Ottoman imperial government organized its population, whether on a
collective or an individuated basis. The absence of race from the official archival records is one reason that racism in Ottoman societies has been so understudied. With no state-sanctioned policies or empire-wide laws that explicitly
discriminated against free people based on race, historians who are mostly
dependent on the Ottoman state archives for sources seldom study race or
racism as a societal phenomenon. That the state archives do not point toward
state-sponsored ethnoracial discrimination, however, does not mean that the
Ottoman metropole was immune to this nineteenth-century phenomenon.

With a few exceptions, discussions of race and racism in the Ottoman
Empire remain tucked away at the margins of research dealing with the royal
court, the institution of slavery, and, more recently, research focusing on the
small Afro-Turkish community.[37] Even discussions of race within the context
of slavery, a deeply rooted institution in the Ottoman Empire that included
Black and White slavery, remains controversial. In particular, slavery and its
connection to Blackness, the traditional argument goes, could not apply considering that enslaved individuals were of various ethnic origins and, in some
cases, Black Ottomans rose to high positions in the imperial state. For example, some of Sadik's colleagues in the Office of the Aides-de-Camp were
listed as Black (*siyahi*) in the official records.[38]

At the risk of oversimplifying these debates, until recently the kneejerk
reaction to any discussion of racism in Ottoman societies was met with an

argument for the exceptionalism of the Ottoman case among global empires. For example, Özgür Türesay, while rightfully arguing against the notion that Ottoman colonialism cannot be understood based simply on analyzing the rhetoric of Ottoman bureaucrats in Istanbul to look for similarities to European notions of "civilizing mission," highlights that no "racist or racial coloring" in Ottoman rhetoric was to be found.[39] It is fair to say that any critical discussions of race, racialization, and racism have often been sidestepped or shut down as topics that were artificially superimposed on the Ottoman case by Western academics grappling with racism in their own backyard. Race and racism, however, did play a role in the way Ottoman imperialists like Sadik perceived themselves and the world around them. The reader will see how ethnoracial categories were not limited to territories beyond the frontiers of the empire. It became a factor in Istanbul, and it impacted the way society was organized and how the various ethnic groups were perceived and treated in the final years of the Ottoman Empire.

Before the travelogue entry describing his arrival in Addis Ababa, Sadik paused to give a relatively detailed guide to the history, geography, administration, military, economy, and population of Abyssinia. He did not mention the source of his information, but it most likely came from travelogues written by explorers who surveyed the area as representatives of European imperial powers interested in the colonial potential of the region, or scientists interested in documenting flora and fauna there. In his description of the people of Abyssinia, he stated that they could not be counted as Negro (*zenci*) and were counted as Semites. He continued: "The people here came out of a mixture of ancient Egyptians and Semite peoples that came from southern Arabia. Thus, some of them look like Arabs, and others look *Sudani*. The earlier are better looking and are superior to the other by appearance and shape and the color that approach white, refined noses and lips, balanced body, and proportional extremities."[40] One might count his attention to racial characteristics as simply a reflection of the adoption of information as it was presented by European colonialists at the time. However, in Sadik's case it betrayed a view he adopted as a self-identified White man whose experiences he interpreted as essential habits based on race.

For example, Sadik recounted an incident in which one of his servants fell ill and came to him asking for help. He assumed that the man must have eaten too much raw meat and thus was in so much pain that he was "rolling on the ground." Sadik pulled out his "mobile pharmacy" and gave the man some medicine that helped with the pain but caused him severe diarrhea. He gave him "Dicentricum," which he recommended to anybody who suffered from diarrhea. He went on to explain that "if one of the people in this land fell ill, he would seek the care of Whites (*beyazlar*), because Whites from their perspective are doctors, surgeons, and capable of doing anything."[41] The rest of Sadik's musings about the Abyssinians' attitude toward "Whites" was left out of the published Ottoman-Turkish and Modern-Turkish versions of the travelogue. In his manuscript, however, he continued to describe what he thought was an illogical anti-White prejudice. Despite thinking that the White man was capable of helping them, Sadik said, "they still hate his color, and if they were ever angry at a White person (*beyaz insan*), they would throw insults at him saying 'taj olaj,' meaning White slave (*beyaz köle*). They generally hate the color white since they are not used to seeing White people, especially Blacks (*Sudanlar*) in the African interior who think it is very ugly. So, they think that a White person was born prematurely, that is before he was fully grown in his mother's belly, or that he became white due to some disease that changed his natural black skin to white (*siyah renk beyaza munk-alip olmuş*)."[42]

Sadik's recounting of this incident and his differentiation based on skin color—counting himself among the *beyazlar*—was about more than appearances. He also assigned differences in behavior or habit based on biological markers associated with what he considered a person's racial characteristics. As historian Suman Seth tells us, attributing specific physical characteristics, including a person's tolerance, or lack thereof, to specific diseases or climatic conditions as a racial characteristic crystalized in the late eighteenth century when race started to be used in scientific debates as an "essential category" that was rigid and unchanging. Of course, physical characteristics such as specific physical features or skin color had been noted since the beginning of recorded history. What was different about the nineteenth century, was that people's racial characteristics were pathologized and essentialized to explain behavior and justify different aspects of colonialism inside and outside the empire.[43]

Sadik's observations fit into this pattern. For example, one of his themes was the notion of an inherent ability of locals to tolerate excessive heat, something that he believed, like many imperialists of the time, could not be tolerated by Whites. This kind of observation started while he was onboard the French navy ship as it entered the Red Sea. The captain had to hire some locals to serve as coal trimmers in the engine room. The reason he cited was that "the European coal trimmers are not able to tolerate the heat in the Red Sea and the Indian Ocean," buying into the notion that somehow locals were born tolerant of heat.[44] Similarly, while he was at a dinner in his honor at the French governor's house in Djibouti, he again mentioned that the Whites could not survive the heat and thus they had big fans operated through a pully system by Somali servants who stood outside in the heat.[45] He insisted that the "weather in Djibouti is extremely hot, and its sun very strong, that if a White person stood for ten minutes in the sun without an umbrella, he would die immediately from sunstroke. Death due to sunstroke is a common incident there."[46] According to Sadik, Somalis not only tolerated the heat better than Whites; they sought the heat and the sun while he always looked for the shade.[47] He even said that babies growing up tied to the backs of their mothers were not affected by the sun, "while a White person can barely stand under the sun for five minutes without an umbrella since the sun of these parts is very harsh. If a person got a sunstroke here, his brain would swell up, and he would die right away."[48]

Perhaps the incident most illustrative of Sadik's disposition toward what he considered an essential biological difference between himself as a White man and the local Abyssinians and Somalis is the following. One day during the journey, he left the caravan and went to what he thought was a secluded part of a river to bathe:

I took off my clothes and put them between two rocks, then I entered the water and started to cleanse my body with a bar of soap and a luffa. There was nobody around at that time, so I lathered some soap on my face and closed my eyes so that the soap would not get in them. When I opened my eyes, I felt a shadow hovering over me like a small cloud. When I looked closer to understand what was going on, I saw that it was an Abyssinian whose color is almost totally black standing on a rock high above me, leaning forward with his hands extended, holding up one side of his shawl, while the other part covered his lower half. Using signs, I asked him what he wanted standing there so strangely. In response, he pointed to the sun and then to my head. That was how I understood that he wanted to protect me from the heat of the sun. I thanked him and decided to no longer bathe in the sun because the sun in these parts has an immediate impact on the heads of Whites who can get sunstroke. I also decided to make sure not to ever stand under an umbrella with a soul [a human umbrella], like the one I found myself standing under that day.[49]

This is yet another example of Sadik interpreting race, and Whiteness, as a point of difference. His assumption was that the man wanted to protect him because of his unique vulnerability to the sun as a White man.

A White Muslim Man?

Anthropologist Ezgi Güner has researched how Ankara, today, deploys the historical connections between Turkey and Muslims in sub-Saharan Africa—real and imagined—coupled with a global brand of White supremacy to produce the trope of the benevolent "White Muslim."[50] A hundred years earlier, Sadik's observations, not simply as a White man but as a self-identified White Muslim man, might help historicize this narrative. The idea of White superiority coupled with his Ottoman Muslim identity, which he constructed in contrast to that of the African locals he encountered, challenged Sadik's perception of his place in the world. Following the lead of many of his European counterparts who traveled in Africa as explorers, at certain times, he wrote with academic distance, and at other times his feelings of wonder and even confusion about what he experienced overtook his narrative. While he was careful to document the date and time of every major part of his journey with scientific accuracy, often giving the reader an hour-by-hour account using both "Turkish" and "European" timekeeping, it was clear that it would be impossible to continue following a model of writing that simply asserted his superiority as a White man with no commonality with the "exotic" subjects he described. After all, he was there as a representative of the Ottoman sultan-caliph, a man who claimed to represent the entirety of the Muslim *ummah*. Many of the locals he traveled with were Muslim and Orthodox Christians, and summarily dismissing them as "ignorant" Others would have required much mental gymnastics on his part. For example, he met Somalis and Abyssinians who had traveled extensively in the Hijaz and could converse with him in Arabic. Yet, instead of looking for their similarities with himself—an Arabic speaker who also traveled in the Hijaz—he focused on differences. For Sadik, even though they were bilingual and were well-traveled, they did not travel extensively enough or speak the "right" kind of foreign language. Similarly, many were Sunni Muslims just like him. However, for him their understanding of Islam was a shallow understanding that allowed them to maintain their "savage" ways. Time and time again, this dilemma of distancing the intimate Other and ignoring the familiar came up.

Autobiographical writing, including travel writing, is often a simultaneous narration of one's "experience" and the "self." This simultaneity allowed Sadik to control the narrative of not only what he saw but how he was redefined by it.[51] Sadik had to negotiate his identification with a global imperial social space by invoking race to explain where he fit in. As a self-identified Muslim Ottoman man, the conflict he must have had to face as he traveled in northeast Africa was that many of the Others, for European imperialists, were often Muslim men like he was. Many of Sadik's influences, travel writers and explorers who wrote in French and German, made a point of describing their difference in terms of their superiority not only on a racial level, but also on a cultural level in a Hegelian notion of Christianity as an inherently superior culture. For example, two influential German travelers "clearly though not expressly influenced by Hegelian categories of development" ranked Islamic cultures below Christian ones but above African traditional polytheistic religions.[52]

Thus, cultural differentiation was not enough; race was a factor that allowed Sadik a way to build distance and produce himself as White without being European. His true puzzlement and frustration and perhaps even confusion may be best expressed in a statement he made about what he perceived as an unjustified pride that Somalis had toward Europeans. He could not understand how they could not see the superiority of the *Efrenc*. He stated: "A Somali is like other nomadic peoples, conceited and thinks highly of himself, and due to his endurance of hardship and difficulties and his being accustomed to the harshness of nomadic life, you can see him being so attached to keeping up his pride in front of the urbanites, who enjoy the comforts of the city. He looks at them with condescension and contempt for being so immersed in a life of comfort and luxury. For example, Somalis who work in base professions . . . as porters, servants, and coal trimmers on steamships. They are exposed to and mix with Europeans (*Frenkler*) and can observe the impact of their civility and the great industrial advances they have achieved, they still look down on them, especially in front of Westerners (*Efrencler*), and they displayed their conceit and put on airs in front of them."[53] Such a statement betrays his insecurities as an Arab-Ottoman man. Although he criticized some of the habits of Europeans in his travelogue, he seemed unable to understand why Somalis, with as little as they had, did not perceive Europeans as superiors—the Europeans that he looked up to and whose language and some aspects of their culture he had worked so hard to adopt.

Similarly, once in Addis Ababa he commented on the fact that the people there resented the Europeans and they only feigned respect out of fear of the Ethiopian emperor. He acknowledged that their resentment came from the wars they had fought with the Italians and the English and because they had been exploited by Europeans for their labor and had had their lands plundered for their mineral wealth. Yet a European man confided in him that foreigners feared what might happen to them if the emperor were to die. They worried that "they might meet the same fate that had befallen their brothers in China." Identifying with his fellow imperialists, Sadik answered: "The emirs and reis (leaders) here would not allow the people here to commit such barbaric acts like those."[54]

Not All Ottomans Get to Come Home

Explicit statements about race hardly reappeared in any of Sadik's writings that I found, because the rest of the documents left behind were official correspondences that did not invite any such introspection. Sadik, Shafiq, and Izzet were part of the same ethnoracial *unsur*, and within a few years they would have to either reinvent themselves or lose the empire for good. The ways they publicly identified themselves would become an existential issue.

The discussion in Chapter 4 and in this chapter is meant to shed light on some of the processes that had already begun well before so called Turki-fication, Arabism, or nationalism(s) came into play. I have argued that the notion that differentiation based on ethnicity and race did not exist before the upheaval of World War I ignores a history of Ottoman participation in the global rise of ethnoracial identification years before the end of the age of empire.

Sadik returned to Istanbul via the Suez Canal, stopping in Alexandria before continuing to the Ottoman capital. There he would find an Abys-sinian delegation that had been there for months. His return was written about in *Thamarat al-Funun*, a Beirut-based Arabic-language newspaper, which stated that Sadik received the highest Abyssinian medal, the Star of Abyssinia, along with a sword and shield made of silver and gold. His two companions, Yasin Efendi from Nablus and Talib Bey from Tripoli, faired very well and received medals and precious gifts before being sent off with an elaborate celebration.[55]

Upon his return to Istanbul, Sadik was received with many honors by the palace as well. His mission was deemed successful, and he could finally reap the rewards of his difficult journey. He wasted no time publishing accounts of his trip in *İkdam*, collecting the praise he felt he was owed. However, his two companions seem to have been forgotten. Neither Yasin nor Talib were paid for this trip. By September of 1904, both of them had sent several letters asking for what they believed was owed to them, including expenses incurred on the road, particularly the cost of transport and hotel stays and what they were promised in payment.[56]

This was not the last word from Yasin. A few years later, mere months after the Young Turk Revolution and the change in regime, he spoke with *Tanin*, a newspaper in Istanbul, about the Ottoman subjects they had met in Abyssinia. They were there as refugees, running away from persecution by the Hamidian regime or local oppressive powers back home in Anatolia. He spoke up because he felt that the original accounts of the trip did not do justice to those people. He urged Ottoman exiles in Abyssinia to con-sider returning so that their children did not have to grow up in a foreign land (Tr. *gurbet*).[57] An Arabic-language newspaper also published a column about the Ottomans who lived in Abyssinia. It reported that their numbers amounted to close to one thousand and that they controlled more than half of the country's trade. However, the newspaper stated that they suffered from discrimination and abuse because of the Abyssinians' hatred for Whites. As a result of these difficulties, with the change in regime in Istanbul, the Ottomans living in Abyssinia reportedly wished to return to Anatolia. Unfortunately, most of them were never able to go back.[58]

CHAPTER 6

THE BEGINNING OF THE END

For the love of God, for the love of the Prophet! In the
name of the sultan and the honor and solemnity of the
state, over and over I have had to request our salaries and to
rescue us from this pitiful state.

—Sadik al-Mu'ayyad Azmzade,
Sofia, 1905[1]

A LETTER OF RESIGNATION FROM A FORMER SPECIAL COMMISSIONER
to Bulgaria and a fellow Arab-Ottoman from the Levant sheds some light
on the kind of difficulties that Sadik was about to encounter in the fall of
1904. Nejib Melhamé,[2] the younger brother of Selim Melhamé whom the
reader encountered earlier, highlighted the challenges that came with the
post of Ottoman special commissioner to Bulgaria. First, Nejib lamented not
being given a diplomatic post in a major European city like Geneva, Paris,
or Berlin, for which he felt he was better suited. Despite his hesitation, he
explained, he accepted the post in Sofia as a service to the empire and did his
best with very little support from the Sublime Porte. Then, he complained
about the obstacles raised by a nonresponsive Office of the Grand Vizier and
the Ministry of Foreign Affairs, which meant that all his recommendations
to Istanbul fell on deaf ears. Nejib said that he was thrust into the middle

of the heated Crete crisis; the Macedonian separatist movement; the issue of the maltreatment of Muslims in Bulgaria; and the smuggling of weapons into Salonica, Kosovo, and Monastir with very little financial or political support. Despite his best efforts, nothing ever changed and so he felt compelled to leave his post, noting that while he patiently waited to be rewarded with a more significant post in Europe, he thought he would tough it out in Sofia. However, he could no longer wait and decided to prioritize his health and being reunited with his family and thus had no choice but to resign.[3] As the epigraph above indicates, Sadik would inherit Nejib's post and all of the problems Nejib had faced, two and a half years later.

After his return from Addis Ababa, Sadik had very little time to prepare for what would arguably be his most important assignment yet—Ottoman special commissioner to the Principality of Bulgaria. His appointment to this critical post made a great deal of sense since he was very familiar with the explosive situation in the Balkans. Between 1899 and 1903, he served as an inspector on at least two commissions on Ottoman Macedonia and as a negotiator in a bilateral summit with the Russian Empire addressing the so-called Macedonian Question. Since then, Istanbul's position had become more difficult as Prince Ferdinand of Bulgaria had garnered further support for complete Bulgarian independence from the Ottoman Empire.

Bulgaria represented the pinnacle of Sadik's career, but it was also the point from which he fell, never to recover his former status in the Ottoman government. The challenges of diplomacy in this turbulent region, getting caught in the middle of quibbling between the Sublime Porte and the palace, and his pride and sense of entitlement would get the best of him.

Sadik's three and a half years in Bulgaria, an autonomous principality that fell under the sultan's suzerainty, were marred by constant struggles. He had the challenge of negotiating with a prince with a maximalist attitude, determined to seek independence and declare himself king. Like Nejib, Sadik was also starved for funds by the Ministry of Foreign Affairs, which seemed determined to challenge every akçe spent by the commission, indirectly accusing him of corruption and embezzlement at every turn. He also faced challenges in his personal life as the age of the palace wound down and the Azmzades of Istanbul began to lose their clout.

It is fair to say that by then Sadik's status as a wealthy statesman, independent of his family's provincial power, had been confirmed. During his tenure in Sofia, Sadik finally reaped the benefits of over two decades in the palace's service and he reached out to his family in Istanbul and the Levant to share his success and display his wealth. However, what lay beneath all of the trappings of monetary success was the impending collapse of the Hamidian regime and with it much of the political capital that Sadik and other Arab-Ottoman imperialists of Istanbul had acquired.

Sadik's fate was tied to the sultan's; he put on extravagant celebrations at the commissioner's residence for every occasion in an attempt at maintaining the sultan's prestige and by extension his own. This meant that, like many statesmen of his generation, the line between his personal benefits and those of the empire often blurred. Sadik's wealth was of the empire's wealth, and his pride came from the dignity of the empire. During this period, however, there were many occasions when his wealth was questioned and his pride injured as the Principality of Bulgaria marched steadily toward independence. Additionally, Sadik's three and a half years as the special commissioner were marked by infighting between the Sublime Porte on one side and Sadik and his supporters in the palace on the other. With the fury of a man raging against the dying light of empire, Sadik lost the fight mere months before the collapse of the old regime.

The Road to Sofia

A month before taking up his post in Sofia, Sadik was assigned the official task of representing the sultan by handing the honorary title of vizier to one of his most loyal civil servants. Sadik took the short trip to Bursa to hand-deliver the official letter from the sultan to the governor-general of the Province of Hüdavendigar, Reşid (Ar. Rashid) Mümtaz Pasha.[4] Reşid had a long track record of loyal service to the sultan, including as governor-general of the Province of Beirut and later as head of the Municipality of Istanbul.[5] As a senior military official and advisor to the sultan, Sadik stood in for the sultan, honoring one of his closest allies in the historical city of Bursa, the site of the first Ottoman capital. Upon his return to the capital, Sadik wrote a long and detailed report enumerating all of the impressive projects that the governor-general had overseen and the wonderful state of the city of Bursa.[6] Soon after, Sadik received the official appointment to Bulgaria by imperial decree at the end of October 1904.[7] It was a permanent position, not a temporary one like so many of his career moves up to that point, meaning that his wife and children, now teenagers, could accompany him to the commissioner's residence in the heart of Sofia.

Sadik arrived in Sofia on the first of November and sent a formal telegram to the grand vizier indicating the commencement of his "sacred duty."[8] The Ministry of Foreign Affairs requested that Sadik be paid 20,000Kr in travel expenses and announced that his salary was set at an agreed on 20,000Kr per month. The massive difference between his salary and that of one of the employees in the embassy, which averaged around 1,500Kr, made the commissioner's salary more than thirteen times that of most of his employees. It was unclear whether the money Sadik was paid constituted his personal salary or if it was also meant to cover the expenses he incurred in his official duties.[9]

Sadik wasted no time in meeting with the Bulgarian prime minister the day after his arrival to present his appointment papers. They discussed matters of mutual importance, expressing hopes that issues such as the return of the refugees to their lands would, "God willing (*insha' Allah ta'ala*)," be resolved.[10] Prince Ferdinand was in Varna when Sadik arrived, but he returned to Sofia within a week.[11] However, he would not meet with Sadik for another month, which some observers, like the British representative in Sofia, took as a slight to the Ottomans.

It is important to remember that Sadik did not arrive in Bulgaria without his own prejudices. As an imperialist and Hamidian loyalist, and as someone who had worked on the several commissions in the Balkans and the eastern provinces of the empire, he was part of a cadre of palace advisors animated by a particular perspective on the world. Sadik internalized the belief that the Christian inhabitants of the empire were not only "well-protected" but even privileged and those who rebelled or complained were traitors working to advance the European powers' goals. The British representative in Sofia between 1903 and 1908, Sir George Buchanan, confirmed this view when he first met Sadik. He reported that, upon meeting with Sadik in November of 1904, he wanted to emphasize the importance of coming together to resolve some of the issues that were still causing "friction" between Bulgaria and the Ottoman Empire:

> His Excellency, however, appears to be so perfectly satisfied that the Christian populations in the Turkish Empire enjoy an enviable and privileged position under the benevolent rule of the sultan that nothing, I fear, which I may say, is likely to convince him that there is any foundation for the complaints raised by the Bulgarian Government.[12]

Once the prince and Sadik met, however, he reported that the meeting was rather pleasant and that it lasted for close to an hour, after which he introduced all of the clerks at the commission, one by one, and the prince engaged each of them individually.[13] Knowing Sadik's history, Charles Marling of the British Special Commission in Sofia breathed a sigh of relief when the first meeting between Sadik and Prince Ferdinand finally took place and was "of perfect cordial nature."[14]

Over his three and a half years of service in Bulgaria, Sadik faced two main problems, which eventually took him down. The first was the Bulgarian stonewalling of any effort to resolve outstanding issues, and there were many, including questions of who in the principality could have an Ottoman passport and vice versa;[15] putting down anti-Muslim insurgencies in eastern Rumelia;[16] the status of Muslims in Bulgaria;[17] cross-border smuggling; customs;[18] post and telegraph agreements; border drawing; and extradition of those who Istanbul considered criminal.[19] Needless to say, that kept Sadik very busy, as reports of Bulgarian violations of agreements made any diplomatic progress practically impossible. Sofia was also the center of Young Turk opposition in the Balkans. This made Sadik the first line of defense against antiregime activities, which came to haunt him in the months that followed the Young Turk Revolution in July of 1908, which I discuss later in this chapter.[20]

The other source of frustration was similar to one of Nejib Melhamé's complaints—the lack of support from the Ministry of Foreign Affairs and the Office of the Grand Vizier. Sadik arrived at the commission while it was in a state of disarray. He was left with large files detailing staffing issues, budgetary problems, and general frustration with the Ministry of Foreign Affairs, which seemed nonresponsive to requests for funds needed to cover the most basic maintenance costs and staff salaries. Sadik inherited debts from his late predecessor, Ali Farrukh (Tr. Farruh),[21] who had died while on duty and had been buried in Sofia, leaving behind his family and many unpaid bills for the commissioner's residence and the doctors who looked after him. The situation was so dire that the electric company threatened to cut the electricity to the commission if it was not paid right away. In addition, the cost of upkeep of Ali's family and funeral expenses were left for Sadik to take care of. All of these debts and the cost of transporting Ali's things, horses, and family back to Istanbul were estimated at 60,000Kr.[22]

The Sublime Porte's lack of responsiveness to Sadik's requests eventually turned into what he perceived as harassment. It started with the initial request of this large estimate to settle bills that had been overdue even before his arrival. It quickly deteriorated from there into a conflict of wills and a comparative moral economy of corruption between the Sublime Porte, the palace, and Sadik.

An Impossible Mission

Sadik found his path filled with obstacles set up by the Bulgarian government and made more difficult by the lack of funds from the Sublime Porte, which he complained prevented him from hiring and retaining essential staff in one of the most sensitive diplomatic missions in Europe. Within a few days of his arrival in Sofia, Sadik sent out the first hiring request: replacing two secretaries who had left after an espionage scandal. The scandal had to do with one of the secretaries' assistants being implicated in the theft of sensitive papers and arrested and thrown in jail on suspicion of espionage on behalf of the Serbians. In addition, the assistant's wife and family were left in dire straits, prompting Sadik to ask for *nafaka* covering basic expenses to make sure that they could survive.[23]

A month later, Sadik had not received money to cover the annual expenses estimated at 50,000Kr, including the cost of basic maintenance and monthly salaries, causing him a great deal of frustration and signaling more stonewalling to come.[24] Every expense seemed to be questioned, every lira delayed. For example, 12,000Kr covering the cost of a fete held at the commission to celebrate the sultan's birthday, an important event on the Ottoman official calendar and an indication of the sovereign's presence in this breakaway principality, was questioned and had to be justified in detail by the commissioner.[25]

One of the main sticking points with the Sublime Porte was the hiring of Sadik's cousin and Shafiq's son Vassik, as a second secretary responsible for French translation and correspondence.[26] At twenty years of age, Vassik had only five months of work experience at his father's workplace, the English and French translations office, where he made a humble 570Kr per month.[27] The Azmzade family network was close to reaching its apex at that point as Sadik and Shafiq shepherded the next generation of Azmzades through the ranks. However, despite their years of experience and influence, this was not to be an easy task. Other statesmen with their own interests were watching as money got tighter, and the seemingly endless flow of benefits from the sultan started to fall under scrutiny. So, when Sadik asked to hire his cousin at a salary of 2,000Kr, he faced immediate resistance, first because that amount was well above the rate for even an experienced second secretary of French (who made 1,500Kr); second, because, according to the Sublime Porte, the Bulgarian commission was already well-staffed with all that was needed to carry out its affairs.[28] As a seasoned statesman, Sadik understood the power he had and the levers he could pull. He often did not take no for an answer.

The Ministry of Foreign Affairs protested Sadik's incessant complaining about not receiving the money he had requested. For example, it complained that he was in the habit of requesting 20,000Kr for expenses every time he took the train to Istanbul. By the second month of his employment, he had done that twice, and in one case the ministry claimed his travel was for personal purposes. Additionally, it made the case that travel, which was one of his duties as a diplomat, should not be covered at such a high rate when he was already being paid a monthly salary of 20,000Kr.[29] However, the Ministry of Foreign Affairs balked under pressure when the palace was ready to issue a decree (*irade*) forcing it to pay the money.[30]

While this was going on, the hiring of Sadik's cousin continued to be stalled by no less than the grand vizier himself. At the same time, the Ministry of Foreign Affairs stopped sending the salary for three secretaries in the employ of the commission. Sadik advocated for his staff, and his letters and telegrams became more exasperated as the salaries were delayed by one, two, and even three months. Sadik was advocating not only for the wages of one family member, namely his cousin Vassik, he was also doing this for another person who was soon to join his family through marriage. Within a few months, his seasoned head secretary for French, a man named Salih, would become his son-in-law, which I will discuss later. After several telegrams and letters, the grand vizier ordered that the commission be paid. However, Vassik's salary remained a sticking point.[31]

Budgetary issues and the mistrust of Sadik's handling of money came up repeatedly. Help came from the very top to support Sadik in paying his cousin the unusually high sum of 1,500Kr (reduced from the original 2,000Kr). It came as a decree from the palace, issued by the head secretary's office, where Vassik's father worked. Whether Shafiq had anything to do with this is hard to tell, but his influence likely helped to exert pressure from above.[32] The Ministry of Foreign Affairs acknowledged the necessity of hiring Vassik in order to comply with the decree, but insisted that since the budget of the commission did not have the extra 1,500Kr to spend, it was up to Sadik to find the money.[33]

It seemed that the confirmation of Vassik in his position could not have come any sooner. A few days earlier, a man claiming to be the secretary of a chief rabbi (*haham başı*) by the name of Solomon Yitzhak had written to report that a man named Vassik had given him a "fake" calling card that stated that he was a second secretary at the commission. This incident took place before Vassik was officially hired. Yitzhak threatened that he would go to the newspapers in Sofia to expose this scandal at the "Turkish" government.[34]

Sadik repeatedly wrote justifying the hiring of extra staff and the raises he gave his existing team to retain them, explaining the vital importance of keeping on top of all the press and current events in Bulgaria as other European countries did. He often complained that the Ottoman government did not even have a military attaché in Sofia, unlike the British, Austro-Hungarians, and Russians, for example. He repeated that even with the new hires he was still barely able to keep up with all that had to be done with everything happening in the Balkans.[35]

Every two months, Sadik sent several letters complaining that the salaries for his employees had not been deposited, and his frustration began to show in his tone.[36] In May, then June, then July, he wrote asking for money for salaries that the employees had not received since March of 1905. He was frustrated because some of his best employees had threatened to quit over the lack of payment. At this rate, he said, even the most essential of services performed at the commission would come to a halt. The situation was, he exclaimed, more than we "can bear." "For the love of God, for the love of the Prophet! In the name of the sultan and the honor and solemnity of the state (*Allah Aşkına! Peygamber Aşkına! Padişah efendimizin ve devleti ebedi müddeti şan ve haşyeti namına!*) over and over I have to request our salaries and to rescue us from this pitiful state."[37] A week later, he wrote yet again, complaining that the withholding of salaries was unacceptable.[38] He would eventually receive the money, but often it would not be the full amount.

In less than a year, an investigation into the expenses of the commission was launched by the Ministry of Foreign Affairs and the Ministry of Finance. A detailed schedule of changes in reported expenses of other Ottoman diplomatic missions, year to year, was produced for comparison. Accusations of exaggerated expenses and unnecessary spending, such as the payment for the housing of single, stranded Muslim men from Bucharest in two rooms, were given as an example of unjustifiable expenses. They showed that the commission had increased its spending by an additional 60,000Kr over the year that had passed, comparing it with yearly increases of other Ottoman diplomatic missions in Europe to highlight the difference.[39]

On the scale of what was considered "favors," it seemed that toward the end of Sultan Abdülhamid's rule, the Azmzades were running out of the ability to make things work outside of official channels. Even when a royal decree was issued approving Vassik's hiring, for example, the Ministry of Foreign Affairs only agreed to pay him 1,000Kr per month. That was 500Kr less than what it had agreed upon a few months earlier. The issue turned into a battle of wills between the ministry and Sadik and his palace supporters. Neither side backed down, even eight months after Vassik started working.[40] Eventually, it seemed that the compromise was to keep Vassik on staff at a much-reduced salary.[41]

Sadik, the Ministry of Finance, and the Ministry of Foreign Affairs continued this power struggle until the very last day of Sadik's tenure in Bulgaria. Whether it was an issue of personal conflict, an attempt to sabotage the commission's work, or a proxy war between the Sublime Porte and the palace men is difficult to pin down. The Sublime Porte attempted to exercise its power by inspecting every expense, every akçe spent, and how it should be covered within the existing commission's budget. If there were any complaints filed about delays in depositing money for salaries or basic operational expenses, the ministries came back with a rebuttal and their own set of complaints about the commission's handling of money.[42] The Sublime Porte made every effort to show that this was not a political power play by producing expense schedules and assigning committees to inspect the commission's ledgers. This meant hundreds of hours of Sadik's and commission employees' time spent answering questions, presenting their ledgers, and justifying why they deserved the money they requested. In the meantime, one has to wonder how this might have impacted the work to bolster the empire's position in the Balkans, which Sadik took seriously, even personally.

In March of 1908, a month before Sadik was fired, there was yet another heated exchange after he complained that the "bit by bit (*ceste ceste*)" sending of money to cover the most basic of expenses—salaries, rent, post, telegraph, and the like—was unbearable. This nickel and diming was a source of frustration that he complained about to the grand vizier himself, over and over.[43] The Ministry of Foreign Affairs went to the granular level to prove that the expenses requested by Sadik were not valid. This was followed by a similarly detailed answer from the commission showing what it believed was a reasonable explanation for every item.[44]

The amount of time and effort put into this fight suggests that it was most likely not about a budget-conscious Sublime Porte. It looked more like a political witch hunt, whether the ministries were correct in their estimates or not. Sadik, for his part, pushed the envelope, even giving raises of 500Kr per month due "to increase in expense of living" in Sofia to three of his secretaries, one of whom was his son-in-law Salih. The answer from the Sublime Porte was that such a raise should have been authorized ahead of time, and that the raises "naturally would not be approved."[45]

In between seemingly endless correspondence investigating the commission's expenses, the usual duties of the commissioner continued. Sadik arrived in Sofia at a time when the principality was emboldened to claim complete independence, on its own terms, with the backing of Western powers. Only one month after his arrival, a lengthy opinion piece claiming to represent "the prince, the intellectuals, and the entirety of the Bulgarian people" demanded the Ottoman government's recognition of the complete "independence" of the principality as "other Europeans" did in order to move forward in taking care of their shared interests. The writer expressed disappointment that the role of the "commissioner" was not equivalent to an ambassador or consul general like that of any other foreign diplomatic representative. He insisted that what he referred to as the "commissioner of *evkaf*" was supposed to look after "Mosque properties and the Muslim community." Instead, he complained, the special commissioner reverted to the role of looking into Bulgarian internal state affairs and following the orders of "his sovereign, the sultan."[46]

Whether it was keeping an ear to the ground by following local and international press coverage,[47] keeping an eye on the Bulgarian prince's travels to meet with European heads of state, sifting through rumors of Bulgaria's impending declaration of independence,[48] or investigating disturbances in Rumelia impacting Muslim inhabitants,[49] there was likely a report dispatched for each occasion. For example, after the prince's tour through Rome, London, Paris, and Berlin, Sadik was sure to point out that in Berlin the prince was treated as a mere "vassal" of the Ottoman state, protecting "the right of the sultan (*hakk-ı Hümayun*)" and giving the sultanate the respect (*hürmet*) it deserved. He explained that even though the prince was expecting a "brilliant" reception in Berlin, London, and Paris, it was known that Bulgaria had leanings toward Russia in the first place (*Rusya'ya mütemayil olan nezdinde esassan*), and thus he did not get what he wanted.[50] This statement was followed by a much more detailed and sober analysis of the visits, possible discussions between the prince and various powers, all the while underplaying the significance of Prince Ferdinand's tour of the European imperial capitals.[51]

In the meantime, rumors about the prince's possible visit to the sultan upon his return from Europe caused a great deal of agitation since such visits should have been planned and announced formally, especially considering the delicate relationship between the sovereign and the prince.[52] The grand vizier wrote to Sadik to state the official stance of the Ottoman Empire and to emphasize the importance of the prince holding up his end of agreements before meeting the sultan, including stopping cross-border attacks among other outstanding issues.[53] Although Sadik had some personal successes during his tenure, receiving a promotion to *birinci ferik* (general) in early 1907,[54] the difficult task of walking a fine line between asserting the empire's suzerainty while maintaining a working relationship with the Bulgarian state proved more than he could handle.

The Wedding of His Dreams

Revisiting accusations of the Ministry of Foreign Affairs of unnecessary expenses from a different perspective, it is easy to see how some of Sadik's lavish displays of wealth at the commission's residence might have made him a target of envy and scrutiny. One of those events continues to be talked about until today in the Azmzade family, several generations later. This was the massive wedding celebration of his daughter, Masune, who married his head French secretary, Salih Bey. Sadik announced this to the palace with a letter stating that the wedding was an excellent occasion for people to come together to praise the sultan and renew their commitment to his rule.[55] Salih was born in Lefçe in the eastern Balkans, just east of Edirne. He was thirty-six years old at the time of his marriage, a considerable age difference between him and Masune. He was a seasoned translator educated in Hungary and Switzerland, who knew German, French, English, and Ottoman-Turkish. He had worked at the Ottoman Embassy in Stockholm and the translation office of the grand vizier before joining the Ottoman commission in Bulgaria in 1902.[56] On the occasion of her wedding, Masune received a second-rank Order of Charity (*Şefkat Nişanı*), and Sadik's wife, Esma, received a first-rank Order of Charity, which Sadik followed with a letter of thanks to the sultan.[57] This order was reserved for women who had made an exceptional contribution to humanitarian causes or who had somehow earned the sultan's appreciation. It was made of a red and gold star with green ornamentation. The words "Humanity, Aid, Charity (*İnsaniyet, Yardım, Hamiyet*)" were engraved. The first-order medal given to Esma was adorned with gold, diamonds, emerald, and rubies.[58] What was not mentioned in the thank-you note to the sultan was that the celebration was in fact a double wedding.

Sadik's grandchild, the late Sadiq Jalal al-'Azm, told me that he grew up hearing about this lavish wedding. Sadik's cousin Badi' and his niece Ghida, who lived in Damascus, also got married that day in what appeared to be an arranged match between a rising star in the imperial administration and his second cousin. Arranged marriages meant to keep Azmzade wealth and power in the family unit were a common occurrence. At the time, Badi' had been working in the Public Debt Administration office, alongside his uncle Shafiq, as an assistant to the head of the Office of Legal Affairs, for five years.[59] He would rise to the position of inspector before being sent to the Mosul office of the Public Debt Administration following the Young Turk Revolution.[60] The double wedding was in reality a family reunion taking place in Sofia, with family members traveling from as far as Damascus and Cairo.

The personal use of the commissioner's residence might have raised the ire of some in the Ministry of Foreign Affairs. However, there might have been more scandalous incidents that would have added up to the level of wanting to dismiss Sadik from his position. One, which Sadik reported, involved a large celebration in 1906 to mark the anniversary of the ascension of the sultan to the throne. In preparation for the event, workers were moving fireworks into the commission building when gun powder ignited. This led to one young woman, the sister of Mustafa Efendi, who was employed at the commission as a guard, sustaining severe injuries and losing her eyesight. Sadik wrote that he got her the best care he could find to try to save her eyesight, but it was not to be. He asked that she be given 2,000Kr as a charitable act (10 percent of what he made in a single month) and that her brother be awarded with a medal to ease the suffering of the aggrieved family.[61]

Another reason the Sublime Porte might have made life difficult for Sadik was his constant questioning of the decisions made by the ministries and his attempt to pressure them by reaching out to the palace for help. We have seen him push back when it came to the hiring of his cousin Vassik. He also sent a letter to the sultan asking for the palace's help in exerting pressure on the Sublime Porte to promote his younger brother Iklil, the *kaymakam* (district governor) of the district of 'Ajlun at the time. A trained lawyer, Iklil served as the *kaymakam* of 'Ajlun, Duma, Der'a, and the Beqaa during his lifetime.[62] Apparently, he had been in his current position for two years and was to be moved to yet another district.[63] Writing on his brother's behalf, Sadik explained that Iklil had been led to believe that he would be promoted and rewarded for all the work he had done in 'Ajlun. Instead, he was being moved laterally, and thus he was now "incredibly miserable and hopeless (*fe-vkalgaye ba'is ve nevmide düşer*)," which was why Sadik wanted to reach out to the sultan to intervene and correct this unfair and unexpected victimization (*mağduriyet*) of his brother.[64] In April of 1906, the governor-general of Syria also sent a telegram recommending a higher rank for Iklil to reward his service. The governor-general stated that Iklil managed to collect taxes, keep order, and conduct the census in the region, and for that he deserved the recognition.[65]

Iklil would stay in his position, even though two years later, all of those who had complaints about him, perceiving him as a man favored by the deposed sultan, would come forward. The mayors of three villages in his district would write to the new administration complaining of his despotism. They stated that since arriving in the district "five or six years earlier," he had done nothing for the benefit of the district but had managed to enrich himself. According to the complaints, he pitted one person against the other for his benefit. That resulted in conflicts that he used as the excuse to act with tyranny (*istibdad*), even ordering the beating of some mayors. The mayors expected justice under the CUP's rule.[66] As the reader will see next, the Azmzade's clout in Istanbul almost disappeared under the new administration. Still, Iklil, unlike his uncle Shafiq and his older brother Sadik, would somehow keep his position until 1913, and after World War I would live for a long time and hold on to a great deal of the family's wealth.

A Fall from Grace

It is difficult to understand precisely how Sadik's tenure in Bulgaria came to an abrupt end. There was an official reason for his dismissal, but as was often the case, the reason given might have been a convenient excuse to remove an official whose political capital had run out. In this case, it all started with a hastily arranged visit to meet with the prince and princess of Bulgaria on April 22, at 7 pm. On April 23, Sadik sent a report on the visit, detailing all of the topics that had been brought up. He was careful to mention that it was a social visit and not an official one, and thus the topics discussed were of that nature. He insisted that it went very well, with them exchanging niceties and mentioning the great hospitality that the sultan had generously shown members of the Bulgarian royal family. Sadik also detailed the preparations made for his visit. After greetings, Sadik sat on the left side of the princess and the prince on his right as custom dictated. Then they went into a "care-free and cheerful (*beşuşane ve laubaliyane*)" conversation. The whole visit was described as an enjoyable one with much discussion about the wonderful relations between the principality and the sultan.[67] This was, at least, the version that Sadik relayed to the palace.

The next day the palace was informed about a complaint from the Bulgarian government about the treatment the prince and princess had received, which they considered a slight that could not be repaired, demanding the immediate removal of the commissioner. According to the Bulgarian report, Sadik had shown up at the palace not dressed in his official uniform and not wearing any of his medals, a *faux pas* that finally did him in. Indeed, within the week he would be sent back to Istanbul.[68] A telegram to the Bulgarian representative in Istanbul from the office of the prince detailed what the prince thought was an unforgivable insult:

> The Ottoman commissioner sent an official request for an appointment with her Excellency, the princess. The office of the prince sent him a date and a time for the audience. It was stated that he must attend in full formal dress. As usual, the prince and princess were waiting in full ceremonial dress in the hallway, and the whole suite of staff greeted Sadik Pasha at the entrance. The prince was very shocked and surprised when he saw the commissioner in a frock-coat without epaulet or medals. That was a show of blatant lack of respect for the prince and a serious affront to him. After this incident, there could be no relations between the palace and the Ottoman commissioner. This rugged and uncouth Turk pretends to be a doyen of the diplomatic corps deserving of a special place in the receptions held at the palace. Please inform the Sublime Porte and Yıldız Palace about this incident.[69]

The response from the palace was quick and unequivocal, stating that "the sultan considers the actions of the commissioner unseemly. He ordered a recall of Sadik Pasha back to Istanbul. . . . The palace offered its apologies."[70]

One can speculate as to the actual reason behind such an abrupt dismissal. Was that matter of unseemly informality, in the early twentieth century, given the delicate balance of diplomacy and assertion of sovereignty, all it took to tip the balance toward a break in relations? Was it an excuse to finally listen to the Sublime Porte, which complained about his handling of the commission's finances? Or was it an excuse by the Bulgarian prince to get rid of Sadik, a staunch imperialist, and gain some leverage in choosing who would be sent to replace him? According to a Bulgarian intelligence report from only one month earlier, there was some discussion of Sadik being reassigned as the Ottoman ambassador in Tehran before any of these events unfolded.[71]

Maybe it was something completely different. An event so scandalous that it was not written down in the official document, but one that has become a thing of legends, passed down from generation to generation in the Azmzade family. Indeed, Sadiq Jalal al-'Azm recounted that the family always talked about Sadik's hot temper, which he displayed, regardless of the person who had caused his anger. In this story, relayed to me in 2009, the prince himself was no match for Sadik's temper. Apparently, during a casual conversation in which Sadik felt that the prince did not seem to understand the perils of breaking away from the empire, he did something truly hard to imagine. Sadik lifted the prince by his collar a few inches off the floor, shouting at him: "Is your skull empty?"

Such an incident might sound unimaginable until one understands that outside of the formalities of diplomacy and official correspondence, the imperial elites who socialized with one another as members of the same global social space, often had an affinity that transcended political boundaries and imperial loyalties. Transimperial elite social spaces in the early twentieth century meant that it was not unimaginable that Sadik and Ferdinand often socialized outside of official functions. In fact, Sadik's eldest son, Jelal, was a childhood friend of the future crown prince of Bulgaria, and they maintained their friendship even after the departure of Sadik from Sofia. Thus, in a casual setting, in the privacy of his home, tempers might have gotten heated, and Sadik could indeed have insulted the prince. A personal insult turned into an international incident when the people involved represented two competing royal dynasties. That might have been what happened in this case, or maybe it was a combination of all of the above that eventually led to Sadik's abrupt dismissal.

A decree was issued six days after the reported incident, officially re-
lieving Sadik of his post and requesting the assignment of an "appropriate
alternative" as soon as possible.[72] Two weeks after, the Ottoman ambassador
to Romania, Kamil Bey, was assigned as the new commissioner.[73] Soon after,
Sadik's travel expenses back to Istanbul were requested. This time they were
calculated according to the Ministry of Foreign Affairs' formula and not according to Sadik's habit of requesting 20,000Kr for every trip he took to Istanbul. It amounted to 10,800Kr, calculated based on a percentage of Sadik's
salary multiplied by a factor of the distance between Sofia and Istanbul. He
was paid by the book, down to the akçe.[74] Sadik also requested the settlement
of salaries to be carried out as soon as possible by the Ministry of Foreign
Affairs.[75]

Surprisingly, his cousin Vassik, a second French secretary at the commission under Sadik's son-in-law Salih, was praised and rewarded with a
promotion in rank, a mere four days after the infamous incident.[76] A strange
revelation that took place just before Sadik's dismissal was that Vassik was
only making 800Kr, about half of what he was promised when he first moved
to Sofia. A few weeks later, he was further rewarded by being assigned as
head secretary for the French language at the Bulgarian commission, one of
the most critical positions in the consulate and the position formerly held by
Sadik's son-in-law.[77] There was a catch, however. He was not to be paid the
salary of a head secretary. He remained at 800Kr, less than one-third of what
the former head secretary of French earned, who had been paid a decent
3,000Kr per month.[78] Why was this the case? No documents give a clear
answer, but one has to wonder whether Vassik helped make a case for the
departure of Sadik and was promised a promotion in return.

One should keep in mind that a whole new administration came into
power within a few months of Sadik's return to Istanbul. Izzet, arguably
the most potent Arab-Ottoman in the palace, ran away when the Young
Turk Revolution took place. In addition, the commission shut down because,
soon after the coup, the Principality of Bulgaria declared independence from
the Ottoman Empire in October 1908. When he left, Vassik was sure to
remind the Ministry of Foreign Affairs of his loyalty, continuing to work
for the humble sum of 800Kr per month, forcing him to spend "twenty to
thirty thousand Kurush" from his personal savings to make ends meet. He

requested a position at the level of second secretary in another diplomatic mission.[79] As we will see in Chapter 8, he would eventually get his wish and his diplomatic career would take off as those of his father and cousin were coming to an end.

The Dissolution

It is hard to overestimate the Young Turk Revolution's impact on the lives of those closest to the eye of the storm, the palace advisors and administrators. Some saw the writing on the wall and jumped ship in the nick of time, like Shafiq, whose ability to reinvent himself as a representative of Syria championing the Arab-Ottoman cause was an impressive chameleon act that spared him for a little while. Sadik was not as lucky, however, for along with many other statesmen in the government's military and civil service, he was initially swept up in a large "purification" dragnet that momentarily looked like the end of his career.

Many of those who felt wronged by the Hamidian regime came forward with complaints against those who had been in charge. Sadik was no exception, with a case brought against him for illegally shutting down the Ottoman-Turkish-language newspaper put out by an anti-Abdülhamid man named Mustafa Ragib (Ar. Raghib), who had played an important role as a Young Turk in the Balkans, based in Bulgaria. Sadik had attempted to convince the Ottoman government to curb Mustafa Ragib's activities by turning him into an asset and giving him a post in the administration. However, this suggestion was rebuffed, and the government chose instead to continue to suppress his influence. After many years, Sadik finally convinced the Bulgarian government to arrest and deport Mustafa Ragib to Istanbul.[80] Now the tables had turned, and a case was opened against Sadik for persecuting a Young Turk revolutionary.[81]

The tables had turned indeed. The *Tasfiye-i Rütebi Askeriye Kanunu* (Purification of Military Ranks Law) was used to punish members of the military who were considered loyal to the sultan. Signed into law in August of 1909, it was touted as a way to demote those that were deemed to have been promoted through corrupt means. According to its preamble, the law was put into place to rectify the undeserved promotions for members of the military who were deemed not to have spent the prescribed time in a certain rank or who were considered not to have the needed training or skills necessary to execute the responsibilities of their position.[82] Sadik, an undoubtedly loyal advisor to the deposed sultan, was caught up in the web of this new law. As I have highlighted before, his promotions from one rank to the next were rather meteoric; sometimes he stayed in one rank for only a few months before being given another promotion. Ranks were handed out to people like Sadik the same way that medals and commendations were, as rewards for a job well done or acknowledgments of loyalty and service to the sultan. Stripping a military man of his rank was not only a public humiliation tactic within the military or professional arena,[83] it could reach into his titles and his status in Ottoman society as a whole. Honorary titles, such as Bey and Pasha signified belonging to an elite class, and even an Ottoman form of "nobility." How one earned these titles changed a great deal over time. In the late nineteenth century, the way one earned such titles became much more regularized and policed. Once earned or conferred, a title became inseparable from how a person was referred to in public, attached to his first name and symbolizing public acknowledgment of belonging to a particular class or profession, in many ways similar to the way surnames came into use. To put it another way, if, as James Scott explains, a surname was meant to make one legible and traceable by the state, titles were there to make the person legible to Ottoman society.[84] The class, professional belonging, and social status inferred by titles were fundamental to one's way of negotiating his place in Ottoman society. A demotion of title, not just of rank, took on meaning well beyond its professional implications. It could be thought of as a psychologically calamitous event, a fracture in one's habitus, similar to being expelled from one's tribe or, to follow Bourdieu's terminology, losing one's place in the social space one had inhabited.

In the case of the military, in the late nineteenth century one earned a title based on one's rank. Sadik earned the title of Pasha, the highest title one could earn in the Ottoman hierarchy of titles, as an outcome of being promoted to the rank of *mirliva* (major general) from the rank of *miralay* (colonel).[85] With the use of a table that dictated the length of time a member of the military had to stay in a specific rank, taking into consideration conditions of service (such as the harshness of the environment he served in) the military court demoted Sadik by three levels, from *birinci ferik* (general) to *miralay*, in the process stripping him of his title of Pasha, which he never regained, and returning to him the title of Bey.[86]

The demotion had financial implications too, not just in terms of salary but also in terms of the pension Sadik would receive and the compensation his widow would get once he passed away. Although he was still relatively young, at just over 50 years of age, Sadik decided to choose retirement over employment at a demoted rank. Nevertheless, within a few months he took up a new challenge, albeit with less pay and a lower rank. Jeddah, one of the most important cities in the Hijaz—the port of entry for those coming for the hajj and the city where all foreign councils set up their operation in Ottoman Arabia—was in tatters after the reign of military governor Ahmed Ratib Pasha. Soon after the revolution, Ratib was taken to Istanbul, where he stood trial for years of corruption.[87] His assets were seized, but his years of rule in the province meant that a great deal of work had to be done to regain the trust of the locals and improve the failing infrastructure of this strategically and symbolically important city. While Ratib's demise was covered closely in the newspapers in Istanbul, the administration was busy trying to find people who could take up the challenges of governance and administration in this Arab-majority province.[88]

A big part of the challenge was to find experienced civil servants and diplomats when so many had been purged in the immediate aftermath of the deposition of Sultan Abdülhamid II. A number of former high-level administrators had run away, been dismissed, demoted, or in some cases imprisoned or executed. That meant that the new regime had to go back on many of its decisions, asking those accused of incompetence, corruption, or of being supporters of "tyranny" to come back and take up posts in the running of the empire. However, finding men with suitable experience who spoke fluent Arabic and French proved much harder than anticipated. Finally, Sadik was assigned as the district governor (*kaymakam*) of Jeddah, which was later changed to *mutasarrıf* of Jeddah after the administrative reorganization of the region. He agreed to come out of retirement for an assignment close to his heart. He was familiar with the region, having worked there less than a decade earlier when he was responsible for the extension of the telegraph line; he was an experienced diplomat who could interact with the European counselors stationed in the city; and he was a proven Arab-Ottoman imperial loyalist in this geopolitically sensitive part of the empire.[89] Years of service in the Ottoman administration came back full circle to his Arabic language skills, allowing him to reenter the service as an "expert" on the conditions of the Arab-majority provinces.

The Final Journey

Sadik passed away in October of 1910, less than a year after his arrival in Jeddah. He had contracted a waterborne disease and left for treatment in Istanbul, or, as *Lisan al-Hal* in Beirut put it more subtly, for a "change of air."[90] He must have known he was gravely ill because a month before he died, he requested that he be moved somewhere near Medina, asking for only a small stipend of a "few hundred Kurush." He wanted to be close to the holy cities in his final days, in an act known a *mücaveret*. A special request was sent to the governor of Medina during Sadik's final days. It was approved, but by then it was too late.[91]

He was buried in Istanbul. His remains would later be moved to his childhood home of Damascus. A note from the Ministry of Interior to the governor-general of Hijaz simply stated, "On the 3rd of October 1326 (October 16, 1910), Sadik al-Mu'ayyad passed away. Find a suitable and honest person to appoint in his place."[92] The governor-general replied with a telegram that praised Sadik's service. He described him as a man who bravely stood up to corruption and was able to plan and start several projects for the good of the city with "purity of heart and competence."[93]

During the short time he was in Jeddah, Sadik worked hard, managing to extend the drinking water supply to the city.[94] Some even said he introduced electricity to the city, but I found no documentary evidence to back this claim. His death was announced in newspapers in Istanbul, Damascus, and Beirut. The obituary in the newspaper was written by his uncle Shafiq, a deputy representing the Province of Syria at the time. *Al-Ittihad al-'Uthmani*, a newspaper published in Beirut, eulogized him, stating that he spent fifty years in the service of the government and the fatherland . . . his loss is a great loss for the Ottoman fatherland in general and the Arab *'unsur* in particular."[95] In the *Musaver Nevsal Osmani* journal, his obituary inaccurately stated that his military rank when he died was *kaymakam*. It read: "He was an aide-de-camp to the sultan for a long time when he was assigned on missions to Abyssinia and Sudan. He was also in the position of commissioner in Bulgaria, and he achieved the rank of general (*birinci ferik*). In the recent purification [of ranks], he was demoted to *kaymakam*. After choosing to retire, he was assigned as the mutasarrıf of Jeddah."[96]

Sadik left all his worldly possessions in Jeddah with the expectation that he would be back. The list of his possessions told of a life filled with finer things, a history of service to the Ottoman government, and a pious existence. Every item he had with him was counted and recorded. Many of them were gold, diamond, and other precious-stone medals, jewelry, kilims, and gold ashtrays. The rest were simpler necessities; prayer rugs, curtains, and various items of clothing. Surprisingly, the list even included children's clothing, cutlery, and bedsheets. They were all recorded and, at the request of his wife, Esma, and his daughter, Masune, were delivered to his son-in-law Salih. Salih, who had left the Ottoman commission in Sofia with his father-in-law a couple of years earlier, landed on his feet in the new administration, working as the head of the privy office in the Ministry of Foreign Affairs.

Among Sadik's possessions was documentation of thousands of Ottoman liras and French francs in bank accounts stretching from Istanbul to Lyon.[97] Tracing the money, which should have been Esma's after his death, proved difficult and disappointing. Letters were left behind asking for the deposit amount in a bank in Lyon and one in Vienna, for example, with some replying that they did not have any accounts in Sadik's name.[98] Sadik's death was unexpected, as he did not seem to have had his affairs in order, causing his wife and children difficulties in trying to get hold of his worldly processions.

Sadik was spared the worst of the persecution that some Arab-Ottomans would later face, whether in the Levant or Istanbul. Sadik's immediate family fared much better than his brothers' families in Damascus and Shafiq's in Istanbul. They were spared the humiliation of internment that his cousins and uncles would face when some Arab-Ottomans became suspect Others in the fog of World War I. In fact, there is evidence that Sadik's family was able to retain the *konak* in which they lived in Teşvikiye, even though, traditionally, once a statesman ended his service, his *konak* should have reverted to the palace. A large fire that swept through the neighborhood in 1919 took down

"Sadik's *konak*," as it was referred to in the newspaper.[99] Some members of the Turkish side of Sadik's descendants, coincidentally, continued to live in Nişantaşı, a few blocks from where his house once stood. His untimely death spared him the agony of the loss of his empire and beloved imperial capital, Istanbul.

In this chapter, Sadik reached the apex of his career followed by an abrupt fall that came mere months before the coup that ended the palace's domination and the Hamidian regime from which he rose. Like many loyalists of his generation, he saw his career cut short, losing much of his clout and his source of power. Not all Arab-Ottoman imperialists disappeared from public life after the Young Turk Revolution. Many, including Shafiq, reinvented themselves as parliamentarians and statesmen in the new regime and as representatives of Ottoman provinces with an Arab *unsur* majority. As Chapter 7 will show, Shafiq managed to build an alternative political career by modeling himself as a defender of Arab-Ottoman rights, only to face obstacles at every turn that ultimately led to his demise.

CHAPTER 7

THINGS FALL APART

A Turk calling an Arab *Arap* as an insult is completely
outside of the realm of possibility. It goes completely
against our hearts, spirit, and ideology.
                              —Hüseyin Cahid, October 3, 1909[1]

THROUGHOUT THE REIGN OF ABDÜLHAMID II, THE AZMZADES
could count on the support of the palace and a network of family members
across the empire. Shafiq was a critical node in this network, with his influence reaching as far as Damascus, Aleppo, Beirut, and Cairo. However, like
many palace men the Azmzades faced an existential threat when Abdülhamid lost control. Many career diplomats, bureaucrats, and administrators of
various stripes had to quickly and convincingly reinvent themselves in order
to survive the revolutionary fervor during the Second Constitutional Period
(*İkinci Meşrutiyet Devri*). This was especially challenging for those perceived
to be closest to the sultan himself.

Out of all Arab-Ottomans who worked in the inner circle of the palace
during the Hamidian period, Izzet, who was referred to by some Turkish-
language press in 1908 as Arap İzzet, was arguably the most powerful. The
appellation *Arap* in this case was a source of great frustration for Arab-
Ottoman politicians in Istanbul. Within days of the coup, they wrote to the

editor-general at *Tanin* complaining about what they considered an inflammatory practice of deploying *Arap* as an insult. As I discussed in Chapter 4, by the late nineteenth century, the signifier *Arap* was not a neutral term denoting a judgment-free place of origin but a practice meant to other through an ethnoracial label in an increasingly ethnoracially differentiated Ottoman Istanbul. Thus, it could not have come as a surprise to the editor when he received a complaint from "Arabs from honorable families," who wrote to the pro–Committee of Unity and Progress (CUP) daily newspaper requesting that it ceases this inflammatory practice. The editor of the newspaper was no other than the deputy from Istanbul, Hüseyin Cahid (Yalçın), who printed a long response, insisting that "A Turk calling an Arab *Arap* as an insult is completely outside of the realm of possibility. It goes completely against our hearts, spirit, and ideology."[2] However, the newspaper acquiesced and agreed to stop referring to him as Arap İzzet.

After fleeing with all his liquid assets safely stored in foreign bank accounts, Izzet became the symbol of the corruption of the Hamidian period and an easy excuse for CUP members to point the finger at Arab-Ottomans who surrounded Sultan Abdülhamid II as part of the problem that ailed the empire. Izzet maintained his innocence of all accusations and went into exile with his family in complete luxury. As a sign of his defiance, soon after he arrived in London, he gave an interview in which he calmly expressed his thanks to the sultan for standing by him. He insisted that he had been planning on leaving Istanbul and retiring much earlier, but out of devotion to his country and at the request of the sultan, whom he portrayed as someone who could not function without him, he stayed until the latest events. He said that one day "I returned home to find an order from the sultan to travel to Europe," producing the note to show it to the reporter. He then thanked the sultan and said, "His majesty did not hand over his servant and has not abandoned him during this crisis. . . . When I received a note informing me that I should not take the postal service boat because the Young Turks were intent on humiliating me, I rented the British ship *Maria*, and left on it to England. My wife and my children, three boys and girls, were on the Princes Islands (*Adalar*) at the time, so we passed on our way and picked them up."[3] What Izzet might have not appreciated at the time was that he had lost Istanbul, and the many homes he built there, forever. Within a decade all other

Arab-Ottoman citizens of the empire would lose Istanbul as their imperial capital as well.

No one can argue that Izzet was not one of the most important influencers in the Hamidian regime, both in Istanbul and in the Arabic-speaking-majority provinces, and dismissing him simply as the corrupt "Arap İzzet" has left one of the most complex characters and loyal imperialists, and his impact on the history of the region, understudied. However, this is where I leave Izzet to return to another Arab-Ottoman imperialist who was more optimistic about the future.

In this chapter, I catch up with Shafiq after he reinvented himself as a parliamentarian representing the Province of Syria. He successfully recast himself long enough to become an influential voice in the Levant and a leader of an Arab-centered political party in Istanbul. He brought with him other Arab-Ottomans who were determined to work within the Ottoman structure of rule, but they were vociferous about what they perceived as growing anti-Arab discrimination. He lasted less than four years, during which he endured very public attacks questioning his loyalty and his recent past as a palace man, and even bringing some of the skeletons out of his personal closet for all of the empire to see. Examining the last few years of Shafiq's life gives the reader the chance to understand the experience of being an Arab-Ottoman politician as cultural identification became an issue of public debate and ethnoracial difference part of the political discourse, leaving no doubt that for some Arab-Ottomans anti-Arab sentiment was a reality well before the beginning of World War I.

Liberté, Égalité, Fraternité

Shafiq left his position in the palace soon after the coup to run as a representative of the Province of Syria in the parliament. His family continued their life in Istanbul, seemingly with no fear of retribution against them. Initially, it seemed that he had escaped the anti-Hamidian witch hunt that had claimed others like Sadik. Years later, Shafiq's son-in-law 'Abd al-Qadir, painted him as a reluctant hero who shunned the limelight of politics but who felt the responsibility of accepting the nomination for the parliament, leaving behind a monthly income of 20,000Kr as a commissioner at the Tobacco Régie for the uncertainty of politics and the humble salary of 2,000Kr. His son-in-law asked him why he had left his well-paying position to become eligible to run for the parliament. Shafiq answered that if he had said no to the nomination, how could he have "faced those that nominated and granted [him] their trust and confidence."[4]

He quickly found out how inhospitable Istanbul political life was. Soon after being elected to the lower chamber, he faced a vicious campaign to discredit him and sow fear and suspicion toward Arab-Ottoman politicians. Shafiq and some other deputies from Arab-majority districts, like Shitwan Bey, the deputy from Benghazi, faced loud shouts of disapproval from other deputies every time they stood up to speak on the floor of the lower chamber, accusing them of being spies for Abdülhamid II or Izzet al-'Abid.[5] The disruptions were often hard to control and parliamentary sessions would have to be suspended for the day. Within days of the opening of the parliament, official reports (*mazbatalar*) questioning the legitimacy and legality of their elections were filed.

The attacks did not seem to stop Shafiq and others from taking a political stance that offered an alternative understanding of the Young Turk's slogan, adopted from the French Republic, "liberté, égalité, fraternité (*hürriyet, müsavat, uhuvvet*)."[6] Protecting the rights of Arab-Ottomans' claim to the Ottoman fatherland as equal citizens became his rallying cry and it placed him in the crosshairs of politicians willing to wage a character assassination campaign to discredit him and his colleagues. They dug deep into his past to find dirt in his personal life that involved his late wife Nimet and their dead infant. They even brought it up on the floor of the lower chamber of deputies, on the steps of the Çırağan Palace, and in the drawing rooms of Istanbul's high society.

Soon after the revolution, members of the Arab *unsur* began to publicly demand "equality." For example, Ibrahim Abu Khater, a resident of Zahleh (in today's Lebanon), lamented the lack of an organized Arab political party even though he stated that ironically that Arabs in Ottoman lands were probably the only group that had not worked toward "nationalist goals." According to Abu Khater, the Greeks, the Armenians, and even the Albanians had organized to demand their rights while "the Turks have worked to dominate the rest."[7] He was expressing a sentiment that many who understood the importance of political organization shared. For the ink was not yet dry on the agreement signed by Sultan Abdülhamid II to reinstate the parliament before Shafiq began to politically organize.

One of his first actions as a deputy was to apply for a license to establish two newspapers to promote his vision of an Ottoman future. He described them as "political, literary, scientific, and sociological" newspapers, one in Arabic titled *al-Ikha'* (*The Brotherhood*) and the other in Ottoman-Turkish called *Uhuvvet-i Osmaniye* (*Ottoman Brotherhood*).[8] Shafiq published an editorial in *al-Ittihad al-'Uthmani* introducing the public to these newspapers, and inviting qualified people from Iraq and Syria and other "Arab regions" to apply. This Ottoman Brotherhood, the editor of the paper stated, was desperately needed, "for if Ottomans are united and work together, then bring them the good news of a bright and prosperous future that could even overtake Japan . . . however, if we insist on discussing the issues at hand as Arabs, Turks, Kurds, and Armenians and each attacks the other to become more fanatical in pursuing the interest of their own team [to the exclusion of other] becoming traitors (like some newspapers do now) then our progress is impossible." The editor continued to discuss the importance of looking out for the good of all and the importance of the fraternity of "Arabs" and "Turks" for the sake of the survival of the empire.[9] This sentiment was pushed by politicians and editors of newspapers in Arab-majority provinces and Istanbul alike, while an undercurrent of mistrust brewed just below the surface.[10] Similarly, *İkdam* addressed parliamentarians warning of the dangers of "*nasyonalizm*," saying, "You are not the representatives of your own people [only] . . . you have the trust of all Ottomans . . . Turks or Greeks, Bulgarians or Armenians, or whomever they might be."[11]

One of Shafiq's cousins, Rafiq Azmzade, initially thought that it was too early to create a new party lest it gives the CUP the wrong impression. He even wrote to Shafiq stating his concerns, but he assured him that the Brotherhood Party was similar to other parties established by other ethnic groups in the empire and that it would allow the Arabs to have a united and strong voice.[12] Rafiq, who was initially a member of the CUP party, felt that it was very poor timing, especially since rumors of Arab separatist activism were making headway in the Turkish-language press, driving some CUP members to become paranoid that their "brothers who have been by their side through

the good and the bad times," might be working against the interests of a
united empire.[13]

Soon after, Rafiq realized that the CUP's mistrust had become a form
of cultural war for domination. He cited examples of discrimination against
Arab-Ottomans across all levels of the government, whether it were in the
distribution of cabinet positions, positions in the upper ranks of the military,
and governorships; or the preferential treatment given to Turkish-speaking
employees even when they were not qualified for the positions they were
hired for.[14] After a short stay in Istanbul in 1909, Rafiq returned to Cairo,
where he published an editorial in which he expressed his alarm at what
he interpreted as opportunistic efforts by the CUP to discriminate against
non-Turkish-Ottomans, especially Arab-Ottomans. He stated that the previous "despotic government," which had maintained its control through "co-
ercion and force" could have forcibly "assimilated" all of the Ottoman peoples
into the "Turkish nationality" or could have usurped all rights of the Arab-
Ottomans and concentrated all mechanisms of "rule and authority" in the
"Turkish race," yet it did not. So how does it make sense, he continued, that
a "constitutional government in the time when people have soaked up democratic principles would try to carry this out? . . . Of course, no sane person
can imagine that our Turkish brothers who were at the forefront of the fight
for personal freedoms, would be the ones subjugating the rest of the Ottoman races, especially the Arabs, who stood shoulder to shoulder with the
Turks since the 3rd century [*Hijri*]." He ended his column by calling all this
a misunderstanding and the work of a few "fanatical" CUP members, and
he warned that people should not make the mistake of judging all Turkish-
Ottomans as being uniformly against Arabs. Simply, "Turks know that they
are Turks first and Ottoman second, so the same goes for the Arabs, Albanians, and the Greeks, and all of the Ottoman races. Yet that does not
negate the fact that we are all one nation working toward the happiness of
the fatherland and raising the standard of the [Ottoman] government whose
shadow protects all of us." Not correcting this misunderstanding could be
catastrophic, he warned, because if divided, everybody would then find themselves at the mercy of Europeans.[15]

A few months later, Rashid Rida, Rafiq's friend and the founder of the *al-
Manar* journal in Cairo, traveled to Istanbul and published an article in *İkdam*,

addressing its readers. He repeated Rafiq's warnings from a few months earlier by quoting the famous Turkish-Ottoman author and intellectual Namık
Kemal: "Turks and Arabs are the twins of the Hanafi tree. They are two brothers in an Ottoman union, the two bases supporting the structure of the Ottoman caliphate. Whoever desires to dissolve the bond between the two is the
devil, and this devil is the enemy of God." Rida said that, instead of one devil,
they were living through the age of two devils, the first was "European political ambitions" and the second was "the ignorance of many people on either
side." He insisted that all that had been happening was a result of paranoia
and "misunderstanding" stating that rumors about efforts to start a competing
Arab caliphate or the notion that Arab-Ottomans wanted to separate were
untrue. He said that both rumors were leftovers from the Hamidian period
and no longer held any truth. Yet they were published and republished, causing paranoia and further misunderstanding in the Turkish-language press.[16]

Whether the CUP's policies were part of a program of Turkification,
forced assimilation, centralization, or none of the above, has been well debated in the field. These debates attempt to analyze the words and deeds of
CUP member to understand if what was taking place was nascent ethnic
nationalism disguised as centralization reforms or was a misguided effort at
bringing the empire together to espouse unity and cultural affinity among
the various ethnic groups that made up the Ottoman Empire. When it came
to the day-to-day lives of Arab-Ottomans living in the provinces, this was
not only an academic or political question. It was an existential one, often
expressed as perceived discrimination against Arab-Ottomans. These accusations exploded onto the public scene soon after the censorship laws were
relaxed after 1908.

Many historians have argued that "Turkification," at least until 1913, was
not a form of Turkish nationalism or anti-Arab assimilationist policy.[17] It
was a form of state centralization that continued Abdülhamid-era policies
in the hope of creating a unified "national" identity. The assumption is that
accusation of forced Turkification was forwarded at the time by politicians
running against the CUP in Arab-majority provinces.[18] I contend that such
an argument assumes that Arab-Ottoman politicians' audiences were limited to provincial Arab-Ottomans while Turkish-Ottoman politicians were
representatives of the central imperial state. It does not take into account

Arab-Ottomans like Shafiq and his family, whose very sense of self was tied to their identification with an Ottoman metropole and the empire *as a whole*. In the lives of the penultimate generation of Arab-Ottomans closest to the center of power, this was about much more than pandering to a limited Arab-Ottoman audience in Arab-majority provinces. It was an existential fight, a struggle to interpret notions of *liberté*, *égalité*, and *fraternité* in a way that empowered them and their families to claim the Ottoman Empire as their own as well and on their own terms. An interpretation of this motto envisioned a "multicultural" imperial citizenship where they could have a place at the table as equals with Turkish-Ottomans and not simply as a tolerated ethnic group in a Turkish-dominated multi-ethnic, multi-confessional empire. That was the only interpretation they were willing to adopt. It is crucial to understand that for Shafiq and his Arab-Ottoman contemporaries in Istanbul, this fight was not only a political struggle; it was a personal one.

Keeping this in mind, it becomes easier to understand why the Azmzades were from the beginning of the CUP era at the forefront of the culture wars, waged with quiet trepidation of what might come in the near future. The wars were carried out on the pages of newspaper trading jabs across the empire from Istanbul to Beirut, at gentlemen's clubs in Beyoğlu, and in the salons of Nişantaşı, Beşiktaş, and Bostancı. It was no longer a matter of which ethnic or religious groups would be counted as part of the Ottoman *millets*. It was about defining the future of Ottoman citizenship: Which forms of performing Ottoman citizenship were considered legitimate? Which spoken language(s) were to be fostered and which were to be relegated to the religious or private spheres, or completely repressed? Which forms of cultural representation and ethnic identification were to be sponsored by the Ottoman state and promoted in the Ottoman education system, military institutions, courts, city halls, and the parliament? Whose version of history was to be elevated above others?

The Significance of Language

Debates raged about multiculturalism, ethnonationalism, and even the virtues and failures of Ottoman assimilation and methods of imperial rule. Only a few weeks after the coup, the issue came up in relation to Turkish-language proficiencies of Arab-Ottoman deputies. The language of discussion in the parliament was Turkish, so for non-native Turkish-speaking deputies, it was impossible to express their opinions in any forceful way without knowing the language fluently. This meant, for example, that the Province of Yemen, a strategic frontier province of the empire, at one point was left with no local representative. None of the Yemeni politicians interested in running for the parliament knew Turkish well enough to qualify, triggering a debate over the language policy at the Ministry of Interior.[19] This was not a new issue. It was codified in the first constitution in 1876 when Turkish—not Ottoman-Turkish—was designated as the official language of the state. Deputies sent to Istanbul were given four years to become fluent. In 1876, wider implications of this policy were not explored because it did not have the chance to be tested before the parliament was suspended. A requirement to make fluency in Turkish mandatory effective immediately was struck down in 1909.[20] However, some CUP members felt a certain urgency to enforce it, not just in the parliament but across the empire.

The language issue was taken up by politicians and some newspapers in the capital, which forwarded a vision of an empire that had to choose one language. For newspapers like *İkdam* and *Tanin,* it was simple: Turkish was the only acceptable choice. They advocated the mandatory promotion of "purified" Turkish as the "logical" official language to be taught across the empire to allow the illiterate majority to become literate quickly, since Ottoman-Turkish was only known by a well-educated few.[21] The editors at *İkdam* made the editorial choice to try to eliminate Arabic and Persian loanwords from their newspaper, to whichever level possible, defending this choice by saying, "Our language has an inherent logic that it is almost mathematical. When we insist on violating its established grammar and rules with Arabic and Persian constructions . . . we will never have an independent language."[22] Similarly, *Tanin* openly advocated the use of a "purified" Turkish, or what others referred to as "pure Turkish" (*Öz Türkçe*) as opposed to new Turkish, that is, Ottoman-Turkish (*Osmanlica*), arguing that it would be easier to teach to a wider swath of the Ottoman population once Arabic and Persian words and grammar had been excised or reduced.[23]

That attitude often put Turkish-language newspapers and their CUP supporters on the defensive, fending off the complaints of Arab-Ottoman politicians and Turkish-Ottoman literary figures. For example, *İkdam*'s editor-general responded to two columns in *al-Iqbal*, published in Beirut, and in *al-Liwa'*, published in Cairo, in a long editorial filled with backhanded insults interspersed with his attestation to the debt of Ottoman-Turkish to Arabic that "every Turk is well aware of." Using famous Arabic quotes and couplets to belittle the ideas presented by the two Arabic-language newspapers and to highlight his knowledge of Arabic, he summed up his dismissal of Arabic-language newspapers' concerns with a famous Arabic saying: "If you got poor testimony about your character from a degenerate, then you should take it as a testimony to your virtue."[24]

Al-Ittihad al-'Uthmani in Beirut and *al-Muqtabas* in Damascus fiercely defended the use of Arabic in public institutions and called out the "purification" of the language as nothing more than a way to further marginalize Arab-Ottomans. They rejected the argument of purification for the sake of simplification, saying that the subject of purifying a language had at one point even been debated for Arabic, which has many Persian loanwords, but it was concluded that "organic" borrowing from other languages made a language richer.[25] Similarly, an article adapted from the French newspaper *Le Temps* recalled the mixing of:

> [the languages] of the Turonian immigrants with Persians who are Arians, and Arabs who are Semites, whose tongues and blood also mixed. To try to disentangle them would be like trying to separate blood platelets flowing through a single body, and attempting to cleanse the language would be like trying to drain blood from a piece of flesh. No Turk, unless they could go back to their simple traditions, conditions, and lifestyle that they had in the Middle Ages (in fact, they would have to go back to their time in Central Asia), would ever be able to strip Arabic and Persian words from their language, regardless of how long their arguing and fighting continues. The needs of the age made them rely on these languages since their mother tongue was incapable of meeting the time's needs.[26]

In the context of the early twentieth century, advocating for a "purified" official language, which assumed a default citizen whose native tongue was "pure Turkish" contradicted a vision of the Ottoman future that considered equality between Turkish- and non-Turkish-Ottomans a foundational principle. The language debate had a direct impact on representation and not only

in the Chamber of Deputies. It quickly trickled down to the various ranks
of the imperial and provincial administration and to the humble clerks in
courthouses in Damascus, Sanaa, and Beirut. This prompted those running
for election in Arab-majority provinces to highlight the issue, promising to
put it at the top of their agenda if they were sent to Istanbul.[27] One writer in
Lisan al-Hal emphasized that everybody in the empire should have access to
learning Turkish but that all judges and government employees sent to places
like "Beirut, Syria, Hijaz, Yemen, and Jerusalem" should know Arabic, the
language of the locals, for without it the government and court staff would
be unable to serve the locals' needs.[28]

Arab-Ottoman-Turk

Haqqi, Esma's brother and the famous politician and writer who would become the prime minister of Syria in 1932, initially supported the CUP and
continued to be a part of the Ottoman political system until World War I.[29]
His name was even put forward as a potential nominee to replace a deputy from Syria who had passed away in 1911.[30] Looking back on this period,
he wrote that opposition to the policies of the CUP had begun only a few
months "after the commencement of the first parliamentary session . . . it
was proven that the unionists [the CUP] were determined to oppress the
Arabs by usurping their rights and treating them unfairly in word and deed.
So, the [Arab] representatives began to complain about this poor treatment,
and the Arabic newspapers began discussing this issue at length, explaining
to the Arab Ottomans the bad policies of the unionists."[31]

In this charged environment, the Ottoman Brotherhood Party was established, with Shafiq and Sadik signing their name as two of the founding
members. They typed their name in its Arabic form—al-'Azm. This was a
significant choice and one that reflected a new kind of self-fashioning, particularly by Shafiq. In 1908, Shafiq added a seal to his official correspondence
featuring his full name in its Arabic form, along with his handwritten signature: "Azmzade, Shafiq al-Mu'ayyad." Other family members in similar
circumstances chose to maintain the Ottoman-Turkish form on their seal
until the end, including his nephew Sadik.[32]

Ethnocentric political groups were illegal, and anything that resembled
a minority political organization was deemed a form of anti-Turkishness.

Rumors often spread in the Turkish-language press about secret Greek and
Arab or Greek and Armenian unified opposition to the Turkish majority in
the parliament.[33] Arab-Ottoman parliamentarians were often the primary
target of these attacks. *Tanin*'s editor and a deputy from Istanbul, Hüseyin
Cahid, often took direct aim at Arab-Ottoman deputies. He wrote that if
news of the establishment of an "Arab party" were true, it would be unconsti-
tutional, citing several articles that prohibited ethnocentric political parties
since they were thought to be a threat to "the unity of the Ottoman people."[34]

Some parliamentarians came to the defense of the Arab-Ottoman politicians. Sinop's deputy, Rıza Nur, wrote explaining that, as in most "civilized
nations," there should be left and right parties. The party that was proposed
was not an Arab-only party, he wrote, but one that was a centrist "moderate"
party, and that anybody was welcome to join.[35] A Greek-language newspaper
attacked the editor of *Tanin* for implying that the newly formed party included sixty-six Arab-only members, and stated that similar slander was directed toward Greeks, Albanians, and Armenians in the parliament, as *Tanin*
seemed to forward a claim of an anti-Turkish conspiracy.[36] *Tanin* continued
to report on meetings in private residences, pointing out that all those in
attendance were indeed only deputies from Arab-majority provinces and administrative zones stretching from (Deir al) Zor to Tripoli and from Yemen
to Mosul.[37]

Hüseyin was one of many who shared the opinion that Arab-Ottoman
politicians organizing or joining political parties outside of the control of the
CUP was the result of a failure of the Ottoman regime to assimilate "Arabs"
into what he considered to be an Ottoman ideal. Non-assimilation was often
discussed as the weakness of the ancient Ottoman conquerors and portrayed
as an issue represented by the "language problem" and the "race problem."[38]
Arabic should have survived, but only as a religious language for "if the con-
quering Ottomans [had] thought of unifying the various ethnicities, then
many peoples whom they ruled, regardless of how varied they were, would
have accepted the tongue of Turkey. . . . Just like when Arabs conquered the
land of Christians who then became marginal and unimportant, it would
have worked in this [the Ottoman] case." Lamenting a missed opportunity
at assimilation was usually followed by a suggestion that it was high time

that the "language of the Ottomans, *Turkish* [my emphasis]" be mandatory in all schools and for everybody. Changing course now because of complaints coming from the "Arabian Provinces (*Arabistan Vilayetleri*)" was not the solution. The solution was to slowly push for change in the education system to create a sense of unity among people. He concluded by stating that the problem was "us, not them" because these policies should have been introduced many years earlier.[39]

An "us versus them" discourse betrayed an attitude that assumed that an Ottoman meant "us," Turkish-speakers, not "them," non-Turkish speakers out there in the provinces, the *taṣra*. "Out there" was increasingly exoticized, repackaged, and introduced to an audience in Istanbul as strange and foreign lands needing to be brought into a Turkish-Ottoman cultural fold. *Tanin* correspondents who traveled through Syria and Iraq lamented how foreign the people felt to them: almost "nobody knew Turkish" and all you saw and heard were discussions of "Arabism" and not "Ottomanism," "Arab" history and culture, and nothing on "Ottomans or Turks." In a series of columns titled "From Damascus," the correspondent stated that he could not even tell who was Christian, Jewish, or Muslim because all go by "Arab." On the one hand, the reporters blamed previous Ottoman governments for not enforcing a uniform cultural and educational program across Arab lands. On the other hand, they blamed what they called false press reports, which they often pinned on Christian Ottomans and the Arab diaspora in Europe, members of which they accused of working to instill the sense that there was anti-Arab prejudice in the government. Politicians like Shafiq were often called out for instilling divisive ideas published in the local newspaper, amounting to "treason against their homeland and their own Syrians."[40] The solution was always to discipline people into feeling a sense of belonging to the wider Ottoman world, and it started with enforcing Turkish language rules.[41]

The Arabic-language press was engaged in direct conversation with the Turkish-language press. Writing in *al-Ittihad al-'Uthmani*, a reporter was clear in stating that the government's efforts "to merge the various ethnic groups have no part in [having] peace, and it is evident now that there is no force stronger than one's fanatic attachment to his own ethnic identity," especially since there was one ethnic group that was trying to dominate the

others. He also stated that ethnic diversity should not be anything to fear, interestingly, giving the example of Germany, which he described as "a collection of national groups" similar to England and the United States. "As long
as the government sanctifies each ethnic group's rights and no one group
has privileges over another, there should be no need to fear for peace."[42] The
paper even printed a translation of Hüseyin's response to *Le Temps*, in which
he accused the French paper of distorting the facts. He said that now it had
backtracked, saying that the only difference between "Arabs" and "Turks" was
that the Arabs wanted a multilingual state, like many countries in Europe:
"Austria-Hungary has six different official languages, Switzerland has three,
and in Belgium, there is two, so what does it really mean that one has to
learn Turkish and to what end?" But Hüseyin then continued to defend his
position of the necessity to eventually adopt Turkish as the only official language, yet agreed that those who spoke Arabic should also be hired if it were
possible.[43]

Language was not simply a political issue of Ottoman national unity; it
had a direct impact on the lives of ordinary non-Turkish speakers in Arab-
majority provinces. It was felt most acutely in the courts, where many of the
local employees were replaced by Turkish-speakers who did not know Arabic.
Not knowing Turkish was used as an excuse to dismiss Arab-Ottomans or
to limit the opportunities available to them in governmental jobs. However,
it proved very difficult to run the courts when most of the locals could not
speak Turkish.[44] This was not limited to Arabic-speaking-majority provinces.
What linguist Michiel Leezenberg calls the "vernacularization" of languages
for the various communities, such as Armenians, Albanians, Greeks, Bulgarians, Kurds, as well as Arabs and Turks, began as early as the mid-seventeenth
century. Vernacular languages were used in locals' day-to-day life, including when communicating with imperial government officials.[45] Thus, while
the language took on a distinctly political significance at the beginning of
the twentieth century, the diversity of languages had been a staple of Ottoman quotidian life for centuries. Therefore, it should come as no surprise that
many other ethnic groups had similar demands as that of Arab-Ottoman
deputies, namely for their vernacular tongue to be taught in schools and to
allow enough decentralization of local administrations to cater to the needs
of specific ethnic communities across the vast empire.[46]

In an opinion piece, a lawyer named Muhammad Zain al-Din made the argument that reasonable people understood that Arab-Ottomans who did not have the right qualifications should not expect to get jobs in the courts. Still, by the same token, "justice cannot be served" if those working in local courts were not proficient in the local language. He cited an anecdote about a new Turkish-speaking policeman who was not proficient in Arabic and was taking down information for a claim a local citizen was making. He asked the claimant his name, to which he answered, "Zaki." Then the policeman asked, "What about your father?" to which Zaki said, "He is dead, Sir (*sayyidi, mat*)." So, the policeman registered his name as "Zaki Son of He-is-dead-Sir (*Zeki Bin Sayyidi Mat*)." A funny anecdote that vividly illustrates how an ideologically driven policy of language centralization was poorly implemented and received on the local level.[47]

As Hasan Kayalı points out, the adoption of Turkish, as opposed to the more complex Ottoman-Turkish as a formal language, had taken place in 1876 with little reaction from the Arab-Ottoman population.[48] However, I argue that the impact of language changes and their perceived forced implementation were much more injurious to Arab-Ottomans in the capital and the provinces in 1908. By 1908 there had been three decades of Ottomanization and centralization to build a sense of belonging to an Ottoman collective and loyalty to the sultan during the Hamidian period.[49] In many ways, the loud reaction to the language policies reflected this centralization—a citizenry that felt it could claim its belonging to the fatherland on its own terms. A sense of belonging that demanded bringing the private—cultural traditions, religious practice, language—into the public sphere to contribute to an imagined empire-state during a short-lived period marked by hope for a shared future.

News of discriminatory practices against employees and students of "Arab origin" filled the newspapers. Rafiq Azmzade took issue with the fact that many Arab-Ottomans in the capital with "nothing in their past that would blemish their honor" were dismissed while Turkish-Ottomans with questionable pasts, "who should have received the harshest penalties," were hired.[50]

The public saw the problem as being more than just a few discriminatory CUP members. It was also the Ottoman-Arab members of the parliament who were called out for not being vociferous enough. In frustration, one writer exclaimed that whenever these members spoke up, it seemed it was to plead "after months of silence" for non-Arab-Ottomans to join the party they called the "moderate" party. A palatable frustration at a perceived lack of effectiveness of their representatives was becoming public.[51] Within a few months of the start of the first parliamentary sessions, *al-Ittihad al-'Uthmani* wondered why Arab-Ottoman deputies were staying so quiet about these issues. *Al-Muqattam*'s reporter interviewed several deputies from the Levant. He concluded that several factors hindered Arab-Ottoman deputies. First, the way they had been ostracized by the ruling party and treated with suspicion by some Turkish-Ottoman deputies blocked their access to cabinet positions. Second, many were new to politics and have not had the time to organize since they were just getting to know one another. Third, they were not given any chance to express their opinion, for they were attacked as soon as they opened their mouths. Last but not least, the language problem was a major hindrance since most of them were not comfortable speaking Turkish in public.[52]

Arab-Ottomans were indeed regularly shut out of cabinet positions. A *Lisan al-Hal* columnist warned of what he considered discrimination against them. He urged all political parties to work toward achieving equality among the various ethnic groups and to "count the Arab as an Ottoman, the way they count a Turk ... otherwise, things will not progress in the right direction and hopes will be dashed and the end of this parliament would be similar to the end of the first parliament, God forbid."[53]

Shafiq was at the center of the language debate as a fluent Arabic and Turkish speaker who was as comfortable writing and giving speeches in Arabic as he was in Turkish.[54] As a longtime resident of the Ottoman capital, Shafiq was very well connected within the social circles of the city where Turkish, Armenian, Greek, Albanian, Turkish, and indeed Arabic intermingled in the salons, hotel lobbies, bars, and cafes. The Hamidian period he lived through was not a multicultural utopian Ottoman existence. Far from it; it was a time when a centralizing Ottoman imperial government resorted to escalating levels of oppression and state-sponsored violence to suffocate any independent notions of self-determination, non-state-sponsored cultural expression, as well as nationalist ideations. Like many people of his time, Shafiq saw the Young Turk Revolution as an opening to assert the role of Arab-Ottomans culturally, politically, and economically. This was not about Arab nationalism, as Hasan Kayalı has so skillful established. Still, neither was it about espousing Arabism or a form of political autonomy under an Ottoman umbrella. For Shafiq, and many others like him, non-Turkish-Ottomans wanted an explicit, publicly acknowledged share in defining what it meant to be an Ottoman citizen. Unfortunately, hope was quickly extinguished for many ethnic groups in the Ottoman Empire who counted on full participation in a new Ottoman system that included and represented them.

Historians have argued for a number of different turning points in Ottoman history that might have announced the death of hopes that non-Turkish-Ottomans had for a form of participation in a new Ottoman Empire. Some place it at the end of World War I, while others put it earlier at the hangings of Arab-Ottoman notables by the military governor of Syria, Cemal Pasha. Still others place it at the second set of elections in 1912 following the defeats in the Balkan wars and the loss of the Libyan province to Italian colonialism.[55] One can look back to analyze where and how Arabism or Turkism became incompatible with Ottomanism, or when Arab separatism became a forgone conclusion, or how colonialism foreclosed the possibility of a future for a federated existence.[56] Here I focus on the experience of these events as they developed over time and not as a reaction to a singular pivotal moment at the end of the empire. As with most major changes, it all happened slowly, and first within the intimacies of daily life.

The experience of being at the center of the action, on the floor of the lower chamber of the parliament, was a lived experience that for Shafiq meant a struggle against his past brought out to discredit him and some of his colleagues. The second part of this chapter tackles the controversies of almost unrelenting accusations thrown at some Arab-Ottoman officials, which ranged from character flaws to treason. The complaints about deputies representing Arab-majority provinces being too quiet in upholding the interests of their constituents, thrown at Shafiq and others like him, become much easier to understand if we take a microhistorical approach to their experience. Shafiq's struggle started on his first day in the parliament and continued until 1912, when he lost his seat as one of the deputies from the Province of Syria.

Character Assassination

The press in Beirut and Damascus kept a close eye on the proceedings of the Ottoman parliament. Starting in the first few sessions, *al-Ittihad al-'Uthmani* gave a blow-by-blow account of what was happening on the lower chamber's floor in Istanbul. The first order of business was to confirm the electoral results and discuss those deputies who had complaints filed against them. Their very character and the validity of their election were to be debated in public, and it seemed that nothing was considered too personal or taboo to bring up. The goal for those arguing against the nominations of some of the deputies was to prove them legally unqualified to serve or to invalidate the results of their elections.

Shafiq had the unfortunate claim to being on a list that included Yusuf Shitwan, the deputy from Benghazi, and Arif (Ar. 'Aref) Pirinççizade, the deputy from Diyarbakir. While members of the parliament could level accusations against these deputies, according to the rules of the Chamber of Deputies the accused were not allowed to speak in their own defense. Having a long political career and a network of allies that one could leverage to speak on one's behalf became invaluable at this early stage. If they did not, Shafiq, Yusuf, and Arif had to wait and hope for some of their colleagues to come to their rescue. Ultimately, it became an issue of popularity and political clout that saved or sank the young career of an Ottoman deputy.

The result was that Yusuf Shitwan's election was declared invalid, and he was asked to run again citing the number of complaints against him. The other two, Arif and Shafiq, had backers who stood up for them in the lower chamber. First, Nafi' Pasha, the deputy from Aleppo, and 'Asem (Tr. Asım) Bey, the deputy from Ma'murat al-'Aziz, came to Arif's defense, testifying to his good character and his reputation for standing up to corruption, which they argued was why he had to defend himself from those with an ax to grind. Ardaks Efendi, a deputy from Erzurum, rebutted, stating that they could not possibly confirm Arif without a proper investigation. He also went after Shafiq, claiming that the chamber took the telegrams from Benghazi, which claimed that Yusuf Shitwan was a spy, at face value. However, the deputies did not investigate the accusations against Shafiq, and now it seemed that they were about to confirm a deputy whose character was questionable. The deputy from Kayseri, Ömer (Ar. 'Umar) Efendi, brought the debate to an end by stating: "We have fair laws we can go by. This person got the majority of the votes in this province [Diyarbakir] legally. . . . As for Yusuf Shitwan Bey, many deputies were against him, and the [bad] reports we received about him were overwhelming. . . . As for Shafiq Bey al-Mu'ayyad, his innocence was proven through a legal decision." The head of the parliament then said, "The majority believe that Syria's representative, Shafiq Bey al-Mu'ayyad, and Arif Efendi Pirinççi were thus confirmed."[57]

This statement does not do justice to the long and heated debate about the confirmation of Shafiq. The legal issue Ömer Efendi referred to was not in fact ruled on by a court of law but dismissed by a royal decree. As it turns out, archival records show that a royal decree went against the recommendations of the Ministry of Justice to pursue an investigation against Shafiq, dismissing the case, which I discuss later. Needless to say, this would not be the end of it.

Rumors of Shafiq being a spy either for Izzet or for the removed sultan continued to circulate. His recent past as an employee of the palace was repeatedly used to discredit him and cast doubts on the motivations behind his political ambitions. The notorious and expansive network of spies in Abdülhamid's time had been officially disbanded in one of the first acts of the newly appointed cabinet, and the signature of the sultan had been obtained to make this kind of spying illegal. Instead, a professional information-gathering system was put in place, similar to those established in European countries. However, as historian Nader Sohrabi tells us, a simple decree did not take care of years' worth of bitter memories of one of the most hated institutions of the old regime. Avenging those wronged by the law and tracking down former spies became an excuse to come after opponents of the CUP.[58]

Shafiq, one of the founders of the Ottoman Brotherhood and a strong critic of CUP policies in the Arab-majority provinces, faced the brunt of those accusations. Any of Shafiq's criticisms of members of the party in power seemed to be shot down by loud accusations of his sympathies with the former regime. In one session, Shafiq angrily defended himself, stating

that accusations that he was a spy for Abdülhamid, which were being published in newspapers in Istanbul and the Balkans, amounted to slander that
should be prosecuted. Shafiq defiantly said, "I ask that the government . . .
examine the [spy] reports in Yıldız Palace, and if they find any to have been
written by me, they should give them to Hüseyin Cahid to publish them in
the newspapers." Cheers arose in support of Shafiq's position, but Hüseyin
insisted that he had seen reports written by Shafiq and the dismissed Benghazi deputy, Shitwan.[59]

This issue came up again when Shafiq spoke against the budget put forward by the cabinet, stating that even Abdülhamid was more careful not to
get into so much debt to European creditors. Again, he was accused of wanting to go back to the way things used to be, leveling the accusation against
him and other deputies from Arab-majority provinces of being spies. Shafiq
insisted that these accusations were about trying to stop him and other deputies from speaking up, scaring them into silence. Newspapers in Damascus
and Beirut followed the details of what they described as a vendetta against
Shafiq.[60] As one of the few experienced Turkish speakers in the chamber
representing Arab-Ottoman constituents, he gave an important speech that
was translated into Arabic and published in the local newspapers.

> In the previous regime, the sultan did not only rule in a way that goes against
> the constitution, but he ruled in a way that made no sense except when un-
> derstood as personal rule whose only goal was to satisfy his every whim and
> desire. . . . All that concerned Abdülhamid was himself. People took this
> opportunity to get close to him by writing these journals, and that was how
> even ministers would ingratiate themselves to him. . . . A committee exam-
> ined the reports, which amounted to over three hundred and fifty boxes of
> material. Some deputies were assigned to examine these journals, and from
> what I understand . . . some were still being cataloged, and it would be im-
> possible to get through them all in the near future, for all they have been able
> to examine so far are one hundred and seventy-five boxes.

Shafiq insisted that any leaked information would compromise the entire investigation at that point.[61] He did not deny or confirm that he was one of the
people who spied on others for the sultan. Instead, he addressed the fairness
of being singled out when the practice was so widespread. This is confirmed

by historian Merih Erol, who argues that "spies belonged to various ethnic groups and diverse ranks of society [including] Greeks, Armenians, Jews, Europeans, Kurds, Tatars, Turks and represented a wide range of occupations from sheiks to street vendors, or simple citizens who spied on people to win the approval and gratitude of the sultan."[62] Shafiq explained that some "have requested a general amnesty be granted to all the spies and have asked that we be satisfied with removing those people from their posts. Others want the reports published because they are all marred by them, and it would make better sense to air them out to remove their shame from this nation ... [so] either publish them all or burn them all!"[63] Calling him and some other deputies who had been employed by the previous administration traitors was just one of the methods used to discredit Shafiq. Next, I turn to more personal and scandalous attacks and accusations leveled against Shafiq.

Skeletons, Closets, and Glass Houses

In July 1910, *Lisan al-Hal* published a column titled "A Painful Incident." In the most somber of tones, it reported: "In the parliament, an incident took place that harms every honest Ottoman who loves his country and hopes for the unity of its men and the extraction of all causes of conflict from the hearts of its sons." It continued to report that a few days earlier Shafiq had been on his way into the parliament when he ran into Halijian (Tr. Halicyan) Efendi, the minister of public works.

> Halijian Efendi greeted him, and he [Shafiq] responded with the utmost respect. Shafiq Bey then apologized for not shaking his hand because he was determined not to shake the hand of any of the ministers before discovering the killer of Ahmed Samim Bey [a reporter who had been critical of the CUP]. So Halijian Efendi said, "and I am one of them?" and Shafiq Bey said "Yes." That was the end of it." As Shafiq was leaving at the end of the day, he ran into Talat Bey, the minister of Internal Affairs, who exchanged verbal greetings with Shafiq and went on his way then "as Talat Bey continued one or two steps further, he stopped and turned to Shafiq Bey and asked him: "Why do you not shake my hand?" He replied: "For the same reason, I have already mentioned to your colleague Halijian Efendi." Talat Bey asked: "What is that, for I am ignorant of it." Shafiq answered, "I will not shake

the hand of any minister before the killer of Ahmed Samim Bey is found."
So, Talat Bey turned pale and got very angry and said to Shafiq Bey, "Can
a man like you who turned his son into Sahurra' [mummy, in reference to
the mummy of a Pharaoh that had a cult of worshipers] have the nerve to
say this?"

The writer followed this with an explanation:

A son of Shafiq's born to him by the widow of Cevad Pasha [Nimet] whom
he had married died two days after his birth and doctors were conflicted as
to the cause of death or the truth behind it, so the body of the son was supposedly preserved with alcohol for a post-mortem examination to take place.

Shafiq answered: "Whoever said this is making it up for their own
good . . . and if you are doing that, then you are no better than those people." That is when Talat Pasha physically attacked Shafiq, and "they got each
other in a lock. As Shafiq Bey's back was up against the wall, he was in a
position to push him down to the ground. By then, several deputies had
gathered when they heard all of the shouting and fighting and were able to
catch the minister before he fell. The two men continued to exchange insults
until one of the deputies from Aleppo, Ali Cenani (Ar. Jenani) Efendi, arrived." Ali Cenani (1872–1934) is best known for his roles in the persecution
of Armenians, in the Armenian Genocide, and for the role he later played in
republican Turkey.[64] Ali Cenani attacked Shafiq, saying, "What you did is a
demonstration of ill manners." So Shafiq replied by forcefully telling him not
to get involved. Ali Cenani replied: "This is an insult!" So Shafiq Bey replied
that Ali Cenani was an ugly man who was blindly defending his "master."

That is when they tried to attack each other but those around them
stopped them. Soon after, Ali Cenani sent Shafiq a note challenging him to
a duel with the following words: "What happened between us can only be
erased with blood." Shafiq replied with a note: "I am ready to meet whenever
you and your witnesses want, and I will stay here [parliament] for a couple
of hours and in the evening, I will be in Club Istanbul and tomorrow I will
be at home." He asked Tawfiq (Tr. Tevfik) Bey, the deputy from Karak (in
today's Jordan), to take the note to Ali. According to the reporter, Shafiq
waited but Ali never showed up at the set time. Shafiq had his witnesses with

him, to whom he allegedly said, "Those people underestimated me because of the grey hair on my head, and they do not know that for *us Arabs* [my emphasis] our hearts are made of iron." The writer then continued: "This is the news that was told to us, and I transcribed it and published it here because those fighting one another are two of the most important men in the government . . . so our wish is that this painful incident is the first and last of its kind and that soon the opponents get into a stable partnership with everlasting affinity for one another."[65]

To those reading about this incident at home in Beirut and Damascus, it seems that no further context for such a bizarre incident was necessary. Thus, it is left to the historian to follow the pieces of the story and understand what drove a deputy to challenge a fellow deputy to a duel. Investigating the allegations presented in the article revealed that the reason given by the reporter for the mummy reference was inaccurate. In fact, it was a much more serious accusation about a crime of fraud against the public interest committed through a manipulation of the body of a dead newborn baby. It was also not the first time the accusation had come up. It had been openly discussed in the lower chamber a few days after the opening of the parliament. After the initial accusation leveled at Shafiq of being a spy for the former secretary and close advisor to the sultan, Izzet, there was a second, much more personal accusation that involved Shafiq's late wife and son.

On January 1, 1909, some deputies pushed to reopen an investigation into Shafiq's election.[66] A general committee read the files, and on January 2, Amir Muhammad Arslan, the deputy from Latakia, stated that Shafiq's "record was read yesterday, and we did not find anything suspicious in it." A murmur arose in the assembly, so Shafiq stood up and said, "Mr. president, it is me, Shafiq al-Mu'ayyad, and I would like to speak." More noise from the crowd, with some deputies even shouting for the president to prevent him from taking the floor. One deputy addressed the president, saying, "The deputy whose record is being discussed does not have the right to speak." Rida (Tr. Rıza) Bey, a deputy from Beirut, protested: "There cannot be a sentence passed against someone who does not get a chance to defend himself." Another deputy interrupted, shouting, "The accused, Shafiq Bey, cannot speak since he is a criminal and a puppet of Izzet Pasha!" Rida Bey retorted: "Article eighty of the internal regulations of the parliament states that if a deputy cannot defend himself, he can designate a colleague to do it on his behalf." Ahmed Mahir (Ar. Maher) Efendi, a deputy from Kastamonu in northeastern Anatolia, complained that previous discussions of Shafiq's file had been full of gossip and hearsay about his past and that two issues had come up. One deputy had accused him of being a spy and an agent of Izzet and another deputy had leveled the charge that he was a criminal and that papers proving his crime were still held at the Ministry of Justice. He continued: "I do not know this man, nor do I know if he is a spy for Izzet Pasha or his men, but through my own investigations, I found out that he did frequent Izzet Pasha's house, but he did not work in spying. As for the crime being referenced here, I happen to have been the legal representative of the claimant who brought the case against him." The claimant was Shafiq's father-in-law, whose daughter, Nimet, had died while giving birth to their child. He said that he had never laid eyes on Shafiq until the day before. He presented what he knew about the case:

> The wife of Shafiq Bey gave birth to a dead baby, so Shafiq Bey hid the body somewhere, and covered it in ice and hid the news of his son's death. He did not kill him as has been rumored. Then his wife died. His issue had to do with her [Nimet's] property and real estate, which he automatically transferred to their son, and from the son, he [Shafiq] would be the real inheritor. It was proven through his interrogation that he did commit this fraud to prove that he is the inheritor of his child even though he had, in reality, died before his mother. So, an order was issued to prosecute Shafiq Bey; however, since he was a governmental employee hired through a royal decree, his trial required a royal decree in order to proceed. The permission was never granted, and the case was stalled. So, the action that is termed a crime is his hiding of the boy's body and nothing else. Even that is still in a grey area between doubt and certitude because it was never adjudicated ... so what Shafiq Bey is accused of, in my opinion, would not have prevented his election according to the electoral law.

Next, Rıza (Ar. Rida) Tevfik, a deputy from Edirne in Rumelia, rose to the podium and said, "The case of this person was transferred to me yesterday, and I approved his election because the charge that he is a spy, according to my investigation, is a false accusation that was not based in reality." He continued that he had even confronted Shafiq about the accusations leveled against him, but he calmly and simply replied that he should read the medical report prepared by Dr. Basim Pasha. Rıza then stated that he followed his advice and went that same evening to Dr. Basim's house, where he learned that this issue was just a collection of delusions:

> The wife of Shafiq Bey had a fever, and her temperature was between 39 and 39.5 C, and that was not that unusual. There is no truth in what has been said about the boy being born dead. However, the boy was suffocating [parts of his lungs were blocked] that he almost passed out. Basim Pasha moved his arms and legs up and down, and that is when he realized that he was still alive, and that is how he left him. As for his mother and whether she died before or after the baby, there are still some disagreements.

Rıza continued to explain that the doctor left with both of them alive and that even though their death was certain, Shafiq called on five other doctors to see if anything could be done out of an abundance of care. "The way I see it," he continued, "the important issue is limited to pinpointing the time of the death of the baby and the mother. As for the rumor that Shafiq Bey had killed his wife and put his child on ice is just a claim that has no proof whatsoever. I have not made these facts up. There is a report from Basim Pasha, and the legal records at the Ministry of Justice are also available and can be checked, and they would confirm what has been said."

Noise rose from the crowds, and Emanuel Karasu Efendi, a deputy from Salonica, stood up to speak against Shafiq, but the head of the lower chamber stopped him and said that since there was no real evidence of these accusations, there was no need to continue debating:

> Article four of the internal regulations of the parliament states that a case should be reviewed in the presence of the general committee and after each case is reviewed and found to meet the regulations and conditions assigned by the electoral law it would be confirmed by the majority. This man, who has had some complaints about his election . . . seems to fall within the legal electoral regulations, and the committee agrees on that. . . . Thus, our response to a man associated with Izzet or Tahsin is outside of our jurisdictional power. The committee which investigates personalities and issue of honor must

show its approval or disapproval, and by respecting what it says and the decision it makes, we keep the respect of this parliament.

Another deputy, Lutfi Bey from Dersim, wanted to say something, but he was stopped by the president of the chamber, stating that the majority had approved Shafiq's election. People clapped, and one deputy said, "My thanks to the justice shown by the general committee."[67]

The tragic circumstances of the death of Shafiq's wife and son were being hashed out in public. They would continue to haunt him as political opponents used the issue repeatedly to hinder his political career. As for the case, the details presented in the parliament were not accurate. Archival records from the Ministries of Justice and Religious Affairs and Yıldız Palace highlight how Shafiq's power to suppress the investigation changed before and after the deposition of the sultan. The incident had taken place five years earlier at Shafiq's house in Teşvikiye on Bostan Street, no 16. Details of the documented investigation are impressively thorough. Interviews were conducted with all those involved, including his family members and servants, the mayor, the doctors on hand, and Shafiq himself. What the investigation revealed was that there was no doubt that Nimet had died before the child, which eliminated any claims to Nimet's inheritance by her father, İsa Efendi, who brought the case against Sadik. However, the investigation continued because questions remained as to whether the child had died before or after he was registered with the state under the name Ahmed Na'im, and an Ottoman identification card was issued to him.[68]

According to the investigator, Shafiq confirmed in written testimony that his son had died on the evening of Wednesday, April 16, 1903, at eleven o'clock, after all the necessary paperwork for his registration with the state had been completed that morning. The inheritance of the child was registered on Tuesday and got him an Ottoman identification card. People noticed that Shafiq was trying to finish the procedures while carrying a map of all the land that would be transferred to the child, going from building to building and from one municipal department to the other, with Badi' Azmzade acting as his witness. His running around wanting everything to be done that day attracted some attention (*celb-i nazar*) since there were so many different places he needed to go; the procedure continued until Wednesday, which was when the accuser, İsa Efendi's son-in-law Cafer (Ar. Ja'far) Bey, found out about the death of the child from the imam of the neighborhood. He said that according to the doctor's report, the child died at eleven o'clock on Wednesday evening. The maid, a certain Nubar Nevzade from Van, believed the boy had died on Tuesday night "because from that point on, Shafiq Bey forbade the servants from going upstairs and into the boy's room. In addition, witnesses who believed the boy died on Wednesday put the time of death at nine, nine-thirty, ten, ten-thirty, and eleven, which is a wide variance."[69]

Because of the discrepancies, the possibility of the child having died before he was registered and inheritance procedures completed, coupled with the fact that there were several charitable endowments involved, including a magnesium mine in the Province of Hüdavendigar in Anatolia in the inheritance, the investigator recommended that the case of fraud proceed. Since Shafiq was an employee of the palace at the time, the case could not proceed without the explicit permission of the sultan. Shafiq's connection helped him escape prosecution as the royal decree to approve the continuation of the case never came, even though the request had been sent to and acknowledged by the Public Debt Commission, where he worked.[70]

The damage to Shafiq's reputation had already occurred, and the protection afforded by the sultan, became a liability after 1908. The accusation that he made his son into a mummy for a couple of days until he registered him to fraudulently inherit his wife's assets would not leave him until his death.

The End of the Road

The short period of relative peace between 1908 and 1911 ended with the Italian-Ottoman war in Libya, resulting in the loss of an Arab-majority province and the last Ottoman territory in Africa. The second Balkan war in 1912 dealt a blow to the dream of a resurgent Ottoman Empire. This, according to Rafiq Azmzade, was one of the main reasons that Arab-Ottoman deputies joined the opposition—the Decentralization Party. Rafiq thought that many Arab-Ottomans were stuck between a rock and a hard place. On the one hand they feared falling victim to European colonial ambitions, and on the other they witnessed the discriminatory approach of the CUP towards Arab-majority provinces. He also stated that it was in 1912 that most Arab-Ottoman politicians became aware that "Arabs needed to have a united word and not be reliant on the [Ottoman] government, whether it was to remain or disappear."[71]

Shafiq ran for election again in 1912 under the Decentralization Party banner and lost. Haqqi, in self-imposed exile in Cairo, supported Shafiq and the Decentralization Party, and his articles were regularly republished in *al-Muqtabas* in Damascus.[72] The loss was a blow, coming on the heels of the loss of Libya to Italian colonialism.[73] The CUP ran on "Ottoman-Islamic rhetoric" and used the panic generated by the Italian bombardment of Beirut in early 1912 to encourage unity in the face of external aggression. Haqqi blamed the CUP's sweeping election victory in Arab-majority provinces on many breaches of electoral laws and intimidation against supporters of the opposition. However, according to Hasan Kayalı, "the fact remains that while the CUP employed unacceptable pressures and was aided by foreign aggression and martial law justified by the war, the mandate it received reflected a political reality that was not in its entirety forged by the Committee."[74] Shafiq's electoral defeat marked his official retirement, followed by complaints about what he considered a misrepresentation of his salary over the years, which impacted his pension.[75]

Shafiq did not quit political life, however, and he paid a high price for it when he was executed by the military governor of the Levant, who accused him and others of plotting to establish an Arab caliphate. Shafiq, along with several other Arab-Ottoman politicians and intellectuals, was held on suspicion of treason. Little information was initially given, and his family and friends and the head of the Chamber of Deputies were forced to write to the Ministry of Interior demanding to know the reason for his arrest.[76] According to the 4th Army Regiment, Shafiq, who had been suspected of having separatist ambitions, was accused of being a member of a secret organization, "The Revolutionary Arab Committee," whose goal was to establish an Arab caliphate, and the military investigators claimed to have documentary evidence to support their claim.[77] He was tried in a hastily assembled military court and publicly executed along with a whole generation of Arab-Ottoman politicians and intellectuals, forever losing the battle for the empire and severing their connection to the imperial capital.[78]

This episode was the final chapter in the life of Arab-Ottoman imperialists who were born and raised in the wake of the Tanzimat period, took advantage of the missionary school systems in the Levant, and relied on their skills and kinship networks to build a life in their imperial capital, Istanbul. Their rise and survival in Istanbul depended on the palace's favor, becoming staunch supporters of an Ottoman imperial system that was simultaneously on the offensive and the defensive as it tried to battle what it considered enemies of Ottoman sovereignty from within and without.

Shafiq remained close to the center, building a network of influence that emanated from Teşvikiye and stretched all the way to the Levant. He survived the harsh transition from the old to the new regime, only to be battered by the reality of an emerging ethnocentric Ottoman system that saw him and some of his Arab-Ottoman colleagues as dangerous figureheads of Arab separatism—dangerous intimate Others.

CHAPTER 8

THE AFTERMATH

SHAFIQ'S FAMILY WOULD DENY THE ACCOUNT OF HIS ALLEGED treason for decades to come. The rush to execute him and other Arab-Ottomans was supposedly part of a plan by the military governor, Cemal Pasha, to eliminate any competition in asserting his control over the Levant.[1] The execution of Arab-Ottoman notables and intellectuals was only one of many wartime atrocities that Cemal (Ar. Jamal) committed, earning him the title Shedder of Blood (*al-Saffah)* in the official history curricula of Syria and Lebanon.

Until today, his has been probably the most well-known name from the Ottoman era in the Levant. This was not by coincidence. He was held up by nationalist historians as "proof" of the oppression that the Arab population suffered under Ottoman rule, making heroes of his victims and villains of his supporters. As historian Salim Tamari puts it, that was how "four centuries of relative peace and dynamic activity, the Ottoman era, with what was known in Arabic discourse as 'the days of the Turks' was replaced with four miserable years of tyranny symbolized by the military dictatorship of Ahmad Cemal Pasha in Syria."[2] Burj Square, where the public executions took place, was later renamed Martyrs' Square. It stands today in the heart of downtown Beirut, where people still gather for political demonstrations against present-day corruption and tyranny of rulers, some of whom come from powerful families that stretch back to the Ottoman period. Some of the streets branching off from the square were named after those who were hanged, including one called "Shafiq al-Mu'ayyad."

Whether it was true that Shafiq never gave up his loyalty to an Ottoman fatherland as his family members claimed, or that he was working to establish an alternative Arab caliphate with the help of enemies of the empire as Cemal and the military tribunal claimed, I do not think can ever be known for sure. For the most part, intentionality remains outside the realm of experiential history. In the desire to understand this traumatic period and the mass violence it engendered by both friend and foe, the search for black-and-white characterization of historical actors becomes attractive, though it is often misleading. The Arab-Ottomans who were hanged became symbols of the Arab *hıyanet* (betrayal) in what historian Selim Deringil refers to as the "stab in the back syndrome" in Turkish nationalist historiography and as *shuhada'* (martyrs) in Syrian and Lebanese nationalist historiography.[3]

For Arab-Ottoman families who were invested in the late imperial project, the years leading up to World War I must have been disorienting and the dissolution of the Ottoman Empire excruciatingly difficult. The war effectively ended the promise of an Ottoman Empire that could have encompassed the multitude of ethnic and religious groups under its umbrella. The war not only brought about the end of an empire and the loss of Istanbul as the capital of an imagined multicultural political entity; it also meant the loss of hope for an alternative future for the region. For the Azmzades of Istanbul, the loss was devastating and deeply personal.

Two-dimensional heroes, victims, villains, and a succession of epic events are how the history of the Ottoman period continues to be discussed in school curricula and popular media. In 2019, on the centenary of the French establishment of "Greater Lebanon," the president of the Lebanese Republic rehashed the trope of "Ottoman atrocities" in a speech that attracted international attention and caused a mini diplomatic incident between Ankara and Beirut.[4] Such an incident highlights two falsities that continue to dominate the telling of Ottoman history. The first is part of a nation-founding myth in which centuries of being a part of the Ottoman Empire are either completely erased or reduced to foreign occupation of a "primordial nation." Beyond the obvious historiographical problems in this approach, I think there is a much more dangerous impact of this kind of unchallenged narrative. It severs the historical connection of Arabic-speaking people of the Levant from the lived experiences of their ancestors in service of an "invented history" designed to legitimize the founding of a new nation-state.[5]

The second, a flip side of denying the Levantine peoples' ownership of *their* Ottoman history, is the unspoken assumption that the history of the Ottoman Empire is fundamentally and exclusively part of the history of the Republic of Turkey. This subtle assumption reinforces the notion that the empire was ruled by and for "Turks," reducing other ethnic groups to simply tolerated subjects or "minorities."[6] In Turkey, like the United Kingdom and France and other nation-states that lay claim to the legacies of "imperial glories," much of what I call the "sins of empire" is also written out, denied, or fiercely defended as a necessary evil for the survival of the fatherland.[7]

Arab-Ottomans not only participated in day-to-day life in imperial Istanbul; they also were members of the ruling elites who contributed to the making of the empire in all its sins and virtues. In many ways, imperial Istanbul, with half of its permanent residents born outside of Istanbul in the 1880s and 1890s, was as much a Turkish city as it was an Arab city.[8] In other words, Istanbul as the imperial capital of the Ottoman Empire is a part of Arab heritage as much as it is a part of Turkish heritage. Denying Arab-Ottoman influence during the late imperial era robs citizens of the Republic of Turkey of a part of their multicultural heritage and denies citizens of Arab-majority successor nation-states the right to *their* imperial history and the history of *their* connection to the imperial capital. When considering history as belonging to people who participated in the making and unmaking of the empire, rather than as a prologue to the history of successor nation-states, it becomes clear that denying the shared and diverse experiences of people from across the region, whether Armenian, Kurdish, Greek, Sephardi or, in this case, Arab, is a form of denying people their own past.

One way of accessing the shared history of people is by changing the unit of analysis by focusing on the *experience* of major and quotidian events and not necessarily the events themselves. I have waded through the remnants of the lives of a few Arab-Ottoman imperialists not because they led exceptional lives but because they provide us with a window into a lived experience that has, so far, been hidden under a thick layer of state-centered political and intellectual narratives. Arab-Ottomans, who constituted a small

yet influential community in Istanbul, have so far been left at the margins of
political and intellectual history of the empire. There continues to be a dearth
of stories of Arab-Ottomans and members of other ethnoreligious groups
who contributed to the shaping of the empire in the provinces, along the
frontiers, and, as I have argued, in the metropole. Why have the important
stories of these imperialists been ignored?

One reason is our fetishization of the Ottoman state archives. Arguably
the richest, best organized, and most accessible archives of Southwest Asia,
the Ottoman archives in Istanbul have boosted the production of historical
monographs about this complex region in the last few decades. However,
reliance on imperial state archives is a double-edged sword. It has led to a
concentration on the history of the imperial state as told by the imperial
and successor state. As the necessity for a critical approach to reading European colonial archives has become clear, the same kind of critical approach
should be applied to the reading of Ottoman imperial archives. Countless
stories from towns, villages, and neighborhoods can be uncovered by reading
the imperial archives against the grain. Stories of common and extraordi-
nary people from Van to Tunis and from Sanaa to Budapest deserve to be
told—stories that could tell us a fuller "Total History," through the peoples'
experiential history, than a study of the state's policies on paper could ever
do. As an historian who has been guilty of over relying on the Ottoman state
archives, I think it is high time that historians start to read them not as they
were organized and presented to us by the state but as they help us understand people's experiences.

Another reason has to do with the concerted efforts by successor nation-
states to draw a hard line between so-called Arab and Turkish histories. If
scholars think of history as belonging to the people and not to a territory,
that of the Ottoman period would become part of the history of all peoples
of the region. The lucky few who had the opportunity to talk with members
of the generation that straddled the Ottoman and post-Ottoman periods,
like my *Teté* Bader and *Jiddo* 'Abed, find stories that abound with how large
Istanbul loomed in their imagination, painting a picture that simply cannot
be crammed into the history of one nation or a pre- versus post-Ottoman
existence. How do societies disentangle their histories, their memories, and
their shared experiences when the political reality changes? The painful and

often violent period of disentanglement awaits scholars who are not afraid to look at recent history, possibly the history of their own ancestors as is the case for me, and bring these decades of transition to light. The "shattering of the empires" was refracted in the lives of shattered communities, peoples, and families.[9]

In this book, I have argued that the Ottoman metropole was not immune to the years of escalating ethnoracial differentiation in the frontiers and beyond.[10] I have shown that racism was not foreign to the Ottoman ruling elites who were part of a global imperial ruling class.[11] The atrocities that took place during World War I and the decade that followed were not a sudden "flick of a switch" or even surprising when one considers that ethnoracial differentiation was also not new. It was, however, weaponized and deployed as a policy of segregation and, in some cases, even ethnic cleansing in the second decade of the twentieth century. One has to take a closer look at social spaces over the period of a few decades leading up to the war in order to understand the societal changes before they manifested as state-sponsored policies of war. The journey from Arab-Ottoman citizens of empire to intimate Others and even enemy aliens might seem jarringly fast, but it did not happen overnight. It simply was never an official policy of the state and thus has too little of a trace in the state archives for it to emerge in conventual Ottoman historiography.

During World War I, some Arab-Ottoman imperialists continued to try to be part of the Ottoman government, or they did what they had to to somehow prove their loyalty by asserting their allegiance to the CUP government and the military governor in the Levant. For example, two Azmzades found success in Istanbul politics during the war years by showing their loyalty to the CUP. Sadik's nephew Badi', who as the reader may recall had had his wedding party in the Bulgarian commissioner's house as discussed in Chapter 6, joined the CUP in 1912 and took his uncle Shafiq's place as a deputy for the Province of Syria in the parliament right through the end of the war. Another nephew, Fawzi, the father of Khaled al-'Azm, whom the reader encountered in Chapter 1, was a close friend of the military governor Cemal Pasha. He was another Azmzade to move back to Istanbul and work in the CUP-led government in a number of positions until at least 1918.[12]

However, the web of suspicion that was cast by the CUP during World War I also caught many members of the Azmzade family in Damascus and Istanbul. They were some of the thousands sent to Anatolia as a form of internment during the war years.[13] With the noted exception of his sons, Vassik and Hisham, Shafiq's children were caught up in the collective punishment that was meted out to some prominent Ottoman-Arabs, including children and women, now treated like enemy aliens. For example, Shafiq's daughters intended to stay in their father's home in Istanbul after his execution. However, they were not allowed to and instead were interned in Bursa, along with as many as five thousand Arab-Ottomans distributed across several cities and towns in Anatolia.[14] Due to their perceived political and security threat, influential citizens from Arab-majority provinces of the Ottoman Empire, according to official propaganda put out by the Ottoman military governor of Syria during this period, had to be turned from "Syrian notables" into "Ordinary Anatolians." Some were even housed in depopulated Armenian villages and neighborhoods following the Armenian Genocide.[15]

In many parts of Europe during World War I, different groups of people were also marked as enemy aliens and interned (figure 12).[16] What made the Ottoman situation unique, however, was that the Arab-Ottomans of the Levant were one of the largest ethnic groups of the Ottoman citizenry. Even Cemal acknowledged their legal rights, stating that, though they were to be interned, they were to be treated as fellow citizens.[17] As such, the Ottoman state gave the family a place to stay and a small stipend to live on. Hisham, Shafiq's younger son, who was twenty-one years old and in the military college in Erenköy at the time, wrote asking that his sisters be spared the hardship of internment in Bursa. Three of them were married, with one single woman who was weak and ailing (*zavallı ve hasta*), and they were accompanied by two young girls. He asked that they not be forced to leave their beloved Istanbul as they would be on their own in Bursa, with no close male relative to help. His brother Vassik, whom the reader last encountered in Chapter 6, had become a second secretary in the Ottoman embassy in Madrid by that time and would not join them in Bursa. Hisham was also concerned that one of his uncles was the only male relative there at the time he wrote the letter.[18] There was no word as to whether Hisham, as an *İstanbul'lu* whose native tongue was Turkish, was spared the discrimination that some

قونیه ده منفیاً بولنان ذوتك ۱۱ نمرزده بختماً بیكدیردكارى رسم
Les ex-exilés à Konia

FF-719122

FIGURE 12. Ottoman men "exiled" in Konya, Central Anatolia, during World War I. *Source*: Salt Research, Feridun Fazıl Tülbentçi Archive, FFT719122.

other Arab-Ottoman cadets suffered during their military training in Eren-köy at that time. However, he would have surely witnessed the discrimination that many of the cadets experienced. For example, some Arab-Ottoman cadets were reportedly called *hain Arap* (Arab traitor) and were mistreated by the commanders, in some cases not being issued proper uniforms or rations of bread, and finally, along with Ashkenazi Ottomans, separated from the rest of the trainees to endure further abuse.[19]

Hisham, however, seemed more concerned about his sisters than himself. He was especially concerned about his uncle Ali, who as the reader may recall, had been convicted of a double murder and, ironically, due to the influence of his brother Shafiq at the time was given a pardon by the palace, as discussed in Chapter 2. But in 1916, his association with Shafiq was what sealed his fate, and he was also exiled to Bursa along with his three adult sons. Ali appointed himself as a chaperon over Shafiq's family. One of Shafiq's sons-in-law 'Abd al-Qadir, approached the *mutasarrıf* (district governor) of Kale-i Sultaniye to intervene on Hisham's behalf, asking that Shafiq's family stay in their house in Teşvikiye. He also brought up the existence of another part of the family that were not mentioned in Hisham's letter—a concubine of Shafiq and two of her children. They too were exiled to Bursa. In total, eleven members of the family had to live out the rest of the war away from their homes along with Arab-Ottomans now also deemed suspicious Others. In his letter, 'Abd al-Qadir mentioned that he also did not trust Ali around the family because he was a degenerate man, a *sefihülahlak*.[20] Ali also wrote on behalf of the concubine and the two children, asking for a stipend of 60Kr per day instead of the 30Kr they were allocated.[21] Two months later, the Ministry of Interior must have lost track of the family, because they wrote asking for confirmation from the local authorities in Bursa that the entire family was still there.[22] The request probably came from Cemal himself, for two weeks later the Ministry of Interior sent him a telegram relaying the news that Shafiq's family was still in Istanbul, but that they would be heading to Bursa in two days.[23]

The request for information about Shafiq's family was most likely prompted by the capture of two Azmzades who were supposed to be in Bursa. At least two of Ali's grown children had run away from Bursa and were later caught in Syria. One of them, Faiz, broke out of prison and made it to the Hijaz, where he joined the British-supported Sharif Hussein army. He was described as a "companion" of Amir Faisal when he was photographed in Bedouin costumes in Ma'an in 1918.[24] Other members tried to escape back to Syria with fake papers after the entry of the Hijazi army into Damascus.[25] Still others requested permission to return to Syria toward the end of the war, in accordance with a law that was passed allowing those not convicted by the military court to go back to their homes.[26] Ali also asked to return to Damascus for health reasons. He submitted a doctor's report stating that the water and air in Bursa did not suit him, causing him to have a great deal of pain and possible blockage in his arteries.[27]

There is no evidence that the government responded to any of Hisham's and 'Abd al-Qadir's pleas. They all remained in Bursa until the end of the war. Four of Shafiq's daughters who had married Turkish-Ottomans remained in what would become the Republic of Turkey and would eventually take on Turkish citizenship. One daughter, who married 'Abd al-Qadir, moved to Damascus with her husband, while Shafiq's sons eventually ended up in

Damascus and Cairo, with Hisham taking on a position in the Syrian government. His other son, Vassik, continued his upward trajectory after leaving the Bulgarian commission. He was first assigned to Tehran, then, for a short period, Tripoli (of Libya), and then Washington and Madrid, before returning after the end of the war to settle in Egypt.[28] Somehow, he managed to maintain his status in the Ottoman government even after the execution of his father, and later moved to Cairo to look after the charitable endowment inheritance of the Azmzade family in Egypt.

Sadik's family fared much better than their cousins since all of his grown children initially stayed in Istanbul. Jelal and Giyas fought in the Ottoman army in World War I and the Turkish war of independence between 1919 and 1923. Jelal married one of his cousins, Neziha, one of Iklil's daughters, and eventually moved to Damascus. As the reader might recall, Iklil was the governor of several districts over a period of several years. Like most of the Azmzades, he was also interned in Bursa but upon his return to Damascus was able to retain most of his wealth and to serve in the Amir Faisal administration.

Sadik's younger son, Giyas, remained in Istanbul and after the war married Olga, the daughter of a White Russian naval officer from Odesa who had fled with her father following the Bolshevik Revolution. Giyas adopted a Turkish surname in accordance with the Surname Law of 1934. Sadik's daughter Masune remained in Istanbul with her husband Salih, whom she had married in Sofia during her father's tenure as the Ottoman special commissioner to Bulgaria. The Azmzades/al-'Azms on both sides of the Turkish-Syrian border maintained some ties over the years, which have weakened considerably over time. In Syria, the family played a substantial role in the governments that ruled there until the 1960s.[29] It seems that, for the most part, the decision to live on the Turkish or Syrian side of the border was inspired not by ideological or identarian considerations, but mostly by practical considerations such as marriage ties, wealth and land inheritance, and career potential.

This is where the trail of the Azmzades as Arab-Ottoman imperialists tapered off. Some Arab-Ottomans who had had their start in the Ottoman military or civil service held on for the possibility of rapprochement between the Arab-majority successor states under colonial occupation and Turkey, but as historian Michael Province has shown, that was foreclosed a few years later. The final blow came in 1938 with the Alexandretta Crisis and the Turkish annexation of the Sanjak of Alexandretta on the eastern Mediterranean coast. What is more significant than territorial expansion for Turkey and contraction for French Syria was the reason given for the Turkish territorial claims.[30] Twenty years after the end of World War I, statesmen from the Turkish republic had fully embraced the concept of racial purity of the "Turk" as a justification for Turkish nationhood and the incorporation of the "Turk"-majority Sanjak of Alexandretta.[31]

The names of Arab-Ottoman imperialists of the late nineteenth and early twentieth centuries are hard to find in an officially sanctioned national curriculum in any of the successor nation-states. If they appear, they are often depicted as proto-nationalists, whitewashing a long history of their participation in Ottoman rule. The history of the late Ottoman Empire is still being written. Explicitly or implicitly, the subject of the majority of monographs continues to be the state. My hope is to encourage fellow students of history to provincialize the state and the European gaze by focusing on the changing habitus of characters like Sadik and Shafiq, whose complex life stories shine a light on the entangled social spaces of the communities that make up the history of the region. Excavating the stories of people, while being careful not to fall into the trap of contemporary identity politics, is a powerful tool for the reassessment of popular notions of history, in order to combat often toxic nationalist historiography, and to humanize our ancestors not as abstract symbols of heroism or victimhood but as flawed and amazing people who lived flawed and amazing lives worth connecting with. Rethinking the history of the region without the seemingly unshakable burden of having to rescue the Ottoman state from orientalist's stereotypes (foreign and domestic) would indeed be a moment of "decolonizing" the field.

A microhistorical approach to uncover the experiential history of the period is one way to do this. At the risk of being accused of encouraging too much navel gazing, I especially want to encourage historians from the region to dig deep into histories of their towns, villages, neighborhoods, streets, and family members. I believe that in the right hands, and with the right set of skills and languages, no story stands alone, no detail is too small, no incident is insignificant, and no individual is ordinary. Only when, as historians, we break our reliance on large state archives and shed the burdens of defending the history from a perceived Western construction of the "M/middle" of the "West's" "E/east" can scholars truly start to make historical connections that resonate with local peoples' experiences today. This will allow the people of the region to start to take ownership of their story, all of their story—the good, the ugly, and the very ugly that has to be uncovered and acknowledged in order for them to gain some agency over their present and future, by reclaiming the entirety of their past.

This book shows that in the final days of the Hamidian period, Arab-Ottomans were a cornerstone of imperial rule, and their lives refracted the privilege, power, and cultural hybridity of global imperialism. They also participated in and were objects of emerging racialization that would be weaponized as the cultural wars for the soul of the empire heated up after the Young Turk Revolution. The loves, fears, hopes, disappointments, frustrations, and tragedy of a family torn apart by the inertia of the breakup of the empire is an intimate history of the hardest kind of loss, the loss of home—Istanbul—symbolizing the loss of hope for an alternative vision of a future that was never to be.

NOTES

Preface

1. Somaiyeh Falahat, *Cities and Metaphors: Beyond Imaginaries of Islamic Urban Space* (London: Routledge, 2018), 81–92.

2. Mostafa Minawi, *The Ottoman Scramble for Africa: Empire and Diplomacy in the Sahara and the Hijaz* (Stanford, CA: Stanford University Press, 2016).

Introduction

1. For all military ranks, I use *Redhouse Yeni Türkçe-İngilizce Sözlük* for an approximation of how turn-of-the-century Ottoman military ranks mapped to American military ranks. They are not exact, but they give a sense of the rank of the military officer for readers more familiar with the American military system. *Redhouse Yeni Türkçe-İngilizce Sözlük*, 8th ed. (Istanbul: Redhouse Yayınevi, 1968).

2. See Baki Tezcan, *The Second Ottoman Empire: Political and Social Transformation in the Early Modern World* (Cambridge, UK: Cambridge University Press, 2010).

3. See Jacob M. Landau, "Abdülhamid II in 1912: The Return from Salonica," in *The Balance of Truth: Essays in Honour of Professor Geoffrey Lewis*, ed. Çigdem Balim-Harding and Colin Imber (Piscataway, NJ: Gorgias Press, 2010), 251–54.

4. The description of Abdülhamid's departure is translated and edited by the author from a column in a newspaper published in Beirut. "Kayfa Safara ila Selanik," *al-Ittihad al-'Uthmani*, June 5, 1909, 3.

5. In cities like Istanbul in the late nineteenth century, even though households employed several people, they were much closer to well-known aristocratic urban households of the Victorian era, where only the immediate family lived. I bring this up so my description will not be confused with historian Jane Hathaway's influential

conceptualization of eighteenth- and early nineteenth-century Egyptian households, which were extended client-patron networks that centered around one family. Jane Hathaway, *The Politics of Households in Ottoman Egypt: The Rise of the Qazdağlis*, Cambridge Studies in Islamic Civilization (Cambridge, UK: Cambridge University Press, 1996).

6. For more on the generation that survived the war and went on to play a role in post-Ottoman Arab nation-states, see Michael Provence, *The Last Ottoman Generation and the Making of the Modern Middle East* (Cambridge, UK: Cambridge University Press, 2017).

7. For a straightforward understanding of the reasons for the 1908 revolution, see Feroz Ahmad, "The Young Turk Revolution," *Journal of Contemporary History* 3, no. 3 (1968): 19–36.

8. I try not to use the problematic "Middle East" as part of my commitment to avoid terms that were imposed on the region by Western powers and have shifted over time as Western policies and geopolitical interests in the region have changed. "Southwest Asia" is a more accurate geographical descriptor that refers to a part of the Asian continent that were under Ottoman rule. For further discussion on the creation of the concept of the Middle East as a geopolitical region and its wider political implications, see for example Michael E. Bonine, Abbas Amanat, and Michael E. Gasper, ed., *Is There a Middle East? The Evolution of a Geopolitical Concept* (Stanford, CA: Stanford University Press, 2012); Guillemette Crouzet, *Inventing the Middle East: Britain and the Persian Gulf in the Age of Global Imperialism*, translated by Juliet Sutcliffe (Montreal, QC: McGill-Queen's University Press, 2022); Karen Culcasi, "Constructing and Naturalizing the Middle East," *Geographical Review* 100, no. 4 (2010): 583–97.

9. Cemil Aydın, "The Emergence of Transnational Muslim Thought, 1774–1914," in *Arabic Thought Beyond the Liberal Age, Towards an Intellectual History of the Nahda*, ed. Jens Hanssen and Max Weiss (Cambridge, UK: Cambridge University Press, 2016), 133–39. For further excellent analysis of the institution of the sultan-caliph during the reign of Abdülhamid II in the global context of racialized religious groups and interimperial competition, see Cemil Aydın, *The Idea of the Muslim World: A Global Intellectual History* (Cambridge, MA: Harvard University Press, 2017), 65–98; Cemil Aydın, "Imperial Paradoxes: A Caliphate for Subaltern Muslims," *ReOrient* 1, no. 2 (2016): 171–91. For a detailed understanding of Islam as a modern political state tool during the reign of Abdülhamid II in the Ottoman Empire, see Kemal H. Karpat, *The Politicization of Islam: Reconstructing Identity, State, Faith, and Community in the Late Ottoman State* (Oxford, UK: Oxford University Press, 2001).

10. Engin Deniz Akarlı, "The Tangled Ends of an Empire: Ottoman Encounters with the West and Problems of Westernization—an Overview," *Comparative Studies of South Asia, Africa, and the Middle East* 26, no. 3 (2006): 353–66.

11. The international treaties that followed World War I and led to a *de jure* partition and colonization of most of Southwest Asia have been written about for decades.

Here are some of the more recent publications: Hamza Karčić, "Sèvres at 100: The Peace Treaty That Partitioned the Ottoman Empire," *Journal of Muslim Minority Affairs* 40, no. 3 (2020): 470–79; Djene Rhys Bajalan, "The First World War, the End of the Ottoman Empire, and Question of Kurdish Statehood: A 'Missed' Opportunity?" *Ethnopolitics* 18, no. 1 (2019): 13–28; Othman Ali, "The Kurds and the Lausanne Peace Negotiations, 1922–23," *Middle Eastern Studies* 33, no. 3 (1997): 521–34; Keith David Watenpaugh, *Being Modern in the Middle East: Revolution, Nationalism, Colonialism, and the Arab Middle Class* (Princeton, NJ: Princeton University Press, 2006), 121–59; Eugene Rogan, *The Arabs: A History* (New York: Basic Books, 2009), 147–74; James Barr, *A Line in the Sand: The Anglo-French Struggle for the Middle East, 1914–1948* (W. W. Norton, 2013); Elizabeth F. Thompson, *How the West Stole Democracy from the Arabs: The Arab Congress of 1920, the Destruction of the Syrian State, and the Rise of Anti-Liberal Islamism* (New York: Atlantic Monthly Press, 2020).

12. Karen Barkey and George Gavrilis, "The Ottoman Millet System: Non-Territorial Autonomy and Its Contemporary Legacy," *Ethnopolitics* 15, no. 1 (2016): 26.

13. Arabism and Arab nationalism are some of the better researched topics in Middle Eastern studies. Most of the studies focus on intellectual history, with a few addressing some political and social manifestations beyond the intellectual and political classes. In English, some books that have taken up this issue as part of Ottoman history include Hasan Kayalı, *Arabs and Young Turks: Ottomanism, Arabism, and Islamism in the Ottoman Empire, 1908–1918* (Berkeley, CA: University of California Press, 1997); William Cleveland, *The Making of an Arab Nationalist: Ottomanism and Arabism in the Life and Thought of Sati' al-Husari* (Princeton, NJ: Princeton University Press, 2016); C. Ernest Dawn, ed., *From Ottomanism to Arabism: Essays on the Origins of Arab Nationalism* (Urbana, IL: University of Illinois Press, 1973); James L. Gelvin, *Divided Loyalties: Nationalism and Mass Politics in Syria at the Close of Empire* (Berkeley, CA: University of California Press, 1999); Rashid Khalidi et al., eds., *The Origins of Arab Nationalism* (New York: Columbia University Press, 1993); James L. Gelvin, "'Arab Nationalism': Has a New Framework Emerged? Pensée 1: 'Arab Nationalism' Meets Social Theory," *International Journal of Middle East Studies* 41, no. 1 (2009): 10–12; Michael Provence, *The Great Syrian Revolt and the Rise of Arab Nationalism* (Austin: University of Texas Press, 2005). For a very popular, albeit linear, Arab-nationalist telling of the rise of Arab nationalism, it is hard to ignore the lasting power of one of the first books to tackle the issue, originally published in 1938: George Antonius, *The Arab Awakening: The Story of the Arab National Movement* (reprint) (Berlin: Allegro Editions, 2015).

14. See Eugene Rogan, *The Fall of the Ottomans: The Great War in the Middle East* (New York: Basic Books, 2016); Sean McMeekin, *The Ottoman Endgame: War, Revolution, and the Making of the Modern Middle East, 1908–1923* (London: Penguin, 2015); Erik Jan Zürcher, *Turkey: A Modern History* (London: I. B. Tauris, 1998).

15. There are many studies on the various tools that the Hamidian state used to inculcate a sense of Ottomanness, or Ottoman loyalty, in its subjects-cum-citizens. Some have focused on education, while others have looked at the mechanics of infiltration of the central state in the day-to-day life of subjects across the empire. For example, see Benjamin C. Fortna, *Imperial Classroom: Islam, the State, and Education in the Late Ottoman Empire* (Oxford, UK: Oxford University Press, 2002); Selçuk Aksin Somel, *The Modernization of Public Education in the Ottoman Empire, 1839–1908: Islamization, Autocracy, and Discipline* (Leiden, Netherlands: Brill, 2001); Selim Deringil, *The Well-Protected Domains: Ideology and the Legitimation of Power in the Ottoman Empire, 1876–1909* (London: I. B. Tauris, 1998); Avner Wishnitzer, *Reading Clocks, Alla Turca* (Chicago: University of Chicago Press, 2015); İpek K. Yosmaoğlu, "Counting Bodies, Shaping Souls: The 1903 Census and National Identity in Ottoman Macedonia," *International Journal of Middle East Studies* 38, no. 1 (2006): 55–77.

16. There are tens of books and articles on the rise of various forms of nationalisms in the wake of the Ottoman Empire. The following is but a small sample, including only sources that do not relate to Bulgarian independence or the Macedonian and Armenian Questions, as those are dealt with in more detail later in the book. Feroz Ahmad, *The Young Turks and the Ottoman Nationalities: Armenians, Greeks, Albanians, Jews, and Arabs, 1908–1918* (Salt Lake City, UT: University of Utah Press, 2014); Isa Blumi, *Rethinking the Late Ottoman Empire: A Comparative Social and Political History of Albania and Yemen, 1878–1918* (Istanbul: İsis Press, 2003); Houri Berberian, *Roving Revolutionaries: Armenians and the Connected Revolutions in the Russian, Iranian, and Ottoman Worlds* (Oakland, CA: University of California Press, 2019); Aslı Iğsız, *Humanism in Ruins: Entangled Legacies of the Greek-Turkish Population Exchange* (Stanford, CA: Stanford University Press, 2018); Umut Ozkirimli and Spyros A. Sofos, *Tormented by History: Nationalism in Greece and Turkey* (London: C. Hurst, 2008); Michelle Campos, *Ottoman Brothers: Muslims, Christians, and Jews in Early Twentieth-Century Palestine* (Stanford, CA: Stanford University Press, 2011); Barbara Henning, *Narratives of the History of the Ottoman-Kurdish Bedirhani Family in Imperial and Post-Imperial Contexts* (Bamberg, Germany: University of Bamberg Press, 2018).

17. Here I am referencing the "notables" as a political concept first introduced by the late Albert Hourani in 1966. Since then, there have been many revisions of the concept and much legitimate critique. However, the concept remains generative, igniting debates and discussions about the power of the so-called notables and how and when it functioned in relation to the Ottoman state. For more on the politics of the notables and some well-known published debates on them, see Albert Hourani, "Ottoman Reforms and the Politics of the Notables," in *Beginnings of Modernization in the Middle East, the Nineteenth Century*, ed. William Polk and Richard Chambers (Chicago: University of Chicago Press, 1968), 41–68; Philip Khoury, "The Urban Notables Paradigm Revisited," *Revue des mondes musulmans et de la Méditerranée* 55, no. 1 (1990): 215–30;

James L. Gelvin, "The 'Politics of Notables' Forty Years After," *Middle East Studies Association Bulletin* 40, no. 1 (2006): 19–29.

18. On the second constitutional period and the representatives in the parliament, see Nader Sohrabi, *Revolution and Constitutionalism in the Ottoman Empire and Iran* (Cambridge, UK: Cambridge University Press, 2011). Also see the edited volume on the postrevolutionary period, with a few pieces on the parliament and politicians after 1908: Noémi Lévy-Aksu and François Georgeon, eds., *The Young Turk Revolution and the Ottoman Empire: The Aftermath of 1908* (London: I. B. Tauris, 2017).

19. Gelvin, *Divided Loyalties*; M. Talha Çiçek, *Syria in World War I: Politics, Economy, and Society* (London: Routledge, 2016).

20. 'Izzet signed his name on French documents preserved in the Ottoman Bank papers as Izzet, which is the spelling I adopt for his name. Salt Research, Ottoman Bank Archives, Sundry Documents, *İzzet*, IMDIV00304352.

21. Izzet Holo al-'Abid, *Abdülhamid'in Kara Kutusu, Arap İzzet Holo Paşa'nın Günlükleri*, ed. Pınar Güven and Birol Bayram, vols. 1 and 2 (Istanbul: İş Bankası Kültür Yayınları, 2019).

22. Michael Harsgor, "Total History: The Annales School," *Journal of Contemporary History* 13, no. 1 (1978): 1–13.

23. Two English-language books give a detailed political and social history of the Azmzades' role in the local power rivalry and provincial structures of power. Linda Schatkowski Schilcher, *Families in Politics: Damascene Factions and Estates of the 18th and 19th Centuries* (Stuttgart: Franz Steiner, 1985); Philip S. Khoury, *Urban Notables and Arab Nationalism: The Politics of Damascus, 1860–1920* (Cambridge, UK: Cambridge University Press, 1983).

24. David Carr, *Experience and History: Phenomenological Perspectives on the Historical World* (Oxford, UK: Oxford University Press, 2014).

25. Additionally, multiculturalism, where settlers are folded into a wider notion of belonging, erases the history of the violence of settler colonialism by ignoring the question of the native Canadians, known as the First Nations people. The First Nations people continue to be politically, socially, and culturally marginalized in their native land. Evelyn I. Légaré, "Canadian Multiculturalism and Aboriginal People: Negotiating a Place in the Nation," *Identities* 1, no. 4 (1995): 347–66; H. Srikanth, "Multiculturalism and the Aboriginal Peoples in Canada," *Economic and Political Weekly* 47, no. 23 (2012): 17–21; David Bruce MacDonald, "Reforming Multiculturalism in a Bi-National Society: Aboriginal Peoples and the Search for Truth and Reconciliation in Canada," *Canadian Journal of Sociology* 39, no. 1 (2014): 65–86; *Canadian Encyclopedia*, s.v. "multiculturalism," https://www.thecanadianencyclopedia.ca/en/article/multiculturalism (accessed May 5, 2021).

26. James W. Redhouse, *A Turkish and English Lexicon*, 4th ed. (Istanbul: Çağrı Yayınları, 2011), 1965. For more on the *millet* system, see Benjamin Braude, ed., *Christians*

and Jews in the Ottoman Empire, abr. ed. (Boulder, CO: Lynne Rienner, 2014); Ergün Çakal, "Pluralism, Tolerance, and Control: On the Millet System and the Question of Minorities," *International Journal on Minority and Group Rights* 27, no. 1 (2020): 34–65; Barkey and Gavrilis, "The Ottoman Millet System"; Karen Barkey, *Empire of Difference: The Ottomans in Comparative Perspective* (Cambridge, UK: Cambridge University Press, 2008).

27. Ussama Makdisi, *Age of Coexistence: The Ecumenical Frame and the Making of the Modern Arab World* (Oakland, CA: University of California Press, 2019), 11–12.

28. Redhouse, *A Turkish and English Lexicon*, 1324. For a discussion of the development of terms for "race" in Arabic and Turkish, see Elise K. Burton, *Genetic Crossroads: The Middle East and the Science of Human Heredity* (Stanford, CA: Stanford University Press, 2021), 15–16.

29. For example, Zouhair Ghazzal's argument that terminology identifying Arab or Turk was not helpful in the context of the Ottoman Empire. As I mentioned, in the last two decades of the empire, those words became meaningful and consequential before the spread of Arab or Turkish nationalism. Zouhair Ghazzal, "The Historiography of Arab-Turkish Relations: A Re-Assessment," review of "al-'Alaqat al-'Arabiyya al-Turkiyya (Arap-Türk Münasebetleri)" by Ekmeleddin İhsanoğlu and Muhammad Safi al-Din Abu al-'Izz, *Turkish Studies Association Bulletin* 24, no. 1 (2000): 124–25.

30. For a critical rethinking of the Nahda and the intellectual history of the Arab world at the turn of the twentieth century, I highly recommend Jens Hanssen and Max Weiss, "Language, Mind, Freedom, and Time: The Modern Arab Intellectual Tradition in Four Words," introduction to *Arabic Thought Beyond the Liberal Age, Towards an Intellectual History of the Nahda* (Cambridge, UK: Cambridge University Press, 2016), 1–37.

31. Erol Ülker, "Contextualizing Turkification: Nation Building in the Late Ottoman Empire 1909–18," *Nations and Nationalism* 11, no. 4 (2005): 615–17.

32. Kayalı, *Arabs and Young Turks*, 113–14.

33. There are many popular recountings of the so-called "Arab Revolt" that tout the heroics of T. E. Lawrence and the Hashemites. A quick Google search produces hundreds of hits. The revolt remains a sensitive topic in Turkey and in most of the Arab world, with the former painting all Arabs with a broad brush of treasonous conspiracy because of it and the latter incorporating it into nationalist accounts of the birth of the various Arab nation-states. There are less sensational treatments of the revolt; see, for example, Rogan, *The Arabs*; Rogan, *The Fall of the Ottomans*; Eliezer Tauber, *The Arab Movements in World War I* (London: Routledge, 2014); Kayalı, *Arabs and Young Turks*.

34. For the latest monograph-length book on this topic, see Hasan Kayalı, *Imperial Resilience: The Great War's End, Ottoman Longevity, and Incidental Nations* (Oakland, CA: University of California Press, 2021).

35. See Campos, *Ottoman Brothers*, 20–92; Bedross Der Matossian, *Shattered Dreams of Revolution: From Liberty to Violence in the Late Ottoman Empire* (Stanford, CA: Stanford University Press, 2014).

36. Selim Deringil, "'They Live in a State of Nomadism and Savagery': The Late Ottoman Empire and the Post-Colonial Debate," *Comparative Studies in Society and History* 45, no. 2 (2003): 311–42; Thomas Kuehn, *Empire, Islam, and Politics of Difference* (Leiden, Netherlands: Brill, 2011).

37. Mostafa Minawi, "Beyond Rhetoric: Reassessing Bedouin-Ottoman Relations along the Route of the Hijaz Telegraph Line at the End of the Nineteenth Century," *Journal of the Economic and Social History of the Orient* 58, no. 1–2 (2015): 74–104.

38. The permeation of colonial discourse and tools of differentiation from the colonies into the metropole has been well studied in the British and French imperial context. Two seminal works tackle this issue: Ann Laura Stoler and Frederick Cooper, "Between Metropole and Colony: Rethinking a Research Agenda," in *Tensions of Empire: Colonial Cultures in a Bourgeois World*, ed. Frederick Cooper and Ann Laura Stoler (Oakland, CA: University of California Press, 1997), 1–56; Kathleen Wilson, ed., *A New Imperial History: Culture, Identity, and Modernity in Britain and the Empire, 1660–1840* (Cambridge, UK: Cambridge University Press, 2004).

39. Deborah Reed-Danahay, *Bourdieu and Social Space: Mobilities, Trajectories, Emplacements* (New York: Berghahn, 2020), 7.

40. Reed-Danahay, *Bourdieu and Social Space*, 23.

41. Reed-Danahay, *Bourdieu and Social Space*, 7.

42. Pierre Bourdieu, "Habitus," in *Habitus: A Sense of Place*, ed. Jean Hiller and Emma Rooksby (Aldershot, UK: Ashgate, 2002), 27–29.

43. I have borrowed this term from Durba Ghosh's discussion of the "Imperial Turn" in 2012. Even though she used this term in reference to accessing the agency of the "subaltern," its use paralleled accessing the personal lives of elites like Sadik, who almost never wrote outside of the gaze of imperial censorship. See Durba Ghosh, "Another Set of Imperial Turns?" *American Historical Review* 117, no. 3 (2012): 772–93.

44. A seminal work on race and racism in the context of the Ottoman Empire is Eve Troutt Powell, *A Different Shade of Colonialism: Egypt, Great Britain, and the Mastery of the Sudan* (Oakland, CA: University of California Press, 2003). Others have studied racism in the context of the institution of slavery in the Ottoman Empire. See for example, Terence Walz and Kenneth M. Cuno, eds., *Race and Slavery in the Middle East: Histories of Trans-Saharan Africans in 19th-Century Egypt, Sudan, and the Ottoman Mediterranean* (Cairo: American University in Cairo Press, 2010); Abdulhamit Avras, "Early Modern Eunuchs and the Transing of Gender and Race," *Journal of Early Modern Cultural Studies* 19, no. 4 (2020): 116–36. More recently the study of race and racism in the late Ottoman Empire and the post-Ottoman states has been the object of much more

attention. Two works that stand out are Ezgi Güner, "The Soul of the White Muslim: Race, Empire, and Africa in Turkey" (PhD diss., University of Illinois at Urbana-Champaign, 2020); Murat Ergin, *Is the Turk a White Man? Race and Modernity in the Making of Turkish Identity* (Leiden, Netherlands: Brill, 2017). Several promising young scholars who work on race and racism in Southwest Asia are waiting in the wings.

45. Frantz Fanon, *Black Skin, White Masks*, translated by Charles Lam Markmann, 2nd ed. (London: Pluto Press, 2008); Homi K. Bhabha, *The Location of Culture*, 2nd ed. (London: Routledge, 2004); Homi K. Bhabha, "Forward to the 1986 Edition," in *Black Skin, White Masks*, 2nd ed. (London: Pluto Press, 2008); Claude Lévi-Strauss, *Structural Anthropology*, rev. ed. (New York: Basic Books, 1974).

46. Here I borrow the term from Edward Said when he described the European fascination with the people of the "Near East" in their travelogues. Edward Said, *Orientalism* (London: Pantheon Books, 1978); Edward W. Said, *Culture and Imperialism* (New York: Vintage Books, 1994).

47. Bourdieu, "Habitus"; Will Atkinson, *Bourdieu and After, A Guide to Relational Phenomenology* (London: Routledge, 2020); Reed-Danahay, *Bourdieu and Social Space*.

48. These are some of the writers in the field who have put the human experience at the center of their work and who have all been an inspiration to me: Christine M. Philliou, *Turkey: A Past Against History* (Oakland, CA: University of California Press, 2021), and *Biography of an Empire: Governing Ottomans in an Age of Revolution* (Oakland, CA: University of California Press, 2010); A. Holly Shissler, *Between Two Empires: Ahmet Ağaoğlu and the New Turkey* (London: I. B. Tauris, 2003); M'hamed Oualdi, *A Slave Between Empires: A Transimperial History of North Africa* (New York: Columbia University Press, 2020); Julia Philips Cohen and Sarah Abrevaya Stein, eds., *Sephardi Lives: A Documentary History, 1700–1950* (Stanford, CA: Stanford University Press, 2014); Eve Troutt Powell, *Tell This in My Memory: Stories of Enslavement from Egypt, Sudan, and the Ottoman Empire* (Stanford, CA: Stanford University Press, 2012); Cornell H. Fleischer, *Bureaucrat and Intellectual in the Ottoman Empire: The Historian Mustafa Ali* (Princeton, NJ: Princeton University Press, 1986); Provence, *The Last Ottoman Generation*.

49. David A. Bell, "Total History and Microhistory: The French and Italian Paradigms," in *A Companion to Western Historical Thought*, ed. Lloyd Kramer and Sarah Maza (Oxford: Blackwell Publishers, 2002), 262–76; Cheng-chung Lai, *Braudel's Historiography Reconsidered* (Lanham, MD: University Press of America, 2004), 1–30; Dale Tomich, "The Order of Historical Time: The Longue Durée and Micro-History," *Almanack*, no. 2 (2011): 38–52.

50. Lai, *Braudel's Historiography Reconsidered*.

51. John-Paul A. Ghobrial, "Introduction: Seeing the World like a Microhistorian," *Past & Present* 242, no. 14 (2019): 13. Some other inspiring examples that convinced me of the validity of this project are classics such as Natalie Zemon Davis, *The Return of Martin Guerre* (Cambridge, MA: Harvard University Press, 1983); Robert Darnton, *The*

Great Cat Massacre: And Other Episodes in French Cultural History (New York: Basic Books, 2009); Carlo Ginzburg, *The Cheese and the Worms: The Cosmos of a Sixteenth-Century Miller*, trans. John Tedeschi and Anne C. Tedeschi (Baltimore: Johns Hopkins University Press, 1980).

52. Thomas V. Cohen, "The Macrohistory of Microhistory," *Journal of Medieval and Early Modern Studies* 47, no. 1 (2017): 53–73.

53. Thomas A. Kohut, *A German Generation: An Experiential History of the Twentieth Century* (New Haven, CT: Yale University Press, 2012); Donna Orange, "Experiential History: Understanding Backwards," in *History Flows through Us: Germany, the Holocaust, and the Importance of Empathy*, ed. Roger Frie (London: Routledge, 2018), 49–60, and "History Flows Through Us: Psychoanalysis and Historical Understanding," *Psychoanalysis, Self and Context* 12, no. 3 (2017): 221–29.

54. Carlo Ginzburg and Carlo Poni, "The Name and the Game: Unequal Exchange and the Historiographic Marketplace," in *Microhistory and the Lost People of Europe*, ed. Edward Muir and Guido Ruggiero (Baltimore, MD: Johns Hopkins University Press, 1991), 1–9. I was inspired by Ginzburg's methodology following the trail of clues across countries and time, often with no idea what I was about to find. Carlo Ginzburg, *Clues, Myths, and the Historical Method*, trans. John Tedeschi and Anne C. Tedeschi, reprint (Baltimore, MD: Johns Hopkins University Press, 2013).

55. Ali Karaca, "Azmzadeler," in *TDV İslam Ansiklopedisi* (Ankara: Türkiye Diyanet Vakfı, 1991), 4:350. Also see Ali Karaca, "Azm-zade Mehmet Paşa," MA thesis, Marmara Üniversitesi, 1986.

56. 'Abd al-Qadir al-'Azm, *al-Usra al-'Azmiyya* (Damascus: Matba'at al-Insha', 1960), 18–21.

57. Salt Research, Ottoman Bank Archives, OFTA0240, https://archives.sal tresearch.org/handle/123456789/168591; OFTA0148, https://archives.saltresearch .org/handle/123456789/155590; OFTM0139, https://archives.saltresearch.org/han dle/123456789/146935.

58. Meltem Türköz, *Naming and Nation-Building in Turkey: The 1934 Surname Law* (New York: Palgrave, 2018).

59. Courtney L. McCluney, Kathrina Robotham, Serenity Lee, Richard Smith, and Myles Durkee, "The Costs of Code-Switching," *Harvard Business Review*, November 15, 2019, https://hbr.org/2019/11/the-costs-of-codeswitching.

60. Historian Khaled Fahmy famously made the convincing argument that it is perhaps more historically accurate to write his name the way he, a Turkish-speaking governor-general of the Province of Egypt, most likely would have: Mehmed Ali. However, the debate continues. Fahmy, *All the Pasha's Men: Mehmed Ali, His Army and the Making of Modern Egypt* (Cairo: American University in Cairo Press, 1997).

61. Salt Research, Ottoman Bank Archives, OFTS0021, https://archives.sal tresearch.org/handle/123456789/172439.

62. BOA, A.MTZ(04)-122/69 (1/11/1904).

63. BOA, A.MTZ(04)-122/69 (1/11/1904). In modern Turkish, it would be rendered as "Şimdi Sofya'ya vasıl ve vazaifi mir köle çakranamın ifasına besmele keşi ibtidar olduğum maruzdur ferman."

64. For a nuanced, historically informed sociological treatment of the surname law and the rupture it introduced in Turkish society, see Türköz, *Naming and Nation-Building in Turkey*.

65. Mehmet İpşirli, "Beylerbeyi," in *TDV İslam Ansiklopedisi* (Ankara: Türkiye Diyanet Vakfı, 1992), 6:69–74; Abdülkadir Özcan, "Paşa," in *TDV İslam Ansiklopedisi* (Ankara: Türkiye Diyanet Vakfı, 2007), 34:182–83; Orhan Köprülü, "Bey," in *TDV İslam Ansiklopedisi* (Ankara: Türkiye Diyanet Vakfı, 1992) 6:11–12.

Chapter 1

1. Sadik's sitting room as described by Mrs. Max Müller. Georgina Adelaide Müller, *Letters from Constantinople, by Mrs. Max Müller* (London: Longmans, Green, 1897), 181–82.

2. I do not engage with historian Albert Hourani's generative use of the term or the debates that followed it, which are mostly centered on how, when, where, and to whom it applies in an analytically meaningful way. However, the term is useful to signal the milieus that the Azmzades came from to students of Ottoman history who are familiar with the nuances of the debate. It will, however, bear no weight on the arguments to be made later in the book that have to do with the Ottoman metropole. For more on the "Notable Paradigm," see Philip Khoury, "The Urban Notables Paradigm Revisited," *Revue des mondes musulmans et de la Méditerranée* 55, no. 1 (1990): 215–30.

3. For an exposé of the Melhamé family as a major player in the Ottoman imperial administration, see Jens Hanssen, "'Malhamé-Malfamé': Levantine Elites and Transimperial Networks on the Eve of the Young Turk Revolution," *International Journal of Middle East Studies* 43, no. 1 (2011): 25–48.

4. See Ussama Makdisi, *The Culture of Sectarianism: Community, History, and Violence in Nineteenth-Century Ottoman Lebanon* (Oakland, CA: University of California Press, 2000); Ilham Khuri-Makdisi, *The Eastern Mediterranean and the Making of Global Radicalism, 1860–1914* (Oakland, CA: University of California Press, 2010); Leila Tarazi Fawaz, *An Occasion for War: Civil Conflict in Lebanon and Damascus in 1860* (Oakland, CA: University of California Press, 1994); Jens Hanssen, *Fin de Siècle Beirut: The Making of an Ottoman Provincial Capital* (Oxford, UK: Oxford University Press, 2005).

5. Linda Schatkowski Schilcher, *Families in Politics: Damascene Factions and Estates of the 18th and 19th Centuries* (Stuttgart, Germany: Franz Steiner, 1985), 29–30.

6. BOA, İ.MVL-99/2138 (26/6/1847); A.TŞF-4/20 (26/2/1848).

7. BOA, C.ZB-74/3680 (1858).

8. For more on sectarian violence in Damascus and neighboring cities, see Makdisi, *The Culture of Sectarianism*; Khuri-Makdisi, *The Eastern Mediterranean*; Fawaz, *An Occasion for War*; Hanssen, *Fin de Siècle Beirut*.

9. Schatkowski Schilcher, *Families in Politics*, 100–102.

10. BOA, İ.DH-494/33565 (13/8/1862).

11. The information on the Lazarist school that was formerly a Jesuit mission is from Ceasar E. Farah, "Arab Supporters of Sultan Abdulhamid II: 'Izzet al-'Abid," *Archivum Ottomanicum* 15 (1997): 197.

12. "Collége Saint Joseph Antoura-Historique," Collège Saint Joseph d'Antoura, www.csja.edu.lb/french/a-propos/historique (accessed April 5, 2021). Antoura gained notoriety for being the site of the orphanage for Armenian genocide survivors in World War I. This was the project of two characters who would try to erase the cultural heritage of children in the orphanage—Cemal Pasha and Halide Edib—Halide Edib was mentioned earlier in this chapter. Cemal Pasha will be discussed in Chapter 7. What they were doing was correctly identified by historian Keith David Watenpaugh, who wrote the introduction to the published memoirs of one of the survivors of the genocide, as an act of genocide. See Karnig Panian, *Goodbye, Antoura: A Memory of the Armenian Genocide* (Stanford, CA: Stanford University Press, 2015).

13. BOA, DH.SAİD-197/173 (24/6/1914) simply puts it as going to "Patriarchate schools and the American College" in Beirut. My thanks to one of the blind reviewers, who noted that the Patriarchate school most likely referred to the Greek Catholic Collège Patriarchal in Beirut, which I later confirmed. Many other members of the family followed a similar path, with some studying at the National School (*al-Madrasa al-Wataniyya*), which was a feeder school to the American College, officially called the Syrian Protestant College. For more on Butrus al-Bustani and Protestant education in Beirut in the 1880s, see Jens Hanssen and Hicham Safieddine, *Butrus al-Bustani: From Protestant Convert to Ottoman Patriot and Arab Reformer* (Oakland, CA: University of California Press, 2019).

14. Bayard Dodge, *The American University of Beirut* (Beirut: Khayyat Publishing, 1958), 13. It was common practice to have a first name that was one of the prophet's many names (Muhammed, Ahmed, etc.), but to go by the more unique second name. In this case, Ahmed al-Mu'ayyad was known as al-Mu'ayyad or Mu'ayyad.

15. Sadik Jalal al-'Azm conveyed information about the land sale during an interview conducted in the winter of 2009 in his Damascus residence.

16. BOA, DH.SAİD-197/173 (24/6/1914); 'Abd al-Qadir al-'Azm, *al-Usra al-'Azmiyya* (Damascus: Matba'at al-Insha', 1960), 59. There are discrepancies between the salary reported by al-'Azm, which he got through hearsay, and information in the public records (*Sicil-i Umumi*, abbreviated as DH.SAİD in the BOA). For the purpose of this chapter, where discrepancies occurred I assumed the public records' information to be

more accurate. The public records were much more detailed and were used to calculate Shafiq al-Mu'ayyad's pension and as such must have been confirmed by him personally at the time.

17. Many other members of the family followed a similar path, with some studying at *al-Madrasa al-Wataniyya*, which was a feeder to the Syrian Protestant College.

18. al-ʿAzm, *al-Usra al-ʿAzmiyya* 67.

19. Schatkowski Schilcher, *Families in Politics*, 140–41.

20. Historian C. E. Farah puts his year of birth at 1854, but later in the same article he puts it at 1850, while the Ottoman archives put his year of birth at 1851–1852. Farah, "Arab Supporters of Sultan Abdulhamid II," 193, 196; BOA, DH.SAİDd.0004 as transliterated into modern Turkish in Izzet Holo al-ʿAbid, *Abdülhamid'in Kara Kutusu, Arap İzzet Holo Paşa'nın Günlükleri*, ed. Pınar Güven and Birol Bayram (Istanbul: İş Bankası Kültür Yayınları, 2019), vol. 1, sec. 1, 21–27.

21. Farah, "Arab Supporters of Sultan Abdulhamid II," 196–97. Al-Yaziji is credited, along with al-Bustani, for reviving Arabic as a language of literature and intellectual discourse. He and al-Bustani founded The Syrian Society for the Sciences and Arts. For more on the importance of al-Yaziji and al-Bustani in the linguistic "awakening," see Christian Junge, "al-Yaziji, Nasif (1800–1871)," in *Routledge Encyclopedia of Modernism* (Leiden, Netherlands: Routledge, 2016), https://www.rem.routledge.com/articles/al-yaziji-nasif-1800-1871.

22. From DH.SAİDd.0004 as transliterated into Modern Turkish in al-ʿAbid, *Abdülhamid'in Kara Kutusu*, vol. 1, sec. 1, 21–27. See the announcement of the members of this commission under "Tevcihat" in *İkdam* (8/5/1900), 1.

23. Farah, "Arab Supporters of Sultan Abdulhamid II," 197.

24. Schatkowski Schilcher, *Families in Politics*, 155–56.

25. al-ʿAzm, *al-Usra al-ʿAzmiyya*, 95.

26. Farah, "Arab Supporters of Sultan Abdulhamid II," 196.

27. Farah, "Arab Supporters of Sultan Abdulhamid II," 196.

28. Philip S. Khoury, *Urban Notables and Arab Nationalism: The Politics of Damascus, 1860–1920* (Cambridge, UK: Cambridge University Press, 1983), 38–39. The usually reliable guide to big families and dynasties of the Ottoman Empire, *Devletler ve Hanedanlar*, contains many mistakes about the life of Izzet, his wife, his children, his family's origins, and his mother. Yılmaz Öztuna, *Devletler ve Hanedanlar, Türkiye (1074–1990)*, vol. 2 (Ankara: Kültür Bakanlığı Yayınları, 1969), 572–73. I cross-referenced several sources I had gathered to come up with the most accurate information at my disposal.

29. There is no evidence of Namık Pasha ever being a governor of Syria, as the writer claims. See Abdullah Saydam, "Namık Paşa (1804–1892), Osmanlı Devlet Adamı," in *TDV İslam Ansiklopedisi* (Ankara: Türkiye Diyanet Vakfı, 2006), 32:379–80.

30. al-ʿAzm, *al-Usra al-ʿAzmiyya*, 49–50.

31. BOA, İ.DH-1016/80203 (19/1/1887); Y.PRK.AZJ-11/106 (22/3/1887).

32. BOA, Y.PRK.AZJ-11/106 (22/3/1887).

33. BOA, Y.MTV-29/15 (13/12/1887).

34. BOA, İ.DH-1094/85804 (26/8/1888).

35. Although I could not find a direct link, the current Arab Republic of Syria and the Lebanese Republic consulates in Istanbul are on the same streets, tens of meters from where Sadik's *konak* used to stand.

36. Banu Bilgicioğlu, "Teşvikiye Camii, İstanbul'da XIX. Yüzyılın Ortalarında İnşa Edilen Cami," *TDV İslam Ansiklopedisi* (Ankara: Türkiye Diyanet Vakfı, 2011), 40:576–78. The column, which was erected to mark the establishment of the new neighborhood, is one of the very few historical landmarks that still stand in Teşvikiye.

37. Yıldız Salman, "'Alafranga'dan 'Moderne' Teşvikiye Nişantaşı," in *Dolmabahçe, Mekan'ın Hafızası*, ed. Bahar Kaya (Istanbul: İstanbul Bilgi Üniversitesi Yayınları, 2016), 118–19; M. Burak Çetintaş, "Osmanlı Sivil Mimarlığı Bağlamında Teşvikiye/Nişantaşı Sarayları ve Konakları," in *Dolmabahçe, Mekanın Hafızası*, ed. Bahar Kaya (Istanbul: İstanbul Bilgi Üniversitesi Yayınları, 2016), 169–90.

38. Alan Duben and Cem Behar, *Istanbul Households: Marriage, Family, and Fertility 1880–1940* (Cambridge, UK: Cambridge University Press, 1991), 31.

39. Salman, "Alafranga," 120–21.

40. In recent years, there has been a renewed interest in Max Müller. For more on his career and life, see John R. Davis and Angus Nicholls, "Friedrich Max Müller: The Career and Intellectual Trajectory of a German Philologist in Victorian Britain," *Publications of the English Goethe Society* 85, no. 2–3 (2016): 67–97.

41. Müller, *Letters from Constantinople*, 181–82.

42. For more on some of the famous residents of Teşvikiye, see M. Burak Çetintaş, *Dolmabahçe'den Nişantaşı'na: Sultanların Ve Paşaların Semtinin Tarihi*, 2nd ed. (Istanbul: Antik A. Ş. Kültür Yayınları, 2012), 248–49. A big thank you goes to Aslıhan Günhan for recommending many books on the architectural and urban history of Nişantaşı and Beşiktaş.

43. Çetintaş, "Osmanlı Sivil," 172, 178–79, 187; Çetintaş, *Dolmabahçe'den Nişantaşı'na*, 150–51; For more on the political thought of Jamal al-Din al-Afghani, see Nikki R. Keddie, *An Islamic Response to Imperialism: Political and Religious Writings of Sayyid Jamal ad-Din "al-Afghani"* (Oakland, CA: University of California Press, 1983).

44. For an excellent book about the life of leisure with a focus on late nineteenth-century Istanbul, see Melis Hafez, *Inventing Laziness: The Culture of Productivity in Late Ottoman Society* (Cambridge, UK: Cambridge University Press, 2021). Also see A. Yumul, "'A Prostitute Lodging in the Bosom of Turkishness': Istanbul's Pera and Its Representation," *Journal of Intercultural Studies* 30, no. 1 (2009): 57–72.

45. K. Mehmet Kentel, "Caricaturizing 'Cosmopolitan' Pera: Play, Critique, and Absence in Yusuf Franko's Caricatures, 1884–1896," *Journal of the Ottoman and Turkish Studies Association* 5, no. 1 (2018): 7–32.

46. Much has been written about Pera nights. One of the most beautifully written books on early twentieth-century Istanbul, centering on the famous Pera Palace Hotel, is Charles King's *Midnight at the Pera Palace: The Birth of Modern Istanbul* (New York: W. W. Norton, 2014). The Grand hotel de Londres's website details its history. Londrahotel.net/about-us/ (accessed November 11, 2020). It was often featured as reporting on its hosting of parties and diplomatic events such as Izzet al-'Abid's reception in honor of the Spanish ambassador. "Şüunat," *İkdam*, April 17, 1900, 2.

47. Merih Erol, "Surveillance, Urban Governance and Legitimacy in Late Ottoman Istanbul: Spying on Music and Entertainment during the Hamidian Regime (1876–1909)," *Urban History* 40, no. 4 (2013): 706–25.

48. For more on the arrival of residential apartments, see Salman, "'Alafranga,'" 137–43. Beylerbey, on the Asian side of Istanbul, was also the neighborhood where Abdülhamid II would spend his final days after he his return from Salonica.

49. Çetintaş, *Dolmabahçe'den Nişantaşı'na*, 321–24.

50. Shafiq al-Mu'ayyad's exact address was mentioned in a petition sent on behalf of his son-in-law Abd 'al-Qadir al-'Azm, in 1916, asking that he be allowed back in his home on Bostan Sokak. See BOA, DH.EUM.4.Şb-7/2 (5/7/1916). Information about the location of Sadik al-Mu'ayyad's Istanbul residence comes from an interview I conducted with Sadiq Jalal al-'Azm in Damascus in February 2009.

51. Müller, *Letters from Constantinople*, 113.

52. The entire description, including the colorful imagery inside the parentheses, is hers. Müller, *Letters from Constantinople*, 100.

53. Müller, *Letters from Constantinople*, 190.

54. Müller, *Letters from Constantinople*, 161.

55. Müller, *Letters from Constantinople*, 161.

56. Laïc Wacquant and Pierre Bourdieu, "The Cunning of Imperial Reason," in *Pierre Bourdieu and Democratic Politics: The Mystery of Ministry*, ed. Laïc Wacquant (Cambridge, UK: Polity Press, 2005), 179.

57. Müller, *Letters from Constantinople*, 130.

58. Müller, *Letters from Constantinople*, 181–83.

59. Müller, *Letters from Constantinople*, 181–83.

60. Müller, *Letters from Constantinople*, 181–83.

61. Schatkowski Schilcher, *Families in Politics*, 138–39.

62. al-'Azm, *al-Usra al-'Azmiyya*, 150; Schatkowski Schilcher, *Families in Politics*, 139. The mausoleum of Haqqi and other Azmzade family members in Cairo, along with

many other elite family mausoleums, is slated to be destroyed in 2022 to make way for a new highway.

63. Walter Scott, *The Heart of Midlothian* (Edinburgh: Edinburgh University Library Walter Scott Digital Archive), http://www.walterscott.lib.ed.ac.uk/works/novels/midlothian.html (accessed April 29, 2022).

64. From an interview with Sadiq Jalal al-ʿAzm conducted in February 2009.

65. Müller, *Letters from Constantinople*, 181–83.

66. Khaled al-ʿAzm, *Mudhakarat Khaled al-ʿAzm* (Damascus: Dar al-Mutahida li-l-Nashr, 1950), 33–34. Düzgün was a lead-based product that women used to lighten their complexion. It was toxic and caused tooth decay. See Berrak Burçak, "Hygienic Beauty: Discussing Ottoman-Muslim Female Beauty, Health, and Hygiene in the Hamidian Era," *Middle Eastern Studies* 54, no. 3 (2018): 343–60.

67. Marmara Üniversitesi Open Access, Taha Toros Arşivi, Ahmet Cevat Paşa-Cevat Şakir Kabaağaçlı, 001560153008, http://hdl.handle.net/11424/141821 (accessed January 18, 2022).

68. Christoph Herzog, "Ahmed Cevad Paşa, Kabaağaçzade," in *Encyclopedia of Islam 3*, ed. Kate Fleet, Gudrun Krämer, Denis Matringe, John Nawas, and Everett Rowson (Leiden, Netherlands: Brill, 2008), http://dx.doi.org.proxy.library.cornell.edu/10.1163/1573-3912_ei3_COM_26308 (accessed January 10, 2020); Taha Toros arşivinden, Son Sadrazamlar, İbnül Emin as discussed in Jiy Zafer Süren, "Karden İsa'nın Kızları (III)–Nimet Hanım'ın Kaderi" *JINEPS*, September 1, 2016, https://jinepsgazetesi.com/2016/09/karden-isanin-kizlari-iii-nimet-hanimin-kaderi/ (accessed October 4, 2020).

69. al-ʿAzm, *al-Usra al-ʿAzmiyya*, 61–62.

70. As quoted in Jiye Zafer Süren, "Karden İsa'nın Kızları (II)," *JINEPS*, August 1, 2016, https://jinepsgazetesi.com/2016/08/karden-isanin-kizlari-ii/ (accessed October 4, 2020).

71. Çetintaş, *Dolmabahçe'den Nişantaşı'na*, 256–67.

72. Yılmaz Öztuna, *Devletler ve Hanelerden, Türkiye (1074–1990), Vol. 2* (Ankara: Kültür Bakanlığı Yayınları, 1989), 694; Marmara Üniversitesi, Taha Toros Arşivi, Ahmet Cevat Paşa-Cevat Şakir Kabaağaçlı, 001512529006, http://hdl.handle.net/11424/148353 (accessed January 16, 2022).

73. This is according to an amateur historian specializing in family histories of famous Circassian-Turkish citizens, who collected this information from an interview he conducted with the grandson of one of Nimet's sisters. See Süren, "Karden İsa'nın Kızları (II)," *JINEPS*, August 8, 2016, https://jinepsgazetesi.com/2016/08/karden-isanin-kizlari-ii/ (accessed October 4, 2020).

74. Ceyda Karamursel, "Transplanted Slavery, Contested Freedom, and Vernacularization of Rights in the Reform Era Ottoman Empire," *Comparative Studies in Society and History* 59, no. 3 (2017): 694–709.

75. Halide Edib Adıvar, *Memoirs of Halidé Edib* (New York: Century, 1926), 16–18.

76. Betül İpşirli Argıt, *Life after the Harem: Female Palace Slaves, Patronage, and the Imperial Ottoman Court* (Cambridge, UK: Cambridge University Press, 2020), 4–7.

77. See Ceyda Karamursel, "The Uncertainties of Freedom: The Second Constitutional Era and the End of Slavery in the Late Ottoman Empire," *Journal of Women's History* 28, no. 3 (2016): 138–61.

78. For a comprehensive treatment of the figure of *Arap Bacı* in Turkish imagination and historical literature, see Wingham Zavier, "Arap Bacı'nın Ara Muhaveresi: Under the Shadow of the Ottoman Empire and Its Study," *Yıllık: Annual of Istanbul Studies* 3, no. 1 (2021): 177–83.

79. Kimberly Wallace-Sanders, *Mammy: A Century of Race, Gender, and Southern Memory* (Ann Arbor, MI: University of Michigan Press, 2008), 4–8.

80. Edib Adıvar, *Memoirs of Halidé Edib*, 49.

81. Edib Adıvar, *Memoirs of Halidé Edib*, 166.

82. Edib Adıvar, *Memoirs of Halidé Edib*, 168.

83. al-'Azm, *Mudhakarat Khaled al-'Azm*, 26.

84. al-'Azm, *Mudhakarat Khaled al-'Azm*, 3, 10.

85. Little else is known about Bilal. How Sadik "brought" him from Sudan is not known. There is one reference to Sadik being in Sudan during his Abyssinian trip, but this trip does not match the time frame: the photo was taken in 1903 and Sadik was in Abyssinia in 1904. An alternative explanation might be that Bilal was from Sudan but became Sadik's *evlatlık* in Istanbul or while Sadik was on assignment in Hijaz in 1900. As the reader might have picked up, the line between "fostering" a child and slavery was very thin indeed, so I am trying not to make any definitive claims about the status of Bilal in Sadik's family because I have no certain answers.

86. Yahya Araz, "Rural Girls as Domestic Servants in Late Ottoman Istanbul," in *Children and Childhood in the Ottoman Empire: From the 15th to the 20th Century*, ed. Gülay Yılmaz and Zachs Fruma (Edinburgh: Edinburgh University Press, 2021), 196.

87. Abdullah Bay, "Osmanlı Toplumunda Evlatlıklar ve Hukukı Durumları," *Turkish Studies, International Periodical for the Languages, Literature, and History of Turkish and Turkic* 9, no. 4 (2014): 149–63.

88. Amr al-'Azm, an archeologist who is the great-grandson of Sadik Azmzade and the son of the philosopher Sadiq Jalal al-'Azm, told me of a similar practice in Ottoman Syria that horrified him. There, a child, usually female, was handed over by a rural Alawite family in return for a financial arrangement to serve in a rich urban household like those of the Azmzades. This arrangement sometimes resulted in terrible abuse of the child. I asked Amr's permission before sharing this anecdote.

89. For more on the complicated end of Circassian slavery, see Karamursel, "Uncertainties of Freedom."

90. Mustafa Olpak, "Osmanlı İmparatorluğu'nda köle, Türkiye Cumhuriyeti'nde evlatlık: Afro-Türkler," *Ankara Üniversitesi SBF Dergisi* 68, no. 1 (2013): 125–26. For more on *evlatlık*, see Ferhunde Özbay, *Türkiye'de Evlatlık Kurumu: Köle Mi, Evlat Mı?* (Istanbul: Boğaziçi Üniversitesi Yayınları, 1999). A special thank you to Ceyda Karamursel (SOAS) who kindly helped me answer some questions I had about *evlatlık*.

91. BOA, ML.EEM-1372/69 (18/1/1903).

92. Sadik al-Mu'ayyad Azmzade, *Rihlat al-Habasha, Min al-Istana ila Addis Ababa*, ed. Nouri al-Jarrah, trans. Rafiq Azmzade (Abu Dhabi: Dar al-Suwaydi li-l-Nashir wa-l-Tawzi', 2001), 25, 34.

93. Çetintaş, *Dolmabahçe'den Nişantaşı'na*, 294.

Chapter 2

1. Izzet Holo al-'Abid, *Abdülhamid'in Kara Kutusu, Arap İzzet Holo Paşa'nın Günlükleri*, ed. Pınar Güven and Birol Bayram (Istanbul: İş Bankası Kültür Yayınları, 2019), vol. 2, sec. 3, 24.

2. For more on the nostalgia for empire and contemporary politics in Turkey, see M. Hakan Yavuz, *Nostalgia for the Empire: The Politics of Neo-Ottomanism* (Oxford, UK: Oxford University Press, 2020). Also see Edward Wastnidge, "Imperial Grandeur and Selective Memory: Re-Assessing Neo-Ottomanism in Turkish Foreign and Domestic Politics," *Middle East Critique* 28, no. 1 (2019): 7–28. For more on the nostalgia for empire in the UK and its relationship to the British exit from the European Union, see Robert Saunders, "Brexit and Empire: 'Global Britain' and the Myth of Imperial Nostalgia," *Journal of Imperial and Commonwealth History* 48, no. 6 (2020): 1140–74; Caroline Koegler, Pavan Kumar Malreddy, and Marlena Tronicke, "The Colonial Remains of Brexit: Empire Nostalgia and Narcissistic Nationalism," *Journal of Postcolonial Writing* 56, no. 5 (2020): 585–92. For more on what drives nostalgia for empire in Britain and France, see Patricia M. E. Lorcin, "The Nostalgias for Empire," *History and Theory* 57, no. 2 (2018): 269–85.

3. Ali Akyıldız, "Mabeyn-i Hümayun," *TDV İslam Ansiklopedisi* (Ankara: Türkiye Diyanet Vakfı, 2003), 27:283. At an earlier time in history, the Mabeyn also referred to the offices which were between the Sublime Porte and the palace.

4. See Betül İpşirli Argıt, *Life after the Harem: Female Palace Slaves, Patronage, and the Imperial Ottoman Court* (Cambridge, UK: Cambridge University Press, 2020), 38–77. Leslie P. Peirce, *The Imperial Harem: Women and Sovereignty in the Ottoman Empire* (Oxford, UK: Oxford University Press, 1993).

5. Akyıldız, "Mabeyn-i Hümayun," 285.

6. S. Tanvir Wasti, "The Last Chroniclers of the Mabeyn," *Middle Eastern Studies* 32, no. 2 (1996): 10.

7. BOA, DH.SAİD-197/173 (24/6/1914), İ.DH-1251/98134 (26/11/1891).

8. BOA, Y.PRK.AZJ-21/101 (26/5/1892). His petition led to a recommendation by the office to promote him to a fourth-rank position. İ.DH-1266/99509 (18/3/1892).

9. BOA, İ.DH-1303/1310-N-37 (17/4/1893).

10. BOA, Y.MTV-88/152 (28/12/1893), DH.SAİD-197/173 (24/6/1914), İ.Tal-65/1312-Ca-13 (10/11/1894).

11. BOA, Y.PRK.AZJ-33/33 (only the year was noted in the file—1313 Hijri, 1895/1896).

12. BOA, DH.SAİD-197/173 (24/6/1914), İ.Tal-99/1314-M-28 (12/6/1896). His son-in-law claimed that Shafiq's salary at that point in his career was 12,000 Kr.

13. BOA, DH.SAİD-197/173 (24/6/1914). İ.Tal-224/1318-Ca-195 (6/9/1900).

14. 'Abd al-Qadir al-'Azm, al-Usra al-'Azmiyya (Damascus: Matba'at al-Insha', 1960), 59.

15. Can Nacar, "The Régie Monopoly and Tobacco Workers in Late Ottoman Istanbul," Comparative Studies of South Asia, Africa, and the Middle East 34, no. 1 (2014): 207–08.

16. BOA, İ.Tal-334/1322-Ra-91 (29/5/1904). Badi' al-Mu'ayyad became director of the Public Debt Administration's office in Mosul and after 1908 was reassigned to the customs inspection office in Istanbul. al-'Azm, al-Usra al-'Azmiyya, 71–72.

17. Tahsin Paşa, Sultan Abdülhamid, Tahsin Paşa'nın Yıldız Hatıraları (Istanbul: Boğaziçi Üniversitesi Yayınları, 1990), 27–28, 186–88.

18. BOA, HR.TO-394/64 (10/9/1890), HR.TO-395/21 (22/11/1890).

19. BOA, Y.MTV-45/34 (3/9/1890). Interestingly, in one of the petitions against the governor, a member of the Quwatli family was engaged with one side of the al-'Azm family in a land case. Y.MTV-49/21 (17/3/1891).

20. BOA, Y.PRK.AZJ-18/80 (16/3/1891).

21. BOA, DH.MKT-1828/18 (13/4/1891).

22. The same person who wrote most of the petitions, and whose sisters and daughters wrote to have him released from detention, appears again in a major case involving an inheritance from one of those sisters, who had passed away in 1904. Again, this person locked legal horns with the local government over classification of the land and thus whether it could be inherited. He petitioned the Şura-yı Devlet in Istanbul, and again his request was taken up by the highest council in the land and an investigation was initiated. BOA, ŞD-229/26 (28/4/1906).

23. BOA, İ.MMS-110/4740 (18/5/1891).

24. BOA, İ.MMS-110/4740 (18/5/1891), DH.MKT-1671/74 (4/11/1889), İ.DH-1172/91599 (27/2/1890).

25. BOA, İ.DH-1159/90577 (12/11/1889), İ.DH-1172/91599 (27/2/1890), DH.MKT-1679/106 (7/11/1889), DH.MKT-1795/92 (27/12/1890), DH.MKT-1679/106 (7/11/1889).

26. BOA, Y.MTV-63/44 (6/6/1892).

27. This is the last trace of this case that I could find. Whether there were protests from the al-Quwatlis, who had the law on their side, I could not determine. BOA, Y.MTV-67/35 (12/9/1892).

28. BOA, DH.H-54/10 (20/7/1914). This land was a major source of dispute. Along with Munira, her husband had a Circassian concubine, Rengigül, whom he eventually married but then left before his death. Rengigül also asked for her rightful share since she claimed that she had never received the right compensation after her husband left her, Y.MTV-50/41 (23/5/1891).

29. Linda Schatkowski Schilcher, *Families in Politics: Damascene Factions and Estates of the 18th and 19th Centuries* (Stuttgart, Germany: Franz Steiner, 1985), 87.

30. Schatkowski-Schilcher, *Families in Politics*, 89, 98.

31. al-'Azm, *al-Usra al-'Azmiyya*, 57–58. It was also around this time that Shafiq asked for a four-month leave to go to Egypt as well, though it is not clear whether this was related to his brother's escape. BOA, Y.PRK.AZJ-33/33 (only the year was noted in the file—1313 Hijri, 1895/96).

32. BOA, Y.MTV-80/27 (18/7/1893), Y.A.HUS-277/132 (13/7/1893).

33. BOA, İ.HUS-81/1317-Z-3 (2/4/1900), İ.HUS-82/1318-S-69 (27/6/1900), DH.MKT-2368/86 (4/7/1900), DH.MKT-2331/28 (10/4/1900).

34. BOA, DH.H-35-1/34 (4/2/1913).

35. BOA, DH.MKT-614/35 (19/11/1902).

36. BOA, İ.TAL-57/65 (1894/7/29), İ.TAL-75/46 (6/4/1895). The military rank of kaymakam should not be confused with the district governor title, kaymakam.

37. Frank Gerard Clemow, *The Cholera Epidemic of 1892 in the Russian Empire. With Notes upon Treatment and Methods of Disinfection in Cholera, and a Short Account of the Conference on Cholera Held in St. Petersburg in December 1892* (London, 1893), 1; National Library of Medicine, http://resource.nlm.nih.gov/3472045oR (accessed May 24, 2022).

38. Nazan Maksudyan, "'This Time Women as Well Got Invovled in Politics!' Nineteenth Century Ottoman Women's Organizations and Political Agency," in *Women and the City, Women in the City: A Gendered Perspective on Ottoman Urban History*, ed. Nazan Maksudyan (New York: Berghahn, 2014), 110–11.

39. Nuran Yıldırım, "A History of Healthcare in Istanbul," in *The Istanbul 2010 European Capital of Culture Agency and Istanbul University Project No. 55–10*, trans. İnanç Özekmekçi (Istanbul: Ajansfa, 2010), 85.

40. The spelling of his name is taken from a bank's "sample of his signature": "S.E. Selim Pacha Melhamé," OFTM0385, Ottoman Bank Records, Salt Research Archives.

41. Erol Makzume, *Sultan II. Abdülhamid'in Hizmetinde Selim Melhame Paşa ve Ailesi* (Istanbul: MD Basım Evi, 2019), 46–47.

42. BOA, Y.A.HUS-323/89 (5/4/1895); Yıldırım, "A History of Healthcare in Istanbul," 43.

43. See M. Exner, "Cholera Epidemic in Hamburg, Germany 1892," in *Routledge Handbook of Water and Health* (London: Routledge, 2015), 644–47.

44. Yıldırım, "History of Healthcare in Istanbul," 91–93.

45. Yıldız Salman, "'Alafranga'dan 'Moderne' Teşvikiye Nişantaşı," in *Dolmabahçe, Mekanın Hafızası*, ed. Bahar Kaya (Istanbul: İstanbul Bilgi Üniversitesi Yayınları, 2016), 121.

46. BOA, Y.MTV-124/50 (10/7/1895).

47. Selim Deringil, "Conversion as Survival: Mass Conversions of Armenians in Anatolia, 1895–1897," in *Conversion and Apostasy in the Late Ottoman Empire* (Cambridge, UK: Cambridge University Press, 2012), 199, 214. Ümit Kurt, "Reform and Violence in the Hamidian Era: The Political Context of the 1895 Armenian Massacres in Aintab," *Holocaust and Genocide Studies* 32, no. 3 (Winter 2018): 404.

48. For more on the violence in Istanbul, see Sinan Dinçer, "The Armenian Massacre in Istanbul (1896)," *Tijdschrift Voor Sociale En Economische Geschiendenis* 10, no. 4 (2013): 20–45.

49. Kurt, "Reform and Violence in the Hamidian Era," 404. For more on the mass forcible conversion that took place during the violence between 1894 and 1897, see Selim Deringil, "'The Armenian Question Is Finally Closed': Mass Conversions of Armenians in Anatolia during the Hamidian Massacres of 1895–1897," *Comparative Studies in Society and History* 51, no. 2 (2009): 344–71. For more on the Hamidiye Light Cavalry Regiments, see Janet Klein, *The Margins of Empire: Kurdish Militias in the Ottoman Tribal Zone* (Stanford, CA: Stanford University Press, 2011); Bayram Kodaman, "The Hamidiye Light Cavalry Regiments, Abdülhamid II and the Eastern Anatolian Tribes," in *War and Diplomacy: The Russo-Turkish War of 1877–1878 and the Treaty of Berlin*, ed. M. Hakan Yavuz and Peter Sluglett, Utah Series in Middle East Studies (Salt Lake City, UT: University of Utah Press, 2011), 382–426.

50. William Miller, *The Ottoman Empire and Its Successors, 1801–1927, with an Appendix, 1927–1936* (Cambridge, UK: Cambridge University Press, 1936); Jean Veber, "Abdul Hamid II, Le Sultan Rouge," *Le Rire*, May 29, 1897, http://www.genocide-museum.am/eng/online_exhibition_5.php (accessed May 24, 2020).

51. M. Hakan Yavuz, "The Transformation of 'Empire' Through Wars and Reforms, Integration vs. Oppression," in *War and Diplomacy, The Russo-Turkish War of 1877–1878 and the Treaty of Berlin*, ed. M. Hakan Yavuz and Peter Sluglett (Salt Lake City, UT: University of Utah Press, 2011), 17–55.

52. Deringil, "Conversion as Survival," 199.

53. Kurt, "Reform and Violence in the Hamidian Era," 407–11. For more on Article 61 of the Treaty of Berlin, see Michael A. Reynolds, *Shattering Empires: The Clash and Collapse of the Ottoman and Russian Empires, 1908–1918* (Cambridge, UK: Cambridge University Press, 2011).

54. For more about the missionary perspective on the aftermath of the massacres, see Deborah Mayersen, "The 1895–1896 Armenian Massacres in Harput: Eyewitness Account," *Études arméniennes contemporaines* 10 (2018): 161–83.

55. BNA, "Armenian Massacres, Zeitun Refugees in London," newspaper clipping from *The Echo*, April 4, 1896, FO 78/4792, 170. For more on Armenian migration to the United States after the Hamidian Massacres, see David Gutman, *The Politics of Armenian Migration to North America, 1885–1915: Sojourners, Smugglers, and Dubious Citizens* (Edinburgh: Edinburgh University Press, 2019). For more on the Armenian community in Addis Ababa, see Boris Adjemian, *La fanfare du Négus: les Arméniens en Ethiopie, XIXe-XXe siècle* (Paris: Éditions de l'École des hautes études en sciences sociales, 2013).

56. "İngilizlerin henüz Transvaal'da uğraşmakta olduklarını gazete tercümelerinden anlıyorum şu hâlde bilistifade İngiltere baş vekiline sürat-i hafiye ve gayr resmide bir adam gönderip, Anadolu'da sakin Ermenileri Transvaal'a göndermek ve anlara bedel Transvaal sekenesi Anadolu'da iskân etmek istiyorum bu babdaki mütalaanızdır," in al-'Abid, *Abdülhamid'in Kara Kutusu*, vol. 2, sec. 3, 24.

57. See for example a collection of reports on the latest in the British war in Transvaal from international newspapers under "Transvaal Muharebesi," *İkdam*, June 3, 1900, 2. Also see the analysis of the war translated from *Le figaro* as "Zanniyat ve Tahminat," *İkdam* January 5, 1900, 1. And see the day-by-day account from mid-June in "Transvaal Muharebesi," *İkdam*, November 6, 1900, 2.

58. al-'Abid, *Abdülhamid'in Kara Kutusu*, vol. 2, sec. 3, 24.

59. See Edip Gölbaşı, "1895–1896 Katliamları: Doğu Vilayetlerinde Cemaatler Arası 'Şiddet İklimi' ve Ermeni Karşıtı Ayaklanmalar," in *1915: Siyaset, Tehcir ve Soykırım*, ed. Oktay Özel and Fikret Adanır (Istanbul: Tarih Vakfı Yurt Yayınları, 2015), 140–63.

60. Sadik al-Mu'ayyad Azmzade, *Rihlat al-Habasha, Min al-Istana ila Addis Ababa*, ed. Nuri al-Jarrah (Dubai: al-Mu'asasa al-'Arabiyya li-l-Dirasat wa-l-Nashr, 2001), 162.

61. See Nuri al-Jarrah, introduction to Sadik al-Muayyad Azmzade, *Rihlat al-Habasha, Min al-Istana ila Addis Ababa*, ed. Nuri al-Jarrah (Dubai: al-Mu'asasa al-'Arabiyya Li-l-Dirasat wa-l-Nashr, 2001).

62. BNA, FO 78/5361 (5/12/1904), 233.

63. BNA, Sir P. Currie to the Marquess of Salisbury, FO 78/4792 (27/3/1896), 149.

64. BOA, İ.ML-1314-S-7 (22/7/1896). Izzet al-Abid wrote at length about the commissions sent to the eastern provinces, but he did not mention Sadik by name. See al-'Abid, *Abdülhamid'in Kara Kutusu*, vol. 2, sec. 1, 4–9.

65. "Evénement d'Orient," *Le Petit Journal, Supplément illustré*, November 24, 1895, cover.

66. "Evénement d'Orient," 375.

67. "Evénement d'Orient," 376.

68. "Evénement d'Orient," 376.

69. Oded Y. Steinberg, "The Confirmation of the Worst Fears: James Bryce, British Diplomacy, and the Armenian Massacres of 1894–1896," *Études arméniennes contemporaines*, no. 11 (2018): 15–39.

70. Sir N. O'Conor to the Marquess of Salisbury, BNA, FO 78/5254 (13/4/1899), 2–3.

71. O'Conor, 1–2.

72. by Mr. Block, memorandum enclosed in O'Conor to Salisbury, BNA, FO 78/5254 (13/4/1899), 3–4.

73. R. P. M., "Armenian Massacre Claims," memorandum, BNA, FO 78/5254 (21/2/1901), 1–4; Naci Yorulmaz, *Arming the Sultan: German Arms Trade and Personal Diplomacy in the Ottoman Empire Before World War I* (London: I. B. Tauris, 2014), 187–89.

74. Yorulmaz, *Arming the Sultan*, 191. For Izzet al-'Abid's comments on how the Italians secured this deal, see al-'Abid, *Abdülhamid'in Kara Kutusu*, vol. 2, sec. 2, 54–58.

75. Sir Nicolas O'Conor to the Marquess of Lansdowne, BNA, FO 78/5254 (2/3/1901), 7–9.

76. O'Conor to Lansdowne, BNA, FO 78/5254 (16/6/1901), 1–8.

77. O'Conor to Lansdowne, BNA, FO 78/5254 (20/11/1901), 1–5.

78. Much has been written on the Armenian Genocide of 1914. One source to consider is Norman M. Naimark, Ronald Grigor Suny, and Fatma Müge Goçek, eds., *A Question of Genocide: Armenians and Turks at the End of the Ottoman Empire* (repr., Oxford, UK: Oxford University Press, 2011).

Chapter 3

1. Sadik al-Mu'ayyad Azmzade, *Rihlat al-Habasha, Min al-Istana ila Addis Ababa*, ed. Nuri al-Jarrah (Dubai: al-Mu'asasa al-'Arabiyya Li-l-Dirasat wa-l-Nashr, 2001), 29–30.

2. See Mostafa Minawi, "International Law and the Precarity of Ottoman Sovereignty in Africa at the End of the Nineteenth Century," *International History Review* 43, no. 5 (2021): 1098–121.

3. A good example of Izzet's attitude toward foreign affairs comes in the form of comments on Muslims in China and European colonial interest in East Asia. He pointed out that Ottomans should be consulted on all issues related to Muslims abroad, as he considered the global Muslim population as within the sphere of influence of the sultan-caliph. For example, he was vocal about his disapproval when it came to the discussion of occupation of part of China. He believed that, since China had a large Muslim population, according to the Treaty of Berlin of 1885, any moves by European powers, allies, or foes should be first discussed with the Ottomans. Izzet Holo al-'Abid, *Abdülhamid'in Kara Kutusu, Arap İzzet Holo Paşa'nın Günlükleri*, ed. Pınar Güven and Birol Bayram (Istanbul: İş Bankası Kültür Yayınları, 2019), vol. 2, sec. 2, 111, 113; sec. 3, 27.

4. Theofanis George Stavrou, *Russian Interests in Palestine, 1882–1914: A Study of Religious and Educational Enterprise* (Thessaloniki, Greece: Institute for Balkan Studies, 1963), 67–68.

5. John D. Windhausen, "Siege of Plevna," in *Salem Press Encyclopedia* (Amenia, NY: Salem Press, 2019).

6. M. Hakan Yavuz, "The Transformation of 'Empire' Through Wars and Reforms, Integration vs. Oppression," in *War and Diplomacy: The Russo-Turkish War of 1877–1878 and the Treaty of Berlin*, ed. M. Hakan Yavuz and Peter Sluglett (Salt Lake City, UT: University of Utah Press, 2011), 25.

7. Yavuz, "Transformation of Empire," 29.

8. Michael A. Reynolds, *Shattering Empires: The Clash and Collapse of the Ottoman and Russian Empires, 1908–1918* (Cambridge, UK: Cambridge University Press, 2011), 15.

9. Stavrou, *Russian Interests in Palestine*, 68–69.

10. Irina Mironenko-Marenkova and Kirill Vakh, "An Institution, Its People, and Its Documents: The Russian Consulate in Jerusalem through the Foreign Policy Archive of the Russian Empire, 1858–1914," in *Ordinary Jerusalem, 1840–1940*, ed. Angelos Dalachanis and Vincent Lemire, vol. 1 (Leiden, Netherlands: Brill, 2018), 18n., https://brill.com/view/book/edcoll/9789004375741/BP000024.xml.

11. "Memorandum on the Orthodox Palestine Society and Its Properties in Palestine—UNCCP's Cttee on Jerusalem—Working Paper, A/AC.25/Com.Jer/W.23," Memorandum, Question of Palestine, October 6, 1949, https://www.un.org/unispal/document/auto-insert-211136/.

12. "Lavrov: Imperial Orthodox Palestine Society Is Important Tool for Positions in Region," TASS [Russian News Agency], July 25, 2016, https://tass.com/politics/890368.

13. Christopher Warwick, *The Life and Death of Ella Grand Duchess of Russia: A Romanov Tragedy*, 3rd ed. (London: Albert Bridge Books, 2014), 149–50.

14. M. M. Yakushev, "Diplomatic Relations between Russia and the Ottoman Empire in the Second Half of the Eighteenth Century," *Russian Studies in History* 57, no. 2 (2018): 151–52.

15. Mujeeb R. Khan, "The Ottoman Eastern Question and the Problematic Origins of Modern Ethnic Cleansing, Genocide, and Humanitarian Interventionism in Europe and the Middle East," in *War and Diplomacy: The Russo-Turkish War of 1877–1878 and the Treaty of Berlin*, ed. M. Hakan Yavuz with Peter Sluglett (Salt Lake City, UT: The University of Utah Press, 2011), 98.

16. Elena Astafieva, *The Russian Empire in Palestine, 1847–1917*, 2016, 4–5, https://hal.archives-ouvertes.fr/hal-01293323.

17. Stavrou, *Russian Interests in Palestine*, 67. Also see Deborah Cadbury, "Ella and Sergei," in *Queen Victoria's Matchmaking: The Royal Marriages That Shaped Europe* (New York: Public Affairs, 2017), 65–93. And see the memoirs of Sergei's niece, who grew up with Sergei and Ella: Marie Grand Duchess of Russia, *Education of a Princess: A Memoir*, trans. Russell Lord (New York: Viking Press, 1930), 9–44. Warwick, *The Life and Death of Ella*, 133–36; Tamar Anolic, *The Russian Riddle: The Life of Serge Alexandrovich of Russia* (East Richmond Heights, CA: Kensington House, 2009), 49–51.

18. Tahsin Paşa, *Sultan Abdülhamid, Tahsin Paşa'nın Yıldız Hatıraları* (Istanbul: Boğaziçi Üniversitesi Yayınları, 1990), 409.

19. As represented in Dilek Kaya Mutlu, "The Russian Monument at Ayastefanos (San Stefano): Between Defeat and Revenge, Remembering and Forgetting," *Middle Eastern Studies* 43, no. 1 (2007): 77.

20. Mutlu, "Russian Monument," 75–78.

21. S. Tanvir Wasti, "The Last Chroniclers of the Mabeyn," *Middle Eastern Studies* 32, no. 2 (1996): 94–96, 147–48.

22. BOA, Y.EE-12/18 (mistakenly dated 1882).

23. BOA, Y.EE-12/18 (mistakenly dated 1882); DH.MKT-1572/70 (10/12/1888). The Slavic and Baltic Division of the New York Public Library holds a collection of forty-three photographs from the grand duke's visit to the Levant titled "Album of the Holy Mission [in Jerusalem]," which is mistakenly dated 1881. The pictures are in fact from his 1888 visit to the Levant, showing his wife, his brother, and the completed church. See Edward Kasinec and Benjamin E. Goldsmith, "The Russian Grand Duke Sergei Aleksandrovich and the Holy Land: A Note," in *Modern Greek Studies Year Book*, ed. Theofanis George Stavrou (Minneapolis: University of Minnesota Press, 1991), 7:463–72.

24. BOA, Y.PRK.ZB-4/47 (10/11/1888).

25. BOA, Y.EE-63/24 (17/10/1888).

26. BOA, Y.A.HUS-218/22 (12/10/1888).

27. BOA, DH.MKT-1561/18 (15/11/1888).

28. BOA, Y.PRK.MYD-10/48 (28/5/1891).

29. Naci Yorulmaz, *Arming the Sultan: German Arms Trade and Personal Diplomacy in the Ottoman Empire Before World War I* (London: I. B. Tauris, 2014), 183.

30. Yorulmaz, *Arming the Sultan*, 23–25.

31. Sean McMeekin, "Benevolent Contempt: Bismarck's Ottoman Policy," in *War and Diplomacy: The Russo-Turkish War of 1877–1878 and the Treaty of Berlin*, ed. M. Hakan Yavuz and Peter Sluglett (Salt Lake City, UT: The University of Utah Press, 2011), 88–89.

32. Yorulmaz, *Arming the Sultan*, 220–24.

33. For more on the history of the cemeteries dedicated to Ottoman military and diplomatic personnel, see Alaattin Uca and Ahmet Hamdi Can, "Berlin Türk Şehitiği ve Mezar Taşları," *Akademik Tarih ve Düşünce Dergisi* 3, no. 6 (2019): 1236–308.

34. Sadik al-Mu'ayyad Azmzade, *Rihlat-ul-Habasha, Min al Istana ila Addis Ababa* ed. Nuri al-Jarrah (Dubai: al-Mu'asasa al-'Arabiyya li-l-Dirasat wa-l-Nashr, 2001), 29–30.

35. Yorulmaz, *Arming the Sultan*, 54–57.

36. Yorulmaz, *Arming the Sultan*, 59.

37. Yorulmaz, *Arming the Sultan*, 58.

38. McMeekin, "Benevolent Contempt," 80.

39. Yorulmaz, *Arming the Sultan*, 5.

40. McMeekin, "Benevolent Contempt," 80–83.

41. Yorulmaz, *Arming the Sultan*, 22. Not the term Turk, as used by Europeans, applied to all Ottoman Muslims, not just Turkish-Ottomans.

42. Yorulmaz, *Arming the Sultan*, 43.

43. Salih Kış, "Alman İmparatoru II. Wilhelm'in Haçlı Rüyası ve 1898 Kudüs Seyahatı," *Selçuk Üniversitesi Türkiyat Araştırmaları Dergisi* (2017): 493. Erol Makzume, *Sultan II. Abdülhamid'in Hizmetinde Selim Melhame Paşa ve Ailesi* (Istanbul: MD Basım Evi, 2019), 57–58.

44. BOA, Y.PRK.HR-13/52 (1900). Paul Vasili's popular letters in *La Nouvelle Revue*, published between 1884 and 1888, include *La Société de Berlin, Augmenté de Lettres Inédites* (1884); *La Société de Vienne, La Société de Madrid,* and *La Société de Londres* (all 1885); *La Société de Paris* (1887); and *La Société de Saint-Pétersbourg* (1888).

45. İrfan Ertan, "The Orient Journey of Kaiser Wilhelm II (1898)" (master's thesis, Middle East Technical University, 2018), 27. "Şüunat: Almanya İmparatoru Hazretleri," *İkdam*, October 17, 1898, 1.

46. Ertan, "Orient Journey," 12–13.

47. Ibrahim al-Aswad, *Kitab al-Rihla al-Imbaratoriyya Fi al-Mamlek al-'Uthmaniyya*, ed. Khayri al-Thahabi (Damascus: al-Hay'a al-'Amma al-Suriyya li-l-Kitab, 1898), 51–52.

48. Ertan, "Orient Journey (1898)," 16–23, Y.PRK.TKM-16/20 (9/11/1889).

49. Kış, "Alman İmparatoru II," nn, 31, 493.

50. "Hayfa'dan İstikbal," *İkdam*, November 4, 1898, 2.

51. See the front pages of *İkdam*, October 20, 21, and 25, 1898; and November 1–3, 8, 10, 14, 15, and 17, 1898.

52. al-Aswad, *Kitab al-Rihla al-Imbaratoriyya*, 99–100.

53. al-Aswad, *Kitab al-Rihla al-Imbaratoriyya*, 103. Wilhelm II's trip made such an impression on the royal family that a few years later the son of Princess Victoria of Baden and the crown princess of Sweden, who was a relative of Empress Victoria, sent her own son to the Ottoman Empire. His name was also Wilhelm after his relative, the emperor. He toured the empire and was equally impressed. His mother sent a personal note to Sultan Abdülhamid to thank him for taking such good care of her son. BOA, Y.PRK.BŞK-75/97 (18/3/1906).

54. "Müsaade-i Seniye," *Suriye*, May 18, 1899, 1.

55. al-Aswad, *Kitab al-Rihla al-Imbaratoriyya*, 2n, 110n, 111n.

56. Leila Tarazi Fawaz, *A Land of Aching Hearts: The Middle East in the Great War* (Cambridge, MA: Harvard University Press, 2014), 124.

57. Linda Schatkowski Schilcher, *Families in Politics: Damascene Factions and Estates of the 18th and 19th Centuries* (Stuttgart, Germany: Franz Steiner, 1985), 141–43.

58. al-Aswad, *Kitab al-Rihla al-Imbaratoriyya*, 105. A picture of Wilhelm II and his entourage sitting in the 'Azm palace courtyard is preserved at İstanbul Üniversitesi, Nadir Eserler Kütüphanesi record no. 90621.

59. Shimon Shamir, "As'ad Pasha al-'Azm and Ottoman Rule in Damascus (1743–58)," *Bulletin of the School of Oriental and African Studies, University of London* 26, no. 1 (1963): 1–28.

60. 'Abd al-Qadir al-'Azm, *al-Usra al-'Azmiyya* (Damascus: Matba'at al-Insha', 1960), 35–36.

61. al-Aswad, *Kitab al-Rihla al-Imbaratoriyya*, 104–05.

62. Jean Richard, "Les transformations de l'image de Saladin dans les sources occidentales," *Revue des mondes musulmans et de la Méditerranée* 89–90 (2000): 177–87.

63. al-Aswad, *Kitab al-Rihla al-Imbaratoriyya*, 112–13.

64. *Suriye*, December 6, 1900, 4.

65. al-'Abid, *Abdülhamid'in Kara Kutusu*, *vol.* 2, sec. 3, 22.

66. According to Amr al-'Azm, Sadik accompanied Wilhelm II all the way back to Berlin, where he stayed for a while. I cannot find the record for this extended trip in the Ottoman archives; however, it is a completely plausible idea.

67. From a column reporting on an item from a German newspaper, "Şüunat," *İkdam*, June 6, 1900, 1.

68. al-Aswad, *Kitab al-Rihla al-Imbaratoriyya*, 122–23, 2n.

69. An example of the many occasions he was tasked with welcoming foreign dignitaries is included in this note form the Ottoman ambassador to France, stating that Sadik was at the train station to welcome the French ambassador and his wife in the Spring of 1899. BOA, Y.PRK.TŞF-5/75 (8/4/1899).

70. Mehmet Hacısalihoğlu, "Muslim and Orthodox Resistance Against the Berlin Peace Treaty in the Balkans," in *War and Diplomacy: The Russo-Turkish War of 1877–1878 and the Treaty of Berlin*, ed. M. Hakan Yavuz and Peter Sluglett (Salt Lake City, UT: University of Utah Press, 2011), 125–43.

71. Borislav Chernev, *Twilight of Empire: The Brest-Litovsk Conference and the Remaking of East-Central Europe, 1917–1918* (Toronto: University of Toronto, 2017), 160–64.

72. İpek Yosmaoğlu, *Blood Ties: Religion, Violence, and the Politics of Nationhood in Ottoman Macedonia, 1878–1908* (Ithaca, NY: Cornell University Press, 2013), 23–25.

73. Yosmaoğlu, *Blood Ties*, 10–11.

74. Keith Brown, *Loyal unto Death: Trust and Terror in Revolutionary Macedonia* (Indianapolis: Indiana University Press, 2013), 4–6.

75. Yosmaoğlu, *Blood Ties*, 29–30.

76. Yosmaoğlu, *Blood Ties*, 16–17.

77. Sevilya Aslanova Saylak, "Osmanlı—Rus İlişkilerinde Makedonya Sorunu (1885–1908)," *Gazi Akademik Bakış* 10, no. 19 (2016): 108.

78. BOA. Y.MTV-200/3 (3/3/1900); İ.TAL-168/1316-Za-7 (15/3/1899).

79. BOA, İ.HUS-81/1314-Z-14 (11/3/1900); Y.PRK.MYD-23/7 (11/3/1900); DH.MKT-2337/92 (27/4/1900).

80. For example, this term was used in reference to local rebels in Mount Lebanon who opposed local and provincial rulers' policies in 1840 and 1860. See Ussama Makdisi, *The Culture of Sectarianism: Community, History, and Violence in Nineteenth-Century Ottoman Lebanon* (Oakland, CA: University of California Press, 2000), 96–117.

81. For more details on this mission consult, the following documents: BOA, Y.PRK.ASK-159/68 (22/3/1900); Y.PRK.ASK-159/71 (23/3/1900); Y.PRK.UM-49/116 (23/3/1900); Y.PRK.UM-49/126 (29/3/1900); Y.MTV-201/29 (8/4/1900).

82. G. Bonham to the Marquess of Lansdowne, September 23, 1902; Great Britain Foreign Office, *Correspondence Respecting the Affairs of South-Eastern Europe and Further Correspondence*, British Library collection, 1903, 202.

83. The details in this file are fascinating for those studying Ottoman-Russian diplomatic relations. BOA, Y.PRK.HR-32/20 (13/11/1902).

84. Translation of "Extract from the 'Journal de Saint-Pétersbourg' of the 1st (14th) December 1902," *Correspondence Respecting the Affairs of South-Eastern Europe and Further Correspondence*, British Library collection, 208.

85. BOA, İ.TAL-289/1320-Ş-15 (6/11/1902); İ-TAL-289/1320-Ş-11 (7/11/1902).

86. Yosmaoğlu, *Blood Ties*, 33–34.

87. The Ottoman archives are full of reports from the field during this mission. Here I list reports that were written by or on behalf of Sadik: BOA, Y.PRK.BŞK -69/15 (31/3/1903); Y.PRK.ASK-193/57 (6/4/1903); Y.PRK.ASK-193/89 (10/4/1903); Y.PRK.ASK-193/114 (13/4/1903); Y.PRK.ASK-194/75 (19/4/1903); Y.PRK.ASK-194/83 (20/4/1903); Y.MTV-243/47 (4/5/1903); Y.PRK.ASK-195/50 (8/5/1903); Y.PRK.ASK -195/86 (16/5/1903); Y.PRK.BŞK-69/71 (18/5/1903).

88. BOA, Y.PRK.ASK-195/131 (21/5/1903).

89. BOA, Y.PRK.BŞK-69/76 (20/5/1903).

Chapter 4

1. Sadik al-Mu'ayyad Azmzade, "Afrika Sahra-yı Kebiri'nde Seyahat (Manuscript)" (1896), 7–8, Nadir Eserler Kütüphanesi, İstanbul Üniversitesi. *Aman Aman* is a reference to an often-repeated expression of being caught up in the emotions of singing traditional or classical Turkish and Arabic songs.

2. Hasan Kayalı, *Arabs and Young Turks: Ottomanism, Arabism, and Islamism in the Ottoman Empire, 1908–1918* (Oakland, CA: University of California Press, 1997); Michael Provence, *The Great Syrian Revolt and the Rise of Arab Nationalism* (Austin, TX University of Texas Press, 2005); James L. Gelvin, "'Arab Nationalism': Has a New Framework Emerged? Pensée 1: 'Arab Nationalism' Meets Social Theory," *International Journal of Middle East Studies* 41, no. 1 (2009): 10–12.

3. BOA, Y.PRK.BŞK-12/59 (3/12/1887).

4. Mostafa Minawi, *The Ottoman Scramble for Africa: Empire and Diplomacy in the Sahara and the Hijaz* (Stanford, CA: Stanford University Press, 2016), 61–78.

5. Minawi, *Ottoman Scramble for Africa*, 41–79.

6. Sadik al-Mu'ayyad Azmzade, *Afrika Sahra-Yı Kebiri'nde Seyahat, Bir Osmanlı Zabitinin Sahra-Yı Kebir'de Seyahati* (Istanbul: Alem Matbaası, 1899), 2.

7. Azmzade, "Afrika Sahra-yı Kebiri'nde Seyahat (Manuscript)," 2.

8. In the copy-edited printed version, some of the words were changed to a more "modern Turkish" form than the one used by the seasoned official accustomed to writing Ottoman reports. For example, *ahbabim*, in the manuscript was changed to *muhibim* in the printed version.

9. Azmzade, "Afrika Sahra-yı Kebiri'nde Seyahat (Manuscript)," 2.

10. It was most likely a translation of an existing source, but he made no reference to the original publisher. Sadik al-Mu'ayyad Azmzade, "Fen-i Fotoğraf," İstanbul Üniversitesi, Nadir Eserler Kütüphanesi, T4363.

11. Sadik al-Mu'ayyad Azmzade, "Al-Kimya' fi Tahlil al-Hawa' wa-l-Ma'," İstanbul Üniversitesi, Nadir Eserler Kütüphanesi, T7003.

12. "Küçük Henri" (Matbu 89223), "Fernando" (Matbu 89176), "Tarikh Futuhat al-Sham" (IBN 1528). His brother-in-law, Haqqi al-Mu'ayyad Azmzade, also gifted the sultan a manuscript translation of "Coğrafya-i Tabiiye" (T4567). İstanbul Üniversitesi, Nadir Eserler Kütüphanesi. One of the Mabeyn secretaries reported in his memoirs that the sultan often made one of the junior chamberlains read a novel to him at night from behind a screen to help him fall asleep. S. Tanvir Wasti, "The Last Chroniclers of the Mabeyn," *Middle Eastern Studies* 32, no. 2 (1996): 3.

13. The manuscript of this travelogue is kept by İklil Bey, a great-grandnephew of Sadik, who was so kind as to give me a photocopy. The Arabic book was republished with a new introduction in 2001. See Sadik al-Mu'ayyad Azmzade, *Rihlat al-Habasha, Min al-Istana ila Addis Ababa*, ed. Nuri al-Jarrah (Dubai: al-Mu'asasa al-'Arabiyya Li-l-Dirasat wa-l-Nashr, 2001). It recently came to my attention that one of Sadik's great-grandchildren, Giyas Gökkent, self-published English translations of some of Sadik's travelogues, along with a sort of hagiography and commentary in late summer 2021, I suspect in anticipation of this book.

14. İ. Hakkı Akyol, "Son Yarım Asrında Türkiye'de Coğrafya," *Türk Coğrafya Dergisi* 1, no. 1 (1943): 7–8.

15. In a handwritten note, Sadik dedicated the published version to Abdülhamid's library. Several other Ottoman travelers who wrote and published their travelogues in Arabic and Ottoman-Turkish on trips to Europe, Africa, South America, and South and East Asia. A good place to start investigating Ottoman travelogues from the second half of the nineteenth century is M. U., "Ottoman Travels and Travel Accounts from an Earlier Age of Globalization: The Introduction," *Die Welt Des Islams* 40, no. 2 (2000): 133–38.

16. BOA, Y.PRK.MYD-21/106 (27/2/1899).

17. Sadik al-Mu'ayyad Azmzade, *Rihla fi al-Sahra' al-Kubra bi-Ifriqya*, ed. Salah al-Din Hassan al-Suri, trans. Abdul Karim Abu Shuwayrib and Silsalat al-Dirasat al-Mutarjama (Beirut: Dar al-Muhit al-'Arabi, 1998).

18. Sadik al-Mu'ayyad Azmzade, *Afrika Sahra-yı Kebiri'nde Seyahat (Bir Osmanlı Zabitinin Büyük Sahra'da Seyahati)*, ed. İdris Bostan (Istanbul: Çamlıca Basım Yayın ve Tic. A.Ş., 2008).

19. Pierre Bourdieu, "Habitus," in *Habitus: A Sense of Place*, ed. Jean Hiller and Emma Rooksby (Aldershot, UK: Ashgate, 2002), 27–28.

20. Jacques Derrida, *Of Grammatology*, trans. Gayatri Chakravorty Spivak, 1st American ed. (Baltimore: Johns Hopkins University Press, 1976), 14.

21. Azmzade, "Afrika Sahra-yı Kebiri'nde Seyahat (Manuscript)," 5. Karnıyarık, literally "split belly," is a staple dish in Anatolian cuisine based on a sautéed eggplant with minced meat and tomato sauce baked in the oven. Özge Samancı, "History of Eating and Drinking in the Ottoman Empire and Modern Turkey," in *Handbook of Eating and Drinking, Interdisciplinary Perspectives*, ed. Herbert L. Meiselman (London: Springer, 2020), 73. For a better appreciation for the level of censorship at the time, in the printed Turkish version, Karnıyarık, was replaced by Börek, an Anatolian savory stuffed pastry dish and one of the oldest recorded types of pastries in the Ottoman court. Azmzade, *Afrika Sahra-Yı Kebiri'nde Seyahat, Bir Osmanlı Zabitinin Sahray-ı Kebiri'nde Seyahati*, 2.

22. Azmzade, "Afrika Sahra-yı Kebiri'nde Seyahat (Manuscript)," 6.

23. Azmzade, *Rihla fi al-Sahra' al-Kubra bi-Ifriqya*, 30.

24. Azmzade, *Afrika Sahra-Yı Kebiri'nde Seyahat, Bir Osmanlı Zabitinin Sahray-ı Kebiri'nde Seyahati*, 22; Azmzade, *Rihla fi al-Sahra' al-Kubra bi-Ifriqya*, 58; Azmzade, "Afrika Sahra-yı Kebiri'nde Seyahat (Manuscript)," 51.

25. Derrida, *Of Grammatology*, 107.

26. Azmzade, "Afrika Sahra-yı Kebiri'nde Seyahat (Manuscript)," 51.

27. Azmzade, *Afrika Sahra-Yı Kebiri'nde Seyahat, Bir Osmanlı Zabitinin Sahray-ı Kebiri'nde Seyahati*, 22–25.

28. Derrida, *Of Grammatology*, 110.

29. Azmzade, "Afrika Sahra-yı Kebiri'nde Seyahat (Manuscript)," 190–92.

30. Azmzade, *Afrika Sahra-Yı Kebiri'nde Seyahat, Bir Osmanlı Zabitinin Sahray-ı Kebiri'nde Seyahati*, 88–89.

31. Homi K. Bhabha, *The Location of Culture*, 2nd ed. (London: Routledge, 2004), 53–54.

32. Edward Said, *Orientalism* (London: Pantheon Books, 1978).

33. Bhabha, *Location of Culture*, 50.

34. Azmzade, *Afrika Sahra-Yı Kebiri'nde Seyahat, Bir Osmanlı Zabitinin Sahray-ı Kebiri'nde Seyahati* 82; Azmzade, "Afrika Sahra-yı Kebiri'nde Seyahat (Manuscript)," 175.

35. Azmzade, *Rihla fi al-Sahra' al-Kubra bi-Ifriqya*, 131.

36. Azmzade, *Afrika Sahra-Yı Kebiri'nde Seyahat, Bir Osmanlı Zabitinin Sahray-ı Kebiri'nde Seyahati* , 73; Azmzade, *Rihla fi al-Sahra' al-Kubra bi-Ifriqya*, 117.

37. Azmzade, *Afrika Sahra-Yı Kebiri'nde Seyahat, Bir Osmanlı Zabitinin Sahra-Yı Kebir'de Seyahatı*, 54; Azmzade, *Afrika Sahra-yı Kebiri'nde Seyahat (Bir Osmanlı*

Zabitinin Büyük Sahra'da Seyahati), 106–07. Azmzade, "Afrika Sahra-yı Kebiri'nde Seyahat (Manuscript)," 103–04.

38. Azmzade, *Afrika Sahra-yı Kebiri'nde Seyahat, Bir Osmanlı Zabitinin Sahray-ı Kebiri'nde Seyahat*, 6.

39. Azmzade, "Afrika Sahra-yı Kebiri'nde Seyahat (Manuscript)," 7–8.

40. Izzet Holo al-'Abid, *Abdülhamid'in Kara Kutusu, Arap İzzet Holo Paşa'nın Günlükleri*, ed. Pınar Güven and Birol Bayram (Istanbul: İş Bankası Kültür Yayınları, 2019), vol. 2, sec. 2, 90–92, 107; sec. 3, 21.

41. al-'Abid, *Abdülhamid'in Kara Kutusu*, vol. 2, sec. 3, 41.

42. "Hicaz Şömendöfer Hattı İanesi," *İkdam*, June 16, 1900, 1.

43. Erol Makzume, *Sultan II. Abdülhamid'in Hizmetinde Selim Melhame Paşa ve Ailesi* (Istanbul: MD Basım Evi, 2019), 83.

44. al-'Abid, *Abdülhamid'in Kara Kutusu*, vol. 2, sec. 2, 76.

45. al-'Abid, vol 2, sec. 2, 11–15, 49–55, 75, 84–87.

46. See Minawi, *Ottoman Scramble for Africa*, 99–115.

47. "Mekke Mükerreme Telegraf Hattı," *İkdam*, April 17, 1900, 1.

48. BOA, Y.MTV-201/29 (8/4/1900); İ.TAL-207/1317-Z-54 (23/4/1900).

49. Mostafa Minawi, "Telegraphs and Territoriality in Ottoman Africa and Arabia during the Age of High Imperialism," *Journal of Balkan and Near Eastern Studies* 18, no. 6 (2016): 567–87.

50. Minawi, *Ottoman Scramble for Africa*, 128.

51. BOA, İ.TAL-289/1320-Ş-11 (7/11/1902); İ.TAL-281/9 (25/7/1902); İ.TAL-281/53 (25/7/1902).

52. Azmzade, *Rihlat al-Habasha*, 37.

53. For more on the construction of the Hijaz telegraph line see Mostafa Minawi, "Beyond Rhetoric: Reassessing Bedouin-Ottoman Relations along the Route of the Hijaz Telegraph Line at the End of the Nineteenth Century," *Journal of the Economic and Social History of the Orient* 58, no. 1–2 (2015): 74–104. Minawi, *Ottoman Scramble for Africa*. For more on the Hijaz Railway see M. Metin Hülagü, *The Hejaz Railway: The Construction of a New Hope* (Clifton, NJ: Bluedome Press, 2010); Murat Özyüksel, *The Hejaz Railway and the Ottoman Empire: Modernity, Industrialisation, and Ottoman Decline* (London: Bloomsbury Publishing, 2014).

54. *İkdam* frequently gave updates about Ottoman progress on the telegraph line. See a report on Sadik leaving Istanbul, along with a large number of soldiers and other engineers, heading by train to Damascus: "Hicaz Şimendifer," *İkdam*, May 17, 1900, 1.

55. The meaning of *Rumeli Beylerbeyi* changed several times between the fifteenth and the twentieth centuries. For more, see Mehmet İpşirli, "Beylerbeyi," in *TDV İslam Ansiklopedisi* (Ankara: Türkiye Diyanet Vakfı, 1992), 6:69–74.

56. BOA, İ.TAL-222/1318-R-167 (26/8/1900); İ.Tal-224/1318-Ca-119 (9/9/1900).

57. Sadik al-Mu'ayyad Azmzade, "Habeş Seyahatnamesi (Manuscript)," 18.

58. James W. Redhouse, *A Turkish and English Lexicon*, 4th ed. (Istanbul: Çağrı Yayınları, 2011), 349.

59. Şamsuddin Sami, *Kamus-ı Türki*, ed. Ahmed Cevdet (Istanbul: İkdam Matbaası, 1899), 248.

60. Redhouse, *Turkish and English Lexicon*, 1292.

61. Sami, *Kamus-ı Türki*, 932.

62. Azmzade, *Rihlat al-Habasha*, 36.

63. Bassam 'Abd al-Salam Batush, *Rafīq al-'Azm, Mufakiran wa Muslihan: Dirasa fi Fikrihi wa Dawrihi fi al-Haraka al-Islahiyya al-'Arabiyya* (Amman: Dar Kunuz al-Ma'rifa, 2007), 29.

64. Azmzade, *Rihlat al-Habasha*, 33.

65. Azmzade, *Rihlat al-Habasha*, 36.

66. Azmzade, "Habeş Seyahatnamesi (Manuscript)," 13–14, 18.

67. M. Burak Çetintaş, *Dolmabahçe'den Nişantaşı'na: Sultanların Ve Paşaların Semtinin Tarihi.*, 2nd ed. (Istanbul: Antik A. Ş. Kültür Yayınları, 2012), 310–13.

68. Çetintaş, *Dolmabahçe'den Nişantaşı'na*, 277–78.

69. Selim Deringil, *The Ottoman Twilight in the Arab Lands: Turkish Memoirs and Testimonies of the Great War* (Cambridge, UK: Cambridge University Press, 2019); M. Talha Çiçek, *War and State Formation in Syria: Cemal Pasha's Governorate During World War I, 1914–1917* (London: Routledge, 2014).

70. Redhouse, *Turkish and English Lexicon*, 1292.

71. Redhouse, *Turkish and English Lexicon*, 1292.

72. BOA, Y.EE-9/13 (14/1/1896). He would continue to advocate for reforms and imperial investment in Benghazi for many years after, as some notes left in the archives show. Y.PRK.MYD-22/104 (11/12/1899).

73. Azmzade, *Rihla fi al-Sahra' al-Kubra bi-Ifriqya*, 23.

Chapter 5

1. Frantz Fanon, *Black Skin, White Masks*, translated by Charles Lam Markmann, 2nd ed. (London: Pluto Press, 2008), 15–16.

2. Fanon, *Black Skin, White Masks*, 14–16.

3. Homi K. Bhabha, "Forward to the 1986 Edition," in *Black Skin, White Masks*, 2nd ed. (London: Pluto Press, 2008), xxix.

4. Sadik al-Mu'ayyad Azmzade, *Afrika Sahra-yı Kebiri'nde Seyahat (Bir Osmanlı Zabitinin Büyük Sahra'da Seyahati)*, ed. İdris Bostan (Istanbul: Çamlıca Basım Yayın ve Tic. A.Ş., 2008), 77.

5. Sadik al-Mu'ayyad Azmzade, *Rihlat al-Habasha, Min al-Istana ila Addis Ababa*, ed. Nuri al-Jarrah (Dubai: al-Mu'asasa al-'Arabiyya Li-l-Dirasat wa-l-Nashr, 2001), 156;

Azmzade, "Habeş Seyahatnamesi (Manuscript)," 181–82; Nándor Dreisziger, "Ármin Vámbéry (1832–1913) as a Historian of Early Hungarian Settlement in the Carpathian Basin," *Hungarian Cultural Studies. e-Journal of the American Hungarian Educators Association* 6 (2013), http://ahea.pitt.edu (accessed May 25, 2022).

6. Tracey Reimann-Dawe, "Time and the Other in Nineteenth-Century German Travel Writing on Africa," *Transfers* 6, no. 3 (2016): 101. Similar attitudes were expressed by American travelers in the Ottoman Empire during the same time. See Kent Schull, "Amalgamated Observations: American Impressions of Nineteenth Century Constantinople and Its Peoples," in *Istanbul—Kushta—Constantinople: Diversity of Identities and Personal Narratives in the Ottoman Capital (1830–1900)*, ed. Christoph Herzog and Richard Wittmann (London: Routledge, 2018), 57–77.

7. Mustafa Serdar Palabıyık, "Ottoman Travelers' Perceptions of Africa in the Late Ottoman Empire (1860–1922): A Discussion of Civilization, Colonialism, and Race," *New Perspectives on Turkey* 46 (n.d.): 210.

8. Azmzade, "Habeş Seyahatnamesi (Manuscript)."

9. Sadik al-Mu'ayyad Azmzade, *Habeş Seyahatnamesi* (Istanbul: İkdam Matbaası, 1904).

10. Azmzade, *Rihlat al-Habasha*.

11. Sadık el-Müeyyed Azmzade, *Habeş Seyahatnamesi*, ed. Serkan Özburun and Mustafa Baydemir (Istanbul: Kaknus Yayınları, 1999).

12. For a popular account of the Battle of Adwa, see Raymond Anthony Jonas, *The Battle of Adwa: African Victory in the Age of Empire* (Cambridge, MA: Harvard University Press, 2011).

13. For more on Ottoman involvement in late nineteenth-century imperialism in the Horn of Africa, see Mostafa Minawi, "International Law and the Precarity of Ottoman Sovereignty in Africa at the End of the Nineteenth Century," *International History Review* 43, no. 5 (2021): 1098–121.

14. Bairu Tafra, *Ethiopian Records of the Menilek Era: Selected Amharic Documents from the Nachlass of Alfred Ilg, 1884–1900* (Wiesbaden, Germany: Harrassowitz, 2000), 25–30.

15. Deborah Reed-Danahay, *Bourdieu and Social Space, Mobilities, Trajectories, Emplacements* (New York: Berghahn, 2020),

16. Reed-Danahay, *Bourdieu and Social Space*, 22.

17. Bhabha, "Forward to the 1986 Edition," xxvii–xxviii.

18. Azmzade, "Habeş Seyahatnamesi (Manuscript)," 1.

19. Azmzade, "Habeş Seyahatnamesi (Manuscript)," 4; Azmzade, *Rihlat al-Habasha*, 27.

20. Azmzade, "Habeş Seyahatnamesi (Manuscript)," 121; Azmzade, *Habeş Seyahatnamesi*, 1904, 126.

21. Azmzade, "Habeş Seyahatnamesi (Manuscript)," 92–93; Azmzade, *Rihlat al-Habasha*, 90; Azmzade, *Habeş Seyahatnamesi*, 1999, 96.

22. Özge Samancı, "History of Eating and Drinking in the Ottoman Empire and Modern Turkey," in *Handbook of Eating and Drinking, Interdisciplinary Perspectives*, ed. Herbert L. Meiselman (London: Springer, 2020), 69; Tülay Artan, "Aspects of Ottoman Elite's Food Consumption: Looking for 'Staples,' 'Luxuries,' and 'Delicacies' in a Changing Century," in *Consumption Studies and the History of the Ottoman Empire, 1550–1922: An Introduction*, ed. Donald Quataert (Albany: State University of New York Press, 2000), 165.

23. John L. Austin, *How to Do Things with Words* (Cambridge, MA: Harvard University Press, 1967).

24. Judith Butler, *Gender Trouble: Feminism and the Subversion of Identity* (London: Routledge, 1990).

25. Azmzade, "Habeş Seyahatnamesi (Manuscript)," 93; Azmzade, *Habeş Seyahatnamesi*, 1904, 179–80; Azmzade, *Rihlat al-Habasha*, 90–91.

26. Azmzade, *Rihlat al-Habasha*, 91.

27. Azmzade, *Rihlat al-Habasha*, 92.

28. Azmzade, "Habeş Seyahatnamesi (Manuscript)," 22; Azmzade, *Habeş Seyahatnamesi*, 1999, 41; Azmzade, *Rihlat al-Habasha*, 38.

29. Azmzade, "Habeş Seyahatnamesi (Manuscript)," 43; Azmzade, *Habeş Seyahatnamesi*, 1904, 82–83; Azmzade, *Habeş Seyahatnamesi*, 1999, 55; Azmzade, *Rihlat al-Habasha*, 54.

30. Azmzade, "Habeş Seyahatnamesi (Manuscript)," 155; Azmzade, *Habeş Seyahatnamesi*, 1904, 166; Azmzade, *Rihlat al-Habasha*, 137.

31. See Minawi, Mostafa Minawi, "Telegraphs and Territoriality in Ottoman Africa and Arabia during the Age of High Imperialism," *Journal of Balkan and Near Eastern Studies* 18, no. 6 (2016): 567–87.

32. Azmzade, "Habeş Seyahatnamesi (Manuscript)," 42; Azmzade, *Habeş Seyahatnamesi*, 1904, 80–81; Azmzade, *Habeş Seyahatnamesi*, 1999, 54–55; Azmzade, *Rihlat al-Habasha*, 53.

33. Azmzade, *Rihlat al-Habasha*, 65; Azmzade, "Habeş Seyahatnamesi (Manuscript)," 59.

34. See Karen Barkey and George Gavrilis, "The Ottoman Millet System: Non-Territorial Autonomy and Its Contemporary Legacy," *Ethnopolitics* 15, no. 1 (2016).

35. See Konstantinos Papastathis, "Arabic and Its Alternatives: Religious Minorities and Their Languages in the Emerging Nation States of the Middle East (1920–1950)," in *Arabic vs. Greek: The Linguistic Aspect of the Jerusalem Orthodox Church Controversy in Late Ottoman Times and the British Mandate* (Leiden, Netherlands: Brill, 2020), 261–86.

36. For a critical perspective on the millet system and its contemporary influence and colonial equivalencies in the Middle East, see Ergün Çakal, "Pluralism, Tolerance and Control: On the Millet System and the Question of Minorities," *International Journal on Minority and Group Rights* 27, no. 1 (2020): 34–65.

37. Michael Ferguson, "Enslaved and Emancipated Africans on Crete," in *Race and Slavery in the Middle East: Histories of Trans-Saharan Africans in Nineteenth-Century Egypt, Sudan, and the Ottoman Mediterranean*, ed. Terence Walz and Kenneth M. Cuno (Cairo: American University in Cairo Press, 2010), 171–95; Y. Hakan Erdem, *Slavery in the Ottoman Empire and Its Demise 1800–1909*, St. Antony's Series (London: Palgrave Macmillan UK, 1996); Ezgi Güner, "The Soul of the White Muslim: Race, Empire, and Africa in Turkey" (PhD diss., University of Illinois at Urbana-Champaign, 2020); Eve Troutt Powell, *Tell This in My Memory: Stories of Enslavement from Egypt, Sudan, and the Ottoman Empire* (Stanford, CA: Stanford University Press, 2012).

38. Out of sixty-four members in the pool of aides-de-camp to the sultan in 1908, for example, one, a *miralay* (colonel) by the name of Bilal Bey, was described as *siyahi* (Black). This was one of three ethnoracial identifications explicitly described. The other two were *Çerkez* (Circassian) and *Arap*. The vast majority of the list were identified by a famous relative, the city of their birth, or the army unit they belonged to. BOA, Y.PRK. MYD-26/104 (14/9/1908). With the rise of the Black Lives Matter movement in the United States, it became more common to discuss anti-Black racism globally, including anti-Blackness in the Muslim world. See Iskander Abbasi, "Anti-Blackness in the Muslim World: Beyond Apologetics and Orientalism," *Maydan* (blog), October 14, 2020, https://themaydan.com/2020/10/anti-blackness-in-the-muslim-world-beyond-apologetics-and-orientalism/ (accessed May 25, 2022). Also see Susan Abulhawa, "Confronting Anti-Black Racism in the Arab World," https://www.aljazeera.com/opinions/2013/7/7/confronting-anti-black-racism-in-the-arab-world (accessed April 28, 2021).

39. Özgür Türesay, "L'empire ottoman sous le prisme des études postcoloniales. À propos d'un tournant historiographique récent," *Revue d'histoire moderne et contemporaine* 60–62, no. 2 (2013): 127–45.

40. Azmzade, "Habeş Seyahatnamesi (Manuscript)," 175; Azmzade, *Habeş Seyahatnamesi*, 1904, 329–30; Azmzade, *Rihlat al-Habasha*, 151.

41. Azmzade, "Habeş Seyahatnamesi (Manuscript)," 101; Azmzade, *Habeş Seyahatnamesi*, 1904, 195; Azmzade, *Habeş Seyahatnamesi*, 1999, 106; Azmzade, *Rihlat al-Habasha*, 97–98.

42. Azmzade, "Habeş Seyahatnamesi (Manuscript)," 101; Azmzade, *Rihlat al-Habasha*, 98. *Sudanlar* (not *Sundanlılar*) in the original manuscript was translated as "Black people," not "Sudanese," in the Arabic version, which is what I chose to keep in the translation. I was not able to find *taj olaj* or any expression similar to it in Amharic or Somali.

43. Suman Seth, *Difference and Disease: Medicine, Race, and the Eighteenth-Century British Empire* (Cambridge, UK: Cambridge University Press, 2018), 167–207.

44. Azmzade, "Habeş Seyahatnamesi (Manuscript)," 17; Azmzade, *Habeş Seyahatnamesi*, 1999, 23; Azmzade, *Rihlat al-Habasha*, 35.

45. Azmzade, "Habeş Seyahatnamesi (Manuscript)," 40; Azmzade, *Habeş Seyahatnamesi*, 1904, 76.

46. Azmzade, "Habeş Seyahatnamesi (Manuscript)," 37–38; Azmzade, *Habeş Seya-hatnamesi*, 1904, 72.

47. Azmzade, *Habeş Seyahatnamesi*, 1904, 99; Azmzade, "Habeş Seyahatnamesi (Manuscript)," 52.

48. Azmzade, *Habeş Seyahatnamesi*, 1904, 199–200; Azmzade, "Habeş Seyahatnam-esi (Manuscript)," 103. Another common theme was the notion that the locals' ability to adapt was inherently limited. For example, Sadik compared what he was wearing to what the Somali servants working for the French governor were wearing. He mentioned that he was dressed in his white ceremonial uniform because of the hot weather. The Somali officers in the service of the French colonial government were also dressed in a white uniform made of a white shirt, a pair of white shorts, and a red fez with a star emblem on the front. However, he pointed out, they were barefoot. Sadik believed that one "can get the Somalis to wear clothes, but they could never get used to wearing shoes." Azmzade, *Habeş Seyahatnamesi*, 1904, 74.

49. Azmzade, "Habeş Seyahatnamesi (Manuscript)," 148; Azmzade, *Habeş Seyahat-namesi*, 1904, 157; Azmzade, *Rihlat al-Habasha*, 132.

50. Güner, "The Soul of the White Muslim."

51. Reimann-Dawe, "Time and the Other," 107.

52. Reimann-Dawe, "Time and the Other," 105–6.

53. Azmzade, "Habeş Seyahatnamesi (Manuscript)," 60; Azmzade, *Rihlat al-Habasha*, 67.

54. Azmzade, "Habeş Seyahatnamesi (Manuscript)," 208; Azmzade, *Rihlat al-Habasha*, 176. This section, forty-four pages of the original manuscript in which Sadik presents a great deal of information about the Abyssinian people, state organization, and international politics, as well as four days of his travelogue, was left out of the Ottoman-Turkish and modern-Turkish publications.

55. "Akhbar al-Jihat, Egypt," *Thamarat al-Funun*, August 8, 1904, 7.

56. BOA, DH.MKT-886/30 (5/9/1904); DH.MKT-891/37 (22/9/1904).

57. "Habeş'teki Osmanlılar," *Tanin*, October 21, 1908, 8.

58. "al-'Uthmaniyoun fi al-Habasha," *Lisan al-Hal*, December 22, 1909, 1. See James De Lorenzi, "A Cruel Destiny: The Armenian Stranger in Twentieth-Century Ethiopia," *International Journal of African Historical Studies* 49, no. 3 (2016): 405–35.

Chapter 6

1. BOA, A.MTZ(04)-131/46 (29/7/1905).

2. Nejib Melhamé did not fare well after the collapse of the Hamidian regime. While his brother Selim was able to escape, Nejib was prosecuted and sent to prison for alleged corruption. Jens Hanssen, "'Malhamé-Malfamé': Levantine Elites and Tran-simperial Networks on the Eve of the Young Turk Revolution," *International Journal of Middle East Studies* 43, no. 1 (2011): 25–26.

3. Nejib Melhamé's letter of resignation, as translated into modern Turkish, appears in Erol Makzume, *Sultan II. Abdülhamid'in Hizmetinde Selim Melhame Paşa ve Ailesi* (Istanbul: MD Basım Evi, 2019), 115.

4. BOA, İ.DH-1427/8 (19/10/1904); İ.DH-1427/33 (1904/10/19).

5. Ruveyda Okumuş, "II. Abdülhamid Devrinde Yıldızı Parlayan Bir Devlet Adamı: Reşid Mümtaz Paşa (1856–1928)," *Hazine-i Evrak Arşiv ve Tarih Araştırmaları Dergisi* 2, no. 2 (2020): 113–40.

6. BOA, YY.EE-58/21 (26/10/1904).

7. BOA, A.MTZ(04)-122/51 (26/10/1904); İ.MTZ(04)-25/1651 (26/10/1904).

8. BOA, A.MTZ(04)-122/69 (1/11/1904).

9. BOA, Y.A.RES-128/46 (1/11/1904). During this period, the letterhead of the Ministry of Foreign Affairs read "The Office of Foreign Affairs of the Sublime Porte." I keep it as the Ministry of Foreign Affairs for consistency.

10. BOA, Y.A.HUS-480/89 (4/11/1904); A.MTZ(04)-122/73 (3/11/1904).

11. BOA, A.MTZ(04)-122/87 (8/11/1904).

12. George Buchanan to the Marquess of Lansdowne, Henry Petty-Fitzmaurice, BNA, FO78/5361-9 (14/11/1904), 182–83.

13. BOA, HR.SFR.04-795/5 (2/12/1904).

14. "Charles Maring to the Marquess of Lansdowne, Henry Petty-Fitzmaurice," BNA, FO78/5361-12 (5/12/1904), 233–34.

15. See a note complaining of the delivery of Bulgarian passports outside of the agreed-on borders. It was instigated by a letter from the Ottoman mission in Bucharest. BOA, HR.ŞFR.04-438/52 (20/5/1905).

16. For an example of correspondence complaining about cross-border insurgencies into eastern Rumelia, see BOA, A.MTZ(04)-140/59 (29/3/1906).

17. For example, see the document from Muslim notables in Vidin asking for an Ottoman medal to be given to the *kaymakam* of the town for his good treatment of the Muslims there. BOA, A.AMD-1081/54 (24/1/1908).

18. BOA, HR.SYS-42/54 (6/2/1906).

19. BOA, A.MTZ(04)-122/73 (3/11/1904).

20. M. Şükrü Hanioğlu, *Preparation of a Revolution: The Young Turks, 1902–1908* (Oxford, UK: Oxford University Press, 2001), 75.

21. BOA, A.MTZ(04)-123/52 (29/11/1904).

22. BOA, A.MTZ(04)-123/28 (21/11/1904).

23. BOA, A.MTZ(04)-122/92 (8/11/1904); A.MTZ(04)-123/3 (10/11/1904); A.MTZ(04)-123/14 (17/11/1904); A.MTZ(04)-126/81 (3/3/1905).

24. BOA, A.MTZ(04)-13/62 (1/12/1904); A.MTZ(04)-123/75 (5/12/1904).

25. BOA, A.MTZ.(04)-124/6 (13/12/1904).

26. BOA, A.MTZ(04)-123/15 (17/11/1904).

27. BOA, DH.SAİD-113/439 (2/3/1904).

28. BOA, Y.A.HUS-486/169 (5/5/1905).

29. BOA, A.MTZ(04)-125/38 (14/1/1905).

30. BOA, İ.MTZ(04)-27/1740 (18/2/1907); A.MTZ(04)-153/19 (19/2/1907).

31. BOA, A.MTZ(04)-129/4 (8/5/1905); Y.PRK.MK-20/138 (23/5/1905).

32. BOA, İ.MTZ(04)-26/1681 (18/6/1905).

33. BOA, A.MTZ(04)-134/1 (2/9/1905).

34. A copy of the letter attached to Vassik's calling card are preserved at the Ottoman archives in Istanbul. BOA, A.MTZ(04)-130/25 (11/7/1905).

35. BOA, A.MTZ(04)-130/14 (8/7/1905); A.MTZ(04)-130/57 (18/7/1905).

36. BOA, A.MTZ(04)-130/31 (12/7/1905); A.MTZ(04)-130/55 (17/7/1905).

37. BOA, A.MTZ(04)-131/46 (29/7/1905).

38. BOA, A.MTZ(04)-133/16 (22/8/1905); A.MTZ(04)-133/42 (28/8/1905); A.MTZ(04)-134/29 (11/9/1905).

39. BOA, A.MTZ(04)-134/81 (23/9/1905).

40. BOA, A.MTZ(04)-134/1 (2/9/1905).

41. BOA, İ.MTZ(04)-30/1975 (16/9/1905); A.MTZ(04)-135/5 (25/9/1905). An additional problem was the exchange rate between Ottoman kurush and French francs when the Ottoman Imperial Bank transferred the money to the Bulgarian General Bank. Somewhere along the way, some of the money meant for the salaries was lost, leading to complaints to the bank and the Office of the Privy Treasury. BOA, HR.SFR.04-812/63 (24/12/1906); ML.EEM-579/71 (9/1/1907); HR.SFR.04-8186 (16/1/1907).

42. For example, see the foreign affairs office answer to a request for delayed salaries by Sadik in early 1908. BOA, A.MTZ(04)-163/47 (21/2/1908), and Sadik's letter to the grand vizier about this issue. BOA, A.MTZ(04)-163/48 (21/2/1908).

43. BOA, A.MTZ(04)-164/18 (10/3/1908).

44. BOA, A.MTZ(04)-165/7 (6/4/1908); A.MTZ(04)-165/44 (7/4/1908).

45. BOA, A.MTZ(04)-164/19 (10/3/1908).

46. Translated into French from the newspaper *Denevnik*, November 24, 1904. BOA, A.MTZ(04)-123/86 (8/12/1904).

47. For a report on how the press covered Prince Ferdinand, see BOA, Y.PRK. MK-21/2 (12/7/1905). For the Ottoman state's complaint about the portrayal of the Ottoman position in the Bulgarian press, see BOA, HR.SFR.3-574/48 (14/5/1907). For a report on Russian, Bulgarian, and even Armenian agitation and the way the press covered it, see BOA, HR.TH-349/12 (22/6/1907).

48. For a detailed analysis of European and local press speculation that Prince Ferdinand was preparing to declare himself king, and declaring independence, see BOA, Y.PRK.MK-21/4 (16/7/1905).

49. For a detailed account of anti-Muslim acts of violence in the Balkans, see BOA, A.MTZ(04)-129/9 (11/5/1905).

50. BOA, HR.SFR.04-256/4 (9/3/1905).

51. BOA, HR.SFR.04-256/8 (28/4/1905).

52. For a very detailed note analyzing internal and external relations of the Bulgarian state, see BOA, A.MTZ(04)-161/46 (26/11/1907).

53. BOA, HR.SFR.04-256/7 (25/4/1905).

54. BOA, İ.TAL-413/1324-Z-26 (10/2/1907).

55. BOA, HR.SFR.04-799/83 (11/6/1905).

56. BOA, HR.SAİD-11/7 (22/11/1902).

57. BOA, İ.TAL-366/17 (8/6/1905); Y.PRK.MK-20/151 (11/6/1905).

58. "Ottoman Medal for 'Compassionate' British Lady to Go under the Hammer," *Hürriyet Daily News*, January 24, 2015, https://www.hurriyetdailynews.com/ottoman-medal-for-compassionate-british-lady-to-go-under-the-hammer-77387 (accessed May 29, 2022).

59. BOA, İ.TAL-334/1322-RA-91 (28/6/29).

60. BOA, DH.SAİD-105/61 (12/5/1914).

61. BOA, A.MTZ(04)-150/106 (2/12/1906).

62. BOA, DH.SAİD-113/483 (12/10/1913).

63. He was awarded a *Mecidiye* of the fourth degree for his work as *kaymakam* of 'Ajlun. BOA, DH.MKT-2215/75 (27/6/1899).

64. BOA, DH.MKT-1137/40 (29/1/1907).

65. BOA, DH. MKT-1074/69 (29/4/1906). Iklil was assigned to the district in a vaguely worded special decree as the *kaymakam* of a yet to be announced *kaza* in the Province of Syria. BOA, İ.HUS-108/1321-ca-10 (18/8/1903).

66. BOA, DH.MTV-22/14 (13/11/1910).

67. BOA, Y.PRK.MK-22/80 (23/4/1908).

68. BOA, Y.PRK.BŞK-78/66 (25/4/1908).

69. Office of the Prince to the Bulgarian Diplomatic Agent in Istanbul, telegram, BHA, F.176K, Opus2, ae.238, 2. (10/4/1908). Generously translated from Bulgarian by Dr. Margarita Dobreva.

70. Bulgarian Diplomatic Agent to the Office of the Prince, telegram, BHA, F.176K, Opus2, ae.238, 3. Generously translated from Bulgarian by Dr. Margarita Dobreva.

71. Bulgarian Diplomatic Office in Istanbul to the Minister of Foreign Affairs in Sofia, telegram, BHA, F.176K, Opus2, ae.238, 1 (2/3/1908). Generously translated from Bulgarian by Dr. Margarita Dobreva.

72. BOA, İ.MTZ(04)-27/1762 (27/4/1908); A.MTZ(04)-165/59 (28/4/1908).

73. BOA, İ.MTZ(04)-27/1765 (6/5/1908); A.MTZ(04)-166/60 (26/5/1908).

74. BOA, İ.MTZ(04)-27/1764 (6/5/1908).

75. BOA, A.MTZ(04)-166/29 (15/5/1908).

76. BOA, İ.TAL-447/1326-RA-45 (26/4/1908).

77. It was announced in a daily column of high-level governmental appointments. "Tevcihat," *İkdam* June 11, 1908, 1.

78. BOA, A.MTZ(04)-165/7 (6/4/1908); İ.MTZ(04) 27/1766 (8/6/1908); A.MTZ(04)-167/35 (9/6/1908).

79. BOA, A.MTZ(04)-173/92 (19/1/1909).

80. Hanioğlu, *Preparation of a Revolution*, 75–76.

81. BOA, ŞD-3062/8 (29/11/1909).

82. BOA, DUİT-165/23 (7/8/1909).

83. The names of people who were demoted were published in "Tasfiye-i Rüteb-i Askeriye," *İkdam*, September 17, 1909, 3.

84. James Scott, *Seeing Like a State: How Certain Schemes to Improve the Human Condition Have Failed* (New Haven, CT: Yale University Press, 1999), 64–71.

85. Abdülkadir Özcan, "Paşa," in *TDV İslam Ansiklopedisi* (İstanbul: Türkiye Diyanet Vakfı, 2007), 32:182–83.

86. The weekly magazine *Servet-i Fünun* detailed the final status of the law and featured drawings and photographs of some of the disgraced members of the former regime who were on the run. Izzet, as the poster man for the corruption of the old regime, was featured. The witch hunt took a multilayered approach, where there was very little room for dissent from the harsh critique of the ancient regime and those who supported it. Public condemnation of the ancient regime and those chosen as its face was often featured in daily newspapers such as *İkdam* and *Tanin* and weekly magazines such as *Servet-i Fünun*. İsmail Suphi and Muhammed Fuad, eds., *Salname-i Servet-i Fünun (10 Temmuz 1324–28 Şubat 1325)* (İstanbul: Ahmed İhsan ve Şürekâsı Matbaa-ı Halk Osmanlı Şirketi, 1910); "Tasfiye-i Rüteb-i Askeriye Kanunu," *İkdam*, October 17, 1910, 5; "Tasfiye-i Rüteb-i Askeriye Kanunu," *İkdam* October 18, 1910, 4.

87. For more on Ragib's time in the Hijaz and his demise, see Mostafa Minawi, "Beyond Rhetoric: Reassessing Bedouin-Ottoman Relations along the Route of the Hijaz Telegraph Line at the End of the Nineteenth Century," *Journal of the Economic and Social History of the Orient* 58, no. 1–2 (2015): 74–104.

88. Daily newspapers spilled a great deal of ink on the corruption of Ahmed Ratib, considered a symbol of a bygone era. "Hicaz Ahvali," *Tanin*, September 19, 1908, 7; "Hicaz Mektubu," *Tanin*, October 12, 1908, 6; "Hicaz Mektubu 2, Ratip Paşa Kaçdı, Kaçamadı mı?" *Tanin*, October 22, 1908, 5.

89. BOA, DH.MTV-3/1 (27/1/1910); İ.DH-1479/37 (31/1/1910).

90. "Mahaliyya," *Lisan al-Hal*, September 1, 1910, 2.

91. BOA, DH.MTV-40-1/79 (24/11/1910).

92. BOA, DH.MTV-14/6 (9/9/1912).

93. BOA, DH.MTV-14/6 (9/9/1912).

94. BOA, DH.MTV-14/6 (9/9/1912).

95. "Wafat Sadik al-Mu'ayyad," *al-Ittihad al-'Uthmani*, October 19, 1910, 2.

96. Akram Reşad and Osman Ferid, eds., *Musaver Nevsal Osmani*, 3rd ed. (İstanbul: Şems Matbaası, 1911), 216.

97. BOA, DH.h-27/10 (21/5/1911).

98. BOA, HR.UHM-79/50 (7/11/1910).

99. In an interview conducted in June 2021, a great grandchild of Sadik and Esma told me that two other family members living in the Bostancı neighborhood had their large home burnt down. They were pushed out of the city where they had made a life to start anew in Damascus, a city they barely knew.

Chapter 7

1. "İzzet Niçin Vapur'dan Alınamadı?" *Tanin*, August 8, 1908, 2; Hüseyin Cahid, "Şayan-ı Teessüf Bir Zühul," *Tanin*, March 10, 1910, 1. Italics and use of the colloquial Turkish pronunciation (Arap) is mine and added for clarity.

2. "İzzet Niçin Vapur'dan Alınamadı?" 2; Cahid, "Şayan-ı Teessüf Bir Zühul," 1.

3. Translated from an article in the British *Daily Mail* by William Maxwell: "Ahmed 'Izzat Basha, Hadithahu wa Tanasuluhu min al-Tabi'a, Tazahurhu bi-l-Mayl ila al-Dustur, Raghbatuhu fi Istitan Ingeltra," *Lisan al-Hal*, September 2, 1908, 1. The *Adalar* are eight small islands close to Istanbul where many of Istanbul's wealthy had second homes. In English they are referred to as the Princess Islands.

4. 'Abd al-Qadir al-'Azm, *al-Usra al-'Azmiyya* (Damascus: Matba'at al-Insha', 1960), 60.

5. "Munaqashat al-Mab'uthan, al-Jalsa al-Thaniya fi 22 min al-Jari," *Lisan al-Hal*, December 31, 1908, 1.

6. Variations of this slogan were used; in some "justice" replaced "fraternity" and in some it was added. Bedross Der Matossian, *Shattered Dreams of Revolution: From Liberty to Violence in the Late Ottoman Empire* (Stanford, CA: Stanford University Press, 2014), 44.

7. "al-'Unsur al-'Arabi Bayna al-'Uthmaniyyin," *Lisan al-Hal*, October 6, 1908, 1.

8. BOA, DH.MKT-2619/73 (1/10/1908), ZB-326/135 (3/10/1908).

9. "al-Ikha' al-'Uthmani," *al-Ittihad al-'Uthmani*, January 13, 1909, 2. For more on nationalism among the Kurdish-Ottoman intelligentsia during this period, see Djene Rhys Bajalan, "Princes, Pashas, and Patriots: The Kurdish Intelligentsia, the Ottoman Empire and the National Question (1908–1914)," *British Journal of Middle Eastern Studies* 43, no. 2 (2016), 140–57.

10. Arab-Ottomans were not the only ethnic group to build a political platform at that time. Armenian-, Jewish-, and Greek-Ottomans established political parties as well. For more see Der Matossian, *Shattered Dreams of Revolution*, 62–64.

11. "Nasyonalizm," *İkdam*, February 3, 1909, 1.

12. 'Uthman al-'Azm (ed.), *Majmu'at Athar Rafiq Bey al-'Azm* (Cairo: Mina Printing Press, 1925), 130. Rafiq al-'Azm claimed that the rumor of an "Arab caliph" was started in Cairo by Murad Bey Dağıstani back in 1897, when he thought this idea might scare the Hamidian administration into accepting his demands for reforms. al-'Azm, *Majmu'at Athar Rafiq Bey al-'Azm*, 122.

13. al-'Azm, *Majmu'at Athar Rafiq Bey al-'Azm*, 125, 127–28.

14. al-'Azm, *Majmu'at Athar Rafiq Bey al-'Azm*, 131–35.

15. "al-'Arab wa-l-Turk," *al-Ittihad al-'Uthmani*, March 22, 1909, 1–2.

16. Muhammad Rashid Rida, "Arablar ve Türkler," *İkdam*, October 30, 1909, 1–2.

17. Erol Ülker, "Contextualizing Turkification: Nation Building in the Late Ottoman Empire 1909–18," *Nations and Nationalism* 11, no. 4 (2005): 615–17.

18. Hasan Kayalı, *Arabs and Young Turks: Ottomanism, Arabism, and Islamism in the Ottoman Empire, 1908–1918* (Berkeley, CA: University of California Press, 1997).

19. *İkdam*, August 13, 1908, 3.

20. Kayalı, *Arabs and Young Turks*, 91.

21. "Mülkümüzde Fakr-ı İrfan: Tedrisat Aliye'miz," *İkdam*, September 9, 1909, 1. In an *al-Ittihad al-'Uthmani* article, the founder of the journal *al-Nebras*, Sheikh Mustafa al-Ghlayyini, argued against the modification of Turkish, stating that since many educated people were already fluent in Ottoman-Turkish, it would not make sense to render them illiterate by changing the language. The solution, he said, was to educate Turkish villagers in Ottoman-Turkish. Mustafa al-Ghlayyini, "Tanqih al-Luga al-Turkiyya al-Haditha," *al-Ittihad al-'Uthmani*, September 25, 1909, 1. For more on the complicated history of the myth of a "pure" Anatolian Turkish culture, ethnicity, and language, in opposition to one corrupted by the Arab or Persian culture of the Ottoman elites, see Murat Ergin, *"Is the Turk a White Man?" Race and Modernity in the Making of Turkish Identity* (Leiden, Netherlands: Brill, 2017), 42.

22. This was written in defense of *İkdam*'s policy on language use, in response to criticism by a writer and poet, Süleyman Latif Bey Efendi. V. Y., "Açık Mektup: Edip ve Şair Muhterem Süleyman Latif Efendi'ye," *İkdam*, September 9, 1909, 1.

23. Muhammed Veled, "Lisan ve İmla Mebhası," *Tanin*, September 9, 1909, 1.

24. Ali Kemal, "Kavm-ı Necib-i Arab," *İkdam*, September 29, 1908, 1.

25. "Tasfiyat al-Lughat wa Kuttab al-Ishtiqaq wa al-Ta'rib," *al-Ittihad al-'Uthmani* September 29, 1909, 2; "al-Ta'lim bi-l-Arabiyya," *al-Muqtabas*, July 26, 1909, 1; "Al-Dakheel fi al-Luga al-'Arabiyya," *al-Muqtabas*, May 2, 1911, 1.

26. "Mas'alat Tanawo' al-Ajnas fi al-Saltana al-'Uthmaniyya," *al-Ittihad al-'Uthmani*, September 24, 1909, 2.

27. Faris al-Khuri, "Idha Sirt Mab'uthan," *al-Muqtabas*, September 1, 1911, 1–2.

28. "Akhbar Mahaliyya," *Lisan al-Hal*, October 2, 1908, 1.

29. al-'Azm, *Majmu'at Athar Rafiq Bey al-'Azm*.

30. "Şam Mebus-i Cedidi," *İkdam*, January 8, 1911, 2.

31. Haqqi al-'Azm, *Haqa'iq 'an al-Intikhabat al-Niyabiyya fi al-'Iraq wa Falastin wa Suriyya* (Cairo: al-Akhbar Printing Press, 1912), 16.

32. See Shafiq's signature on a September 23, 1908, letter asking for a permit to publish a newspaper. BOA, DH.MKT-2619/73 (1/10/1908). His nephew Sadik chose the Ottoman-Turkish version for his official seal and signature when writing in French. See

any of his letters sent from Sofia in the *Eyalet-i Mumtaze Bulgaristan Evrakı* (A.MTZ-04), as in BOA, A.MTZ(04)-144/29 (9/6/1908).

33. See a letter attributed to Muhammad Arslan, a deputy representing Latakia, which the newspaper *Tanin* published and which Arslan denied even having written. Muhammad Arslan, "Arablar ve Rumlar: Garib İftira," *Tanin*, December 7, 1908, 2.

34. Hüseyin Cahid "Arab Fırkası?" *Tanin*, December 11, 1909, 1. For a flattering treatment of Hüseyin Cahid's political philosophy and thoughts on Ottoman language and culture, see Banu Turanoğlu, *The Formation of Turkish Republicanism* (Princeton, NJ: Princeton University Press, 2017), 121–22. *Al-Muqtabas*, a daily newspaper published in Damascus, often locked horns with *Tanin*, taking offense to what its editors considered to be *Tanin*'s insulting representation of Arabs and anti-Arab-Ottoman deputy sentiments. "Musajala ma' Makatib Tanin," *al-Muqtabas*, June 7, 1911, 1.

35. Rıza Nur, "Mebussan-ı Arabiye Fırkası," *İkdam*, February 13, 1909, 2.

36. As published by *Tanin* claiming that the attack by Greek papers was unjust. "Meclis-i Mebusan'da Fırkalar," *Tanin*, February 13, 1909, 2.

37. Jön Türk, "Arap Grubunun İçtimai," *Tanin*, March 27, 1911, 2.

38. The expression was translated into Turkish from the French newspaper *Le Temps* and published in *İkdam*. The article paints the Young Turks as reformers who gave minorities freedoms but could not seem to catch a break. "Türkiye'de Irk Meselesi," *İkdam*, September 15, 1909, 1.

39. "Devlet-i Osmaniye Esbab-ı Zufu: Vüsat-ı Arazı—Kesret-i Anasır," *İkdam* May 2, 1909, 2. The sentiment that there is no real discrimination and nobody is to blame for poor patriotism derived from previous administrations that did not work harder to teach Turkish and to instill a sense of unity. Hüseyin Cahid, "Mahkemel-erde Lisan Meselesi," *Tanin*, November 11, 1909, 1; "Türkçe Nasıl Lisan Umumi Olur?" *İkdam*, November 13, 1909, 2; "Şam'da," *Tanin*, March 28, 1910, 1; Hüseyin Cahid, "Yanlış Bir Telakki," *Tanin*, November 13, 1909, 1; "Arablar ve Türkler," *Tanin*, April 8, 1910, 1; "Hissiyat-ı Milliye," *İkdam*, May 6, 1911, 1; Ismail Hakki Babanzade, "Irak Mektupları: Türk ve Arab," *Tanin*, October 16, 1910, 1.

40. Ahmed Şerif, "Suriye'deki Tanin: Suriye'deki Matbuat ve Hissiyatta Tezahürat, Hükümet, 1, Beyrut, 23 Mart, 1327," *Tanin*, April 15, 1911, 1-2; Şerif, "Suriye'deki Tanin," *Tanin*, April 4, 1911, 1.

41. Şerif, "Suriye'deki Tanin," *Tanin*, December 12, 1910, 1.

42. M., "Ma Wara' al-Hawadeth," *al-Ittihad al-'Uthmani*, September 28, 1909, 1. Often, there was some backpedaling by *Tanin* and *İkdam* of their criticism of "the Arabs," but it was rejected as disingenuous by the Arabic-language press, which in return asked the editors of Istanbul-based dailies to change their attitude toward Arab-Ottoman deputies instead of publishing the occasional complimentary piece. For example, see Hüseyin Cahid, "Suriye Ahvalı ve Arablar," *Tanin*, October 25, 1909, 1. This article was followed by "Ahwal Surya wa-l-'Arab aw Tanin wa-l-'Arab," *al-Ittihad*

al-'Uthmani, November 5, 1909, 1; and "Mas'alat al-Masa'il," *al-Ittihad al-'Uthmani*, November 8, 1909, 1.

43. Hüseyin Cahid, "al-'Arab wa-l-Atrak, 2" *al-Itthad al-'Uthmani*, May 2, 1910, 1. *Tanin* published a number of articles during the month of April in 1910 combating claims by the president of the Paris Syrian Arab Society, Shukri Ghanim, in which he gave evidence of discrimination against Arab-Ottomans. See Cahid, "Arablar ve Türkler," *Tanin*, April 8, 1910, 1; 'Arab Mebuslardan: Halil Amirzade,' "Arablar ve Türkler," *Tanin*, April 10, 1910, 2; Cahid, "Bir Makale Münasebetiyle," *Tanin*, April 15, 1910, 1; Cahid, "Arablar ve Türkler," *Tanin*, April 19, 1910, 1. Also see Kayalı, for a detailed analysis of Ghanim's role in the context of Arabism and Syrian and Arab nationalism. Kayalı, *Arabs and Young Turks*, 87–88.

44. Discussions of the problematic impact on the lives of local employees and residents in Arabic-speaking-majority cities are plentiful. See Hüseyin Cahid, "Mahkemelerde Lisan Meselesi," *Tanin*, November 11, 1909, 1; Cahid "Yanlış Bir Telakki," *Tanin*, November 13, 1909, 1; Also see, "Siyasa," *Lisan al-Hal*, November 25, 1909, 1; "al-Lugha al-Turkiyya," *Lisan al-Hal*, January 21, 1910, 1; [illegible], "Al-Lugha al-'Arabiyya fi Nadhar Hukumatina li-Ahad 'Ulama' Halab," *Ittihad al-'Uthmani*, February 29, 1910, 1; "al-'Arab wa al-Atrak," *Lisan al-Hal*, April 28, 1910, 2. Hassan Kayalı provides an analysis of the court language debacle in *Arabs and Young Turks*, 92.

45. Michiel Leezenberg, "The Vernacular Revolution: Reclaiming Early Modern Grammatical Traditions in the Ottoman Empire," *History of Humanities* 1, no. 2 (2016): 251–75.

46. Bedross Der Matossian, *Shattered Dreams of Revolution: From Liberty to Violence in the Late Ottoman Empire* (Stanford, CA: Stanford University Press, 2014), 106–07.

47. Muhammad Zain al-Din, *"Bayna al-'Arab wa-l-Atrak wa-l-'Adliyya," Lisan al-Hal*, December 30, 1910, 1–2.

48. Kayalı, *Arabs and Young Turks*, 91.

49. One of the ways that the Hamidian regime implemented measures to bring Sunni Muslims into the fold of Ottoman loyalty was through a centralized education system designed to inculcate the Ottoman population with a strong sense of belonging to a wider Ottoman citizenry with loyalty to the dynasty as its unifying central concept. See Benjamin C. Fortna, *Imperial Classroom: Islam, the State, and Education in the Late Ottoman Empire* (Oxford, UK: Oxford University Press, 2002). For a comprehensive and concise summary of the processes of instilling imperial nationalism alongside the rise of ethnonationalism in the Ottoman Empire, see Howard Eissenstat, "Modernization, Imperial Nationalism, and the Ethnicization of Confessional Identity in the Late Ottoman Empire," in *Nationalizing Empires*, ed. Alexei Miller and Stefan Berger (Budapest: Central European University, 2015), 429–59.

50. Rafiq al-'Azm, *"al-'Arab wa-l-Atrak," al-Ittihad al-'Uthmani*, March 22, 1909, 1–2.

51. "al-Istana al-'Ulya li-Makatibina: Nuwwab al-'Arab," *al-Ittihad al-'Uthmani*, April 5, 1909, 1. Jar Sadjik and Amin al-Hashimi, "Madha Yujab," *al-Itthihad al-'Uthmani*, January 14, 1910, 1.

52. "Nuwab al-Wilayat al-'Arabiyya: Ara'uhm fi Sukutihim La'al Lahum 'Udhran wa Anta Taloum," *al-Ittihad al-'Uthmani*, March 29, 1909, 2–3.

53. "Akhbar Mahaliyya ila Majlis al-Nuwwab Aydan; al-Diq al-Mali fi al-Bilad; al-Tamyiz Bayna al-'Anasir; La Turki wa La 'Arabi,'" *Lisan al-Hal*, March 30, 1909, 1.

54. Shafiq's speeches were often translated into Arabic and published in *al-Muqtabas* in Damascus. See "Khitab Shafiq Bek al-Mu'ayyad," *al-Muqtabas*, February 12, 1911, 1–2. Another fluent Arabic speaker was Nafi' Pasha of Aleppo. Der Matossian, *Shattered Dreams*, 135.

55. See Der Matossian's conclusion in *Shattered Dreams*, 173–78; Kayalı, *Arabs and Young Turks*, 207–12; Philip Khoury, *Urban Notables and Arab Nationalism: The Politics of Damascus, 1860–1920* (Cambridge, UK: Cambridge University Press, 1983), 53–75.

56. An excellent intervention by historian Alp Yenen about imagined futures, when a Turco-Arab political coexistence was still a possibility, is part of a groundswell of political and intellectual history in the final decade of the Ottoman Empire. See Alp Yenen, "Envisioning Turco-Arab Co-Existence between Empire and Nationalism," *Die Welt des Islams* 61 (April 2021): 72–112. For Turkish readers also see Gülsüm Polat's research on post-1914 "Arab-Turkish" relations, after the effective collapse of the empire and a time of visions of alternative possible futures that ended with 1923. U. Gülsüm Polat, *Türk-Arap İlişkileri: Eski Eyaletler Yeni Komşulara Dönüşürken* (1914–1923) (Istanbul: Kronik, 2019).

57. "Majlis al-Nuwab aw al-Mabusan," *al-Ittihad al-'Uthmani*, January 9, 1909, 1; "Muthakarat Majlis al-Nuwwab," *al-Ittihad al-'Uthmani*, January 10, 1909, 1–2.

58. Nader Sohrabi, *Revolution and Constitutionalism in the Ottoman Empire and Iran* (Cambridge, UK: Cambridge University Press, 2011), 137.

59. "al-Jurnalat," *Lisan al-Hal*, May 21, 1910, 1.

60. See *al-Muqtabas*, May 16, 1910, 2.

61. "al-Jurnalat," *Lisan al-Hal*, May 21, 1910, 1; "al-Jurnalat," *Lisan al-Hal*, May 23, 1910, 1–2.

62. "al-Jurnalat," *Lisan al-Hal*, May 23, 1910, 1–2.; Merih Erol, "Surveillance, Urban Governance, and Legitimacy in Late Ottoman Istanbul: Spying on Music and Entertainment during the Hamidian Regime (1876–1909)," *Urban History* 40, no. 4 (2013): 712.

63. "al-Jurnalat," *Lisan al-Hal*, May 21, 1910, 1; "al-Jurnalat," *Lisan al-Hal*, May 23, 1910, 1–2.

64. Ümit Kurt, "The Curious Case of Ali Cenani Bey: The Story of a Génocidaire During and After the 1915 Armenian Genocide," *Patterns of Prejudice* 52, no. 1 (2018): 58–77.

65. "Mahalliya, Hadith Mu'lim," *Lisan al-Hal*, July 1, 1910, 1 (originally published in *al-Muqattam*).

66. "Muthakarat Majlis al-Nuwab," *al-Ittihad al-'Uthmani*, January 14, 1909, 1.

67. "Muthakarat Majlis al-Nuwab," *al-Ittihad al-'Uthmani,* January 16, 1909, 1.

68. BOA, DH.MKT-794/68 (17/11/1903), Y.A.RES-125/104 (28/4/1904).

69. BOA, DH.MKT-794/68 (17/11/1903), Y.A.RES-125/104 (28/4/1904).

70. BOA, Y.A.RES-125/104 (28/4/1904); İ.AZN-59/1322-L-55 (17/12/1904); I.HUS-125/1322-Za-69 (26/1/1905). Information about Nimet's properties obtained from A.DVN.MKL-34/3 (8/10/1892) as discussed in Jiy Zafer Süren, "Karden İsa'nın Kızları (III)—Nimet Hanım'ın Kaderi," *JINEPS,* September 9, 2016, https://jinepsgazetesi.com/2016/09/karden-isanin-kizlari-iii-nimet-hanimin-kaderi.(accessed October 4, 2020)

71. al-'Azm, *Majmu'at Athar Rafiq Bey al-'Azm.*

72. Haqqi Azmzade, "Al-Lamarkaziyya, al-Idara al-Mu'tadila," *al-Muqtabas,* January 9, 1912, 1.

73. "Junun al-Isti'mar," *al-Muqtabas,* January 20, 1912, 1.

74. Kayalı, *Arabs and Young Turks,* 121.

75. BOA, ŞD-3127/68 (1/12/1914).

76. BOA, DH.ŞFR-57/415 (13/11/1915); DH.ŞFR-58/22 (16/11/1915).

77. BOA, DH.SFR-58/222 (9/12/1915).

78. Selim Deringil, *The Ottoman Twilight in the Arab Lands: Turkish Memoirs and Testimonies of the Great War* (Cambridge, UK: Cambridge University Press, 2019), xlii.

Chapter 8

1. Abd al-Qadir Al-'Azm, *'al-Usra al-'Azmiyya* (Damascus: Matba'at al-Insha', 1960), 61.

2. Salim Tamari, *The Year of the Locust: A Soldier's Diary and the Erasure of the Ottoman Past* (Oakland, CA: University of California Press, 2011), 5.

3. Selim Deringil, *The Ottoman Twilight in the Arab Lands: Turkish Memoirs and Testimonies of the Great War* (Cambridge, UK: Cambridge University Press, 2019), xiv. Also see Veysel Şimşek, "'Backstabbing Arabs' and 'Shirking Kurds': History, Nationalism, and Turkish Memory of the First World War," in *The Great War: From Memory to History,* ed. Kellen Kurschinski et al. (Waterloo, ON: Wilfrid Laurier University Press, 2015), 99–126.

4. "Lebanon Envoy Summoned Amid War of Words Between Beirut and Ankara," *Middle East Eye,* http://www.middleeasteye.net/news/lebanon-envoy-summoned-amid-war-words-between-beirut-and-ankara (accessed June 16, 2021).

5. The invention of history, much like "invention traditions," is part of the scaffolding of many nation-states that claim a continuous and seemingly unbroken link to a past in a particular territory. Of course, the term comes from the famous edited volume by the same title, which mostly deals with the British Isles, but it has been extrapolated on many occasions to a number of places around the world. Eric Hobsbawm and Terence O. Ranger, eds., *The Invention of Tradition* (Cambridge, UK: Cambridge University Press, 1983).

6. The use of *Turk* as opposed to *Turkish* or *Türkiyeli* has a complicated, evolving, and charged history of meanings that lies at the intersection of nationalism, regional

and historic identification, ethnoreligious identification, and race. Its complicated and multilayered meaning during the late Ottoman period, the early republican period, and today is why I have put the term in quotation marks. For more on this, see for example Soner Çağaptay, *Islam, Secularism, and Nationalism in Modern Turkey, Who Is a Turk?* (London: Routledge, 2006). Similarly, "minorities" has a complicated history in the region that goes back to the late Ottoman period, often in reference to Christians of the empire and not specific ethnic groups. See Benjamin Thomas White, *The Emergence of Minorities in the Middle East: The Politics of Community in French Mandate Syria* (Edinburgh: Edinburgh University Press, 2011).

7. Even though the Armenian Genocide and its subsequent denial receive the lion's share of attention in Western media, it is no secret that such atrocities of the late imperial age were not limited to the Ottoman Empire. Other major empires such as the French, British, and German Empires have worked very hard at denying or hiding the "sins" of their empires until today. I believe that an important part of "decolonizing history" is allowing a critical investigation of imperialism, in all its dimensions, of European and non-European empires alike, including the Ottoman Empire. Some of the readings that have influenced my thinking about this topic include Robert Aldrich and Stuart Ward, "Ends of Empire: Decolonizing the Nation in British and French Historiography," in *Nationalizing the Past: Historians as Nation Builders in Modern Europe*, ed. Stefan Berger and Chris Lorenz (London: Palgrave Macmillan UK, 2010), 259–81; Ruqaya Izzidien, "It Is Time to Teach Colonial History in British Schools," https://www.aljazeera.com/opinions/2018/8/30/it-is-time-to-teach-colonial-history-in-british-schools (accessed June 16, 2021); Matthew P. Fitzpatrick, "Colonialism, Postcolonialism, and Decolonization," *Central European History* 51, no. 1 (2018): 83–89; Raymond F. Betts, "Decolonization: A Brief History of the Word," in *Beyond Empire and Nation: The Decolonization of African and Asian Societies, 1930s–1970s*, ed. Els Bogaerts and Remco Raben (Leiden, Netherlands: Brill, 2012), 23–38; Aline Sierp, "EU Memory Politics and Europe's Forgotten Colonial Past," *Interventions* 22, no. 6 (2020): 686–702; François Lantheaume, "The Empire in French History: From a Promise to a Burden," in *School and Nation: Identity Politics and Educational Media in an Age of Diveristy*, ed. Peter Carrier (New York: Peter Lang Publishing, 2013), 134–42.

8. Alan Duben and Cem Behar, *Istanbul Households: Marriage, Family, and Fertility 1880–1940* (Cambridge, UK: Cambridge University Press, 1991), 24.

9. I borrow the term from Michael A. Reynolds's brilliant book, which offers a comparative look into the collapse of the Russian and Ottoman Empires between 1908 and 1918. *Reynolds, Shattering Empires: The Clash and Collapse of the Ottoman and Russian Empires, 1908–1918* (Cambridge, UK: Cambridge University Press, 2011).

10. See Thomas Kuehn, *Empire, Islam, and Politics of Difference* (Leiden, Netherlands: Brill, 2011).

11. The impact of racism and racialization of overseas colonies on the European metropole has garnered much-needed attention in European historiography, particularly

in the relationship of German and French anti-Semitism to the use of race and racist policies toward colonized subjects in Africa. See Dorian Bell, *Globalizing Race: Antisemitism and Empire in French and European Culture* (Evanston, IL: Northwestern University Press, 2018); Christian Davis, *Colonialism, Antisemitism, and Germans of Jewish Descent in Imperial Germany* (Ann Arbor, MI: University of Michigan Press, 2012); Isabel V. Hull, *Absolute Destruction: Military Culture and the Practices of War in Imperial Germany* (Ithaca, NY: Cornell University Press, 2005). In the next few years, there will be more exciting studies to come out about race and its treatment in the late Ottoman Empire. I met many scholars at the African in the Middle East/Middle East in Africa Workshop I organized with Jim Ryan in Fall 2019, in partnership with the Clarke Initiative for Law and Justice in the Middle East and North Africa at Cornell University and the Hagop Kevorkian Center for Near Eastern Studies at New York University. They included scholars such as Beeta Baghoolizadeh, Ezgi Çakmak, Michael Ferguson, and Ayşegül Kayagil, among others. Their work will add to the rich scholarship of pioneers in the field of racism and slavery in the Ottoman Empire like Ceyda Karamursel, Eve Trout Powell, Civan Çelik, and others.

12. BOA, MV-227/126 (16/5/1912); İ.DUİT-72/64 (2/3/1918); HR.SYS-2448/7 (2/12/1918); İ.DUİT-69/23 (10/9/1918).

13. The total numbers are not clear, with estimates ranging from a few thousand to tens of thousands. M. Talha Çiçek, *War and State Formation in Syria: Cemal Pasha's Governorate During World War I, 1914–1917* (London: Routledge, 2014), 51; Eugene Rogan, *The Fall of the Ottomans: The Great War in the Middle East* (New York: Basic Books, 2016), 291.

14. The use of "internment" might raise the ire of some readers who associate it with the violence inflicted on Japanese Americans, for example, during World War II. However, once we look at the facts, we see that Bursa and other cities in Anatolia served as places where a subset of Arab-Ottoman citizens and their families were forcibly moved, their movement curtailed, into houses assigned by the state, and kept under the watchful eyes of the police during the war—in other words, the definition of internment.

15. M. Talha Çiçek, "From 'Notable Syrians' to 'Ordinary Anatolians': The Politics of 'Normalization' and the Experience of Exile During World War I," *New Perspectives on Turkey*, no. 65 (2021): 3.

16. For more on internment during World War I, including a chapter on Armenians in the Ottoman Empire, see Stefan Manz, Panikos Panayi, and Matthew Stibbe, eds., *Internment during the First World War: A Mass Global Phenomenon* (London: Routledge, 2018).

17. Çiçek, "From 'Notable Syrians,'" 7.

18. BOA, DH.EUM.4.ŞB-6/44 (17/6/1916).

19. Malek Sharif, "Istanbul and the Formation of an Arab Teenager's Identity: Recollections of a Cadet in the Ottoman Army in 1914 and 1916–1917," in *Istanbul-Kushta-Constantinople: Narratives of Identity in the Ottoman Capital, 1830–1930*, ed. Christoph Herzog and Richard Wittmann (London: Routledge, 2018), 83–86.

20. BOA, DH.EUM.4.Şb-7/1 (5/6/1916).

21. BOA, DH.EUM.4.Şb-6/44 (17/6/1916).

22. BOA, DH.ŞFR-67/128 (28/8/1916).

23. BOA, DH.ŞFR-68/34 (16/9/1916).

24. He came back to Syria with the invading army and was married to a Turkish woman. They were soon divorced, and she left with their daughter for Ankara. He moved to Beirut, where he spent the rest of his life. 'Abd al-Qadir, al-Usra, 73, 89. I was not given permission to reprint his photo, in which he is dressed in Ma'an, but it is available online at https://opendata.hauts-de-seine.fr//explore/datase…anete/files/4a8 a82a7438e6fbc062e6f3ec7d43997/300/.

25. BOA, DH.ŞFR-78/248 (13/7/1917).

26. BOA, DH.ŞFR-87/34 (4/5/1918); DH.ŞFR-87/33 (5/5/1918); DH.EUM.4.Şb-21/44 (28/8/1918).

27. BOA, DH.EUM.4.Şb-13/16 (19/8/1917).

28. Vassik received the Hürşid Medal from the Iranian government while he worked at the Ottoman embassy in Tehran. BOA, İ.TAL-473/1329-b-33 (22/7/1911). Then he was assigned as a representative of the sultan in Tripoli (Libya). BOA, İ.MBH-13/1331-N-1 (4/8/1913). He was next hired as the head secretary in the Ottoman embassy in Madrid. BOA, İ.HR-432/1331-ZA-15 (18/10/1913). Lastly, he was assigned as the second secretary in the Ottoman embassy in Washington. BOA, İ.HR-432/1331-Z-1 (28/10/1914). He was still in Washington in 1916, where he was awarded a medal from the Spanish government for his previous work at the Ottoman embassy in Spain; BOA, İ.DUİT-72/6 (22/8/1916), notably after his father's execution.

29. al-'Azm, al-Usra al-'Azmiyya, 75–76). The families on either side of the border maintain loose ties with one another, with a few members having dual citizenship. The information about Giyas's wife was relayed to me in an interview with one of Sadik's great granddaughters, who preferred that I not mention her name. I am indebted to her for her generosity and openness.

30. Michael Provence, *The Last Ottoman Generation and the Making of the Modern Middle East* (Cambridge, UK: Cambridge University Press, 2017), 263–65.

31. On the "scientific" efforts by many to reinvent "Turks" as a distinct "race" in the first half of the twentieth century, see Elise K. Burton, *Genetic Crossroads: The Middle East and the Science of Human Heredity* (Stanford, CA: Stanford University Press, 2021), 47–55.

BIBLIOGRAPHY

Primary Sources

American University of Beirut Library
Jafet Library, Newspaper Collection
Lisan al-Hal (Beirut)
Al-Ittihad al-ʿUthmani (Beirut)
Thamarat al-Funun (Beirut)

Başbakanlık Osmanlı Arşivi (BOA)
A.AMD: Amedi Kalemi
A.MTZ (04): Sadaret Eyalat-ı Mümtaze Kalemi Belgeleri, Bulgaristan Prensliği
A.TŞF: Muhtelif Eşhasa Verilen Nişan, Tevcih, Mansıb, Rütbe, Mazulin ve Memurin Esami Kayıt Defteri
C.ZB: Cevdet Zabtiye
DH.EUM.4.Şb: Emniyet-i Umumiye Müdüriyeti Dördüncü Şube
DH.H: Dahiliye Nezareti Hukuk Kalemi Evrakı
DH.MKT: Dahiliye Nezareti Mektubi Kalemi
DH.SAİD: Dahiliye Nezareti Sicill-i Ahval İdare-i Umumiyesi
DH.ŞFR: Şifre Kalemi Belgeleri
DUİT: Dosya Usulü İradeler Tasnifi
HR.SFR.3: Hariciye Nezareti Londra Sefareti Belgeleri
HR.SFR.04: Hariciye Nezareti Sofya Sefareti Belgeleri
HR.SYS: Hariciye Nezareti Siyasi Kısım Evrakı
HR.TH: Hariciye Nezareti Tahrirat

HR.TO: Tercüme Odası Belgeleri

HR.UHM: Umur-ı Hukukiye-i Muhtalita Müdiriyeti

İ.AZN: İrade Adliye ve Mezahib

İ.DH: İrade—Dahiliye

İ.DUİT: İrade Dosya Usulü

İ.HR: İrade—Hariciye

İ.HUS: İrade—Hususi

İ.MBH: İrade—Mabeyn-i Hümayun

İ.ML: İrade—Maliye

İ.MMS: İrade—Meclis-i Mahsus

İ.MTZ(04): İrade—Eyalet-i Mümtaze Bulgaristan

İ.MVL: İrade—Meclis-i Vala

İ.TAL: İrade—Taltif

ML.EEM: Maliye Nezareti Emlak-ı Emiriyye Müdüriyeti

MV: Meclis-i Vükela Mazbatları

ŞD: Şura-yı Devlet Maruzatı

Y.A.HUS: Yıldız Sadaret Hususi Maruzat Evrakı

Y.A.RES: Yıldız Sadaret Resmi Maruzat Evrakı

Y.EE: Yıldız Esas Evrakı

Y.MTV: Yıldız Mütenevvi Maruzat Evrakı

Y.PRK.A: Yıldız Perakende Sadaret Maruzatı

Y.PRK.ASK: Yıldız Perakende Askeri Maruzat

Y.PRK.AZJ: Yıldız Perakende Arzuhaller ve Jurnaller

Y.PRK.BŞK: Yıldız Perakende Mabeyn Başkitabeti Maruzatı

Y.PRK.HR: Yıldız Perakende Hariciye Nezareti Maruzatı

Y.PRK.MK: Yıldız Perakende Müfettişlik ve Komiserlikler Tahriratı

Y.PRK.MYD: Yıldız Perakende Yaveran ve Maiyet-i Seniyye Erkan-ı Harbiye
    Dairesi

Y.PRK.TKM: Yıldız Perakende Tahrirat-ı Ecnebiye ve Mabeyn Mütercimliği

Y.PRK.TŞF.: Yıldız Perakende Teşrifat-ı Umumiye Dairesi

Y.PRK.UM.: Yıldız Perakende Umum Vilayetler Tahriratı

Y.PRK.ZB: Yıldız Perakende Zabtiye Nezareti Maruzâtı

ZB: Zabtiye Nezareti Belgeleri

British Library

Great Britain Foreign Office. *Correspondence Respecting the Affairs of South-Eastern
    Europe and Further Correspondence*, 1903.

[British] National Archives (BNA),

Records of the Foreign Office.

Beyazıt Kütüphanesi
Rare Newspaper Collection
İkdam (Istanbul)
Suriye (Damascus)

Bibliothèque nationale de France
Gallica.bnf.fr/Historic Journal Archives
Le Petit Journal.

David Rumsey Map Collection (Davidrumsey.com)
Historical Map Collection

İstanbul Üniversitesi
Nadir Eserler Kütüphanesi
Azmzade, Haqqi al-Mu'ayyad. "Coğrafya-i Tabiiye (Manuscript)"
Azmzade, Sadik al-Mu'ayyad. "Afrika Sahra-yı Kebiri'nde Seyahat (Manuscript)"
————. *Al-Kimya' fi Tahlil al-Hawa' wa-l-Ma'* (Manuscript)
————. *Küçük Henri* (Manuscript)
————. *Tarikh Futuhat al-Sham* (Manuscript)
————. Fen-i Fotoğraf (Manuscript)
————. *Fernando* (Manuscript)
Historic Photo Albums

İBB Atatürk Kitaplığı
Rare Newspaper Collection
İkdam (Istanbul)
Tanin (Istanbul)

İSAM Arıştırma Merkezi, Istanbul
Rare Journals Collection
Servet-i Fünun (Istanbul)

Library of Congress
Digital Photo Collection

Marmara Üniversitesi
Taha Toros Archives

New York Public Library
Digital Photo Collection

Private Family Collection
Azmzade, Sadik al-Mu'ayyad. "Habeş Seyahatnamesi" (Manuscript)
Family Photos

SALT Research, Istanbul
Ottoman Bank Records
Feridun Fazıl Tülbentçi Archives

SS. Cyril and Methodius National Library, Sofia
Bulgarian Historical Archives (BHA)
Diplomatic correspondence between Sofia and Istanbul

Al-Asad Library (Syrian National Library), Damascus
Newspaper Collection
al-Muqtabas (Damascus)

Secondary Sources

Abbasi, Iskander. "Anti-Blackness in the Muslim World: Beyond Apologet-
    ics and Orientalism." *Maydan* (blog), October 14, 2020. https://themaydan
    .com/2020/10/anti-blackness-in-the-muslim-world-beyond-apologetics-and
    -orientalism/ (accessed December 13, 2021).
Al-'Abid, Izzet Holo. *Abdülhamid'in Kara Kutusu, Arap İzzet Holo Paşa'nın Gün-
    lükleri*. Edited by Pınar Güven and Birol Bayram. Vols. 1 and 2. İstanbul: İş
    Bankası Kültür Yayınları, 2019.
Abulhawa, Susan. "Confronting Anti-Black Racism in the Arab World." *Al-Jazeera*,
    July 7, 2013. https://www.aljazeera.com/opinions/2013/7/7/confronting-anti
    -black-racism-in-the-arab-world.
Adjemian, Boris. *La fanfare du Négus: les Arméniens en Ethiopie: XIXe–XXe siècle.*
    En temps & lieux; 47. Paris: Éditions de l'École des hautes études en sciences
    sociales, 2013.
———. "Ras Tafari in the Memory of Armenian Immigration to Ethiopia." *Annales
    d'Éthiopie* 28, no. 1 (2013): 391–93.
Ahmad, Feroz. "The Young Turk Revolution." *Journal of Contemporary History* 3,
    no. 3 (1968): 19–36.
———. *The Young Turks and the Ottoman Nationalities: Armenians, Greeks, Albanians,
    Jews, and Arabs, 1908–1918.* Salt Lake City, UT: University of Utah Press, 2014.
Akarlı, Engin Deniz. "The Tangled Ends of an Empire: Ottoman Encounters with
    the West and Problems of Westernization—an Overview." *Comparative Studies
    of South Asia, Africa, and the Middle East* 26, no. 3 (2006): 353–66.

Akyıldız, Ali. "Mabeyn-i Hümayun." In *TDV İslâm Ansiklopedisi*, 27:283–86. Ankara: Türkiye Diyanet Vakfı, 2003.

Akyol, İ. Hakkı. "Son Yarım Asrında Türkiye'fr Coğrafya." *Türk Coğrafya Dergisi* 1, no. 1 (1943): 4–15.

Al-'Azm, 'Abd al-Qadir. *Al-Usra al-'Azmiyya*. Damascus: Matba'at al-Insha', 1960.

Aldrich, Robert, and Stuart Ward. "Ends of Empire: Decolonizing the Nation in British and French Historiography." In *Nationalizing the Past: Historians as Nation Builders in Modern Europe*. Edited by Stefan Berger and Chris Lorenz, 259–81. London: Palgrave Macmillan UK, 2010.

Alemdaroğlu, Ayça. "Politics of the Body and Eugenic Discourse in Early Republican Turkey." *Body & Society* 11, no. 3 (2005): 61–76.

Ali, Othman. "The Kurds and the Lausanne Peace Negotiations, 1922–23." *Middle Eastern Studies* 33, no. 3 (1997): 521–34.

Ali Sipahi, Dzovinar Derderian, and Yasar Tolga Cora. *The Ottoman East in the Nineteenth Century: Societies, Identities and Politics*. London: I. B. Tauris, 2016.

Allen, Roger. *Studying Modern Arabic Literature: Mustafa Badawi, Scholar and Critic*. Edinburgh: Edinburgh University Press, 2015.

Altıntaş, Toygun. "The Placard Affair and the Ankara Trial: The Hunchak Party and the Hamidian Regime in Central Anatolia, 1892–93." *Journal of Ottoman and Turkish Studies Association* 4, no. 2 (2017): 309–37.

Anderson, Scott. *Lawrence in Arabia: War, Deceit, Imperial Folly and the Making of the Modern Middle East*. New York: Doubleday, 2013.

Anolic, Tamar. *The Russian Riddle, The Life of Serge Alexandrovich of Russia*. East Richmond Heights, CA: Kensington House Books, 2009.

Antonius, George. *The Arab Awakening: The Story of the Arab National Movement*. Reprint. Berlin: Allegro Editions, 2015.

Appiah, Kwame Anthony. "Why Are Politicians Suddenly Talking about Their 'Lived Experience'?" *Guardian*. November 14, 2020. http://www.theguardian.com/commentisfree/2020/nov/14/lived-experience-kamala-harris

Araz, Yahya. "Rural Girls as Domestic Servants in Late Ottoman Istanbul." In *Children and Childhood in the Ottoman Empire: From the 15th to the 20th Century*. Edited by Gülay Yılmaz and Zachs Fruma, 196–219. Edinburgh: Edinburgh University Press, 2021.

Argit, Betül İpşirli. *Life after the Harem: Female Palace Slaves, Patronage and the Imperial Ottoman Court*. Cambridge, UK: Cambridge University Press, 2020.

Artan, Tülay. "Aspects of Ottoman Elite's Food Consumption: Looking for 'Staples,' 'Luxuries,' and 'Delicacies' in a Changing Century." In *Consumption Studies and the History of the Ottoman Empire, 1550–1922: An Introduction*. Edited by Donald Quataert, 107–99. Albany, NY: State University of New York Press, 2000.

Aslanova Saylak, Sevilya. "Osmanlı-Rus İlişkilerinde Makedonya Sorunu (1885–1908)." *Gazi Akademik Bakış* 10, no. 19 (2016): 107–39.

Astafieva, Elena. "The Russian Empire in Palestine, 1847–1917." *HAL Open Science*, November 14, 2016. https://hal.archives-ouvertes.fr/hal-01293323.

al-Aswad, Ibrahim. *Kitab Al-Rihla al-Imbaratoriyya Fi al-Mamlek al-'Uthmaniyya*. Edited by Khayri al-Thahabi. Damascus: al-Hay'a al-'Ama al-Suriyya li-al -Kitab, 1898.

Atkinson, Will. *Bourdieu and After, A Guide to Relational Phenomenology*. London: Routledge, 2020.

Austin, John L. *How to Do Things with Words*. Cambridge, MA: Harvard University Press, 1967.

Avras, Abdulhamit. "Early Modern Eunuchs and the Transing of Gender and Race." *Journal of Early Modern Cultural Studies* 19, no. 4 (2020): 116–36.

Aybers, Orhan. *Eugenics in Turkey During the 1930's*. Istanbul: Libra Kitap, 2017.

Aydin, Cemil. "Imperial Paradoxes: A Caliphate for Subaltern Muslims." *ReOrient* 1, no. 2 (2016): 171–91.

———. "The Emergence of Transnational Muslim Thought, 1774–1914." In *Arabic Thought Beyond the Liberal Age, Towards an Intellectual History of the Nahda*. Edited by Jens Hanssen and Max Weiss, 121–41. Cambridge, UK: Cambridge University Press, 2016.

———. *The Idea of the Muslim World: A Global Intellectual History*. Cambridge, MA: Harvard University Press, 2017.

al-'Azm, Khaled. *Mudhakarat Khaled Al-'Azm*. Damascus: Dar al-Mutahida li-al-Nashr, 1950.

al-'Azm, 'Uthman, ed. *Majmu'at Athar Rafiq Bek al-'Azm*. Cairo: Matba'at al-Manar, 1926.

Azmzade, Sadik al-Mu'ayyad. *Afrika Sahra-yı Kebiri'nde Seyahat (Bir Osmanlı Zabitinin Büyük Sahra'da Seyahati)*. Edited by İdris Bostan. Istanbul: Çamlıca Basım Yayın ve Tic. A.Ş., 2008.

———. *Afrika Sahra-Yı Kebiri'nde Seyahat, Bir Osmanlı Zabitinin Sahra-Yı Kebir'de Seyahatı*. Istanbul: Alem Matbaası, 1899.

———. *Habeş Seyahatnamesi*. Istanbul: İkdam Matbaası, 1904.

———. *Rihla fi al-Sahra' al-Kubra bi-Ifriqya*. Edited by Salah al-Din Hassan Al-Suri. Translated by Abdul Karim Abu Shuwayrib. Silsilat al-Dirasat al-Mutarjama. Beirut: Dar al-Muhit al-'Arabi, 1998.

———. *Rihlat Al-Habasha, Min al-Istana Ila Addis Ababa*. Edited by Nouri al-Jarrah. Translated by Rafiq Azmzade. Abu Dhabi: Dar al-Suwaydi li-al-Nashir wa al-Tawzi', 2001.

Azmzade, Sadık el-Müeyyed. *Habeş Seyahatnamesi*. Edited by Serkan Özburun and Mustafa Baydemir. Istanbul: Kaknus Yayınları, 1999.

Bajalan, Djene Rhys. "The First World War, the End of the Ottoman Empire, and Question of Kurdish Statehood: A 'Missed' Opportunity?" *Ethnopolitics* 18, no. 1 (2019): 13–28.

Barkey, Karen. *Empire of Difference: The Ottomans in Comparative Perspective.* Cambridge, UK: Cambridge University Press, 2008.

Barkey, Karen, and George Gavrilis. "The Ottoman Millet System: Non-Territorial Autonomy and Its Contemporary Legacy." *Ethnopolitics* 15, no. 1 (2016): 24–42.

Barr, James. *A Line in the Sand: The Anglo-French Struggle for the Middle East, 1914–1948.* W. W. Norton, 2013.

Batush, Bassam 'Abd al-Salam. *Rafiq al-'Azm, Mufakiran Wa Muslihan:Dirasa Fi Fikrihi Wa Dawrihi Fi al-Haraka al-Islahiyya al-'Arabiyya.* Amman: Dar Kunuz al-Ma'rifa, 2007.

Bay, Abdullah. "Osmanlı Toplumunda Evlatlıklar ve Hukukı Durumları." *Turkish Studies* 9, no. 4 (2014): 149–63.

Bell, David A. "Total History and Microhistory: The French and Italian Paradigms." In *A Companion to Western Historical Thought.* Edited by Lloyd Kramer and Sarah Maza, 262–76. Oxford, UK: Blackwell Publishers, 2002.

Bell, Dorian. *Globalizing Race: Antisemitism and Empire in French and European Culture.* Evanston, IL: Northwestern University Press, 2018.

Berberian, Houri. *Roving Revolutionaries: Armenians and the Connected Revolutions in the Russian, Iranian, and Ottoman Worlds.* Oakland, CA: University of California Press, 2019.

Betts, Raymond F. "Decolonization: A Brief History of the Word." In *Beyond Empire and Nation: The Decolonization of African and Asian Societies, 1930s–1970s.* Edited by Els Bogaerts and Remco Raben, 23–38. Leiden, Netherlands: Brill, 2012.

Bhabha, Homi K. "Forward to the 1986 Edition." In *Black Skin, White Masks.* 2nd ed. London: Pluto Press, 2008.

———. *The Location of Culture.* 2nd ed. London: Routledge, 2004.

Bilgicioğlu, Banu. "Teşvikiye Camii." In *TDV İslâm Ansiklopedisi,* 40:576–78. Ankara: Türkiye Diyanet Vakfı, 2011.

Blumi, Isa. *Rethinking the Late Ottoman Empire: A Comparative Social and Political History of Albania and Yemen, 1878–1918.* Istanbul: İsis Press, 2003.

Boddice, Rob. *The History of Emotions.* Manchester, UK: Manchester University Press, 2018.

Bonine, Michael E., Abbas Amanat, and Michael E. Gasper, ed. *Is there a Middle East? The Evolution of Geopolitical Concept.* Stanford: Stanford University Press, 2012.

Bourdieu, Pierre. "Habitus." In *Habitus: A Sense of Place.* Edited by Jean Hiller and Emma Rooksby, 27–34. Aldershot, UK: Ashgate, 2002.

Braude, Benjamin, ed. *Christians and Jews in the Ottoman Empire*. Abridged edition. Boulder, CO: Lynne Rienner Publishers, 2014.

Brown, Keith. *Loyal unto Death: Trust and Terror in Revolutionary Macedonia*. Indianapolis: Indiana University Press, 2013.

Burçak, Berrak. "Hygienic Beauty: Discussing Ottoman-Muslim Female Beauty, Health, and Hygiene in the Hamidian Era." *Middle Eastern Studies* 54, no. 3 (2018): 343–60.

Brummett, Palmira. "Review of *An Ottoman Statesman in War and Peace: Ahmed Resmi Efendi, 1700–1783, The Ottoman Empire and Its Heritage: Politics, Society, and Economy*, by Virginia H. Aksan." *International Journal of Middle East Studies* 28, no. 3 (1996): 450–51.

Burton, Elise K. *Genetic Crossroads: The Middle East and the Science of Human Heredity*. Stanford, CA: Stanford University Press, 2021.

Butler, Judith. *Gender Trouble: Feminism and the Subversion of Identity*. London: Routledge, 1990.

Cadbury, Deborah. *Queen Victoria's Matchmaking: The Royal Marriages That Shaped Europe*. New York: Public Affairs, 2017.

Campos, Michelle. *Ottoman Brothers: Muslims, Christians, and Jews in Early Twentieth-Century Palestine*. Stanford, CA: Stanford University Press, 2011.

Carmichael, Joel. *The Shaping of the Arabs: A Study in Ethnic Identity*. London: Routledge, 2020.

Carr, David. *Experience and History: Phenomenological Perspectives on the Historical World*. Oxford, UK: Oxford University Press, 2014.

Chaubet, François. "L'Alliance Française Ou La Diplomatie de La Langue (1883–1914)." *Revue Historique* 632, no. 4 (2004): 763–85.

Chernev, Borislav. *Twilight of Empire: The Brest-Litovsk Conference and the Remaking of East-Central Europe, 1917–1918*. Toronto: University of Toronto, 2017.

Chojnacki, Stanislaw. "Some Notes on Early Travellers in Ethiopia." *University College Review* 1, no. 1 (1961): 71–89.

Clemow, Frank Gerard. *The Cholera Epidemic of 1892 in the Russian Empire. With Notes upon Treatment and Methods of Disinfection in Cholera, and a Short Account of the Conference on Cholera Held in St. Petersburg in December 1892*. London: Longmans, Green, 1893. http://hdl.handle.net/2027/mdp.39015012534304.

Cleveland, William. *The Making of an Arab Nationalist: Ottomanism and Arabism in the Life and Thought of Sati' al-Husri*. Princeton, NJ: Princeton University Press, 2016.

Cohen, Julia Phillips. *Becoming Ottomans: Sephardi Jews and Imperial Citizenship in the Modern Era*. Oxford, UK: Oxford University Press, 2014.

Cohen, Julia Philips, and Sarah Abrevaya Stein, eds. *Sephardi Lives: A Documentary History, 1700–1950*. Stanford, CA: Stanford University Press, 2014.

Cohen, Thomas V. "The Macrohistory of Microhistory." *Journal of Medieval and Early Modern Studies* 47, no. 1 (2017): 53–73.

Crouzet, Guillemette, *Inventing the Middle East: Britain and the Persian Gulf in the Age of Global Imperialism*. Translated by Juliet Sutcliffe. Montreal: McGill-Queen's University Press, 2022).

Culcasi, Karen. "Constructing and Naturalizing the Middle East." *Geographical Review* 100, no. 4 (2010): 583–97.

Çağaptay, Soner. *Islam, Secularism, and Nationalism in Modern Turkey: Who Is a Turk?* London: Routledge, 2006.

Çakal, Ergün. "Pluralism, Tolerance, and Control: On the Millet System and the Question of Minorities." *International Journal on Minority and Group Rights* 27, no. 1 (2020): 34–65.

Çetin, Gülser. "Le français dans le contexte des réformes en Turquie à la fin du XIXe siècle: un témoignage." *Documents pour l'histoire du français langue étrangère ou seconde*, no. 38/39 (2007): 159–68.

Çetintaş, M. Burak. *Dolmabahçe'den Nişantaşı'na: Sultanların Ve Paşaların Semtinin Tarihi*. 2nd ed. Istanbul: Antik A.Ş. Kültür Yayınları, 2012.

———. "Osmanlı Sivil Mimarlığı Bağlamında Teşvikiye, Nişantaşı Sarayları ve Konakları." In *Dolmabahçe, Mekanın Hafızası*. Edited by Bahar Kaya, 169–90. Istanbul: İstanbul Bilgi Üniversitesi Yayınları, 2016.

Çiçek, M. Talha. "From 'Notable Syrians' to 'Ordinary Anatolians': The Politics of 'Normalization' and the Experience of Exile During World War I." *New Perspectives on Turkey* 65 (2021): 1–29.

———. *Syria in World War I: Politics, Economy, and Society*. London: Routledge, 2016.

———. *War and State Formation in Syria: Cemal Pasha's Governorate During World War I, 1914–1917*. London: Routledge, 2014.

Darnton, Robert. *The Great Cat Massacre: And Other Episodes in French Cultural History*. Illustrated edition. New York: Basic Books, 2009.

Davis, Christian. *Colonialism, Antisemitism, and Germans of Jewish Descent in Imperial Germany*. Ann Arbor, MI: University of Michigan Press, 2012.

Davis, John R., and Agnus Nicholls. "Friedrich Max Müller: The Career and Intellectual Trajectory of a German Philologist in Victorian Britain." *Publications of the English Goethe Society* 85, no. 2–3 (2016): 67–97.

———, ed. *Friedrich Max Müller and the Role of Philology in Victorian Thought*. London: Routledge, 2018.

Davis, Natalie Zemon. *The Return of Martin Guerre*. Cambridge, MA: Harvard University Press, 1983.

Davison, Roderic H. "'Russian Skill and Turkish Imbecility': The Treaty of Kuchuk Kainardji Reconsidered." *Slavic Review* 35, no. 3 (1976): 463–83.

———. "The 'Dosografa' Church in the Treaty of Küçük Kaynarca." *Bulletin of the School of Oriental and African Studies, University of London* 42, no. 1 (1979): 46–52.

Dawn, C. Ernest, ed. *From Ottomanism to Arabism: Essays on the Origins of Arab Nationalism.* Champaign, IL: University of Illinois Press, 1973.

De Lorenzi, James. "A Cruel Destiny: The Armenian Stranger in Twentieth-Century Ethiopia." *International Journal of African Historical Studies* 49, no. 3 (2016): 405–35.

De Vito, Christian G. "History Without Scale: The Micro-Spatial Perspective." *Past & Present* 242, no. 14 (2019): 348–72.

Delgado, Richard, and Jean Stefancic, eds. *Critical Race Theory, The Cutting Edge.* 3rd ed. Philadelphia: Temple University Press, 2013.

Demirkol-Ertürk, S., and S. Paker. "Beyoğlu/Pera as a Translating Site in Istanbul." *Translation Studies* 7, no. 2 (2014): 170–85.

Der Matossian, Bedross. *Shattered Dreams of Revolution: From Liberty to Violence in the Late Ottoman Empire.* Stanford, CA: Stanford University Press, 2014.

Deringil, Selim. *Conversion and Apostasy in the Late Ottoman Empire.* Cambridge, UK: Cambridge University Press, 2012.

———. "'The Armenian Question Is Finally Closed': Mass Conversions of Armenians in Anatolia during the Hamidian Massacres of 1895–1897." *Comparative Studies in Society and History* 51, no. 2 (2009): 344–71.

———. *The Ottoman Twilight in the Arab Lands: Turkish Memoirs and Testimonies of the Great War.* Brighton, MA: Academic Studies Press, 2019.

———. *The Well-Protected Domains: Ideology and the Legitimation of Power in the Ottoman Empire, 1876–1909.* London: I. B. Tauris, 1998.

———. "'They Live in a State of Nomadism and Savagery': The Late Ottoman Empire and the Post-Colonial Debate." *Comparative Studies in Society and History* 45, no. 2 (2003): 311–42.

Derrida, Jacques. *Of Grammatology.* Translated by Gayatri Chakravorty Spivak. 1st American ed. Baltimore: Johns Hopkins University Press, 1976.

Dinçer, Sinan. "The Armenian Massacre in Istanbul (1896)." *Tijdschrift Voor Sociale En Economische Geschiedenis* 10, no. 4 (2013): 20–45.

Dodge, Bayard. *The American University of Beirut.* Beirut: Khayyat Publishing, 1958.

Doğan, Orhan. "Ottoman Soldiers Martyred by Zeytun (Suleymanlı) Armenians." *Gaziantep Üniversitesi Sosyal Bilimler Dergisi* 10, no. 1 (2011): 509–46.

Dreisziger, Nándor. "Ármin Vámbéry (1832–1913) as a Historian of Early Hungarian Settlement in the Carpathian Basin." *Hungarian Cultural Studies. e-Journal of the American Hungarian Educators Association* 6 (2013).

Duben, Alan, and Cem Behar. *Istanbul Households: Marriage, Family, and Fertility 1880–1940.* Cambridge, UK: Cambridge University Press, 1991.

Duindam, Jeroen. "A Plea for Global Comparison: Redefining Dynasty." *Past & Present* 242, no. 14 (2019): 318–47.

Edib Adıvar, Halide. *Memoirs of Halidé Edib*. New York: Century Co., 1926.

Erdem, Y. Hakan. *Slavery in the Ottoman Empire and Its Demise 1800–1909*. St Antony's Series. London: Palgrave Macmillan UK, 1996.

Ergin, Murat. *Is the Turk a White Man? Race and Modernity in the Making of Turkish Identity*. Leiden, Netherlands: Brill, 2017.

Erol, Merih. "Surveillance, Urban Governance, and Legitimacy in Late Ottoman Istanbul: Spying on Music and Entertainment During the Hamidian Regime (1876–1909)." *Urban History* 40, no. 4 (2013): 706–25.

Ertan, İrfan. "The Orient Journey of Kaiser Wilhelm II (1898)." Master's thesis. Middle East Technical University, 2018.

Etensel Ildem, Arzu. "Le français langue diplomatique de la Sublime Porte: le cas de la légation ottomane de La Haye." *Documents pour l'histoire du français langue étrangère ou seconde*, no. 38/39 (2007): 215–39.

Exner, M. "Cholera Epidemic in Hamburg, Germany 1892." In *Routledge Handbook of Water and Health*, 644–47. London: Routledge, 2015.

Fahmy, Khaled. *All the Pasha's Men: Mehmed Ali, His Army and the Making of Modern Egypt*. Cairo: American University in Cairo Press, 1997.

Falahat, Somaiyeh. *Cities and Metaphors: Beyond Imaginaries of Islamic Urban Space*. London: Routledge, 2018.

Fanon, Frantz. *Black Skin, White Masks*. Translated by Charles Lam Markmann. 2nd ed. London: Pluto Press, 2008.

Farah, Caesar E. "Arab Supporters of Sultan Abdulhamid II: 'Izzet al-'Abid." *Archivum Ottomanicum* 15 (1997): 189–219.

Fawaz, Leila Tarazi. *A Land of Aching Hearts: The Middle East in the Great War*. Cambridge, MA: Harvard University Press, 2014.

———. *An Occasion for War: Civil Conflict in Lebanon and Damascus in 1860*. Oakland, CA: University of California Press, 1994.

Ferguson, Michael. "Enslaved and Emancipated Africans on Crete." In *Race and Slavery in the Middle East: Histories of Trans-Saharan Africans in Nineteenth-Century Egypt, Sudan, and the Ottoman Mediterranean*. Edited by Terence Walz and Kenneth M. Cuno, 171–95. Cairo: American University in Cairo Press, 2012.

———. "White Turks, Black Turks and Negroes: The Politics of Polarization." In *The Making of a Protest Movement in Turkey: #occupygezi*. Edited by Umut Özkırımlı, 77–88. London: Palgrave Macmillan UK, 2014.

Firchow, Peter Edgerly. *Envisioning Africa: Racism and Imperialism in Conrad's Heart of Darkness*. Lanham, MD: Lexington Books, 2000.

Fitzpatrick, Matthew P. "Colonialism, Postcolonialism, and Decolonization." *Central European History* 51, no. 1 (2018): 83–89.

Fleischer, Cornell H. *Bureaucrat and Intellectual in the Ottoman Empire: The Historian Mustafa Ali*. Princeton, NJ: Princeton University Press, 1986.

Fortna, Benjamin C. *Imperial Classroom: Islam, the State, and Education in the Late Ottoman Empire*. Oxford, UK: Oxford University Press, 2002.

Frechette, Julie, Vasiliki Bitzas, Monique Aubry, Kelley Kilpatrick, and Mélanie Lavoie-Tremblay. "Capturing Lived Experience: Methodological Considerations for Interpretive Phenomenological Inquiry." *International Journal of Qualitative Methods* 19 (2020): 1–12.

Frie, Roger. "Psychoanalysis, Experiential History, and Empathy." *Psychoanalysis, Self and Context* 14, no. 1 (2019): 53–61.

Fursov, Kirill A. "Russia and the Ottoman Empire: The Geopolitical Dimension: Guest Editor's Introduction." *Russian Studies in History* 57, no. 2 (2018): 99–102.

Gawrych, George. *The Crescent and the Eagle: Ottoman Rule, Islam and the Albanians, 1874–1913*. London: Bloomsbury Publishing, 2006.

Gelvin, James L. "'Arab Nationalism': Has a New Framework Emerged? Pensée 1: 'Arab Nationalism' Meets Social Theory." *International Journal of Middle East Studies* 41, no. 1 (2009): 10–12.

———. *Divided Loyalties: Nationalism and Mass Politics in Syria at the Close of Empire*. Oakland, CA: University of California Press, 1999.

———. "The 'Politics of Notables' Forty Years After." *Middle East Studies Association Bulletin* 40, no. 1 (2006): 19–29.

Ghazzal, Zouhair. "The Historiography of Arab-Turkish Relations: A Re-Assessment. *Turkish Studies Association Bulletin* 24, no. 1 (2000): 121–28.

Ghobrial, John-Paul A. "Introduction: Seeing the World like a Microhistorian." *Past & Present* 242, no. 14 (2019): 1–22.

Ghosh, Durba. "Another Set of Imperial Turns?" *American Historical Review* 117, no. 3 (2012): 772–93.

Ginzburg, Carlo. *Clues, Myths, and the Historical Method*. Translated by John Tedeschi and Anne C. Tedeschi. Reprint. Baltimore: Johns Hopkins University Press, 2013.

———. *The Cheese and the Worms: The Cosmos of a Sixteenth-Century Miller*. Translated by John Tedeschi and Anne C. Tedeschi. Baltimore: Johns Hopkins University Press, 1980.

Ginzburg, Carlo, and Carlo Poni. "The Name and the Game: Unequal Exchange and the Historiographic Marketplace." In *Microhistory and the Lost People of Europe*. Edited by Edward Muir and Guido Ruggiero, 1–9. Baltimore, MD: Johns Hopkins University Press, 1991.

Gölbaşı, Edip. "1895–1896 Katliamları: Doğu Vilayetlerinde Cemaatler Arası 'Şiddet İklimi' ve Ermeni Karşıtı Ayaklanmalar." In *1915: Siyaset, Tehcir ve Soykırım*.

Edited by Oktay Özel and Fikret Adanır, 140–63. Istanbul: Tarih Vakfı Yurt Yayınları, 2015.

Marie, Grand Duchess of Russia. *Education of a Princess: A Memoir.* Translated by Russell Lord. New York: The Viking Press, 1930.

Güner, Ezgi. "The Soul of the White Muslim: Race, Empire, and Africa in Turkey." PhD diss. University of Illinois at Urbana-Champaign, 2020.

Gürpınar, Doğan. *Ottoman Imperial Diplomacy, A Political, Social, and Cultural History.* London: I. B. Tauris, 2014.

Gutman, David. *The Politics of Armenian Migration to North America, 1885–1915: Sojourners, Smugglers, and Dubious Citizens.* Edinburgh: Edinburgh University Press, 2019.

Hacısalihoğlu, Mehmet. "Muslim and Orthodox Resistance Against the Berlin Peace Treaty in the Balkans." In *War and Diplomacy: The Russo-Turkish War of 1877–1878 and the Treaty of Berlin.* Edited by M. Hakan Yavuz and Peter Sluglett, 125–43. Salt Lake City, UT: University of Utah Press, 2011.

Hafez, Melis. *Inventing Laziness: The Culture of Productivity in Late Ottoman Society.* Cambridge, UK: Cambridge University Press, 2021.

Hanioğlu, M. Şükrü. *Preparation of a Revolution: The Young Turks, 1902–1908.* Oxford, UK: Oxford University Press, 2001.

Hanssen, Jens. *Fin de Siècle Beirut: The Making of an Ottoman Provincial Capital.* Oxford, UK: Oxford University Press, 2005.

———. "'Malhamé-Malfamé': Levantine Elites and Transimperial Networks on the Eve of the Young Turk Revolution." *International Journal of Middle East Studies* 43, no. 1 (2011): 25–48.

Hanssen, Jens, and Hicham Safieddine. *Butrus al-Bustani: From Protestant Convert to Ottoman Patriot and Arab Reformer.* Oakland, CA: University of California Press, 2019.

Hanssen, Jens, and Max Weiss, eds. *Arabic Thought Beyond the Liberal Age: Towards an Intellectual History of the Nahda.* Cambridge, UK: Cambridge University Press, 2016.

———. "Language, Mind, Freedom, and Time: The Modern Arab Intellectual Tradition in Four Words." In *Arabic Thought Beyond the Liberal Age: Towards an Intellectual History of the Nahda.* Edited by Jens Hanssen and Max Weiss, 1–37. Cambridge, UK: Cambridge University Press, 2016.

Harsgor, Michael. "Total History: The Annales School." *Journal of Contemporary History* 13, no. 1 (1978): 1–13.

Hathaway, Jane. "Amir al-Hajj." *Encyclopaedia of Islam,* January 1, 2015. https:// referenceworks.brillonline.com/entries/encyclopaedia-of-islam-3/amir-al-hajj -COM_24219?s.num=316&s.start=300.

———. *The Chief Eunuch of the Ottoman Harem: From African Slave to Power-Broker.* Cambridge, UK: Cambridge University Press, 2018.

————, ed. "The Household." In *The Politics of Households in Ottoman Egypt: The Rise of the Qazdaglis*, 17–31. Cambridge Studies in Islamic Civilization. Cambridge, UK: Cambridge University Press, 1996.

————. *The Politics of Households in Ottoman Egypt: The Rise of the Qazdağlis*. Cambridge Studies in Islamic Civilization. Cambridge, UK: Cambridge University Press, 1996.

Henley, Jon. "French Angry at Law to Teach Glory of Colonialism." *Guardian*, April 15, 2005. http://www.theguardian.com/world/2005/apr/15/highereducation .artsandhumanities.

Henning, Barbara. *Narratives of the History of the Ottoman-Kurdish Bedirhani Family in Imperial and Post-Imperial Contexts*. Bamberg, Germany: University of Bamberg Press, 2018.

Hobsbawm, Eric, and Terence O. Ranger, eds. *The Invention of Tradition*. Cambridge, UK: Cambridge University Press, 1983.

Hourani, Albert. "Ottoman Reforms and the Politics of the Notables." In *Beginnings of Modernization in the Middle East, The Nineteenth Century*. Edited by William Polk and Richard Chambers, 41–68. Chicago: University of Chicago Press, 1968.

Hülagü, M. Metin. *The Hejaz Railway: The Construction of a New Hope*. Clifton, NJ: Bluedome Press, 2010.

Hull, Isabel V. *Absolute Destruction: Military Culture and the Practices of War in Imperial Germany*. Ithaca, NY: Cornell University Press, 2005.

Iğsız, Aslı. *Humanism in Ruins: Entangled Legacies of the Greek-Turkish Population Exchange*. Stanford, CA: Stanford University Press, 2018.

İpşirli Argıt, Betül. *Life after the Harem, Female Palace Slaves, Patronage, and the Imperial Ottoman Court*. Cambridge, UK: Cambridge University Press, 2020.

İpşirli, Mehmet. "Beylerbeyi." In *TDV İslam Ansiklopedisi*, 6:69–74. Ankara: Türkiye Diyanet Vakfı, 1992.

Izzidien, Ruqaya. "It Is Time to Teach Colonial History in British Schools." *Al Jazeera*, August 30, 2018. https://www.aljazeera.com/opinions/2018/8/30/ it-is-time-to-teach-colonial-history-in-british-schools.

Jonas, Raymond Anthony. *The Battle of Adwa: African Victory in the Age of Empire*. Cambridge, MA: Harvard University Press, 2011.

Junge, Christian. "Al-Yaziji, Nasif (1800–1871)." In *Routledge Encyclopedia of Modernism*. Leiden: Routledge, 2016. https://www.rem.routledge.com/articles/ al-yaziji-nasif-1800-1871.

Karaca, Ali. "Azmzadeler." in *TDV İslam Ansiklopedisi*, 4:350. Ankara: Türkiye Diyanet Vakfı, 1991.

————. "Azm-zade Mehmet Paşa." Master's thesis. Marmara Üniversitesi, 1986.

Karamursel, Ceyda. "The Uncertainties of Freedom: The Second Constitutional Era and the End of Slavery in the Late Ottoman Empire." *Journal of Women's History* 28, no. 3 (2016): 138–61.

———. "Transplanted Slavery, Contested Freedom, and Vernacularization of Rights in the Reform Era Ottoman Empire." *Comparative Studies in Society and History* 59, no. 3 (2017): 690–714.

Karčić, Hamza. "Sèvres at 100: The Peace Treaty That Partitioned the Ottoman Empire." *Journal of Muslim Minority Affairs* 40, no. 3 (2020): 470–79.

Karpat, Kemal H. *The Politicization of Islam: Reconstructing Identity, State, Faith, and Community in the Late Ottoman State.* Oxford, UK: Oxford University Press, 2001.

Kasinec, Edward, and Benjamin E. Goldsmith. "The Russian Grand Duke Sergei Aleksandrovich and the Holy Land: A Note." In *Modern Greek Studies Year Book.* Edited by Theofanis George Stavrou, 7:463–72. Minneapolis: University of Minnesota Press, 1991.

Kastoryano, Riva. "Multiculturalism and Interculturalism: Redefining Nationhood and Solidarity." *Comparative Migration Studies* 6, no. 1 (2018): 17.

Kaya, Bahar, ed. *Dolmabahçe: Mekânın Hafızası.* İstanbul: Bilgi Üniversitesi Yayınları. 2016. https://bilgiyay.com/kitap/dolmabahce-mekanin-hafizasi/.

Kaya, Zeynep N. *Mapping Kurdistan: Territory, Self-Determination and Nationalism.* Cambridge, UK: Cambridge University Press, 2020.

Kayalı, Hasan. *Arabs and Young Turks: Ottomanism, Arabism, and Islamism in the Ottoman Empire, 1908–1918.* Oakland, CA: University of California Press, 1997.

———. *Imperial Resilience, The Great War's End, Ottoman Longevity, and Incidental Nations.* Oakland, CA: University of California Press, 2021.

Keddie, Nikki R. *An Islamic Response to Imperialism: Political and Religious Writings of Sayyid Jamal ad-Din "al-Afghani."* Oakland, CA: University of California Press, 1983.

Kentel, K. Mehmet. "Caricaturizing 'Cosmopolitan' Pera: Play, Critique, and Absence in Yusuf Franko's Caricatures, 1884–1896." *Journal of the Ottoman and Turkish Studies Association* 5, no. 1 (2018): 7–32.

Kettell, Steven, and Alex Sutton. "New Imperialism: Toward a Holistic Approach." *International Studies Review* 15, no. 2 (2013): 243–58.

Khalidi, Rashid, Lisa Anderson, Muhammad Muslih, and Reeva S. Simon, eds. *The Origins of Arab Nationalism.* New York: Columbia University Press, 1993.

Khan, Mujeeb R. "The Ottoman Eastern Question and the Problematic Origins of Modern Ethnic Cleansing, Genocide, and Humanitarian Interventionism in Europe and the Middle East." In *War and Diplomacy, The Russo-Turkish War of 1877–1878 and the Treaty of Berlin.* Edited by M. Hakan Yavuz, 98–128. Salt Lake City, UT: The University of Utah Press, 2011.

Khoury, Philip. "The Urban Notables Paradigm Revisited." *Revue des mondes musul-mans et de la Méditerranée* 55, no. 1 (1990): 215–30.

———. *Urban Notables and Arab Nationalism: The Politics of Damascus, 1860–1920.* Cambridge, UK: Cambridge University Press, 1983.

Khuri-Makdisi, Ilham. *The Eastern Mediterranean and the Making of Global Radical-ism, 1860–1914.* Oakland, CA: University of California Press, 2010.

Killingray, David, and Martin Plaut. "Race and Imperialism in the British Empire: A Lateral View." *South African Historical Journal* 72, no. 1 (2020): 1–28.

King, Charles. *Midnight at the Pera Palace: The Birth of Modern Istanbul.* Reprint. New York: W. W. Norton, 2014.

Kış, Salih. "Alman İmparatoru II. Wilhelm'in Haçlı Rüyası ve 1898 Kudüs Seyahatı." *Selçuk Üniversitesi Türkiyat Araştırmaları Dergisi* 42 (2017): 487–506.

Kış, Salih. *Osmanlı Ordusunda Alman Ekolü: Von Der Goltz Paşa (1883–1895).* Konya, Turkey: Palet Yayınları, 2017.

Kırmızı, Abdulhamit. "Experiencing the Ottoman Empire as a Life Course: Ferid Pasha, Governor and Grandvizier (1851–1914)." *Geschichte und Gesellschaft* 40, no. 1 (2014): 42–66.

Klein, Janet. *The Margins of Empire: Kurdish Militias in the Ottoman Tribal Zone.* Stanford, CA: Stanford University Press, 2011.

Kodaman, Bayram. "The Hamidiye Light Cavalry Regiments, Abdülhamid II and the Eastern Anatolian Tribes." In *War and Diplomacy: The Russo-Turkish War of 1877–1878 and the Treaty of Berlin.* Edited by M. Hakan Yavuz and Peter Sluglett, 382–426. Salt Lake City, UT: University of Utah Press, 2011.

Koegler, Caroline, Pavan Kumar Malreddy, and Marlena Tronicke. "The Colonial Remains of Brexit: Empire Nostalgia and Narcissistic Nationalism." *Journal of Postcolonial Writing* 56, no. 5 (2020): 585–92.

Kohut, Thomas A. *A German Generation: An Experiential History of the Twentieth Century.* New Haven, CT: Yale University Press, 2012.

Kuehn, Thomas. *Empire, Islam, and Politics of Difference.* Leiden, Netherlands: Brill, 2011.

Kurt, Ümit. "Reform and Violence in the Hamidian Era: The Political Context of the 1895 Armenian Massacres in Aintab." *Holocaust and Genocide Studies* 32, no. 3 (2018): 404–23.

———. "The Curious Case of Ali Cenani Bey: The Story of a Génocidaire During and After the 1915 Armenian Genocide." *Patterns of Prejudice* 52, no. 1 (2018): 58–77.

Lai, Cheng-chung. *Braudel's Historiography Reconsidered.* Lanham, MD: University Press of America, 2004.

Landau, Jacob M. "Abdülhamid II in 1912: The Return from Salonica." In *The Balance of Truth: Essays in Honour of Professor Geoffrey Lewis*. Edited by Çigdem Balim-Harding and Colin Imber, 251–54. Piscataway, NJ: Gorgias Press, 2010.

———. *The Hejaz Railway and the Muslim Pilgrimage: A Case of Ottoman Political Propaganda*. London: Routledge, 2016.

Lantheaume, François. "The Empire in French History: From a Promise to a Burden." In *School and Nation: Identity Politics and Educational Media in an Age of Diversity*. Edited by Peter Carrier. Frankfurt am Main, Germany: Peter Lang, 2013.

Laremont, Ricardo. "Race, Islam, and Politics: Differing Visions Among Black American Muslims." *Journal of Islamic Studies* 10, no. 1 (1999): 33–49.

Latimer, Elizabeth Wormeley. *Russia and Turkey in the Nineteenth Century*. Chicago: A. C. McClurg, 1895.

Leezenberg, Michiel. "The Vernacular Revolution: Reclaiming Early Modern Grammatical Traditions in the Ottoman Empire." *History of Humanities* 1, no. 2 (2016): 251–75.

Légaré, Evelyn I. "Canadian Multiculturalism and Aboriginal People: Negotiating a Place in the Nation." *Identities* 1, no. 4 (1995): 347–66.

Lehmann, Jörg. "School and Nation. Identity Politics and Educational Media in an Age of Diversity." *National Identities* 18, no. 2 (2016): 237–39.

Levi, Giovanni. "Frail Frontiers?" *Past & Present* 242, no. 14 (2019): 37–49.

Lévi-Strauss, Claude. *Structural Anthropology*. rev. ed. New York: Basic Books, 1974.

Lévy-Aksu, Noémi, and François Georgeon, eds. *The Young Turk Revolution and the Ottoman Empire: The Aftermath of 1908*. London: I. B. Tauris, 2017.

Lorcin, Patricia M. E. "The Nostalgias for Empire." *History and Theory* 57, no. 2 (2018): 269–85.

M. U. Introduction to "Ottoman Travels and Travel Accounts from an Earlier Age of Globalization." *Die Welt Des Islams* 40, no. 2 (2000): 133–38.

MacDonald, David Bruce. "Reforming Multiculturalism in a Bi-National Society: Aboriginal Peoples and the Search for Truth and Reconciliation in Canada." *Canadian Journal of Sociology* 39, no. 1 (2014): 65–86.

Makdisi, Saree. *Making England Western: Occidentalism, Race, and Imperial Culture*. Chicago: University of Chicago Press, 2014.

Makdisi, Ussama. *Age of Coexistence: The Ecumenical Frame and the Making of the Modern Arab World*. Oakland, CA: University of California Press, 2019.

———. *The Culture of Sectarianism: Community, History, and Violence in Nineteenth-Century Ottoman Lebanon*. Oakland, CA: University of California Press, 2000.

Maksudyan, Nazan. "'This Time Women as Well Got Involved in Politics!' Nineteenth Century Ottoman Women's Organizations and Political Agency." In

Women and the City, Women in the City, A Gendered Perspective on Ottoman Urban History. Edited by Nazan Maksudyan, 107–35. Oxford, NY: Berghahn, 2014.

Makzume, Erol. *Sultan II. Abdülhamid'in Hizmetinde Selim Melhame Paşa ve Ailesi*. Istanbul: MD Basım Evi, 2019.

Manz, Stefan, Panikos Panayi, and Matthew Stibbe, eds. *Internment during the First World War: A Mass Global Phenomenon*. London: Routledge, 2018.

Mayersen, Deborah. "The 1895–1896 Armenian Massacres in Harput: Eyewitness Account." *Études arméniennes contemporaines*, no. 10 (March 2018): 161–83.

McCarthy, Justin. *Death and Exile: The Ethnic Cleansing of Ottoman Muslims, 1821–1922*. London: Darwin Press, 2021.

McCluney, Courtney L., Kathrina Robotham, Serenity Lee, Richard Smith, and Myles Durkee. "The Costs of Code-Switching." *Harvard Business Review*, November 15, 2019. https://hbr.org/2019/11/the-costs-of-codeswitching.

McMeekin, Sean. "Benevolent Contempt: Bismarck's Ottoman Policy." In *War and Diplomacy: The Russo-Turkish War of 1877–1878 and the Treaty of Berlin*. Edited by M. Hakan Yavuz and Peter Sluglett, 79–97. Salt Lake City, UT: University of Utah Press, 2011.

———. *The Ottoman Endgame: War, Revolution, and the Making of the Modern Middle East, 1908–1923*. London: Penguin, 2015.

Menegon, Eugenio. "Telescope and Microscope. A Micro-Historical Approach to Global China in the Eighteenth Century." *Modern Asian Studies* 54, no. 4 (2020): 1315–44.

Miller, William. *The Ottoman Empire and Its Successors, 1801–1927, with an Appendix, 1927–1936*. Cambridge, UK: Cambridge University Press, 1936.

Minawi, Mostafa. "Beyond Rhetoric: Reassessing Bedouin-Ottoman Relations along the Route of the Hijaz Telegraph Line at the End of the Nineteenth Century." *Journal of the Economic and Social History of the Orient* 58, no. 1–2 (2015): 74–104.

———. "International Law and the Precarity of Ottoman Sovereignty in Africa at the End of the Nineteenth Century." *International History Review* 43, no. 5 (2021): 1098–1121.

———. "Telegraphs and Territoriality in Ottoman Africa and Arabia during the Age of High Imperialism." *Journal of Balkan and Near Eastern Studies* 18, no. 6 (2016): 567–87.

———. *The Ottoman Scramble for Africa: Empire and Diplomacy in the Sahara and the Hijaz*. Stanford, CA: Stanford University Press, 2016.

Mironenko-Marenkova, Irina, and Kirill Vakh. "An Institution, Its People, and Its Documents: The Russian Consulate in Jerusalem through the Foreign Policy Archive of the Russian Empire, 1858–1914." In *Ordinary Jerusalem, 1840–1940*.

Edited by Angelos Dalachanis and Vincent Lemire, 200–222. Leiden, Netherlands: Brill, 2018.

Müller, Georgina Adelaide. *Letters from Constantinople, by Mrs. Max Müller*. London: Longmans, Green, 1897.

Mutlu, Dilek Kaya. "The Russian Monument at Ayastefanos (San Stefano): Between Defeat and Revenge, Remembering and Forgetting." *Middle Eastern Studies* 43, no. 1 (2007): 75–86.

Nacar, Can. "Labor Activism and the State in the Ottoman Tobacco Industry." *International Journal of Middle East Studies* 46, no. 3 (2014): 533–51.

———. "The Régie Monopoly and Tobacco Workers in Late Ottoman Istanbul." *Comparative Studies of South Asia, Africa, and the Middle East* 34, no. 1 (2014): 206–19.

Naimark, Norman M., Ronald Grigor Suny, and Fatma Müge Göçek, eds. *A Question of Genocide: Armenians and Turks at the End of the Ottoman Empire*. Reprint. Oxford, UK: Oxford University Press, 2011.

Okumuş, Ruveyda. "II. Abdülhamid Devrinde Yıldızı Parlayan Bir Devlet Adamı: Reşid Mümtaz Paşa (1856–1928)." *Hazine-i Evrak Arşiv ve Tarih Araştırmaları Dergisi* 2, no. 2 (2020): 113–40.

Olpak, Mustafa. "Osmanlı İmparatorluğu'nda köle, Türkiye Cumhuriyeti'nde evlatlık: Afro-Türkler." *Ankara Üniversitesi SBF Dergisi* 68, no. 1 (2013): 123–41.

Oualdi, M'hamed. *A Slave Between Empires: A Transimperial History of North Africa*. New York: Columbia University Press, 2020.

Özbay, Ferhunde. *Türkiye'de Evlatlık Kurumu: Köle Mi, Evlat Mı?* Istanbul: Boğaziçi Üniversitesi Yayınları, 1999.

Özcan, Abdülkadir. "Paşa." in *TDV İslam Ansiklopedisi*, 34:182–83. İstanbul: TDV İslâm Araştırmaları Merkezi, 2007.

Özkırımlı, Umut, and Spyros A. Sofos. *Tormented by History: Nationalism in Greece and Turkey*. London: C. Hurst, 2008.

Öztuna, Yılmaz. *Devletler ve Hanedanlar, Türkiye (1074–1990)*. Vol. 2. Ankara: Kültür Bakanlığı Yayınları, 1969.

Özyüksel, Murat. *The Hejaz Railway and the Ottoman Empire: Modernity, Industrialization, and Ottoman Decline*. London: Bloomsbury, 2014.

Palabıyık, Mustafa Serdar. "Ottoman Travelers' Perceptions of Africa in the Late Ottoman Empire (1860–1922): A Discussion of Civilization, Colonialism, and Race." *New Perspectives on Turkey* 46 (2012): 187–212.

Panian, Karnig. *Goodbye, Antoura: A Memory of the Armenian Genocide*. Stanford, CA: Stanford University Press, 2015.

Papastathis, Konstantinos. "Arabic and Its Alternatives: Religious Minorities and Their Languages in the Emerging Nation States of the Middle East (1920–1950)." In *Arabic vs. Greek: The Linguistic Aspect of the Jerusalem Orthodox Church*

Controversy in Late Ottoman Times and the British Mandate, 261–86. Leiden, Netherlands: Brill, 2020.

Paşa, Tahsin. *Sultan Abdülhamid, Tahsin Paşa'nın Yıldız Hatıraları*. Istanbul: Boğaziçi Yayınları, 1990.

Peirce, Leslie P. *The Imperial Harem: Women and Sovereignty in the Ottoman Empire*. Oxford, UK: Oxford University Press, 1993.

Philliou, Christine M. *Biography of an Empire: Governing Ottomans in an Age of Revolution*. Oakland, CA: University of California Press, 2010.

———. *Turkey: A Past Against History*. Oakland, CA: University of California Press, 2021.

Polat, U. Gülsüm. *Türk-Arap İlişkileri: Eski Eyaletler Yeni Komşulara Dönüşürken (1914-1923)*. Istanbul: Kronik, 2019.

Polatcı, Türkan. *Osmanlı Diplomasisinde Oryantalist Memurlar, Osmanlı Belgeleriyle Diloğlanları ve Tercümanlar*. Ankara: Akçağ Yayınları, 2013.

Polatel, Mehmet. "The Complete Ruin of a District: The Sasun Massacre of 1894." In *The Ottoman East in the Nineteenth Century: Societies, Identities, and Politics*. Edited by Ali Sipahi, Dzovinar Derderian, and Yaşar Tolga Cora. London: I. B. Tauris, 2016.

Provence, Michael. *The Great Syrian Revolt and the Rise of Arab Nationalism*. Austin: University of Texas Press, 2005.

———. *The Last Ottoman Generation and the Making of the Modern Middle East*. Cambridge, UK: Cambridge University Press, 2017.

Redhouse, James W. *A Turkish and English Lexicon*. 4th ed. Istanbul: Çağrı Yayınları, 2011.

Reed-Danahay, Deborah. *Bourdieu and Social Space: Mobilities, Trajectories, Emplacements*. Oxford, NY: Berghahn, 2020.

Reimann-Dawe, Tracey. "Time and the Other in Nineteenth-Century German Travel Writing on Africa." *Transfers* 6, no. 3 (2016): 99–116.

Reşad, Akram, and Osman Ferid, eds. *Musavver Nevsal-i Osmani*. 3rd ed. Istanbul: Şems Matbaası, 1911.

Reynolds, Michael A. *Shattering Empires: The Clash and Collapse of the Ottoman and Russian Empires, 1908–1918*. Cambridge, UK: Cambridge University Press, 2011.

Richard, Jean. "Les transformations de l'image de Saladin dans les sources occidentales." *Revue des mondes musulmans et de la Méditerranée*, no. 89–90 (2000): 177–87.

Rogan, Eugene. *The Arabs: A History*. New York: Basic Books, 2009.

———. *The Fall of the Ottomans: The Great War in the Middle East*. New York: Basic Books, 2016.

Saada, Emmanuelle. "Race and Empire in Nineteenth-Century France." In *The Cambridge History of French Thought*. Edited by Jeremy Jennings and Michael Moriarty, 353–62. Cambridge, UK: Cambridge University Press, 2019.

Said, Edward. *Orientalism*. London: Pantheon Books, 1978.

———. *Culture and Imperialism*. New York: Vintage Books, 1994.

Salman, Yıldız. "'Alafranga'dan 'Moderne' Teşvikiye Nişantaşı." In *Dolmabahçe, Mekanın Hafızası*. Edited by Bahar Kaya, 115–44. Istanbul: İstanbul Bilgi Üniversitesi Yayınları, 2016.

Samancı, Özge. "History of Eating and Drinking in the Ottoman Empire and Modern Turkey." In *Handbook of Eating and Drinking: Interdisciplinary Perspectives*. Edited by Herbert L. Meiselman, 55–74. London: Springer, 2020.

Sami, Şamsuddin. *Kamus-ı Türki*. Edited by Ahmed Cevdet. Istanbul: İkdam Matbaası, 1899.

Saunders, Robert. "Brexit and Empire: 'Global Britain' and the Myth of Imperial Nostalgia." *Journal of Imperial and Commonwealth History* 48, no. 6 (2020): 1140–74.

Saydam, Abdullah. "Namık Paşa (1804–1892), Osmanlı Devlet Adamı." In *İslam Ansiklopedisi*, 32:379–80. Ankara: Türkiye Diyanet Vakfı, 2006.

Saylak, Sevilya Aslanova. "Osmanlı—Rus İlişkilerinde Makedonya Sorunu (1885–1908)." *Gazi Akademik Bakış* 10, no. 19 (2016): 107–39.

Schatkowski Schilcher, Linda. *Families in Politics: Damascene Factions and Estates of the 18th and 19th Centuries*. Stuttgart, Germany: Franz Steiner Wiesbaden, 1985.

Schull, Kent. "Amalgamated Observations: American Impressions of Nineteenth Century Constantinople and Its Peoples." In *Istanbul—Kushta—Constantinople: Diversity of Identities and Personal Narratives in the Ottoman Capital (1830–1900)*. Edited by Christoph Herzog and Richard Wittmann, 57–77. London: Routledge, 2018.

Scott, James. *Seeing Like a State: How Certain Schemes to Improve the Human Condition Have Failed*. New Haven, CT: Yale University Press, 1999.

Seed, David. "Nineteenth-Century Travel Writing: An Introduction." *Yearbook of English Studies* 34 (2004): 1–5.

Seth, Suman. *Difference and Disease: Medicine, Race, and the Eighteenth-Century British Empire*. Cambridge, UK: Cambridge University Press, 2018.

Shamir, Shimon. "As'ad Pasha al-'Azm and Ottoman Rule in Damascus (1743–58)." *Bulletin of the School of Oriental and African Studies, University of London* 26, no. 1 (1963): 1–28.

Sharif, Malek. "Istanbul and the Formation of an Arab Teenager's Identity: Recollections of a Cadet in the Ottoman Army in 1914 and 1916–1917." In *Istanbul-Kushta-Constantinople: Narratives of Identity in the Ottoman Capital, 1830–1930*. Edited by Christoph Herzog and Richard Wittmann, 78–90. London: Routledge, 2018.

Shissler, A. Holly. *Between Two Empires: Ahmet Ağaoğlu and the New Turkey*. London: I. B. Tauris, 2003.

Sierp, Aline. "EU Memory Politics and Europe's Forgotten Colonial Past." *Interventions* 22, no. 6 (2020): 686–702.

Şimşek, Veysel. "'Backstabbing Arabs' and 'Shirking Kurds': History, Nationalism, and Turkish Memory of the First World War." In *The Great War: From Memory to History*. Edited by Kellen Kurschinski, Steve Marti, Alicia Robinet, Matt Symes, and Jonathan F. Vance, 99–126. Waterloo, ON: Wilfrid Laurier University Press, 2015.

Sipahi, Ali. "Deception and Violence in the Ottoman Empire: The People's Theory of Crowd Behavior During the Hamidian Massacres of 1895." *Comparative Studies in Society and History* 62, no. 4 (2020): 810–35.

Smidt, Wolbert. "Glossary of Terms and Events of the Lij Iyasu Period— Controversial and Non-Controversial Facts and Interpretations." In *The Life and Times of Lij Iyasu of Ethiopia: New Insights*. Edited by Wolbert Smidt and Éloi Ficquet, 181–205. Berlin: Lit Verlag, 2014.

Sohrabi, Nader. *Revolution and Constitutionalism in the Ottoman Empire and Iran*. Cambridge, UK: Cambridge University Press, 2011.

Somel, Selçuk Aksin. *The Modernization of Public Education in the Ottoman Empire, 1839–1908: Islamization, Autocracy, and Discipline*. Leiden, Netherlands: Brill, 2001.

Srikantha, H. "Multiculturalism and the Aboriginal Peoples in Canada." *Economic and Political Weekly* 47, no. 23 (2012): 17–21.

Stavrou, Theofanis George. *Russian Interests in Palestine, 1882–1914: A Study of Religious and Educational Enterprise*. Thessaloniki, Greece: Institute for Balkan Studies, 1963.

Steinberg, Oded Y. "The Confirmation of the Worst Fears: James Bryce, British Diplomacy, and the Armenian Massacres of 1894–1896." *Études arméniennes contemporaines*, no. 11 (2018): 15–39.

Stepanov, V. L. "The Russo–Turkish War, 1877–1878: Guest Editor's Introduction." *Russian Studies in History* 57, no. 3–4 (2018): 181–84.

Stoler, Ann Laura, and Frederick Cooper. "Between Metropole and Colony: Rethinking a Research Agenda." In *Tensions of Empire: Colonial Cultures in Bourgeois World*. Edited by Frederick Cooper and Ann Laura Stoler, 1–56. Oakland, CA: University of California Press, 1997.

Süren, Jiy Zafer. "Karden İsa'nın Kızları (Part 2)." *JINEPS*, August 1, 2016. https://jinepsgazetesi.com/2016/08/karden-isanin-kizlari-ii/.

Tafra, Bairu. *Ethiopian Records of the Menilek Era: Selected Amharic Documents from the Nachlass of Alfred Ilg, 1884–1900*. Wiesbaden, Germany: Harrassowitz, 2000.

Tamari, Salim. *The Year of the Locust: A Soldier's Diary and the Erasure of the Ottoman Past*. Oakland, CA: University of California Press, 2011.

Tauber, Eliezer. *The Arab Movements in World War I*. London: Routledge, 2014.

Tezcan, Baki. *The Second Ottoman Empire: Political and Social Transformation in the Early Modern World*. Cambridge, UK: Cambridge University Press, 2010.

Thompson, Elizabeth F. *How the West Stole Democracy from the Arabs: The Arab Congress of 1920, the Destruction of the Syrian State, and the Rise of Anti-Liberal Islamism*. New York: Atlantic Monthly Press, 2020.

Timur Agildere, Suna. "Les 'élites' de la Sublime Porte ou les médiateurs francophones du Bureau de traduction (Tercüme Odası) au XIXe siècle." *Documents pour l'histoire du français langue étrangère ou seconde*, no. 38/39 (2007): 183–91.

Tokay, Gül, and Sinan Kuneralp. *Ottoman Diplomatic Documents on the Origins of World War One*. Istanbul: İsis Press, 2008.

Tomich, Dale. "The Order of Historical Time: The Long Durée and Micro-History." *Almanack*, no. 2 (2011): 38–52.

Topal, Ali E. "The Effects of German Military Commission and Balkan Wars on the Reorganization and Modernization of the Ottoman Army." Master's thesis, Naval Postgraduate School, 2013.

Trouillot, Michel-Rolph. *Silencing the Past: Power and the Production of History*. Boston: Beacon Press, 1997.

Troutt Powell, Eve. *A Different Shade of Colonialism: Egypt, Great Britain, and the Mastery of the Sudan*. Oakland, CA: University of California Press, 2003.

———. *Tell This in My Memory: Stories of Enslavement from Egypt, Sudan, and the Ottoman Empire*. Stanford, CA: Stanford University Press, 2012.

Tullett, William. "Grease and Sweat: Race and Smell in Eighteenth-Century English Culture." *Cultural and Social History* 13, no. 3 (2016): 307–22.

Türesay, Özgür. "L'empire ottoman sous le prisme des études postcoloniales. À propos d'un tournant historiographique récent." *Revue d'Histoire Moderne et Contemporaine* 60–62, no. 2 (2013): 127–45.

Türköz, Meltem. *Naming and Nation-Building in Turkey: The 1934 Surname Law*. London: Palgrave, 2018.

Uca, Alaattin, and Ahmet Hamdi Can. "Berlin Türk Şehitiği ve Mezar Taşları." *Akademik Tarih ve Düşünce Dergisi* 3, no. 6 (2019): 1236–308.

Ülker, Erol. "Contextualising 'Turkification': Nation-Building in the Late Ottoman Empire, 1908–18." *Nations and Nationalism* 11, no. 4 (2005): 613–36.

Ünal, Hasan. "Ottoman Policy during the Bulgarian Independence Crisis, 1908–9: Ottoman Empire and Bulgaria at the Outset of the Young Turk Revolution." *Middle Eastern Studies* 34, no. 4 (1998): 135–76.

Van Nieuwenhuyse, Karel, and Joaquim Pires Valentim, eds. *The Colonial Past in History Textbooks—Historical and Social Psychological Perspectives*. Charlotte, NC: Information Age Publishing, 2018.

Vries, Jan de. "Playing with Scales: The Global and the Micro, the Macro and the Nano." *Past & Present* 242, no. 14 Supplement. (2019): 23–36.

Wacquant, Laïc, ed. *Pierre Bourdieu and Democratic Politics*. Cambridge, UK: Cambridge University Press, 2005.

Wacquant, Laïc, and Pierre Bourdieu. "The Cunning of Imperial Reason." In *Pierre Bourdieu and Democratic Politics: The Mystery of Ministry*. Edited by Laïc Wacquant, 178–98. Cambridge, UK: Polity Press, 2005.

Wallace-Sanders, Kimberly. *Mammy: A Century of Race, Gender, and Southern Memory*. Ann Arbor, MI: University of Michigan Press, 2008.

Walz, Terence, and Kenneth M. Cuno, eds. *Race and Slavery in the Middle East: Histories of Trans-Saharan Africans in 19th-Century Egypt, Sudan, and the Ottoman Mediterranean*. Cairo: American University in Cairo Press, 2010.

Warwick, Christopher. *The Life and Death of Ella Grand Duchess of Russia: A Romanov Tragedy*. 3rd ed. London: Albert Bridge Books, 2014.

Wasti, S. Tanvir. "The Last Chroniclers of the Mabeyn." *Middle Eastern Studies* 32, no. 2 (1996): 1–29.

Wastnidge, Edward. "Imperial Grandeur and Selective Memory: Re-Assessing Neo-Ottomanism in Turkish Foreign and Domestic Politics." *Middle East Critique* 28, no. 1 (2019): 7–28.

Watenpaugh, Keith David. *Being Modern in the Middle East: Revolution, Nationalism, Colonialism, and the Arab Middle Class*. Princeton, NJ: Princeton University Press, 2006.

White, Benjamin Thomas. *The Emergence of Minorities in the Middle East: The Politics of Community in French Mandate Syria*. Edinburgh: Edinburgh University Press, 2011.

Wilson, Kathleen, ed. *A New Imperial History: Culture, Identity, and Modernity in Britain and the Empire, 1660–1840*. Cambridge, UK: Cambridge University Press, 2004.

Windhausen, John D. "Siege of Plevna." In *Salem Press Encyclopedia*. Amenia, NY: Salem Press, 2019.

Wishnitzer, Avner. *Reading Clocks, Alla Turca*. Chicago: University of Chicago Press, 2015.

Yakushev, M. M. "Diplomatic Relations between Russia and the Ottoman Empire in the Second Half of the Eighteenth Century." *Russian Studies in History* 57, no. 2 (2018): 146–61.

Yasamee, F. A. K. "Colmar Freiherr von Der Goltz and the Boer War." In *The International Impact of the Boer War*. Edited by Wilson Keith, 193–210. London: Palgrave, 2001.

———. *Ottoman Diplomacy, Abdülhamid II and the Great Powers, 1878–1888*. Studies in Ottoman Diplomatic History 7. Istanbul: İsis Press, 1996.

Yavuz, M. Hakan. *Nostalgia for the Empire: The Politics of Neo-Ottomanism*. Oxford, UK: Oxford University Press, 2020.

———. "The Transformation of 'Empire' Through Wars and Reforms, Integration vs. Oppression." In *War and Diplomacy: The Russo-Turkish War of 1877–1878 and the Treaty of Berlin.* Edited by M. Hakan Yavuz and Peter Sluglett, 17–55. Salt Lake City, UT: University of Utah Press, 2011.

Yenen, Alp. "Envisioning Turco-Arab Co-Existence between Empire and Nationalism." *Die Welt des Islams* 61 (April, 2021): 72–112.

Yıldırım, Nuran. "A History of Healthcare in Istanbul." In *The Istanbul 2010 European Capital of Culture Agency and Istanbul University Project No. 55–10.* Translated by İnanç Özekmekçi and Reiner Brömer. Istanbul: Ajansfa, 2010.

Yorulmaz, Naci. *Arming the Sultan: German Arms Trade and Personal Diplomacy in the Ottoman Empire Before World War I.* London: I. B. Tauris, 2014.

Yosmaoğlu, İpek. *Blood Ties: Religion, Violence, and the Politics of Nationhood in Ottoman Macedonia, 1878–1908.* Ithaca, NY: Cornell University Press, 2013.

———. "Counting Bodies, Shaping Souls: The 1903 Census and National Identity in Ottoman Macedonia." *International Journal of Middle East Studies* 38, no. 1 (2006): 55–77.

Yumul, A. "'A Prostitute Lodging in the Bosom of Turkishness': Istanbul's Pera and Its Representation." *Journal of Intercultural Studies* 30, no. 1 (2009): 57–72.

Zaïmova, Raïa. "Le français en Bulgarie dans le contexte de la politique culturelle de la France aux XIXe et XXe siècles." *Documents pour l'histoire du français langue étrangère ou seconde,* no. 38/39 (2007): 149–56.

Zavier, Wingham. "Arap Bacı'nın Ara Muhaveresi: Under the Shadow of the Ottoman Empire and Its Study." *Yıllık: Annual of Istanbul Studies* 3, no. 1 (2021): 177–83.

Zemmin, Florian. "Validating Secularity in Islam: The Sociological Perspective of the Muslim Intellectual Rafiq al-'Azm (1865–1925)." *Historical Social Research/ Historische Sozialforschung* 44, no. 3 (2019): 74–100.

Zürcher, Erik Jan. *Turkey: A Modern History.* London: I. B. Tauris, 1998.

INDEX